PELICAN BOOKS

A HISTORY OF THE UNITED STATES

VOLUME TWO

Russel B. Nye was born in Wisconsin in 1913 and educated at Oberlin College, Ohio, and at the University of Wisconsin. He began teaching English and American Literature at the University of Wisconsin and is now Director of Languages and Literature at Michigan State University. His interest in American history led to a biography of the historian George Bancroft, which won a Pulitzer Prize, and to studies of the Anti-Slavery Movement and of Midwestern politics. His latest book is a study of the American Constitutional and Early Republican period.

J. E. Morpurgo is Professor of American Literature at the University of Geneva, Visiting Lecturer at Leeds and Deputy Chairman of the National Book League. Born in London in 1918 and educated at Christ's Hospital and the College of William and Mary in Virginia, his first academic career began in 1939 and lasted for only six months before the War turned him into an artillery officer. In the next three decades before returning to an academic life he was a publisher, General Editor of the Pelican Histories from their inception until 1960, Assistant Director of the Nuffield Foundation, adviser on book matters to various Asian governments and for fifteen years Director General of the National Book League. He also built up a considerable reputation on radio and television, wrote several books on American topics and on English literature as well as two travel books. He holds three honorary doctorates from American universities.

A HISTORY OF
THE UNITED STATES

BY

R. B. NYE AND J. E. MORPURGO

VOLUME TWO

THE GROWTH OF
THE U.S.A.

*

PENGUIN BOOKS

Penguin Books Ltd, Harmondsworth, Middlesex, England
Penguin Books Inc., 7110 Ambassador Road, Baltimore, Maryland 21207, U.S.A.
Penguin Books Australia Ltd, Ringwood, Victoria, Australia

—

First published 1955
Reprinted 1961
Second Edition 1964
Reprinted 1967
Third Edition 1970

—

—

Made and printed in Great Britain
by Hazell Watson & Viney Ltd, Aylesbury, Bucks
Set in Monotype Baskerville

CONTENTS OF VOLUME I

LIST OF MAPS

CONTENTS OF VOLUME II

LIST OF MAPS

CHAPTER 22

THE AGE OF GOOD FEELINGS
1814–28

THE reaction of war-weary Americans to news of the Treaty of Ghent was swift and spontaneous; bells rang, parades formed, schools dismissed, newspapers broke out headlines to proclaim the passage 'from gloom to glory'. Yet 'Mr Madison's War' accomplished nothing in a military or a political sense. The Treaty realized none of the United States' war aims, neither the officially-pronounced policies of Madison nor the privately-expressed hopes of the 'War Hawks', whose clamours for blood and soil had been loudest. The slogan of victory, 'Not one inch of territory lost or ceded!' had a different ring from the Westerners' triumphant 'On to Canada!' of 1812. The conflict cost a huge sum of money, dislocated business and foreign trade, raised the national debt to astronomical figures, deranged currency values, and exposed glaring cracks in the national political façade. Its record of fumbling, bickering, and unpreparedness remains unmatched by any subsequent American military experience.

But still the war seemed to be a victory, and marked a turning point in American history. It gave a tremendous lift to national morale; after all, American forces had met and presumably defeated for the second time (or at least had not been defeated by) the world's greatest military and naval power, albeit that that power's right hand was elsewhere engaged at the time. True, the war might have been avoided if American statesmanship had been of sufficient skill and calibre to avoid it. True, it might have been fought with France, on possibly better grounds. But from an American viewpoint, the war gave notice to the rest of the world that the United States had arrived as a nation, with aims of its own to be fought for. In it Americans proved something to themselves: that they could fight in defence of their interests, that they could blunder and vacillate, and still not lose the war. The bumbling campaigns, the incompetent commanders, the charred remnants of White House and Capitol, the solid ring of the British blockade, the captured merchantmen and impressed seamen – these could be forgotten if one chose to remember the *Constitution* and the *Guerriere*, Perry's gallant 'We have met the enemy and they are ours', or Pakenham's veterans littering the field at New Orleans, cut down by the long rifles of the Kentuckians. 'Who would not be an American?' trumpeted *Niles' Register*. 'Long live the republic! All hail! Last asylum of oppressed humanity!' If the eagle screamed, the indecisiveness of the conflict left little real ill-feeling between American and Briton. When the newspaper talk died down and the orators stilled, old imprecations and recent insults were more or less forgotten, and British-American relations remained fairly friendly until disturbed by the Civil War.

The conclusion of the war came close to marking the end of a lingering American colonial complex. It was hardly 'a second war of independence', but in a subtle, metaphysical sense there is some reason for so calling it. The 'submission' policies of Jefferson, which had clearly engendered a national feeling of uncertainty and inferiority in foreign affairs, promptly disappeared in the waving folds of Francis Scott Key's 'Star-spangled Banner'. Out of the old clash between a growing national self-consciousness and the old persistent feeling of dependence on Europe, came a newer spirit of self-reliance. Troops from different states and sections fought side by side under the command of Scott, a Virginian, and Jackson, a Tennessean, and the raw troops from the new Western settlements won some memorable victories they were not likely to forget. The sectional grievances and selfish demands of certain states and groups had been dragged into the open, the malcontents exposed to public view in wartime; 'Hartford Convention' and 'Bluelight Federalist' were political terms of contempt for twenty years. The war knit the nation together and matured it. 'It has renewed,' said the Swiss Albert Gallatin, who had served in Jefferson's cabinet, 'and reinstated the national feeling and character which the Revolution had given, and which were daily lessening. The people now have more general objects of attachment. ... They are more Americans, they feel and act more as a nation.'

Hitherto, despite its political independence, America had faced east. Until 1815 its trade was foreign trade, its problem in foreign affairs that of maintaining neutrality in European muddles, its problems of statesmanship those of foreign diplomacy, even its political theory conditioned by a preference either for Britain or for France. After the Treaty of Ghent America turned to the great hazy untouched West, where half a continent lay empty and exposed, ready for exploitation. America could concentrate on its domestic problem of perfecting political and social organization, and of western expansion, with less concern for European standards, ideals, and entanglements. American indifference to European affairs after 1815 was such that even Napoleon's return from Elba excited little attention in the press. Isolationism had begun.

Nineteenth-century America believed in two contrasted worlds, the Old and the New. The Old World of Britain and Europe was corrupt, tyrannical, regressive, plagued by wars and ancient hatreds. The New World was democratic, free, progressive, hopeful. The objective of American diplomacy, it was assumed, must be to keep these worlds apart, lest the taint of the Old besmirch the *tabula rasa* of the New.

The first generation of American statesmen – Washington, Adams, Jefferson, Hamilton, Richard Henry Lee, and others – insisted that the United States should avoid whenever possible entanglements in Old World politics. Washington's Farewell Address (written with Hamilton's aid) was the classic statement of the view which set the prevailing pattern of American foreign policy.

At the same time it was apparent that the United States had close commercial, political, and cultural ties with the Old World, and that to follow a private path would be difficult if not impossible. In winning their independence, Americans had found it necessary to seek an ally in France, and powerful European nations – Britain, Spain and France – had large territorial possessions on America's doorstep. There were certain accepted positions on foreign affairs that the United States believed it must maintain – freedom of the seas, freedom of foreign trade, neutrality in European disputes, national integrity, and above all others, the promotion of the cause of liberty throughout the world. In practice, American diplomats often found these principles difficult and even paradoxical. Did maintenance of freedom of the seas, for example, justify involvement in a European war? Did assistance to South American or European revolutions justify entanglement in European affairs? If so, how far should the United States go in aiding Greeks and Hungarians in throwing off oppression? Should American policy, when it agreed with that of a European power, be pursued jointly or alone? Ought the United States to assume responsibility for a hemispheric pan-American bloc?

In answering these and similar questions, the makers of American foreign policy during the first half of the nineteenth century followed closely the principles laid down by Washington and the first generation. Nearly every statement of foreign policy after 1815 was predicated on the assumption that the United States was detached from Europe, should remain so, and must always be free to pursue its own special diplomatic ends. American diplomats during the period had to find within this framework solutions to increasingly complex issues of foreign policy.

After the War of 1812, however, the American public was much less interested in external foreign relations than it was in the business of augmenting and expanding the nation it had constructed out of two wars and a generation of experiment; in other words, developing modern America. Certain factors operated in that development, producing in pre-Civil War America a particular intellectual and cultural pattern, shaped in time and place by the facts of the present and of the immediate past. Two of these factors, nationalism and romanticism, impressed themselves deeply on the personality of the period.

The feeling of 'Americanism' was of course not recent nor its roots shallow. The Revolution, Americans believed, created a new nation fullborn, and the War of 1812 simply completed its independence. Politically there was no doubt of America's separate national existence. Economically, the most pressing problem since 1776 had been to develop that nation into an economic unit, the more effectively to compete in foreign trade with the established mercantile nations – another reason for a nationalistic trend. At the same time, it was apparent that those British institutions, manners, and *mores* transplanted to American soil in the seventeenth century were subtly and surely flowering into something indigenous and American. Geographically far removed from the parent nation for more than a hundred and fifty years, America had already modified and changed English ideas, law, theology, manners, language, literature, society, and custom into a recognizably native culture long before the revolutionary break, which merely speeded up the process. And there had been, especially since 1790, growing migration to the United States of non-British peoples, further intensifying the cultural cleavage with the mother country. In addition, within this cultural framework sectional differences were beginning to appear, growing sharper as time passed, in dialect, manners, economics, society, tastes, needs – the citified commercial Middle States of New York, Pennsylvania, and New Jersey; rural, Calvinist New England; the semi-feudal agrarian South; the bumptious, sprawling West – not one America, but many in one, the *e pluribus unum* of the coinage made real. Amidst all this was the plain hard fact of the frontier, which as it moved westward became the hither edge of a civilization more and more removed from Europe and increasingly American. Early eighteenth-century Boston, though by no means culturally or temperamentally British, was only a ship's voyage from London; nineteenth-century Pittsburgh and Wheeling, behind the mountain wall, grew in a new and alien world. And beneath the rising tide of nationalism lay the shreds of the old colonial sense of mission and destiny, the idealism of those who came to the shores of Massachusetts to make a new Jerusalem in this green and pleasant land. Small wonder that by 1815 America resounded with cries for a native culture, a native tradition, a realization of its native self.

Early nineteenth-century America, of course, grew up in an age of romanticism, with a tendency to exalt the common man, to stress the potentialities of the individual, to break the rigid bonds of tradition and form. The romantic movement of the late eighteenth century, as it reached America in the early nineteenth century, wrought profound and significant changes in the temper of American life. The legacy of belief in inevitable progress, left behind by the preceding generation, buttressed the nation's romantic faith in its own powers and blew on it the breath of hope. America faced the future with dynamic eagerness, confident of solving its problems. 'We are the pioneers of the world,' reflected Herman Melville. 'God has predestined, mankind expects, great things from our race, and great things we feel in our soul. The most of the nations must soon be in the rear. We are . . . the advance guard, sent on through the wilderness of untried things.'

The optimistic nationalism that characterized the period was not wholly narrow or insular. The literate population of the United States was still for the most part British in origin and old ties with England and Europe were not easily broken. After concluding two wars against Britain, separated by a brief period of internal adjustment, the United States felt sufficiently secure to take another look at England and Europe – but with a self-consciously American attitude, neither imitative nor colonial. After 1814 American scholars, writers, and travellers eagerly sought out and brought back with them from abroad the ideas, treasures, and attitudes of the Old World, yet always with the accepted underlying assumption that they were not copying Europe, but absorbing it. Young men like Motley, Bancroft, Ticknor, and Everett studied at German universities; Emerson visited Wordsworth and Coleridge; Longfellow travelled in Germany, Italy, and Spain; Irving went to England, Spain, and Germany. These and others like them re-established enthusiastic communication with older civilizations. American culture of the period therefore displayed all the hallmarks of contemporary European thought, with the addition of such characteristic American traits as a belief in the superiority of democracy, an optimistic and expansive attitude, and a greater sense of an older Puritan moralism and rigidity. America must 'prove to the world', wrote Charles Ingersoll in 1823, 'that the best patronage of religion, science, literature, and the arts, of whatever the mind can achieve, is SELF-GOVERNMENT'.

This blending of nationalism and cosmopolitanism is aptly illustrated by the literary trends of the period. American authors and critics, groping for some concept of a national culture, could not quite decide whether to be Americans or geniuses; in them the hope lingered that they might be both. With their military and political affairs for the moment apparently stabilized, they turned energetically to the problem of establishing a national culture, though not at all certain what it should be. The journals of the time were filled with laments for the lack of a native cultural tradition, coupled with loud demands for its creation. Under pressure of the nationalistic urge from at home, and the drive of European romanticism from abroad, American critics hopefully awaited the appearance of an American Scott or an American Wordsworth. In their haste to acclaim him, they were often premature, hailing every dull poem as a 'new American epic' or every tedious novelist as an 'American Austen' or a 'native Scott'.

In attempting to create a native culture, the American of the first three decades of the century felt it his patriotic duty to answer the attacks of European (especially British) writers on America. Badgered by foreign critics, uncertain of their own status in the world, and subjected to the abuse of magazines such as the Tory *Quarterly* and *Blackwood's*, they displayed an exaggerated but understandable pugnacity and sensitivity – *le patriotisme irritable* that de Tocqueville noted.

Replies to foreign attacks were not easily fashioned, for American literary and artistic production was hardly distinguished. If Britain could display Burns, Byron, Scott, Wordsworth, Coleridge, Jane Austen, and a myriad of others, to whom could America point with pride? Dwight, Barlow, Dennie, Paulding, Drake, Freneau, Halleck, and company. The shadow of Byron and Wordsworth lay over American verse; Scott, whose books had by 1823 sold a half-million copies in the United States, dominated American fiction. Sydney Smith's sneering query, 'Who reads an American book?' was hard to answer.

Yet there was something developing. Americans discovered that the frontier blockhouse was as satisfactory a background for romantic fiction as a castle on the Rhine or in the Scottish lowlands; Deerslayer in his buckskin was as exciting a figure as a knight in armour; Indians were adversaries as worthy as Moors or clansmen. Cooper, Bryant, young Longfellow, Poe, and a few others provided a partial answer to Smith, and Washington Irving one much more convincing. Irving, who showed that art could be both good and national, pointed the way toward the development of a native cultural tradition. William Ellery Channing expressed the hope that Irving and a few others seemed to justify, that America, with its concept of liberty and with its freedom from much of the Old World's corruption and error, might yet evolve a cultural tradition that would 'give new impulses to the human mind'.

The place of religion in American life in the early nineteenth century was still secure, though not so central as it had once been. The Revolutionary War disrupted churches and weakened their position by shifting interest from religious to political affairs. The separation of church and state, begun by the Bill of Rights and completed by the states, became a fact, while the dominance of Calvinism in American life, already threatened during the later eighteenth century, was further endangered by a growing trend towards secularism.

Seventeenth-century Puritanism, exemplified in the New

England colonies of Plymouth and Massachusetts Bay, was a unified, internally balanced system of beliefs and practices, embracing ethics, politics, science, economics, and social beliefs. It controlled the thought of the American seventeenth century. After 1750 Calvinistic Christianity was gradually buried beneath a heavy coating of political and economic facts to which its theology had little relevance. But for fifty-odd years it was neither effectively disputed nor openly discarded, despite the inroads made into its domain by the Methodism of the 1740s and the Deism of the 1790s. It was simply ignored as something of little consequence in practical living, although occasional flares of revitalization might occur within it. By the time of the War of 1812 Puritanism had lost its hold on American life, though its impression remained on generations to come.

The decline and fall of American Puritanism came as the result of a variety of internal and external causes. It was always a difficult creed to hold, containing seemingly irreconcilable principles which had to be kept in alignment by constant argument and adjustment. Its concepts of God, free will, knowledge and revelation, sin, and moral duty were maintained throughout the seventeenth century in delicate intellectual and imaginative balance; to later generations of ministers and laity they seemed less capable of proof or reconciliation. As the concepts themselves came under the scrutiny of a rationalistic, hard-headed age, the system they supported disintegrated – like Holmes's 'one-hoss shay', which pure logic could no longer hold together.

Puritanism was, of course, under constant pressure from without. As the nation turned to a mercantile and industrial economy, the emphasis of living shifted from other-worldliness to this-worldliness. Cities grew, a new wealthy, sophisticated urban class rose and prospered, while piety suffered. The single-minded purpose of the original Puritans disappeared in the mercantile economics of a maturing eighteenth-century society, where neither Jonathan Edwards nor Cotton Mather could recall it. As one observer noted, it became difficult for reasonable folk to regard their decent, orderly, and wealthy neighbours as inherently sinful and lost, even though they did not belong to the proper orthodox church. 'Protestantism,' remarked Lowell later, 'had made its fortune and no longer protested.' The rationalism of Newton and Franklin had no place for Puritan logic, nor for its concepts of the universe and human nature. Deism, Methodism, Baptism, and Unitarianism were better equipped to meet the needs of the times, and more adaptable to the rational, individualistic, secular spirit of the late eighteenth and early nineteenth century. By substituting an optimistic, expansive religious philosophy for one of gloomy determinism, the newer sects freed the active spirit of the age from the inhibitions imposed on it by traditional Calvinism.

For that matter, the whole drift of contemporary political thought moved directly away from the Puritan idea of the state and its function. The concept of natural rights, the social compact theory, the new feeling of equality, liberty, and fraternity – all these were incompatible with the Puritan tradition of oligarchy. The early Puritans' conviction that they were God's chosen people faded with the rise of nationalism; the wedge driven between church and state by eighteenth-century constitutional thinkers weakened the older system still more. By 1814, after a half-century's defence, Puritanism found itself in contradiction to the main trends of American political thought. Its theology was opposed to contemporary science; its theocracy in conflict with contemporary ideas of democracy; its basic ethic at variance with nineteenth-century social, political, and economic facts.

At the close of the eighteenth century the strength of the long-established American churches was at a low ebb. The Great Awakening of mid century split the Congregationalists into warring wings of 'New Lights' and 'Old Lights', while Methodism and Deism sapped their strength. Presbyterians noted the decline of their churches with alarm; in 1782 only two students at Princeton, long a Presbyterian stronghold, professed the true faith. President Timothy Dwight at Yale inveighed against 'infidelity', while the Congregationalist-

Unitarian controversy split Harvard's theological faculty and led later to the founding of Andover by the defeated conservatives. The Episcopal Church in the South had lost its economic strength, its political privilege and its heart at the time of the Revolution. It was, thought Chief Justice Marshall, 'too far gone to be revived'. Timothy Flint, a frontier missionary, reported from the West that 'in these new regions, too, of the most absolute independence, you see all the wanderings of human thought, every shade of faith . . .' There were a good many frontiersmen who swore by Tom Paine and proudly called themselves 'nullifidians', and a preacher could never be sure how he would be received in the hinterlands. Even in Catholic Louisiana Voltaire and Diderot were popular, while a visitor to St Louis left it with the firm impression that every Frenchman was an infidel.

In the chaos following the breakdown of the old faiths, several new ones or variations of older ones appeared on the theological scene. Unitarianism, whose appeal in America, as in England, was largely limited to the cultivated classes, became an influential force in New England and the East. The visit of the great Hazlitt's father to New England in 1783-5, and the work of liberal Congregationalists such as Thomas Barnard and John Prince before him, had direct consequences. The Episcopal King's Chapel in Boston took a Unitarian stand in 1784; in the next sixteen years all but a few of the city's churches followed suit. The appointment of a Unitarian, Henry Ware, as Hollis Professor of Divinity at Harvard in 1805, marked the end of Puritan dominance in the cradle of New England Calvinism. Universalism, called derisively for its simple creed 'the poor man's Unitarianism', established itself in Massachusetts as early as 1779. Both of these sects, with their stress on the worth of human nature, their emphasis on the social and humanitarian rather than the credal aspects of religion and their belief in the efficacy of the individual, were in closer agreement with the mood of the period than was orthodox Calvinism. They gave respectability and organized status to

347

liberal religious thought as deism had failed to do. Not long after 1800 the majority of existing churches from Maine to Maryland made the transition to Unitarian-Universalist principles without a serious break in church organization.

Neither the older Puritanism nor the newer Unitarianism carried religion to the West. The opening of the transmountain areas and the swift rush of settlement westward meant great new opportunities for church expansion. Of the older sects, the Presbyterians were best situated to take advantage of it, since the last wave of pre-Revolutionary migration scattered Scotch-Irish Presbyterians north and south along the mountain frontier. In 1801 the Congregationalists and Presbyterians joined in a 'Plan of Union' to Christianize the West, and pushed their brands of orthodoxy into Ohio, Michigan, western New York, and Illinois, where migration from New England and the Middle States was largest.

The greatest successes in the West, however, were those of the Baptists and Methodists, whose organization, doctrines and temperament were admirably fitted to frontier conditions. Both were loosely organized, flexible in creed, simple in theology. Both stressed religious elements particularly appropriate to the frontier – emotionalism, personal conversion, directness – emphasizing the importance of the individual in religion, rather than church or creed. The shouting, hymn-singing, camp-meeting of the itinerant evangelist made theology a personal and communal matter; the week-long revivals were social as well as religious events. Bishop Francis Asbury, the superb administrator and organizer who introduced into the West the 'circuit rider' system used by the Wesleys in England, found it perfectly adapted to the scattered settlements, just as the Baptists found their 'lay preacher' system equally well suited. Asbury, who travelled over 300,000 miles in the saddle, sent hundreds of circuit-riding ministers like the redoubtable Peter Cartwright into remote backwoods areas, and created a string of Methodist outposts. The Baptists and Methodists captured the lower Northwest and the Southwest, and pushed churches far into the New England-settled Great Lakes areas.

Probably the greatest factor in the death of Puritanism was the wave of evangelism that swept like a prairie fire across America after 1800. In the Northeast, where Unitarianism and even Universalism never really appealed to the ordinary man, the Methodists sparked a rebirth of religious fervour that eventually evangelized half of the area – by 1802 one third of the students at godless Yale affirmed conversion. Revivalist techniques, worked out in the Great Awakening a half-century before, fired Congregational and Presbyterian churches all over New England with what Timothy Dwight called 'that strange new-birth, that Methodistic grace'. The wave rolled swiftly west, where the Baptists and Methodists held sway. The great evangelist James McGready carried the flame of 'old time religion' through the Carolinas into Kentucky and Tennessee, followed by torchlit camp-meetings, shouting, singing, hysteria, and other stigmata of sudden public conversion. From the mountainous Southwest it spread west and north into the lower fringes of Ohio, Indiana, Michigan, and Illinois, cutting across sectarian lines and striking impartially into all the churches. The Methodists and Baptists, accustomed as they were to emotionalism, welcomed the evangelistic torch-bearers eagerly. The Presbyterians hung back, and the Congregationalists opposed them for a quarter of a century, but revivalism flourished none the less. The largest meeting was probably that at Cain Ridge, Kentucky, in 1801, where roughly 20,000 people gathered for a week in fervent hysterical worship, egged on by Baptist, Methodist, and Presbyterian exhorters. The Second Awakening shook orthodoxy on its already unsteady foundations, broke up into an astonishing variety of new schismatic sects, and left the Baptists and Methodists the undisputed masters of the West. From it came the Christian Church, the Campbellites, the United Brethren, the Rappites, and many more.

The evangelism of the early nineteenth century was in effect a theological manifestation of the democratizing temper of the era. With the old faiths apparently out of touch with the people and the times, the newer and less orthodox churches – by appealing to the common man and emphasizing ideas of individual worth, progress, and equality of believers – met the religious demands of the day as surely and squarely as Jacksonian democracy met contemporary political desires. Splitting the old sects and creating new ones, the wave of revivalism encouraged the dissenting factions to challenge directly the domination of the orthodox churches of the East as well as of the West, and of the conservative, federalist classes who supported them. The break with Puritanism was clean and complete, as clear and certain as Jacksonian democracy's break with the older political tradition.

After 1800 Calvinism no longer dominated American life and thought. Yet its stamp remained strong on the American character – its moral fervour or 'Yankee conscience', its crusading spirit, its dreams of social reconstruction, its tremendous driving energy. The United States was still under the control of an aggressive Protestantism. Congregationalists, Baptists, Presbyterians, Methodists and the others might argue matters of creed interminably, but they all frowned on deviations from the moral, the accepted, the pious – a check on the rebelliousness and individualism of romanticism. There was no American Byron to scandalize New England, no atheist Shelley at Harvard, no illicit romance in Emerson's past. The disputatious diversity of American sects carried to the ultimate the implications of the Reformation, but never denied them; no American could escape the effects of nearly two hundred years of Puritanism.

America was optimistic, nationalistic, romantically hopeful, self-consciously young, trying hard to find the stability, confidence and maturity of the older nations, hoping to establish itself as a nation in the shortest possible time. Perhaps it flexed its muscles in public too much, chased 'refinement' and sensibility too eagerly, played the pugnacious youngster too hard. But it was, or at least believed itself to be, an achieved democracy possessed of something that England, France and the rest of the world did not have.

At the close of 'Mr Madison's War' the United States turned with a sigh of relief to the matter at hand, that of realizing its self-made promises. Mr Madison's party, having concluded its inept prosecution of an unpopular and inconclusive war, surprisingly enough emerged from it covered with popular glory, its Federalist opposition melted away. The Republican party, taking a stronger nationalistic position than even Hamilton's party had maintained in its palmiest days, attracted to it all but the most irreconcilable Federalists, whose popularity had rapidly declined since the Hartford Convention. The Presidential election of 1816, a colourless affair, showed that party politics had reached very nearly a dead level. To decry partisanship became the fashion of the day, and even that king of partisans, Andrew Jackson, advised that 'Now is the time to exterminate the monster called party spirit . . . and perhaps have the pleasure of uniting a people heretofore politically divided.' Madison chose Secretary of State Monroe as his successor, while the Federalists did not bother to name an official candidate. Monroe carried all but three states, whose electors supported Rufus King of New York.

James Monroe of Virginia was neither a distinguished statesman nor an acute politician, though he had, as John Quincy Adams phrased it, 'a mind sound in its ultimate judgements and firm in its final conclusions'. He did have wide experience in politics – Senator from Virginia, Governor of Virginia, Minister to France and England, Secretary of State – a solid but not brilliant record. A congenital middle-of-the-roader, he was so eminently fitted to govern the United States during a period of indecision that his two terms as President became known as 'the era of good feelings'. There was, of course, an internal balance of powers from 1816 to 1824 that lent some logic to the name, but the period was more accurately one of transition rather than of 'good feelings', peaceful only because political forces were busy regrouping for new conflict. For the placid soil of

Date of Inclusion in the Union

Alabama	1819	Iowa	1846	Nebraska	1867		
Arizona	1912	Kansas	1861	Nevada	1864		
Arkansas	1836	Kentucky	1792	New Hampshire	1788		
California	1850	Louisiana	1812	New Jersey	1787		
Colorado	1876	Maine	1820	New Mexico	1912		
Connecticut	1788	Maryland	1788	New York	1788		
Delaware	1787	Massachusetts	1788	N. Carolina	1789	Rhode Island	1790
Florida	1845	Michigan	1837	N. Dakota	1889	S. Carolina	1788
Georgia	1788	Minnesota	1858	Ohio	1803	S. Dakota	1889
Idaho	1890	Mississippi	1817	Oklahoma	1907	Tennessee	1796
Illinois	1818	Missouri	1821	Oregon	1859	Texas	1845
Indiana	1816	Montana	1889	Pennsylvania	1787	Utah	1896

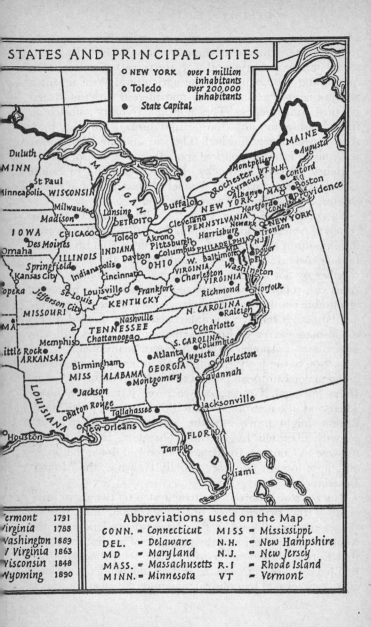

STATES AND PRINCIPAL CITIES

○ NEW YORK — over 1 million inhabitants
○ Toledo — over 200,000 inhabitants
● State Capital

Duluth
MINN
St Paul
Minneapolis WISCONSIN
Milwaukee
Madison
IOWA
CHICAGO
Des Moines
Omaha
ILLINOIS INDIANA
Springfield
Kansas City Indianapolis
opeka St Louis Louisville
MISSOURI Jefferson City KENTUCKY Frankfort
MA Nashville
Little Rock Memphis Chattanooga
ARKANSAS
Birmingham
MISS ALABAMA
Jackson
Baton Rouge
LOUISIANA
Houston New Orleans
Lansing
DETROIT
Toledo Akron
Dayton Pittsburg
OHIO Columbus
Cincinnati
W.
VIRGINIA
Charleston
TENNESSEE
GEORGIA
Montgomery
Tallahassee
MICHIGAN
Buffalo
Cleveland
NEW YORK
PENNSYLVANIA
Harrisburg
PHILADELPHIA
MD baltimore
Washington
VIRGINIA
Richmond Norfolk
N. CAROLINA
Raleigh
Charlotte
S. CAROLINA
Columbia
Atlanta Augusta Charleston
Savannah
Jacksonville
FLORIDA
Tampa
Miami
MAINE
Augusta
Montpelier
Rochester VT N.H. Contord
Syracuse
Albany MASS Boston
Hartford Providence
Newark CONN NEW YORK
Trenton
N.J.
Dover
DEL

Abbreviations used on the Map

CONN. = Connecticut   MISS = Mississippi
DEL. = Delaware   N.H. = New Hampshire
MD = Maryland   N.J. = New Jersey
MASS. = Massachusetts R.I = Rhode Island
MINN. = Minnesota   VT = Vermont

Monroe's era contained the seeds of sectional interests, soon to germinate. The rise of manufacturing in New England, stimulated by embargo and war, the spread of cotton in the South, and the opening of the agricultural West meant a readjustment of sectional economic interests with unforeseen political consequences. The 'Virginia Dynasty', stretching from Washington to Monroe and broken only by John Adams, was nearly finished. The war and the West ended it, bringing into the political spotlight a new cast of leaders – Henry Clay of Kentucky, John C. Calhoun of South Carolina, New England's Daniel Webster, John Quincy Adams, and of course Andrew Jackson.

Except for the delivery of the Monroe Doctrine, the record of American foreign affairs from 1816 to 1840 showed few important developments. The whole of Spanish Florida became American property in 1819, and the problem of whether or not to recognize the new revolutionary South American republics was deferred by observing a policy of favourable neutrality until their recognition seemed expedient. Although relatively uninterested in the tangled diplomatic manoeuvres of Europe, the United States still saw a threat to its power in the Western hemisphere in the formation of the Holy Alliance, and in the apparent design of the major European powers to crush revolution in Spain, Italy, Portugal, Greece, or wherever it raised its head. There was also a strong suspicion that Europe, particularly Britain, might move into the South American republics recently liberated by Bolivar. Therefore, in his annual message to Congress in 1823, Monroe laid down the broad outline of foreign policy eventually known as the Monroe Doctrine.

The basis of Monroe's doctrine rested on two main principles – the principle of non-colonization, that Europe should not be allowed to found new dependencies in the western hemisphere; and the principle of non-intervention, that Europe should never so interfere with the nations of that hemisphere as to endanger their independence or form of government. 'The political system of the allied powers is essentially different . . . from that of America,' Monroe wrote, '. . . . We should consider any attempt on their part to extend their system to any portion of this hemisphere as dangerous to our peace and safety', thus drawing a sharp line of political demarcation between Europe and both Americas. The fundamental ideas of the Doctrine were implicit in the foreign policies of Washington, John Adams and Jefferson. Monroe's message, however, clarified matters by stating in precise and explicit terms the principles of hemispheric separation, non-intervention, and avoidance of foreign entanglement. His forthright enunciation of American dominance over the whole Western half of the world irritated and annoyed Europe (particularly Canning and Metternich) and Canada. It was received at best with mixed feelings by those South American republics whose future it was designed to safeguard. Nevertheless the Monroe Doctrine remained a basic principle of American foreign policy and was brought to issue in the Mexican troubles some thirty years later.

The ultra-nationalistic trend of the 'era of good feelings' was evident in the programme of legislation laid out by Congress during Monroe's administration. His inaugural address of 1815 asked for a stronger military, a solid uniform national currency, a protective tariff for war-born American industry, and a system of roads and canals to improve communications between the seaboard ports and the West. All these requests were speedily granted, the moribund Federalist party acceding with alacrity to what was essentially its own historic programme. New England's commercial interests objected, fearing that a tariff would damage foreign trade and that the road-canal system might favour the agricultural West, but they received short shrift. Meanwhile, as the Republicans strengthened the position of the federal government in political and commercial affairs, the Supreme Court, under the able and obstinate Chief Justice John Marshall of Virginia, gave them legal assistance.

Marshall, one of John Adams's appointees, dominated the Court for thirty-four years (1801–35). An avowed Federalist, he lost no opportunity, in both important and obscure cases, to emphasize the supremacy of federal power and interest over that of the states, and the supremacy of the judiciary over the executive and legislative branches of the government. Hardly learned in law, Marshall was less the technical jurist than the juridical statesman, willing to look beyond the case at hand to the needs of a new people and of an expanding nation. During his term of office he handled more than fifty cases involving important constitutional issues, and decided each from the point of view of Federalist political philosophy. As a result Marshall became the greatest single influence on the shape of American constitutional law.

Marbury versus Madison (1803) established the principle of judicial review, that is, the right of the Supreme Court to declare void and unconstitutional an act or portion of an act of Congress or state legislature. *Fletcher versus Peck* (1810) established the inviolability of contracts, placing them beyond the reach of state courts and governments, while in *Dartmouth College versus Woodward* (1819) he maintained that corporation charters were also contracts, a decision that later proved important to an expanding industrial economy. *McCulloch versus Maryland* (1819) and *Osburn versus Bank of the United States* (1824) affirmed the superiority of federal over state law and the Hamiltonian principle of implied constitutional power – that the federal government may do things not specifically stated in the Constitution that it may do, if its purpose agrees with the spirit of the Constitution and with the national interest. Hammering at these principles in decision after decision, with the majority of the Court behind him, Marshall's idea of federal supremacy fitted the prevailing nationalistic trend. Whatever the fate of the Federalist party, he wrote its ideas into constitutional law and won its old fight with the Jeffersonians.

From the Louisiana Purchase to the entry of Wisconsin (the last state east of the Mississippi to enter the union) in 1848, the area added to the nation was larger than all

Europe west of Russia. 'The rise of the new West,' remarked a later historian, Frederick Jackson Turner, 'was the most significant fact in American history in the years immediately following the War of 1812.'

The West grew with phenomenal speed. In the first thirty-six years of the Republic, five new states joined the Union – Vermont, Tennessee, Kentucky, Ohio, and Louisiana. But six new states entered in only seven years after the close of the War of 1812 – Indiana (1816), Mississippi (1817), Illinois (1818), Alabama (1819), Maine (1820), and Missouri (1821) – five of them carved from frontier territory. The centre of population swiftly shifted westward. At the time of Washington's Inauguration, less than six per cent of the country's population lived west of the Allegheny–Appalachian mountain ranges. By 1820 the figure stood at twenty-seven per cent and was still growing; Ohio's population exceeded that of Massachusetts, while Louisiana and Missouri, the most western of the new states, had more than fifty thousand inhabitants. As early as 1796 a British traveller in Pennsylvania reported seeing 'ten and twenty waggons at a time . . . on their way to Pittsburgh and other parts of Ohio, from thence to descend down the river to Kentucky'. Another observer, watching the flatboats loaded with wagons dotting the Ohio river, remarked that 'there is scarcely a day . . . but that there is a greater or less number of boats floating down its gentle current', to the tune of 'Hi-O, away we go Floating down the river on the O-Hi-O'.

The great migration flowed down established waterways, through convenient mountain passes, and over the new national turnpikes that were built after 1818. New Englanders followed the Connecticut and Housatonic rivers into Maine and over into upper New York State, where the Great Genesee Road began. The Hudson and Mohawk valleys opened up on western New York, joining lake and river routes that continued on to Ohio and Michigan. From Philadelphia and the Middle States Braddock's Road led to Pittsburgh, where the Allegheny and Monongahela rivers met to form the Ohio, the gateway to Ohio, Kentucky, Tennessee, southern Indiana and Illinois, and the Southwest. Migrants from Virginia and the southern seaboard could follow Boone's Wilderness Road through Cumberland Gap into Kentucky, or the new National Pike from Maryland to Wheeling and on into Ohio, Indiana, and Illinois. The Jonesboro Road carried migrants from North Carolina into Tennessee, while another route ran from South Carolina through Georgia into Alabama, Mississippi, and Louisiana. These roads seemed to be always full. At Zanesville, Ohio, fifty wagons a day crossed the Muskingum river; during one nine-day period in 1817, two hundred and sixty wagons passed a given point on the turnpike in upper New York State. On the southern route a traveller coming eastward counted 3,800 persons headed west towards Alabama and Mississippi. In its first year of operation, the Erie Canal carried 13,111 boats and 40,000 persons west. 'Old America,' commented an observer in 1817, 'seems to be breaking up and moving westward.'

Some families travelled alone, with a single horse and wagon piled high with furniture and children, a barefooted wife walking behind. Others banded together for mutual assistance, and occasionally groups as large as 200 from a single area planned and made the trip, electing a leader and appointing trail committees. Cattle, horses, sheep, and hogs were driven before the caravan, tended by slaves in the case of the few wealthy Southerners who made the trip. For those able to afford it, flatboat or steamboat transportation made travel swifter; the poor simply walked, going West 'because everybody says it's good land'. From Virginia and the Carolinas, Southerners moved into Tennessee, Kentucky, Alabama, Mississippi, and Louisiana (and later into Arkansas and Texas), taking with them cotton economies and slavery. A few, like Lincoln's father, filtered north into southern Ohio, Illinois, and Indiana, giving that region a slightly Southern cast that it still retains. The rich flat loam of the Northwest drew New England farmers, tired of the hard-scrabble acreage of Maine and Massachusetts, and attracted frustrated labourers and artisans from the densely-populated

Eastern cities – giving a Puritan, Yankee stamp to the towns of Ohio, Michigan, northern Indiana and Illinois, and later Wisconsin. Though most of them stopped at the Mississippi, the nation sent probing fingers into the huge, vaguely-known, rolling plains of the trans-river area, hitherto the domain of trappers, hunters, fur companies, and Indians. Jefferson sent Meriwether Lewis and William Clark up the Missouri to the Pacific Northwest in 1804, while John Jacob Astor sent two expeditions to the Oregon country and planted a post of his Pacific Fur Company at Astoria in 1811-12. The Wisconsin–Minnesota–Dakota territory was already the base of a highly organized fur trade, and missionaries, both Catholic and Protestant, followed the trappers into the westernmost reaches of the wilderness.

Behind the westward push was the desire for good, cheap land. The long argument over the disposal of the public domain, dating back to the Articles of Confederation, was settled by a series of decisions that favoured the settler rather than the private company or speculator. The Ordinance of 1785, coupled with the Northwest Ordinance of 1787, provided a pattern for surveying, selling, and settling the western lands. Successive changes in land laws led finally to the act of 1820 which established the minimum size of grants at 80 acres, the minimum price at $1.25 an acre, and certain favourable credit terms. Whilst the new laws did not entirely eliminate the speculator, at least they made his job more difficult and the emigrant's acquisition of a good-sized farm somewhat easier.

Cheap land was lure enough, but, to drive men West, there was also the pressure of economic conditions in the crowded, war-dislocated cities of the East. American manufacturing, hurt by embargo and blockade, faltered uncertainly for nearly a decade after the War of 1812. Periodic business recessions, as the national economy adjusted to peace, were immediately reflected by increases in the westward flow, at its highest during the depression years of 1819 to 1821. The shipping interests of New England ran into stiff competition from European merchantmen, while the growth of New York, New Orleans and Baltimore, and the opening of canals and turnpikes, almost killed off the lesser New England ports. Western wheat, sheep, cattle, and even vegetables – especially as transportation routes opened to them Eastern markets – pushed the New England farmer hard; freight rates between Buffalo and New York dropped from $100 to $8 a ton when the Erie Canal opened. From the seaboard South, where tobacco quickly wore out soil, the lush bottom lands of the West attracted farmers who raised cotton, tobacco, and wheat. The Southern yeoman farmer, artisan, and non-slaveholder often found the West a convenient and attractive escape from the economic and political domination of the great planters and merchants of the seaboard cities; the old conflict between back-country and coastal areas in Pennsylvania, Virginia, and the Carolinas helped to drive back-country men farther west in search of political and economic independence.

After 1800 the removal of the Indian threat in the Northwest and Southwest provided an additional impetus to the westward movement. 'Mad Anthony' Wayne's victory over Little Turtle's Miamis at Fallen Timbers in northwestern Ohio in 1794 broke the back of Indian resistance in the Ohio–Michigan–Indiana area, impressing the British so much that they speeded up evacuation of their Great Lakes military outposts, and with the failure of Tecumseh's confederacy after Harrison's inconclusive clash with him at Tippecanoe in 1811, the Indian menace virtually came to an end. The Indians gave ground grudgingly in a series of bloody minor actions; it was not until after the Black Hawk War in 1832 that the westernmost settlers could forget the torch and scalping knife.

American institutions and American character received their shape and pattern from diverse influences – from Europe, from Puritan protestantism, from the environment of the land itself – but certainly one of the most powerful of these influences was the frontier. The growth and development of modern European nations has been conditioned by the fact that their expansion was confined within fairly definite limits, marked by national boundaries; in order to continue expansion one nation was forced to absorb or conquer others. This was not true of the United States. The early seventeenth-century colonies fringing the sea coast found only a negligible Indian civilization between them and seemingly illimitable space. The early settlers came, subdued the wilderness and the Indian, evolved a government, and progressed from primitive agricultural society to complex industrial or agricultural civilization within a few years. Inland, perhaps only a few miles, the process was being repeated again and again, over a period of nearly 250 years, until it was stopped by the Pacific Ocean. Conflict with neighbouring nations was indirect rather than direct. There were no equal states to meet and subdue, no established or well-developed cultures to absorb or dominate – and the frontier could always move West. The settlement itself was fortunately accomplished by a homogeneous people, of the same race, language, stock, religion, and political and social ideals, whose minor cultural differences were easily assimilated.

The frontier meant a constant return to primitive conditions at the edge of the settlement line, a constant repetition of an evolutionary development from simple to complex civilization as that line moved westward. This perennial rebirth of civilization, perennial contact with primitive conditions, perennial social fluidity, had much to do with the distinctive temper of America and Americans. For as the frontier moved westward it became more and more native, geographically and culturally more removed from Europe, less subject to Old World intellectual, religious, and economic influences. In Hawthorne's extravagant phrase, beyond the mountains lay land 'on which the damned shadow of Eurpoe had not fallen'. This is the difference between William Bradford and Abraham Lincoln, between John Smith and Daniel Boone, between Thomas Jefferson and Andrew Jackson, between George Washington and William Jennings Bryan – all Americans, yet as unlike as the ages that produced them, the country they lived in, and – most of all – as diverse as the frontiers that shaped them.

The Atlantic Coast, the frontier of Smith and Bradford, was an English frontier, retaining much of British culture, habits, manners and modes of thought. In the late seventeenth century the line of settlement moved inland up the waterways to the mountain fall line and beyond, to the Wyoming Valley of Pennsylvania, Pittsburgh, eastern Tennessee, the Georgia uplands, Boone's Kentucky. By the late eighteenth century it had moved on – despite efforts to stop it by the Proclamation of 1763 – into the Ohio country, western Tennessee and Kentucky, to the threshold of the Northwest. A quarter of a century later the frontier lay at the Mississippi; then swiftly leaping to the Pacific, it worked slowly across the plains behind the Rocky Mountains, filling in the Missouri basin and the desert Southwest. The census of 1890 noted that there existed no more arable free land with a population density of less than two per square mile. Thus the frontier was declared officially dead, but its imprint on America is eternally present.

The men who went West with this frontier were a varied group, but contemporary observers and later historians identified five main types. A spectator standing at Cumberland Gap in 1790, or at Zanesville in 1810, or at South Pass in the Rockies in 1870, might have seen them pass by in almost the same order. First came the explorer, half-Indian, half-adventurer, driven west by his desire to see what lay beyond the next mountain range or across the hazy plain. He brought back tales of great virgin pine and of hardwood trees a hundred feet high, stretching in a tremendous forest belt four hundred miles long and three hundred miles wide; of fertile tall-grass prairies and black bottom lands; of clear streams and thousands of blue lakes; of deer and turkeys and squirrels and rabbits. After him came the hunter and trapper, living by his rifle and bringing his skins back to some trading outpost, there to stand mute and uncomfortable until he had received his salt, powder, and bullets and could disappear into the wilderness again. He marked trails, found passes and fords, and knew which Indians were friendly and which savage. The pioneer farmer followed him, to build a rude cabin on squatter's land, clear a plot for a few vegetables, hunt, trap, and raise a family. When he heard the sound of a neighbour's axe, he moved on, or his sons did. On his heels came the settler, who bought his land and built a better house with a chimney, rooms and perhaps glass windows. He cleared more acres, drove a well, built bridges, mills, stores, schools, and churches, organized an elementary government, raised grain, fruit, and cash crops. When others came he might sell his land at a higher price and move on, or he might stay to merge with the growing community. In 1840 there were men in Michigan and Wisconsin who had moved five times, each time farther west. (Lincoln's father liked to tell, with typical Western hyperbole, about a family that moved so often that the chickens were trained to walk to the wagon, lie down, and put their feet up to be tied for the trip.) Last to arrive were the men of capital or professional skill – lawyers, bankers, editors, ministers, artisans, speculators, and politicians, the men who rounded out the social, political, and economic society, the men who stayed. They built handsome houses of frame or brick, better churches and schools, distilleries, factories, warehouses; they put up fences and laid out streets and roads, introduced better strains of livestock and seed. Thus the cycle was complete, but beginning all over again somewhere to the west, a cycle accomplished with incredible speed. Some of Chicago's first settlers were still alive when it had become one of the nation's five largest cities.

What sort of man did this process produce? He was, first of all, nationally minded. The Atlantic coast was strongly influenced by Europe, but the area west of the mountains was much less so – it was simply American, a blend of Yankee, Southerner, Scotch-Irish, Pennsylvania Dutch, city man, farmer, and whatever else came West. None of the new states short of the Pacific coast had any colonial history. They were children of the Federal Government, which surveyed their land and sold it to them, helped them finance it, protected them against Indians and British (sometimes none too well), governed them as territories, and admitted them as states. Both Southwest and Northwest were nationalistic in thought until split by slavery and states-rights. The frontier American was, by past and present circumstances, a strong believer in equality. European travellers noted that even in the cities workmen did not tip their hats or say 'Sir', that servants ate at the family table, that titles such as 'Judge' and 'Colonel' were so liberally bestowed as to be meaningless. Together runaway servant and earl's son faced starvation, Indians, the forest, and opportunity; the frontier gave every man his chance. Each man counted as one, and how much he counted depended on his own brain and hands. And by *equality* the frontier meant not only social and political equality, but equality of economic opportunity – each to his own, and the devil take the hindmost.

Frontier man was a self-reliant individualist. He was his own master, and had only himself to blame for failure. There was no store to sell salt to the pioneer who travelled to the nearest salt-lick or trading post to get it. If his axe-handle broke, he whittled a new one. Illness he simply waited out or cured with what herb remedies he could devise. He built his own house, made many of his own tools, raised most of his food, and made much of his clothing. As the Philadelphia *Inquirer and Daily Courier* pointed out in an editorial on prospects in Illinois:

The tendency of a new country being to develop and bring forward youthful talent, exerts a highly favorable influence upon boldness, force, and originality of intellect.

This feeling of self-reliance carried over into political, social and economic life. It was no accident that the West soon became known as an area of political intransigence. From the farmers of Daniel Shays to Jefferson's back-country supporters, to Jackson's muddy-booted followers and on to Bryan's embattled farmers, the line of Western political revolt is clear and marked.

Yet with all his individualism, the pioneer developed a

fairly strong feeling of social solidarity and recognized the value of cooperative effort in dealing with the ever-present problems of frontier life – the wilderness, the Indians, loneliness, isolation. Organization was almost as much a characteristic of the frontier as individualism. He organized militia, fire companies, barn- and house-raisings, cornhusking bees, and so on, as testimony to his feeling of group responsibility. The dances held on the green with bran or sawdust scattered on the ground (the 'brandance' and later 'barndance') with the fiddler scraping away at 'Old Dan Tucker' or 'Zip Coon', the rooster and gander pulls, the horse-races and camp-meetings, all helped to temper frontier individualism with a sense of social unity.

Frontier man was also a convinced optimist. If things went badly, there was always the chance that somewhere to the West they might go better. Thus the New Englanders sang on their way west:

> Come all ye Yankee Farmers who wish to change your lot,
> Who've spunk enough to travel beyond your native spot,
> And leave behind the village where Ma and Pa do stay,
> Come follow me and settle in Michigania –
> Yea, Yea, in Michigania.

Or the pioneers of Wisconsin:

> When we've wood and prairie land,
> Won by our toil,
> We'll reign like kings in fairy land,
> Lords of the soil!

He was also a materialist, accustomed to dealing in the concrete and the present, for the frontier afforded little time for reflection and placed little value on abstractions. 'Men must learn the languages of the rifle, the axe, and the plough,' remarked a frontier minister, 'before they learn the lessons of Grecian and Roman philosophy and history.' There was much to be done simply to survive; the tomahawk, wet powder, starvation, and sickness were real and imminent. He had his vices as well as his virtues. Individualism and self-reliance could turn into plain disregard for law and order. Justice on the frontier could be primitive and self-administered, a matter of fist, knife, or gun. Theft was common, murder or rape not unusual, eye-gouging and ear-biting fights normal. Frontier life in its early stage could be unruly. brutal, and irreligious, though this phase usually did not last long when the church and women moved in. The Baptist, Methodist, Presbyterian, Congregational, and Campbellite circuit-riding preachers, their faiths founded on the rigid moral standards of old-fashioned Calvinism, carried law and order into backwoods settlements, and exerted a powerful force against gambling, vice, drunkenness, and violence. The influence of the frontier wife was even greater. As early as the mid eighteenth century, foreign observers noted the growing importance of women in American life, especially in the West. As soon as the settler arrived with his wife and family, she subtly but emphatically began to impose standards of discipline, refinement, morality, and order on frontier chaos – as Tom Sawyer's Aunt Sally civilized Tom and Huckleberry Finn.

The lack of self-discipline, typical of the frontier, never quite disappeared from its character. The frontiersman liked to do things in a hurry and often regarded careful, finished work as a waste of time; he slashed the forests, gutted the soil, threw up jerry-built buildings, polluted the streams, and exterminated the game. In one large midwestern city two of the largest buildings actually fell down because of poor construction; firebells clanged nightly as matchbox houses flamed; bridges fell in; roads were lost in mire; trains collided and steamboats blew up. At least some of the defeats of the Revolution and the War in 1812 can be laid to the Westerner's dislike of training and discipline, while the tone of legislative debates, punctuated by fist-fights and knife-brandishings, was sometimes hardly statesmanlike.

As Emerson noted in *Self-Reliance*, the American admired the jack-of-all-trades, the man who could farm, keep store, argue in court, serve in Congress, speculate in land, and run a bank. The specialist he viewed with dim suspicion; the learned man, the artist, the thinker he dismissed as an impractical theorist. Frontier society was produced by and organized for the average man, and those with unusual talents or highly developed sensitivities sometimes found it an uncomfortable and frustrating environment.

All in all, the frontiersmen were exuberant, vital, proud, and ambitious. Those who crossed the mountains were engaged in one of the greatest enterprises in history. Within two generations they transformed millions of acres of forest into farms, villages, and cities, and tamed a vast tract larger than Western Europe. The pioneer sensed the magnificence of the undertaking, and took pleasure in his part in it. It is not to be wondered, therefore, that he became fiercely proud of himself and his homeland, and convinced of the superiority of both. It was this feeling that led the Kentucky preacher to define Heaven as 'a real Kentuck of a place', or the frontiersman to create legends around Davy Crockett, who could swallow thunderbolts and ride lightning bareback. 'The coarseness and strength combined with acuteness and inquisitiveness; that practical, inventive turn of mind, quick to find expedients; that masterful grasp of material things, lacking in the artistic but powerful to effect great ends; that restless, nervous energy, that dominant individualism, working for good and evil; and withal that buoyancy and exuberance which comes with freedom – these,' wrote Frederick Jackson Turner, 'are the traits of the frontier, or traits called out elsewhere because of the existence of the frontier.'

The impact of the new West on the national economy was great. The War of 1812 revealed serious weaknesses in the national financial structure, and the settlement of the West intensified them. After the Bank of the United States was refused a renewal of its charter in 1811, national banking business fell to the state banks, many of them small and shaky. The demand for credit from speculators and land-buyers pushed them to the limit, with the result that Western banks over-extended themselves in making loans to settlers who needed money not only to purchase land but to buy tools, seeds, and finished goods. Cheap, fast, easy credit –

and hang the consequences – was exactly to the Westerner's liking. Careless banking practices produced so-called 'wild-cat' banks, until in 1814 all state banks except those in thrifty New England stopped specie payments. With credit and currency gyrating wildly, the Federal government in 1817 created the Second Bank of the United States to stabilize credit and to inaugurate more conservative lending policies. The course pursued by the Second Bank placed the national credit on a more even keel, but in the process it wrecked many of the smaller banks in the West and South, collapsing land values, forcing mortgage foreclosures, and precipitating the depression of 1819–21. For example, when the bubble burst a large part of the city of Cincinnati, including hotels, iron-works, buildings, and lots, fell into the hands of the Bank. Since the panic that followed hit the West particularly hard, and removed the easy credit the West wanted, the Bank became a bitterly hated thing west of Pittsburgh. Western states fought back with debtor-relief and loose banking laws, but the Supreme Court usually overruled them. The roots of the conflict between debtor West and creditor East, between farmer and 'Wall Street', a conflict that flared up again and again until Bryan's time, lay in this post-war push to the West.

A second economic problem, partially though not wholly of the West's creating, was the tariff. Manufacturers, working at forced draft behind the walls of embargo and blockade, demanded tariff protection against European competition. British ships in American ports sometimes auctioned off whole cargoes to the highest bidder, undercutting American prices and robbing the middleman. In addition, the West was rapidly becoming a producing and consuming area of great importance. Demands for a protective tariff grew louder through the post-war years, until Henry Clay of Kentucky believed the time ripe for a planned national economy centred on such a tariff. Clay's 'American system' was intended to make the United States as nearly as possible into a closed, self-supporting economic unit. A tariff that encouraged and developed industry would, it was presumed, provide employment for displaced non-agricultural workers. The agricultural West would feed the industrial East and the cotton–tobacco South, while the textile mills of the South clothed the West and East, both West and South serving as consumer markets for the manufacturing East. The revenue from the tariff, on the other hand, could be used to provide the roads and canals that the West and South needed. Clay's system, which some New Englanders and Southerners considered anything but American, was in effect a cloudy recognition of growing economic sectionalism, a way of balancing sectional interests against each other for a common good.

Sectional interests were far too strong, however, for any such careful compromise, though elements of Clay's system appeared in the tariffs of 1816, 1824, and 1828. The strongest demands for a protective tariff came from the Middle and Western States, which were anxious to develop home markets. The South, which bought manufactured articles from Europe and sent much of its cotton abroad, wanted no part of it. New England's manufacturing interests deemed protection a necessity; its merchants and shippers feared a looser tariff policy would ruin their trade entirely.

Economic development of the West also created a demand for cheap and easy trade routes back to the East and to the sea. The West therefore demanded aid from the Federal and state governments, since these were the only agencies with sufficient capital to underwrite huge road and canal projects. There was some doubt in the East whether Federal monies could be used for purposes benefiting but one or a few States, but Western clamour was too loud to disregard. As a result, construction of the Cumberland National Road started in 1811, partially financed by Federal funds, and was completed in 1818. Six hundred miles long, sixty feet wide with a twenty-foot macadamized strip down the middle, the 'National Pike' stretched from Cumberland, Maryland, over the mountains to Wheeling, Virginia, where it met the Ohio river. It continued on to Zanesville, Ohio, Terre Haute in Indiana, and eventually to the Mississippi at Vandalia, Illinois – a huge artery pulsing with commercial traffic moving at eight miles an hour. Meanwhile, in 1817, the State of New York began construction of the Erie Canal, completing it in 1825 and linking the Atlantic and the Hudson river with the Great Lakes. The 'Big Ditch', 363 miles long (only four feet deep), connected New York and Europe with the thriving Western cities of Buffalo, Chicago, Cleveland, and Detroit; Governor Clinton's ceremonial pouring of two kegs of Lake Ontario water into New York Harbour was not a meaningless gesture.

Pennsylvania organized an intricate system of rivers, canals and roads (even a steam-powered winch to haul boats up an inclined plane and over the mountains) connecting Pittsburgh with Philadelphia. Within twenty years a network of canals covered Ohio and portions of Indiana, linking the Ohio directly to the Great Lakes. Then, as the states built better toll roads, a stage-coach system sprang up, linking cities where canals and rivers could not. Steamboats appeared on the Western lakes and rivers; a scheduled steamboat run between Pittsburgh and New Orleans started in 1811. Later, when railroads pushed into the plains states across the Mississippi, the process was repeated with minor variations.

The effect of the new West in politics was particularly strong. The 'era of good feelings' drew to an end. The five new frontier states added to the Union after the War of 1812 had definite political desires of their own, and their entrance upset the delicate balance of sectional politics. It was no longer Northeast against South, but a three-cornered conflict among North, South, and West, with the West throwing its weight to whatever side it felt most advantageous. Western ways and interests were not those of the older states; the Federalist aristocracy of the Northeast and the planter-politicians of the Southern seaboard feared the bumptious and aggressive frontiersmen. These Westerners were arrogantly democratic, jealous of their individual prerogatives, insistent on their own interests, and suspicious of centralized government unless they wanted something from it. They wanted a good many things – new laws of voting franchise and governmental representation; easy credit and elastic currency; internal improvements; tariffs; political power – and they raised a good many questions about such matters as slavery, the political rights of minorities, equalizing processes, economic opportunities. The farmers in the western counties of New York and Virginia, for example, forced a redrafting of their state constitutions, while the constitutions of the new Western states, with provisions for manhood suffrage, weak executives, short-term offices, and open election laws, reflected a determination to keep government close to the settler. The day of Andrew Jackson was not far off.

The imbalance caused by the emergence of the West in political affairs was evidenced by the first serious appearance of the slavery question in national politics. Before the close of the War of 1812, slavery was considered, North and South alike, as a temporary and regrettable rather than a permament and desirable institution; both non-slaveholders and slaveholders were quite willing to subject the system to critical examination. Washington and Jefferson, among other Virginians, had freed their slaves. The elimination of the slave trade, beginning in 1808 under Constitutional guarantee, aroused little opposition from the South at the time; for that matter, neither did the anti-slavery provisions of the Northwest Ordinance of 1787. By 1804 most Northern states had abolished slavery, while in various Southern states, especially in back-country and border areas, active anti-slavery societies campaigned openly against it. Yet after 1816 there was a noticeable asperity in discussions of the slavery question – a warning, said Jefferson, 'like a fireball in the night'.

There were several reasons for this. Slowly but surely after 1800 the great Virginian tradition of liberalism lost ground to the aristocratic tradition of South Carolina; the South, during the 'era of good feelings', was in the process of transferring its allegiance from the tradition of Jefferson to the tradition of Calhoun. Further differences between North and South on other matters – on the tariff, on the war, on trade – indicated an approaching clash of sectional economic and political interests. Most important of all, however, were the problems connected with the spread of cotton culture. Eli Whitney's cotton 'gin', the development of new strains of cotton, a growing post-war market, and the opening of the rich 'Black Belt' lands of the Southwest made cotton an extremely lucrative cash crop. England's textile industry, revolutionized by the introduction of new machinery, demanded raw cotton in increasing quantities, and by 1815 New England had also developed textile mills of its own. How cotton became King in the South is graphically shown by the production figures. In 1791–5 the South raised five million pounds of cotton. In the period 1800–1805 production jumped to sixty million pounds; by 1845 it rose to four hundred million pounds; by 1850 to one thousand million pounds. Cotton required a large, steady supply of cheap unskilled labour, and the Negro slave fitted the need perfectly. At the same time, it was found that the hot lands of Louisiana and Mississippi delta country were ideal for sugar-cane, while tobacco culture moved into Kentucky and Tennessee. All needed cheap labour. In 1800 there were about one million Negroes in the U.S., almost wholly concentrated in the Southern states. In 1808, when the importation of slaves ceased, the figure stood at one and three-quarter millions. By 1840 there were two and three-quarter millions, and by 1860 four and a half millions. The property value of all slaves in the South was estimated at one thousand three hundred and fifty million dollars in the 1840s, and at four thousand million by 1860.

By 1820 it was perfectly clear to the South that abolishing slavery meant abolishing the economic foundation of Southern society. In the South anti-slavery sentiment could be muzzled or diverted, but not in the North, nor could action by the Federal government against slavery in the South and Southwest be avoided if the free states unanimously supported it. Preservation of their political power in Congress therefore became a matter of utmost importance to the slave-holding states as the nation moved West. The tendency had been to maintain a rough balance of power between slave and free state blocs in Washington since the 1790 census. The Northeast and Northwest had gained a million more than the South and the Southwest in population however, thereby gaining proportionately more seats in the House; in addition a slave counted only three-fifths of a free labourer in determining that representation. Only in the Senate were all sections equally represented.

Of the original thirteen colonies, seven became free states and six slave. Between 1791 and 1819 four more free states were admitted and five slave. When Missouri applied for entrance to the Union in 1819, both Northerners and Southerners in Congress carefully scrutinized the terms of its admission. Tallmadge of New York introduced a House bill requiring Missouri to enter the Union with a plan for emancipating its slaves; the bill immediately started an argument that some feared might flare into actual war. The question was actually much larger than Missouri. Slavery was already barred from the Northwest Territory, but not from those lands acquired by the Louisiana Purchase. Should Missouri and all other states subsequently carved from the Purchase be admitted as slave states, the balance of Federal political power would tip toward the South and slavery. If they were to be free states, their entry favoured the North and emancipation. At stake lay the political control, present and future, of the Union.

In 1820 it was still possible to find a compromise. Henry Clay of Kentucky arranged a plan whereby Missouri entered as a slave state, but Maine, the next addition, would be free, thus preserving the existing balance. At the same time Congress agreed to exclude slavery forever from all Louisiana Purchase territory north of the Parallel 36° 30′, a continuation of the Mason and Dixon line (the boundary between Pennsylvania and Maryland) and the Ohio river. But the Missouri Compromise delayed rather than settled the solution to the problem of slavery and its extension westward, and everyone knew it. 'It is hushed, indeed, for the moment,' wrote Jefferson from Monticello, 'But this is a reprieve only, not a final sentence.' The tocsin of disunion had already sounded.

The election of 1824 brought the 'era of good feelings' to an abrupt end. Outwardly, as the campaign year approached, the virtual one-party government of the preceding eight years seemed to be unopposed. The old Federalist party was practically dead, but within the Republican party there was a three-way struggle for control among representatives of Northeastern manufacturers, Southern cotton-planters, and Western farmers. Their clashing sectional interests were thrown into bold relief by the variety of candidates they put forward and by the campaign they waged.

Among the numerous aspirants to the Presidency who jockeyed for position after 1822, the choice narrowed down to four – one New Englander, one Southerner, and two Westerners. John Quincy Adams of Massachusetts, son of the second President, had probably the best qualifications of anyone in America for the office, though he was a poor practical politician. William Crawford of Georgia, who had the support of the seaboard South, was a Southern aristocrat of the states-rights school; his ill-health made him a doubtful candidate. John C. Calhoun of South Carolina, the most brilliant Southerner in Congress, declared himself out of the running in exchange for the vice-presidential nomination.

The two men from the West, Henry Clay and Andrew Jackson, presented an interesting study in contrasts and similarities. Clay, whose father was a back-country Baptist preacher, was as much a typical product of the Kentucky frontier as Jackson was of neighbouring Tennessee. As a young man Clay had been one of the leading 'War Hawks' and an ardent supporter of Western regional interests. In middle age, as he came into greater contact with the East and Europe, he shifted toward a nationalist position. Clay had all the charm and personal magnetism that Adams lacked; the true politician's ability to adjust, placate, and compromise; and a clear and able mind. Of all the candidates for the office he was the single one with what would today be called a platform – that is, his 'American System'.

Andrew Jackson of Tennessee was the most colourful and controversial figure of the four. Born in poverty in South Carolina to a Scotch-Irish linen-draper, Jackson fought as a boy in the Revolution and carried to his grave the scar of a British officer's sword-cut. After the war he wandered to Tennessee, picked up a smattering of law, traded in horses, farmed, served on the bench and in Congress, and ran into debt keeping a store. His services in the War of 1812 and later against the Indians made him a national military hero. A proud, hard-driving man, Jackson had a violent temper, strong principles, and a keen political sense. He was very nearly the perfect exemplification of Western man, with all his faults and virtues – suspicion of the rich and well-born, faith in the crowd, belief in equality, hatred of special privilege, nationalistic pride – traits present in different mixtures in other Westerners such as Clay, Benton, and Lincoln, but most thoroughly mixed in Jackson.

The election of 1824 revealed how sharply the nation was split on sectional lines. Adams carried New England and New York; Crawford, who suffered a stroke shortly before the election, took only Virginia and Georgia. Clay won in Ohio, Kentucky, and Missouri. Jackson, who received the largest number of electoral votes – ninety-nine to Adams's eighty-four – was the only candidate whose following cut across regional boundaries. He divided the Western states with Clay and the South with Crawford, pulled in the Scotch-Irish of Pennsylvania, the Middle States, and the upland South; but his vote was not enough to secure an overall majority. The election went to the House of Representatives. Clay, having been eliminated, advised his friends to vote for Adams; the Kentucky representatives disobeyed the instructions of their State Legislature and also voted for Adams who was elected by a vote of thirteen states to seven for Jackson and four for Crawford. Clay became Secretary of State in Adams's cabinet, drawing charges of 'bargain' and 'fraud' from the Jacksonians.

Adams's narrow victory foreshadowed a new alignment in American politics. Jackson became the symbol of the common man, those who opposed him symbolized aristocracy. Jackson's supporters frankly appealed to the democratic elements in American society for a broadening of government – held too long, they said, in the hands of New England and Virginia dynasties. The Western farmer, the Eastern labourer, and the Southern yeoman, dimly conscious of their potential political power, surged to Jackson's support and bitterly attacked the 'stolen' election. Shrewd political leaders like Martin Van Buren of New York and Thomas Hart Benton of Missouri capitalized on the groundswell of opinion to begin building a new party, called without subtlety the 'Democratic' party. The remnant Federalists, the industrialists and shippers of the Northeast, and the planters of the South formed an unstable alliance behind Adams and Clay, calling themselves 'National Republicans'. The lines of division were drawn immediately after the vote in the House, and Adams's administration became one long campaign for Jackson in 1828.

'I am a man of reserve, cold, austere, and forbidding manners,' wrote John Quincy Adams in his diary. Selfcontained, arrogant, quite unaware of the arts of blandishment, Adams was constitutionally unable to win personal friends or popular support. His four years in the White House were unhappy and embattled ones, yet the way he handled events proved him an intelligent, farsighted, and statesmanlike President. He refused to play cheap party politics or to dally with boodle; Thurlow Weed of New York exclaimed hotly, 'Mr Adams . . . failed to cherish, strengthen, or even recognize the party to which he owed his election; nor so far as I am informed with the great power he possessed did he make a single influential friend.' He offered cabinet posts to his political enemies if they were able men, attempted to evolve a just and honest Indian policy, agreed with Clay on cooperation with the South and Central American nations, and tried on every political and foreign issue to pursue the wisest and most objectively advantageous policy. Whatever he did, Jacksonians and men from his own party frustrated him at every turn, discredited what little he did accomplish, and attacked him for not doing more. No President was ever more thoroughly sabotaged than John Quincy Adams.

Adams's first annual message outlined a programme of canal, harbour, and road improvements; military schools and a stronger militia; and a national university – all Federally financed. This was attacked as a 'spendthrift programme' even by the nationally-minded Jacksonians, and much was made of the fact that the fourteen million dollars spent by his administration represented the nation's highest peacetime budget. With his long experience in international affairs Adams might have been expected to produce some improvements in foreign policy; however, his appointment of Clay and the accusation of 'corrupt bargain' hurt Adams's prestige at home and nullified much of Clay's effectiveness abroad. Canning, the British Foreign Secretary, the Monroe Doctrine in mind, won his government over to recognition of the Spanish American republics and refused to open the West Indies to American commerce except under conditions unsatisfactory to America; and Adams noted Canning's death in his diary with some relief, for Canning had outwitted him badly. In the same way Adam's attempt to guarantee just treatment to the Indians alienated the South. Southerners wanted the Cherokees, Creeks, Choctaws, and others moved west to open their lands to white settlement. Adams rejected the fraudulent Indian treaties and demanded new and better ones and thereby aroused Southern anger and cries of 'states' rights'.

The tariff was a particularly sharp thorn in the administration's side. The tariff of 1816 satisfied the West, but helped neither New England commerce nor Southern agriculture. The tariff of 1820, asking higher protection for manufacturing, failed by one Senate vote but passed in

1824, while one with still higher rates failed in 1827. The Jacksonians in Congress then evolved a devious plan to win support for Jackson and undermine Adams, without really committing themselves. A tariff bill would be introduced with such high rates on raw materials that both Northeast and South would join to oppose it: the Jackson men would vote down amendments to it, and thus claim credit in the North for having sponsored a high tariff and in the South for having helped vote it down. The bill had nothing to do with manufacturing, said John Randolph of Virginia, except 'the manufacture of a President', Andrew Jackson. Actually, enough support appeared for the bill to ensure its passage, and Adams was blamed for it all.

Jackson's backers used the four years of Adams's reign to good advantage. By 1828 the harassed New Englander had lost the support of many of his own party leaders, while the public at large was regaled with gossip and innuendo. It was rumoured that Adams was a nasty aristocrat, a spendthrift, pro-British, that he kept a billiard table in the White House, that he had once sold a pretty American girl to a Russian. At the same time, the Jackson men spent four years building and perfecting their party machinery, adopting some of the methods originated by the revolutionary Committees of Correspondence. Using conventions, caucuses, committees, and clubs, they evolved an implacably efficient organization that reached down into townships and even rural school districts. They had also more voters to organize. Manhood suffrage increased from 1816 to 1828, as the older states lowered the requirements for voting and the new frontier states almost wholly eliminated them. By 1828 New Hampshire, Maryland, and Connecticut dropped property qualifications, while New York and Massachusetts retained only nominal ones. The ballot opened up to nearly a million new voters in the lower economic brackets, a potential that Jackson's adherents recognized at once. They developed new techniques of party politics, promising this here and denying it there, playing interest against interest, prejudice against prejudice, weaving it all into a national party pattern. Adams stood very little chance against them.

That was the way it was. The campaign was unusually malicious, issues forgotten, rumour rampant, personalities smeared, with Adams's National Republicans winning the palm for scurrility. Jackson was called murderer (his military and duelling record), adulterer (his irregular marriage to Mrs Rachel Robards), corruptionist (his dealings with politicians), and worse. The bitterness of the campaign hurt and angered him and he held to the end that it caused the death of his wife a few months later. He never forgave Adams, who he believed could have stopped the stories but did not, nor did he ever again give quarter to his opponents. Memories of the campaign of 1828 were the driving force in Jackson's politics ever after, colouring his political relationships and some of his policies. Nevertheless, despite the mudslinging, 'aristocratic' John Quincy Adams was no match for 'democratic' Andrew Jackson, who swept into the Presidency with the electoral votes of all states except New Enland, Delaware, Maryland, and New Jersey.

How sharply American politics had changed, and how clean a break the election of 1828 made with the past, showed at Jackson's inauguration. Gone were the Federalist decorum of Washington and John Adams, the courtly Virginia democracy of Jefferson. Rough, rowdy, back-country people in homespun flooded Washington, shouting and carousing in the streets. Gentlemen drew aside from the jostling, motley crowds on Pennsylvania Avenue; 'It was like the inundation of northern barbarians into Rome,' remarked one of them. Jackson walked bareheaded and erect through the muddy streets to the Capitol for his oath-taking, and as he finished it, 'the peal of shouting that arose rent the air and seemed to shake the very ground'. At the reception after, hordes of enthusiastic Democrats jammed the White House, muddied the rich damask furniture with their boots, broke crystal, ruined carpets, and drove Jackson into a corner where men linked arms to guard him from the crush. 'I never saw such a mixture,' wrote Justice Story. 'The reign of King Mob seemed triumphant.'

CHAPTER 23

THE AGE OF JACKSON AND EMERSON
1828–52

ANDREW JACKSON, elected to the Presidency by 'ordinary men', was not one of them. The contemporary campaign picture of him as an illiterate, irascible, rabble-rousing radical was far from the truth. He was not learned, but he was by no means ignorant, and his mind was sharp. He was a pragmatic man (like Lincoln and Franklin Roosevelt) who recognized and seized opportunities with an almost incredibly accurate sense of timing. He possessed, as one contemporary remarked, a scent for the trail of political opinion as delicate as a gun-dog's; he was peculiarly adept at following when he seemed to lead. Social, economic and political forces beyond Jackson's control really shaped the Jacksonian movement, to which he contributed practically nothing until he was elected to the Presidency. Yet he stepped in at the head of the procession, became its symbol, gave it a name, and impressed it with his own powerful personality, a feat only a man of uncommon ability could achieve. The yeoman and small planter of the South, the Western farmer, and the Eastern urban worker constructed about him a political machine more compact and militant than even Jefferson built. The circumstances and the times combined to make Jackson what he liked to call himself, 'the tribune of the people', and few Americans have led political movements with greater skill or success.

Jacksonian democracy remains as difficult to analyse and as paradoxical as Jackson himself. The French observer Alexis de Tocqueville, himself an aristocrat, saw Jackson's America as the final achievement of an egalitarian society, full of crude energy and destructive as well as creative, and did not wholly approve of it. American historians of the later nineteenth century, looking back at it, found it a disorderly and complex time and tended to view it as a prelude to the issues of the Civil War. Historians of the Beard–Turner–Theodore Roosevelt era saw Jackson's time as the 'Age of the Common Man' and Jackson as a kind of progressive folk-hero; the historians of Franklin Roosevelt's time found in Jacksonian democracy prefigurations of the coalition of working man and farmer that culminated in the New Deal. More recently, historians have begun to suspect that Jackson's party was, like any other successful nationalized party, a mixture of inconsistent and disparate interests that represented more or less a cross-section of American society.

However it was to be interpreted, Jackson's victory marked the beginning of a transformation of American society that appeared not only in politics, but in nearly every other area of American thought. The prevailing philosophy of the period can be called 'Jacksonian' only to the extent that Jackson represented the political phase of a larger movement. 'Old Hickory' himself was as much a creation of the movement as he was its spokesman; the democratic or 'Jacksonian' trend manifested itself in many other spheres of action with which he had little or no connexion.

The heyday of Jacksonian democracy came in the 1830s and 1840s, before it was broken by questions of slavery and union that it was not equipped to solve. Stripped of its external political apparatus, it was essentially a system based on an expanding agrarianism – a democracy of independent property owners. In Jackson's words, government existed for the benefit of 'the planter, the farmer, the mechanic, and the laborer' who 'form the great body of the people of the United States'. His party's concern, he said, was for 'the liberty of men owning independent means of livelihood', for the so-called 'common man' – meaning the small independent merchant, farmer, or artisan. Jackson had great faith in the uncommon ability of the common man to discharge all his functions in a democratic society. Any man of average intellectual substance could, in his opinion, handle the business of government; as he once said, 'The duties of public office are, or at least admit of being readily made, so plain and simple that men of intelligence

A History of the United States

may readily qualify themselves for public office.' As more and more farmers, workers, and debtors gained the right to vote, widening the base of popular political activity, the Jacksonian idea of 'mass politics' took root.

Jacksonian democracy held that government was the creature of the majority will. The whole purpose of National Republican and Whig politics, in Jackson's opinion, appeared to be to grant the wishes of the minority without consulting the majority. If the common man were so trustworthy and responsible, as the Jacksonian judged him to be, it was therefore necessary and right that government be under the direct control of the majority, sensitive to its demands and receptive to its desires. The constitutions adopted by the new Western states during the Jacksonian period reflected this belief. Their short-term governors, frequent elections, large grants of power to lower legislative houses, and restrictions on executive and judicial branches were all devices intended to make government dependent rather than autonomous.

The Jacksonian belief in the adequacy of the common man to perform all political duties had its corollary in a belief in every man's right to equality of economic opportunity; in the notion that if this right were safe-guarded, some sort of equal sharing of economic goods would inevitably result. An integral part of Jacksonian politics was its opposition to any special interest, monopoly, or favouritism that might deny equality of opportunity. Jackson himself had been several times heavily in debt. The party slogan 'Equal rights for all, special privileges for none' had economic as well as political connotations; political power, said the Jacksonians, must not be used to gain economic privilege.

The Jacksonian view of economic life exactly fitted the needs of an expanding nation. With the opening of the West and the mushrooming of industry, opportunities were great in the thirties and forties. An important aspect of Jacksonian political philosophy was its desire to keep the door to wealth open by cancelling out any special privileges which gave economic advantages to the favoured few. Jacksonism was the classic philosophy of a rising middle class, aimed at encouraging creative individual enterprise, at developing a more fluid and open economic society. Daniel Webster caught the essence of the prevailing spirit in his statement, 'Society is full of excitement; and intelligence and industry ask only for fair play and an open field.' The Jacksonians believed deeply in *laissez-faire*, holding that an overdevelopment of governmental power, state or federal, crushed individual enterprise and smothered individual opportunity. In the forties, they could not foresee that concentrated economic power might close the doors of opportunity as tightly as the most controlled bureaucracy. After the Civil War, from this cherished Jacksonian doctrine, came an economic oligarchy more potent than anything dreamed of by Hamilton, or Fisher Ames, or Nicholas Biddle. The Gilded Age had its roots in Jacksonism.

Jacksonian democracy was national-minded. Although Jackson and John Marshall were political enemies, they agreed that the power of the Federal government must be defended against encroachment by the states. Old Hickory's famous toast, 'Our Federal Union – it *must* and *shall* be preserved!' was his own and his party's central principle, one never compromised in his long battle with the states' rights school of South Carolina's Calhoun. But at the same time, the Jacksonians vaguely realized that the consolidation of power in Washington might bring centralization, stratification, classification, and possibly special privilege and hierarchy. The Jacksonians therefore held a somewhat bifurcated view of federalism, involving on the one hand a profound attachment to the national government, but on the other a deep suspicion of the centralized or bureaucratic state. It was not that the Jacksonian really feared the State; he feared instead that the *control* of that State might some day be vested in a minority group of special interests.

The differences between Jacksonianism and Jeffersonianism were fundamentally great. Both, it is true, were based on an agrarian economy. But Jefferson's system, founded on a static agrarianism, suited an era of relatively stable land values and of a unified agricultural system. Jackson built on a dynamic agrarianism; his political philosophy reflected an era of expanding land values, rich speculative opportunities, and a much more diversified agriculture. Its economic spirit was totally different. In another sense, the Jeffersonian and the Jacksonian differed in their concept of federalism. Jefferson, a child of revolution, taught that an increased centralized power was inimical to democracy; intent upon restraining government, the Jeffersonians concentrated on keeping it within carefully prescribed limits. To Jackson the federal government was not simply a policeman to keep order, but a parent who gave a helping hand when it was needed – but only when the citizen asked for it. The Jacksonian did not want the government to control his affairs except to the degree that he requested it to do so. He was never loth (nor were the Grangers and Populists later) to call on Washington for assistance, for roads, canals, credit, or subsidies; yet at the same time he fiercely resented any intrusion of federal power into his own domain of authority.

Jefferson and Jackson held quite different estimates of mankind. Jefferson's faith in the people was genuine and sincere, but it was the substance of things hoped for rather than achieved. He was not a believer in absolute equality, but in a graded equality, led by a natural aristocracy (as he told Adams) of education, talent, and worth. Jackson's faith in humanity was of another sort, an unequivocal confidence in the common man's innate natural wisdom and in his ability to cope with almost any problem – a belief shared alike by Western frontiersman and Eastern labourer. The temper of Jacksonian democracy was rude, vociferous, powerful, aggressive; Jefferson's democracy decorous, orderly, dignified. The Jeffersonians of 1800 looked hopefully toward the finer civilization to come. The Jacksonians of the 1830s gloried proudly in the civilization they had made, in its strength, its freedom, its liveliness.

The politics of the Jacksonian period, and for that matter of the ante-bellum decades generally, may be understood best in terms of the developing sectionalism that characterized the age. In the major land areas new social, economic and political relationships were in the process of formation, altering in turn the political attitudes men held on contemporary issues. It is always difficult to establish hard and fast boundaries for sections in American history; such demarcation lines have a habit of fading when too definitely drawn. But at the same time it is apparent that there existed in pre-Civil War America a Northeast, a Northwest, and a South.

In the Northeastern states of New England, New York, Pennsylvania, New Jersey, and Delaware, great changes took place after the turn of the century. Farming, once the mainstay of New England economy, decreased in importance as the rich lands of the West drained off the young men and outproduced the small farms of the East. More and more, as cities like New York, Philadelphia, and Boston grew in size and importance, the area turned to manufacturing. Cheap water power promoted the growth of a great textile industry, concentrated in Massachusetts and lower New Hampshire. Northeastern capital, once heavily invested in shipping, poured into factories. Old ports, such as Salem, Newburyport and Marblehead, faded rapidly before the rise of new factory towns like Lowell and Lawrence. The great mercantile firms and the new industrial corporations linked themselves with banking and shipping interests to establish fairly complete urban control over the political and economic life of the area. And as New England shifted from an agricultural to an urban-industrial economy, conflict between capital and labour grew sharper, while the tremendous flow of immigrants into the cities created new economic and social problems. It was not accidental that the loudest contemporary cries for reform came from the Northeast, nor that labour unions, utopian communities, and humanitarian movements found their centre there. The clash between have and have-not, between conservative and radical, was strongest in the Northeast.

The Northwest (Ohio, Indiana, Illinois, Michigan, Wisconsin, Iowa, and the new Territory of Minnesota) grew rapidly in population during the Jacksonian era and continued to grow even more swiftly after the Civil War. Settlers from the upland South gave the Ohio river country a Southern tinge; in the Great Lakes region settlers from New York and New England predominated, mixed with numbers of German and Scandinavian immigrants. With its tremendous diversity of peoples, creeds, backgrounds and interests, the Northwest was the least unified of the three major sections, less rigid, less cohesive in its social and intellectual patterns. The Northwest had cities like Cleveland, Cincinnati, Detroit, Chicago and Milwaukee, but it was chiefly a land of farms, many of them not far from the pioneer stage. An aggressively democratic area, with a legacy of Jeffersonianism and a strong predilection for Jacksonism, the politics of the Northwest were self-interested, concrete, practical.

The South encompassed thirteen states with at least four subdivisions: the upland South of Kentucky, Tennessee, and Western Virginia; the tidewater South of Maryland, Virginia, North and South Carolina; the Gulf South of Georgia, Alabama, Mississippi, Florida, and Louisiana; the Southwest of Missouri, Arkansas and, later, Texas. It was chiefly an agricultural section, with few important cities other than Baltimore, Charleston, Mobile, and New Orleans – a varied land of swamp, plain, mountain, forest, town, farm, and plantation with a climate ranging from temperate cold to tropic heat. Virginia, Kentucky, Tennessee, and Maryland raised tobacco; the Carolina coast depended on rice; Louisiana on sugar cane. But fundamental to the South was the huge cotton empire that stretched from Virginia to Texas – and with it, slavery. The settling of the Gulf States and of the Southwest produced no break in the Southern pattern. Cotton culture simply moved west with the migrants, and the Southwest, unlike the Northwest, displayed few real sectional variations from the parent states.

Southern life, based on a definite social and economic order, exhibited far more coherence than that of either of the other two sections. At the top of the order, giving Southern civilization its distinctive complexion, stood the great planters who owned fifty or more slaves, one or more plantations, most of the South's best land, and three-quarters of its wealth. There were never many of them, probably fewer than fifty thousand out of the South's population of eight million. Only 300 planters held more than 200 slaves each; there were, of course, a few exceptions, such as Wade Hampton of South Carolina (who had 3,000) or Nathaniel Hayward of South Carolina (who had fourteen plantations and 2,500 Negroes). The plantations averaged perhaps 500 acres; a few planters owned as many as 15,000. These men provided the South with its intellectual, social, and cultural leadership. They built huge white-columned Greek revival houses, wintered on the Gulf Coast or in Europe, hunted the fox, attended balls, raced horses, served in the legislatures and the courts, in Congress and the Army.

The planter-aristocrat educated his sons and daughters with private tutors or at fashionable academies, the young men continuing at West Point, Yale, Harvard, at Jefferson's new University of Virginia (his own *alma mater*, William and Mary, having lost its aristocratic status with the Revolution), above all at Princeton, or abroad. He owned a good private library, respected his Anglican church, took the Grand Tour, and bought his family's clothes in London or Paris. His pride of family was strong and sensitive, his fondness for tradition legendary. Gallantry in gentlemen, purity in ladies, proper assumption of cultural and political responsibilities – these were his passions. At its best the class produced a humane, educated, courtly, cultured aristocrat. At its worst it produced the 'cotton snob' or the bullying, arrogant 'fire-eater', infected with what Mark Twain called 'the Sir Walter Scott disease' of chivalry. There was something in his life of the crisp rustle of crinoline, of magnolias in the moonlight, of court-balls and happy darkies tinkling banjoes in the dusk – but not much. He was above all a hard-working agricultural capitalist with a huge investment in the complex cotton business, facing difficult problems of crop prices, credit, export, labour, and worn-out land. Slavery, despite its cheapness, was neither an efficient nor an economically sound labour system, and slaves were a constant source of trouble.

Below the great planter in the scale was the small planter who owned from one to twenty slaves. He held less land and that less fertile, owned a frame house (or a log one) and lived a simple, unostentatious life of hard work. Though he often sweated in the fields beside his own slaves, ate the same fare, and (except on Sunday) dressed not much better, he was violently anti-Negro and pro-slavery. Culture, fashion, travel, the legislature, West Point, and magnolias in the moonlight were not for him, but his great dream was to acquire them by obtaining more land, more slaves, and entry into the upper stratum of aristocracy.

Next to him came the yeoman farmer, the 'redneck' or 'woolhat boy' who made up more than 75 per cent of the South's population. He owned no slaves. His farm was small and poor, located in the mountains, the barrens, or on the margin of the rich cotton belt. His house was often a ram-shackle cabin, and his days were spent in the backbreaking job of trying to scrabble a living from the obstinate red clay. An earnest, solid man, he too was violently anti-Negro and pro-slavery. He feared the Negro as a social and economic competitor; slavery provided his only means of keeping the black under control.

Lastly, in the lowest social and economic bracket were the 'crackers', 'poor whites', or 'sand-hillers', scattered on the poorest land, illiterate, shiftless, living on the bare edge of subsistence – not a large group, but extremely vocal in its hatred of the Negro, for its members realized subconsciously that the barrier of slavery alone kept them from hitting the bottom of the scale.

Such was the ante-bellum South, a varied yet peculiarly unified section, a state of mind as much as a geographical area, a pattern of life shaped always by cotton and slavery. During the first half of the nineteenth century the South became acutely aware of the fact that it *was* a section, with a culture, tradition, and interests of its own, and its leaders made strenuous efforts to preserve and develop them. It had a closely-guarded set of values, a way of life deemed worth protecting and defending; it had also an extremely difficult set of political, social, and economic problems, all tied up with slavery, the one-crop system, and a rigid social order. Its literacy rate was low (80 per cent as compared with the Northeast's 99.58 per cent and the Northwest's 97 per cent) and not all of its illiterates were Negroes. Some of its universities were excellent – Virginia, William and Mary (although it no longer enjoyed its pre-Revolutionary eminence throughout the nation), the College of South Carolina, several good state institutions – but its educational record was poor. Intellectually the South in the nineteenth century produced nothing to match the Northeast. Only one of America's great writers, Edgar Allan Poe, was a Southerner, and he was scarcely typical of the region. Its great political leaders were too often dedicated to the single aim of defending the *status quo*.

Jackson entered office uncommitted to any specific platform, for part of the Democratic campaign strategy had been to make varied promises to various sections. His first message to Congress recommended 'cautious modification' of the tariff, the removal of the Indian population to lands west of the Mississippi, and a programme of such Federally-financed internal improvements as might be 'constitutional'. It was a conciliatory message, calculated to stir up no immediate reactions. Jackson's cabinet selections, however, boded little peace for the future. Major John Eaton of Tennessee, Secretary of War, had recently married Peggy Timberlake, a handsome young widow whose acceptance into Washington society seemed doubtful in the light of current gossip. Eaton, Attorney-General Berrien, Secretary of the Navy Branch, and Secretary of State Van Buren were all friends of Jackson. Postmaster General McLean and Secretary of the Treasury Ingham were close to Vice-President Calhoun. When Peggy Eaton was soundly snubbed by the cabinet wives, Jackson, remembering his own dead Rachel, sprang to her defence, aided by Van Buren, a bachelor who had nothing to lose. Calhoun and his friends abetted the tea-table gossip, and for a time the battle over Peggy Eaton took on real political importance, splitting the cabinet wide open. When tempers reached the limit, Jackson persuaded his entire cabinet to resign. New appointments pointedly ignored Calhoun's friends, making the break between Jackson and Calhoun final and complete. Van Buren's insistent championing of the maligned Peggy brought him closer than ever to Jackson, who turned more and more frequently to the New Yorker for advice.

Jackson's first term was principally occupied with political manoeuvrings designed to consolidate his party. His lieutenants, working on the principle that spoils belong to the victor, demanded that 'the barnacles be scraped clean off the Ship of State' and that all offices held by Adams's appointees be redistributed among loyal Democrats. Actually, the shift was not so sweeping as the cries of dispossessed office-holders indicated; in Jackson's first term about 900 changes were made in a total of 10,000 positions, not always for political reasons. The 'spoils system' did, however, serve as a concrete illustration of the Jacksonian idea that one man was as good as another, and did prove to be a practical method of solidifying the party structure. Whereas earlier Presidents had been chary of removing incumbents, the Jacksonians quickly recognized the potentialities of political patronage and used it, thus opening the way for its abuse in later years.

Towards the end of Jackson's first term one issue appeared that he met squarely. The Second Bank of the United States, chartered in 1816, needed a renewal of its charter before 1836. Controlled by a group of Eastern financiers, the Bank had long been a target for the Democrats, who accused it of dabbling in politics and claimed that it existed for the primary purpose of enriching a few capitalists. Henry Clay believed the Bank to be a good political issue, and with the help of George McDuffie, a friend of Calhoun's, he fashioned a new pro-Bank political party. The National Republicans met in Baltimore in late 1831, declared themselves for the Bank, and nominated Clay as their candidate for the presidency in 1832. Meanwhile a bill for rechartering the Bank passed both houses of Congress and came to Jackson for his approval. The plan was to confront Jackson with an insoluble dilemma; he either signed a bill he did not like, or he took the blame for an unpopular veto. In either case Clay felt that he could make capital of the Bank issue in the forthcoming campaign.

Clay's guess could hardly have been more wrong. Jackson vetoed the rechartering bill and sent it back to Congress with one of the most astute veto messages ever penned. The Bank, said Jackson, was simply a huge monopoly, controlled by rich men like Nicholas Biddle of Philadelphia, a few wealthy Englishmen, and 'others of the richest class'. It plundered the poor and lined the pockets of the rich; constitutional or not, the Bank must go – Jackson, the poor man's friend, would not have it. The veto was shrewd politics, if not brilliant finance, for it vividly dramatized the issue of special privilege versus public interest. Working men in the cities sang in the streets:

> Yankee Doodle, smoke 'em out
>   The proud, the banking faction –
> None but such as Hartford Feds
>   Oppose the poor and Jackson.

Old Hickory's popularity skyrocketed, and his re-election in 1832 was practically assured.

The election of 1832 was briefly complicated by the appearance of the first organized third party in American history. In 1826 one William Morgan of Western New York State published a pamphlet allegedly revealing the secrets of Freemasonry; his subsequent disappearance seemed to indicate he was a victim of Masonic reprisal. When public furor against the Masons and other secret orders reached a high pitch, Jackson's opponents attempted to divert it into political channels. An anti-Masonic party was quickly formed, appealing to the large Catholic immigrant population of the cities and eventually embracing all of Clay's 'American System' and most of the National Republican platform. This rag-tag party met in convention to nominate William Wirt of Virginia for President on an anti-Jackson, anti-Masonic, anti-almost-everything platform. Since its views were practically indistinguishable from those of the National Republicans (except for its frank appeal to prejudice) it carried little weight in the elections. For that matter, neither did Clay and the National Republicans. The Jackson–Van Buren ticket swept the nation. Even solid New England broke up, with Maine and New Hampshire voting for Jackson and Vermont for Wirt, while in the South only South Carolina failed to vote for Old Hickory. The result seemed to be a complete endorsement of Jackson, his party, and his principles.

But the silent intra-mural war between Jackson and Calhoun was by no means over. South Carolina, divided between back-country Jacksonians and seaboard Calhoun men, had long opposed a protective tariff. The mercantile interests of the state believed (with some justice) that its economy had suffered because of the tariff of 1828; Southern Congressmen worked ceaselessly against it while Calhoun, a brilliant political theorist, worked out an intricate and ingenious method of disposing of it. A state, he affirmed, might nullify an act of Congress within its borders by appealing to the principle of state sovereignty. If three-quarters of the states nullified it, then the act was void everywhere, although what happened if the Federal Government failed to agree seemed not to enter into Calhoun's calculations. When J. Q. Adams (now in the House) and Henry Clay engineered the passage of a new tariff bill in 1832, Calhoun judged it time for action. Late that year a state convention met in South Carolina, declared the 1828 and 1832 tariff bills inoperative, ordered non-compliance, and opened the state's ports to free trade. Calhoun resigned the Vice-Presidency and went home, where the voters promptly sent him back to the Senate.

To a devout nationalist such as Jackson South Carolina's act was intolerable. Seven revenue cutters quickly appeared in Charleston harbour with a battleship to protect them.

Jackson bluntly proclaimed that 'the laws of the United States must be executed', that nullification of a federal law by a state amounted to disunion, and that disunion was treason. Only Henry Clay's compromise tariff bill, rushed through Congress in early 1833, prevented a head-on conflict, and Jackson, who was quite willing to hang Calhoun for treason, always rather regretted that he did not. Not quite thirty years later, as Lincoln prepared to write his inaugural address in the face of secession, he placed both the Constitution and a copy of Jackson's Nullification Proclamation on his desk before him.

Jackson assumed that his decisive victory in 1832 was a mandate to proceed against the Bank. 'I shall not shrink from my duty,' he said, 'until I can strangle this hydra of corruption.' As soon as he had disposed of Calhoun and South Carolina, he turned his attention to Nicholas Biddle. By reshuffling the cabinet he obtained Roger Taney of Maryland as Secretary of the Treasury, who, at Jackson's orders, began to withdraw federal deposits from the Bank and to deposit new revenues in state banks, chiefly in the South and West. Biddle retaliated by reducing the Bank's discounts and call-in loans, and by presenting state bank notes for immediate redemption. New England suffered from a money shortage, while the state banks, encouraged by Taney's policies, happily returned to some of their old wild-catting practices. Credit tightened, businesses crashed, and a small panic started that snowballed with the passing months. Jackson blamed it all on Biddle. 'We have no money here, gentlemen,' he told a delegation of worried businessmen who called at the White House. 'Biddle has all the money. He has millions of specie in his vaults, lying idle . . .' The pressure of public opinion was too great. Biddle gave in, railing at the 'gang of Banditte' in Washington, and began to negotiate for a charter from the state of Pennsylvania. His scalp joined Clay's and Calhoun's at Jackson's belt.

Fortunately Jackson encountered no real diplomatic problems in foreign affairs during his eight years in office. Lord

Aberdeen, the British Foreign Secretary, was much easier to deal with than his predecessor George Canning, and Jackson, despite his vehement Anglophobia, got along well with him. Jackson's administration wisely decided not to emphasize the Monroe Doctrine and allowed matters at issue with Britain to settle down. The United States reopened discussion of the West Indian trade and, with British cooperation, evolved a workable though not wholly satisfactory compromise. Jackson's only real problem, largely of his own making, lay in American relations with France. For more than twenty years the United States had vainly attempted to collect redress from France for damages suffered by American shipping during the wars following the French Revolution. Eventually France in 1831 agreed to pay twenty-five million francs in six annual instalments, but in 1833 the French defaulted, and in 1834 they flatly refused to pay at all. Jackson, who disliked France only a trifle less than he did England, threatened to expropriate French property in the United States if the instalments were not paid, salting his threat with a few hot-tempered remarks on Gallic perfidy. The French government took immediate offence and replied in kind. The exchange of notes continued, until in 1835 the two nations very nearly broke off diplomatic relations. A year later Jackson, on advice from his State Department, offered a rather stiff-necked apology, and with the British government serving as mediator France arranged a satisfactory schedule of payment. The affair underlined Jackson's great weakness as a diplomat. A man of strong anti-European bias, a believer in direct, soldierly action, he was neither trained nor equipped to handle foreign affairs with tact; on the other hand, his firmness and vigour in the French incident did help to arouse respect for the United States in foreign chancelleries.

Jackson, old and tired, designated Martin Van Buren of New York as his successor for the election of 1836. A descendant of an early Dutch family of poor farmers, Van Buren was a slick little professional politician who built and controlled the Democratic organization in New York State, where he practised politics with such dexterity that he earned the name of 'The Little Magician'.

The National Republicans, who had absorbed most of the anti-Masonic, anti-Jackson elements, lacked the unity to provide much resistance. Since one of their party's chief planks was opposition to Jackson's 'Tory' assumption of authority, they styled themselves 'Whigs'. The Whigs actually put four candidates in the field for the presidency, among them Daniel Webster and Indian-fighter William Henry Harrison, but four were hardly enough. The smooth-working Democratic machine swept Van Buren in by a respectable margin, and Jacksonian democracy seemed safe for another four years.

Van Buren's magic could not ward off the disaster that struck the Democrats almost at once. The loose finances of Jackson's time, plus inflated Western land values, wildcat banking, paper speculation, easy money, and heavy public debts (incurred for canals and roads) blew the lid off the national economy in 1837. By September, with Van Buren barely installed in office, nine-tenths of all the factories in the East were closed. Before the panic was over 33,000 business firms collapsed with losses amounting to 440 million dollars; it was estimated later that half the property in the United States changed hands within two years. Mobs of unemployed roamed the streets, and troops had to be called into New York City to protect stores and warehouses from plundering gangs. The manufacturing Northeast stopped dead in its tracks; the debtor West and South were hit almost equally hard. Van Buren, sticking to the *laissez-faire* principle that hard times wore themselves out, did little to relieve the situation, and indeed there was little that he could do. The brunt of the blame for the panic fell on him, and when the Whigs seized control of Congress in 1838 his days were numbered.

As the election year of 1840 approached the Whigs had victory practically assured if their party could only hold together. Henry Clay was willing and eager to run for the presidency, but the convention of 1839 picked William

Henry Harrison, the hero of Tippecanoe. Harrison was Virginian-born but a Westerner by domicile, a military man and a comparative unknown who could be advertised as another Jackson to attract the 'common man' into the Whig party. John Tyler of Virginia, a close friend of Clay's, took second place on the ticket.

A chance remark by a disappointed Clay man gave the Whigs their campaign strategy. Harrison, he said, was so shiftless that if somebody gave him a barrel of hard cider and a log cabin he would rest content for the rest of his days. The Whigs pounced on the statement. General Harrison, a simple, kindly Westerner would henceforth be the 'log cabin, hard cider' candidate, in contrast to the aristocratic Van Buren, who lived in elegance on his Kinderhook estate in New York, used gold spoons on his table, wore imported lace on his cuffs, and drank expensive foreign wines. The fact that Harrison was a courtly, dignified old man who lived comfortably on a 2,000-acre farm made no difference. It was coonskin cap against beaver hat, common man against aristocrat; the Whigs had no other platform and needed none. They made a circus out of the campaign. '6¼ cts. a day and sheep's pluck to the laborer under Van Buren – $2 a day and roast beef under General Harrison!' read the inscription on the banners. The Whig convention at Baltimore shouted, 'Tippecanoe and Tyler too!' and sang lustily,

> Make way for old Tip, turn out, turn out!
> 'Tis the people's decree, their choice shall be,
> So Martin Van Buren – turn out, turn out!

One Whig delegation rolled a huge ball from Alleghany, Pennsylvania, inscribed 'Farewell dear Van – you're not the man – to guide the ship – we'll try Old Tip'. Processions of Harrison men carrying smoking torches paraded the city streets at night to the beating rhythm of 'Van, Van, is a used-up man!' Harrison won by 234 to 60 electoral votes, although his popular majority was less decisive. So ended the dynasty of Jackson.

The period of Jacksonian political ascendancy lasted for

only a little more than a decade. After its defeat by the Whigs, the Democratic party came more and more under Southern control, until it turned eventually into a pro-slavery instrument. Jacksonian democracy, originally an expression of faith in the common man, became the political agent of the Southern planter. The new Whig party, until the break-up of the major parties in the fifties, remained dominant but never really unified. In the Northeast, in Daniel Webster territory, the Whigs attracted those manufacturing interests who favoured a protective tariff and those bankers and merchants who had suffered under Jacksonian fiscal policy. New England anti-slavery men and the remnants of anti-Masonry went Whig, by and large. In the South, some of the sugar and cotton planters, led by Tyler and Calhoun, went Whig, for only the Whig party seemed to offer protection against the rising political power of back-country dissidents and debtors. Even some of Clay's Western followers, resentful of Old Hickory's extreme nationalism and 'executive tyranny', joined the Whigs. The Whig party was in effect a party of 'cons', not 'pros', a party of talent, wealth, and conservatism, but an unstable alliance at best. It was impossible to find any common factor that would bind together Eastern manufacturing capitalist, slave-holding Southern planter, and prosperous Western farmer.

After 1830 both major parties were forced to recognize the existence of two increasingly important elements in politics – business and labour. The United States, like the rest of the world during the first half of the nineteenth century, saw the Industrial Revolution brought to completion by numerous new inventions which revolutionized communication, transportation, and industry. Morse's telegraph, which linked the nation together by 1860, made communication among far-flung settlements swift and efficient. Cyrus McCormick's improved reaper changed the economy of the wheat-growing West, while Lane's steel mouldboard plough (later improved by Oliver) provided a better means of breaking the tough virgin sod of new lands. Colt's revolving pistol, according to popular legend, 'civilized the West'. At the same time, the twin principles of standardization and interchangeability of parts, developed by the ubiquitous Yankee Eli Whitney, stimulated the rise and spread of the factory system. New British techniques of refining iron, joined with huge and accessible coal-fields, made Pennsylvania the centre of an expanding iron and steel industry. The clipper, unquestionably the most perfect ship of its kind, reached its highest development in the forties and fifties. Outspeeding the bluff-bowed British and Dutch merchantmen on the India or China run, the American clippers dominated world trade until driven out by steam. Railroads, especially important in a nation of tremendous distances, tied East and West closely together by the 1860s. The Baltimore and Ohio was incorporated in 1827, and shortly afterwards the first links were made in what became the great New York Central and Pennsylvania systems. From 3,000 miles of track in 1840, the railroads grew to more than 30,000 by 1860, chiefly in the North and Northwest.

The rise of industrialism created a new type of American businessman, quite different from the eighteenth-century colonial merchant or landed gentleman. It was the day of the entrepreneur, of the Lowells, Lawrences, Appletons, Vanderbilts, and others like them. There was an entire continent of illimitable natural resouces to exploit, a constantly expanding market, and a rapidly growing industrial system to feed it. America was the businessman's oyster. After 1820 business became a national, transcontinental affair, so complex and so richly rewarding that it demanded a man's entire time and energy. The man of business no longer had the leisure to cultivate the arts or serve in Congress; he might miss something if he failed even for a moment to attend to his affairs. Yet the businessman had to pay close attention to politics to get what he wanted – tariffs, access to resources and markets, cheap and tractable labour, other favours and necessities. Without the time (and in some cases the skill) to play politics himself, he found it advantageous to establish a working relationship with those who did. The alliance between business and politics, which reached its climax after the Civil War, had its beginnings in the industrial expansion of the period 1830–60, and remains a vital constituent of American politics.

The growth of the factory system in the Northeast created a labour problem with direct political implications. The disappearance of the domestic labour system and of the older trade guilds, as workmen went into factories, created a new kind of labour-management relationship. Working conditions under the factory system were often less than desirable; a workday of thirteen to fifteen hours was common, health and safety rules usually non-existent, child and female labour shamelessly exploited. In the twenties a few labour groups, patterned after British models, formed to agitate for better conditions. A serious carpenter's strike in 1827 in Philadelphia emphasized the need for better labour organization and resulted in the establishment of the Mechanics' Union, a federation of several trades union groups. The federation principle spread, national labour conventions met annually, and some unity of purpose was imposed on the unions scattered through the Northeast.

Labour leaders saw at once the value of organization for bargaining purposes. They also discovered the strike and used it; one hundred and sixty-eight strikes occurred between 1833 and 1837. However, strikers were often prosecuted under the laws of conspiracy and the strike never became a really effective weapon until the courts reinterpreted the statutes after 1842. Most significant, however, was labour's gradual perception of its political potential; what could not be gained by bargaining or striking, its leaders realized, might be won at the polls. Working-men's parties appeared in several Northern states, while other labour groups endorsed candidates for office on the basis of their stand on labour problems – the principle of 'reward your friends and punish your enemies' subsequently followed by the modern American Federation of Labor and C.I.O. Political Action Committees. The Locofoco movement of the 1830s marked the actual entrance of labour into party politics, when the labour element attempted to gain a place in the Democratic organization. (The name came from the 'locofoco' matches once used to light a meeting after an anti-labour group cut off the gas.) Though the labour movement was temporarily broken by the panic of 1837, it forced the old parties, before the Civil War, to put into effect many of the reforms the working-men's parties desired, thus nipping in the bud a national political labour organization. Many industries established a ten-hour day; a few states adopted health and safety regulations; imprisonment for debt, long a union target, was abolished in the North, though not in the South. Recognizing the potency of the labour vote, both major parties began to insert attractive planks in their platforms, with the result that after 1840 no party could afford to neglect the working-man' sdemands.

The American sense of nationality, born during the War of 1812, came of age during these pre-Civil War years. Americans speculated on what made a nation, and what made it great, deepening and strengthening their feelings of patriotism. 'Uncle Sam', who emerged in caricature during the War of 1812, became firmly fixed as a national symbol, a tall, loose-jointed, shrewd, good-hearted man who represented the American spirit. Francis Scott Key's 'Starspangled Banner', a product of the same war, held equal popularity with Samuel L. Smith's 'My Country 'tis of Thee', written in 1832 to a tune which the author later claimed he had not known to be 'God Save the King'. Monuments, beginning with one at Bunker Hill, were raised to commemorate national heroes and events, scattering a rash of equestrian figures through the public parks. It was a time of national self-confidence, of zest for American living and thinking, of bombastic Fourth of July orations and of flag-worship.

This exaggerated nationalism of the Jacksonian period produced a reaction against the wave of immigration that flooded the nation before the Civil War. Economic and political conditions in Europe, particularly in Ireland and

Germany, sent nearly four and a half million immigrants across the Atlantic before 1860. The Irish left Ireland in their thousands during the 1830s and 1840s because of political oppression (real or imaginary), overpopulation, depression, crop failure, and plain famine. Almost unanimously Catholic, clannish, usually uneducated, these Irish settled in the populous Eastern cities as a cheap labour pool. The Native American or 'Knownothing' movement was an attempt to put anti-foreign, anti-Catholic nativism into politics on an 'America for Americans' platform; the Knownothing Party even ran a presidential candidate, ex-President Millard Fillmore, in the election of 1856. Victims of both economic and social discrimination for a generation or more, the Irish meanwhile found American politics tailored to their talents, and drastically changed the entire pattern of urban political life, particularly in Boston and New York.

During the same period the number of German immigrants increased until nearly a million and a half had arrived in the United States by 1860. Those who came were usually somewhat higher in the social and cultural scale than the Irish. Some, such as Carl Schurz and Franz Sigel, were political refugees escaping the abortive revolutions of the forties; others hoped to avoid military service; factory hands left after the collapse of the German textile industry; cheap land in the West attracted land-hungry farmers. The majority of Germans went West, giving cities such as St Louis, Cincinnati, and Milwaukee a highly Teutonic flavour.

Stable citizens, good farmers, excellent businessmen, and skilful artisans, the German migrants were easily absorbed into the prevailing economic and social pattern and were rarely bothered by anti-foreign movements. Also, between 1840 and 1860, some 64,000 settlers arrived from the Scandinavian countries, most of them headed for the Middle West of Illinois, Wisconsin, and Minnesota.

The great migrations of the mid nineteenth century gave the tradition of nationalism its severest test. The influx of Catholic population into a traditionally Protestant society raised serious problems, not the last among them a recon-

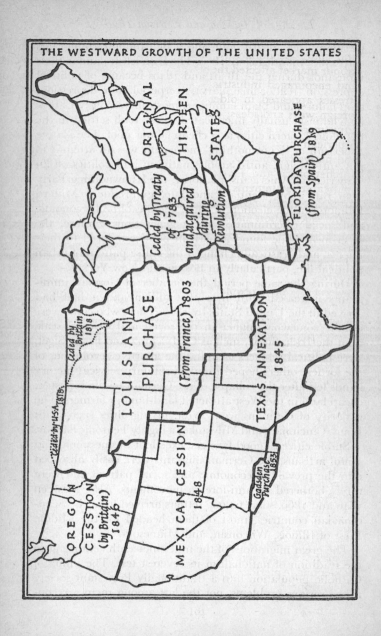

THE WESTWARD GROWTH OF THE UNITED STATES

ORIGINAL THIRTEEN STATES

FLORIDA PURCHASE (from Spain) 1819

Ceded by Treaty of 1783 and acquired during Revolution

LOUISIANA PURCHASE (From France) 1803

Ceded by Britain 1818

Ceded by USA 1818

TEXAS ANNEXATION 1845

OREGON CESSION (by Britain) 1846

MEXICAN CESSION 1848

Gadsden Purchase 1853

sideration of the American principle of separation of church and state. Economically, the presence of a large cheap-labour market affected the status of native American labour and encouraged industrial expansion. Social tensions and stresses appeared in older communities unaccustomed to foreign ways and ideas, eased only after several decades of adjustment. The 'melting pot' concept took hold slowly in American thought, until the initial conflict of foreign culture and native nationalism wore off.

Jeffersonian and Jacksonian democracy were primarily political re-statements of eighteenth-century doctrines of natural goodness and human perfectibility, already expressed in the Declaration and the Bill of Rights. Manifestations of the same faith in man appeared in nineteenth-century religious, social, and economic thought. William Ellery Channing, who in 1830 hailed the arrival of 'a great age of progress', saw evidence all about him of 'a tendency and a power to exalt a people'. The theme of the new age, he believed, would be 'devotion to the progress of the whole human race' by the religious emancipation of man's spirit, the amelioration of his social and economic ills, the removal of obstacles to his steady upward march towards a state of political perfection. The central themes of the Jacksonian epoch were trust in man and certainty of his progress. 'Progressive development does not end with us,' wrote Theodore Parker. 'We have seen only the beginning; the future triumph of the race must be vastly greater than all accomplished yet.'

The democratic drive of the Jacksonian era generated tremendous activity in American intellectual life. Particularly in New England, the new spirit flowered in literature, which for the first time felt itself free of bondage to Europe. 'Our day of dependence, our long apprenticeship to the learning of other lands,' wrote Ralph Waldo Emerson in 1837, 'draws to a close.' During the next quarter of a century, as Emerson predicted, there emerged a native, indigenous, American literature, combined with the best of the European tradition. Oliver Wendell Holmes, John

Greenleaf Whittier, Henry Wadsworth Longfellow, James Russell Lowell, Henry Thoreau, and Emerson himself, among a host of others, were all men who drew inspiration from their native environment, yet kept in touch with the intellectual currents of the rest of the world. The South contributed fewer great names, but among them was Edgar Allan Poe, the Ishmael of American letters. New England's George Bancroft, a Jacksonian by preference, started to write the history of the United States in order to glorify American democracy as 'the culmination of God's wonder-working in the life of mankind'. Jared Sparks began his lifelong task of collecting all the significant documents of American history, pausing meanwhile to write glowing biographies of great Americans but so editing his materials that the founding fathers, as he put it, might never appear in public 'in *déshabille*'. William Hickling Prescott and John Lothrop Motley chose to write histories of Spanish America and the Dutch Republic, Francis Parkman those of New France and the Oregon Trail. Washington Irving, having exhausted Dutch New York and Moorish Spain, found fresh material in the West of Astor and Captain Bonneville. American science, like history and letters, gained greater stature. Benjamin Silliman and Asa Gray established world-wide reputations in geology and botany; Louis Agassiz, a transplanted Swiss, pioneered in zoology; Captain Matthew Maury of the Navy did excellent research in oceanography. Surveying all these accomplishments, Robert Breckenridge of Kentucky exclaimed that 'no mortal power could estimate the heights of grandeur waiting to receive us as a nation'.

There were those who doubted. James Fenimore Cooper, heir to New York aristocracy, could not go the way of enthusiasm. Almost the first considerable imaginative writer of the new nation, he was also the first to deny that nation's right to its artists. 'There is scarcely an ore,' he wrote, 'which contributes to the wealth of the author, that is found, here, in veins as rich as in Europe.' At the very moment of bursting confidence Cooper expressed for the first time that lack of faith in American artistic life which was to make self-criticism a principal factor in American culture. Yet ironically, even while he doubted, Cooper invented an American mythology and might even be said to have invented the American novel. His novels, more than thirty of them, for the first time identified and treated in fiction the great themes of the American adventure – the wilderness versus civilization, the clash of red and white American, the westering conquests of the continent. When Leather-stocking walked into literature and leaned on his long rifle he opened a whole new terrain of American literary material, not yet fully explored.

The most dramatic affirmation of the prevailing belief in progress appeared in the religious ferment of the period, a series of upheavals already foreshadowed by the Unitarian triumph over Calvinism a decade and more earlier. Transcendentalism, a philosophico-religious system current in New England from 1830 to 1860, staked out the route of the new trend. Never an established sect or creed, but rather a somewhat fluid agreement on certain religious matters arrived at by a relatively small group of intellectuals clustered about Boston and its environs, transcendentalism did not play directly on the main stream of American thought, though through Emerson, Thoreau, and a few others it undoubtedly had a powerful indirect impact on contemporary ideas. What Emerson thought and said was what America, in cruder and less intellectual terms, believed; transcendentalism, on a high spiritual and intellectual level, caught and expressed the spirit of the age. The Jacksonian Democrat need not have read Kant or Coleridge to believe as Emerson did in the worth of the individual, in self-reliance, in the integrity of one's own mind – but transcendentalism buttressed his faith in such things and extended it into the realm of philosophical and religious speculation.

The guiding spirit of the transcendental movement was Ralph Waldo Emerson. Born in 1803, the descendant of several generations of Calvinist divines, Emerson, after studying theology at Harvard, entered the ministry as a Unitarian. Dissatisfied with the confinements of even his own liberal sect, he soon resigned his pulpit to travel in Europe. On his return to New England he began to evolve, through lectures and essays, the central doctrines of a new, free, individualistic religious philosophy, disdaining any organized philosophical system and ranging through the whole wide world of thought for his ideas. Emersonian thought, indeed transcendentalism in general, rested on the single belief that every man had within him a spark of divinity. 'In all my lectures,' Emerson wrote, 'I have taught one doctrine, namely, the infinitude of the private man.' In a series of essays and books Emerson built his system about the principle that all men possess both the power to discern intuitively God-given truth and the ability to govern themselves by it. *Nature* (1836), *The American Scholar* (1837), *Self-Reliance* (1841), and all their successors explored and expanded that principle. In effect, Emersonian transcendentalism was a mystical affirmation of the prevailing American belief in freedom and equality, a re-emphasis of frontier individualism, a nineteenth-century modification of the old Puritan doctrine of election, and an assertion of the divine election of every man. His volumes were one great paean to Jacksonian America, Emerson himself its lay preacher. 'We will walk with our own feet,' he wrote. 'We will work with our own hands; we will speak with our own minds.'

Though Emerson was popularly regarded as spokesman for the transcendentalist group, it gathered in as well most of the freshest and most brilliant minds of New England. Most of all, Emerson's doctrines impressed young Henry David Thoreau of Concord, Massachusetts. Thoreau, fifteen years younger than Emerson, practised the doctrines of self-reliance and self-sufficiency that the older man preached. He retired to a rude cabin on the shores of Walden Pond, near Concord, to test to his own satisfaction the values of an independent existence. 'I went to the woods,' he wrote in *Walden*, 'because I wished to live deliberately, to front only the essential facts of life, and to see if I could learn what it had to teach, and not, when I came to die, discover that I had not lived.' An arch-individualist, Thoreau attempted to carry the moral idealism of transcendentalism to its logical conclusion in a sort of philosophical anarchism.

Thoreau's emphasis on individualism brought him into open conflict with organized society, which he found sadly lacking in moral and spiritual values. His experiment in living at Walden Pond he intended to serve both as protest against and proof of the inadequacy of contemporary American society's materialistic, anti-individualistic goals. By the same token his doctrine of the absolute freedom of the individual led him to reject the authority of government; he changed Jefferson's concept of 'that government is best which governs least' to read 'that government is best which governs not at all'. The individual, thought Thoreau, possessed an absolute and inherent right to nullify laws made by ignorant, wrong-headed majorities, if those laws conflicted with his own inner convictions. If the State follows an immoral policy, reasoned Thoreau, the moral individual must perforce disobey it: 'Any man more right than his neighbors constitutes a majority of one.' Thus he preferred to go to gaol rather than pay a tax to support a State engaged in what he regarded as immoral actions – in particular, the Mexican War and the continuance of slavery. His reasoning, as explained in *Civil Disobedience*, was simple and direct. 'If the alternative is to keep all just men in prison, or give up war and slavery, the State will not hesitate which to choose,' he wrote, thus implementing a doctrine that was later to influence Gandhi and other exponents of passive resistance. Emerson stressed the nobility of the individual, the innate authority of the average man. Thoreau emphasized the duties and capabilities of that man in society.

Transcendentalism was an integral part of the American Romantic movement of the early nineteenth century, originating primarily in the discovery by New England intellectuals of German and British Romantic philosophy. It derived from Coleridge and Carlyle, from Kant and his followers, from Cousin and French eclecticism, from Oriental sources, and from native Calvinist, Unitarian, and Quaker roots, all bent to nineteenth-century Yankee uses. It was at bottom a

manifestation in philosophy and religion of the same optimistic, individualistic, egalitarian spirit that produced Jacksonian democracy, although Emerson could never quite
bring himself to unqualified approval of Old Hickory.
Transcendentalism really meant, as one of its followers
phrased it, 'that men are free, and claim the right to think
for themselves in religious as well as in political matters'.
It emphasized the worth of the individual and the principle
of self-reliance; it admired the man of action and original
thought, not the man bound by tradition or formal creed;
it believed in the values of instinctive and individual judgement, rather than in those of authority and convention. It
said, in Emersonian terms, 'God is in every man', which
in the final test was not far removed from what Jackson
meant.

Transcendentalism, however, was a highly specialized
philosophical system, its appeal limited to a small group
of cultivated New Englanders. The average American
applauded the transcendentalists' conclusions about his
indisputable worth and inherent ability, but the Kantian–
Coleridgean–Platonic background of the Emersonian system
was well beyond hisken. Neither Emerson nor his followers
were able to translate their beliefs into familiar terms, whatever their Jacksonian implications. On the popular level, the
translation was accomplished by a different kind of movement, 'come-outism'.

'Come-outism' was the name applied to those dissident,
unorthodox sects that dotted America during the pre-Civil
War period, sects that demonstrated religious independence
by 'coming out' of the orthodox churches. The 'come-
outer' sects stressed individualism, self-expression, equali-
tarianism in religion, thus affirming transcendental–Unitarian principles on a lower, more common, direct level.
Dozens of these new religious societies, some of them on the
lunatic fringe, appeared during the later eighteenth and
earlier nineteenth centuries. The Shakers, more properly
titled The United Society of Believers in Christ's Second
Coming, gathered about 'Mother' Ann Lee, an English-

woman influenced by Quakerism and evangelism. Mother Ann built up a small American following that increased after her death in 1784 to a sizeable body of believers. Rejecting most of the traditional Calvinist doctrines, condemning marriage, the Shakers retired from the world into a number of self-sustaining communities in Pennsylvania, Ohio, New England, New York, and Kentucky. In 1831 William Miller of western New York, who preached the imminent second coming of Christ, established the sect of Millerites, whose churches were soon scattered from Maine to Wisconsin. According to Miller, Christ would appear in the year 1843, at which time there would be a second judgement, a terrible condemnation of the sinful, and the founding of a literal Kingdom of God on earth for true believers. By 1843 Miller claimed nearly a million followers, many of whom that summer waited vainly on hilltops for Christ's arrival. Extremist though the Shakers and Millerites were, the numbers of adherents they were able to attract indicated how strongly the promise of utopia appealed to the common man.

Another facet of 'come-outism' appeared in the religious communities which were established in the United States between 1820 and 1850. The Rappites, led by George Rapp, settled in Pennsylvania and later Ohio and Indiana; William Keil established his Bethel Community in Mississippi and moved it to Oregon; the German Separatists settled at Zoar, Ohio; the Amana Society of New York was transferred to Iowa; Eric Janson's Bishop Hill Colony chose Illinois; the transcendentalist-inspired Brook Farm community in Massachusetts owed its leadership to Emerson's friend George Ripley. All of these communal groups were bent on making religion a personal, individual matter, bringing it into the daily social and economic life of the average man. They were socialistic or communistic by necessity rather than intent. Many of the sects, it is true, originated in the pietistic movements that flourished in Europe after the French Revolution, but their transplantation to the American scene coincided with the democratizing spirit of the times.

Mormonism provides perhaps the best illustration of the religious ferment of the period. Its membership was drawn almost wholly from those lower and lower middle classes that Unitarianism and transcendentalism never touched. Joseph Smith, a shrewd, semi-literate young man from upper New York State, announced in 1827 that he had received an angelic visitation which led in turn to his discovery of some golden plates inscribed with sacred scriptures. Translated and published, these appeared in 1830 as *The Book of Mormon*. That same year Smith established the Church of Jesus Christ of Latter Day Saints under a state charter. Converts flocked to him. A few years later the Saints moved to Ohio, where the revivals of the Second Awakening had already ploughed fertile recruiting grounds. When his church numbered several thousand members, Smith moved its headquarters to Missouri and later to Nauvoo, Illinois, which had a population of nearly 15,000 by the mid-forties. However, neighbouring 'gentiles' frequently clashed with the Mormons (over commercial as well as religious matters) and during an armed attack on Nauvoo Smith and his brother were killed.

After Smith's death leadership of the Mormons passed to Brigham Young, an intelligent, authoritative man who immediately imposed unity and purpose on the church. Despairing of ever finding peace and security in Illinois, Young led the Mormons in 1846 and 1847 on a great migration across the plains to the promised land of Deseret, where they might live in isolation on the shores of Great Salt Lake. Certain members of the Smith family broke off from Young's group to create the Reorganized Mormons, while another faction followed 'King Jesse' Strang to a chain of islands in upper Lake Michigan. Mormonism, unlike many other 'come-outer' sects, was a strong and disciplined movement with powerful and purposive leadership. It appealed to the common man and especially to the poor, stressed an orthodox and old-fashioned Calvinistic morality, established an almost Puritanic theocracy, and furnished its followers with a simple, easily grasped, and highly effective socio-economic code. Mormon leaders placed great emphasis on group cooperation and attempted to develop in their society a strong sense of social responsibility. Alone among these new American sects, the Mormon Church had almost immediate success as a missionary force in Europe. The practice of polygamy, which caused most of the Mormons' troubles, was never really an important part of Mormon faith, being intended instead as a sensible solution to certain practical problems of frontier life.

The most important influence on the religious thought of the period was the 'perfectionist' movement of the thirties and forties. Despite the Unitarian triumphs in New England and the transcendentalist revolt against Unitarianism, orthodox Congregational, Presbyterian, and Methodist churches still dominated the religious life of the West. Neither Congregationalism nor Presbyterianism was especially well suited to Western life, since both possessed views of human nature and hierarchical organization that failed to agree with either frontier egalitarianism or Jacksonian democracy. The Methodists' evangelistic doctrine of 'momentary sanctification' and their loose church structure always met greater approval in the new settlements. As a result, western Congregational and Presbyterian churches soon found Methodist ideas creeping into their creeds. In 1825 reports reached the Eastern church bodies of a wave of revivals sweeping western New York under the leadership of a young Presbyterian named Charles Grandison Finney.

Investigation revealed that Finney, some five years earlier, had committed himself to a doctrine of 'free and full salvation', quite similar to Methodist doctrine. After some difficulties in getting ordained, Finney then began preaching his theory that sin was selfishness and virtue benevolence. Conversion, he said, is a normal experience, accomplished by the sinner himself under the stimulus of emotional excitement; conversion simply meant exchanging sinful selfishness for virtuous selflessness. Any human being can, said Finney, attain a state of perfection by his own efforts, but salvation alone was not enough. The 'perfected' one must make his religion directly active; he should, said Finney, 'have the determination to aim at being useful in the highest degree possible'. Salvation was not the end, but the beginning of a useful life.

Finney's doctrine violated practically every tenet of orthodox Congregational and Presbyterian creed – sin, salvation, election, good works, free will. Equally disturbing were the 'new measures' of worship that he adapted from traditional Methodist and Baptist camp-meeting techniques. Finney, it was claimed, held 'protracted meetings' lasting from three to ten days; permitted women to pray publicly; encouraged 'groaning and posturing' among the congregation; instituted an 'anxious seat' for sinners; and used new converts as lay preachers.

Despite opposition from the Eastern churches, Finney's doctrines swept the West and later the East. He penetrated into strongly Congregational New England, gathering thousands of converts; in New York City the wealthy Tappan brothers built a huge church, the Broadway Tabernacle, especially for him. Oneida Seminary in New York turned into a training school for Finneyite preachers, and Lane Seminary in Cincinnati and later Oberlin in Ohio (where Finney himself was professor of theology) trained perfectionist ministers for the West. Though denounced as heresy by the orthodox Congregational and Presbyterian churches, perfectionism was successful.

Finney's beliefs had more than a religious significance. Like transcendentalism and Unitarianism, perfectionism stressed individual ability, egalitarianism, and self-reliance couched in terms that the ordinary man could easily grasp. The perfectionist ideal was in essence another affirmation of the contemporary belief in optimism, progress, and democratic individualism. It was 'come-outism' with a vengeance, a sharp break with authoritarianism in religion, a theological restatement of Jacksonism. In particular, Finney's idea of 'usefulness' reinforced the numerous humanitarian-reform movements of the time. Many of Finney's followers were attracted to the abolition movement, which was gaining ground in the thirties, simply transferring Finney's revivalistic techniques to this new and different crusade. It was no accident that Lane Seminary produced thirty-two agents for abolition societies (among them Theodore Weld, who trained nearly all the anti-slavery lecturers in the West) or that Oberlin College became the Western centre of abolitionism. The abolitionist movement in its early phases had a strong religious cast that was a direct result of perfectionist influences.

The religious upheavals of pre-Civil War America were merely parts of a wider search for economic equality and justice. The period proved to be a happy hunting ground for utopian experiments in living, particularly for those patterned after the theories of Robert Owen in England and Charles Fourier and Etienne Cabet in France. Twelve communities based on Owenite socialism were established in 1825 and 1826, among them the New Harmony, Indiana, colony supervised by Owen himself. Owen, who bought out a Rappite group for $140,000, at one time had nearly a thousand persons in his colony, though it dissolved in dissension within a few years. Fourierism, popularized by Arthur Brisbane (who had studied in Paris under Fourier) fared not much better, though it attracted support from such prominent men as William Ellery Channing, Horace Greeley, Parke Godwin, George Ripley and Charles A. Dana. Twenty-seven Fourieristic communities were founded between 1843 and 1853, some as far west as Michigan and Wisconsin. Brook Farm Colony, near Boston, was supervised by Ripley and patronized by Nathaniel Hawthorne, Margaret Fuller, and others from the Massachusetts transcendentalist group. It operated with indifferent success for six years until it was destroyed by fire in 1847. The North American Phalanx in New Jersey, the most prosperous of the Fourieristic colonies, lasted for thirteen years and was able to pay off its stockholders at 65 cents on the dollar when it dissolved. A total of sixty-one utopian communities were established in the United States between 1825 and 1860, some religious in origin, some socialistic after the manner of Owen, Fourier, or Cabet, and others simply independent. 'Not a man you meet,' Emerson wrote in his journals, 'but has the draft of a new community in his pocket.'

The search for perfection took other forms as well. Horace Mann, convinced that if the average American were to assume his social responsibilities he must be properly educated, worked tirelessly for free, tax-supported public schools. The educational theories of Pestalozzi, Fellenberg, Froebel and other European innovators were transplanted to American soil; kindergartens, teacher-training schools, and public high schools appeared everywhere. German-trained scholars like Edward Everett, George Ticknor, George Bancroft, and Joseph Cogswell introduced new methods into higher education, while Mary Lyon founded Mount Holyoke in 1837, the first women's college to be planned as a true equivalent of men's education. In the western states, state universities were established almost as soon as the states themselves were ready for admission to the Union – Ohio (1804), Indiana (1820), Michigan (1821), Missouri (1839), Iowa (1847), Wisconsin (1848), and others. Meanwhile the Sunday School, the Lyceum, the subscription library and the literary or debating society served as educational media on the popular level.

At the same time, the plight of the criminal, the deaf, blind, and poor attracted attention. Jefferson redesigned the Richmond gaol on more humanitarian principles, while in 1816 New York commissioned two new prisons at Auburn and Ossining, using the new cell-block system. Connecticut, which used an abandoned copper mine as a state prison, followed suit, and by 1840 eight other states completed new ones. In the prisons themselves routine and discipline became less dreary and harsh; flogging, stocks, and solitary confinement were gradually abandoned. Samuel Gridley Howe of Boston and T. H. Gallaudet of Philadelphia pioneered in the education of the blind and deaf. Gallaudet opened the American Asylum in Connecticut in 1815, and before 1851 thirteen states founded similar institutions. Poor relief in 1800 was handled in a manner not much different from that of 1600. The fact that in early America land was cheap and labour scarce gave currency to the persistent American idea that poverty must be the result of indolence, but after the growth of cities and the emergence of industrial economy, thinking on the matter slowly changed. A few states passed poor relief laws, usually inadequate, while some of the larger cities established charity houses, as in New York (1825), Boston (1826), and Philadelphia (1828).

Not until the third decade of the nineteenth century did the insane attain the status of human beings, to be treated as individuals worth saving. Agitation for the elimination of the traditional Bedlam came after the work of Philippe Pinel in Paris had become known in America through the writings of Dr Benjamin Rush. The most effective reformer was a young Boston girl, Dorothea Dix, a friend of William Ellery Channing. With the support of Samuel Howe and Charles Sumner, she began in 1841 a two-year survey of gaols, asylums, and reform schools in the state of Massachusetts. Her report to the legislature in 1843 shocked the nation and touched off an immediate reform programme. She made similar surveys in Rhode Island, New Jersey, and Pennsylvania, leaving behind her new and better hospitals for the insane wherever she went. By 1854 Dorothea Dix had travelled 30,000 miles and had reported on the institutions of every state east of Indiana; by 1860 she had covered the rest.

The temperance movement stemmed from several sources. Evangelistic revivalists of the early nineteenth century, believing in Finney's doctrines of perfectibility and usefulness, viewed alcoholic beverages as a major obstacle to social progress. Interest in the creation of an enlightened electorate, stimulated by the spread of manhood suffrage, provided another impetus toward temperance reform. At the same time, social workers interested in eliminating poverty and crime in the cities found overwhelming evidence that excessive drinking was a major cause of both. The great temperance crusade came after 1810, under the leadership of the

clergy. In 1811 the Presbyterian Church took an official
stand on the use of alcohol, followed by the Methodists in
1816; earlier, in 1813, the Congregationalists and Presbyterians joined to form a state temperance society in Massachusetts. By 1825 more than a million were enrolled in state
and local church-sponsored societies throughout the nation,
and in 1826 the American Society for the Promotion of
Temperance began work on a national scale. It established
a missionary system, published pamphlets, sent out speakers,
employed professional organizers, and in general copied
the revivalist methods of the evangelical churches. The
Washington Temperance Society, formed in 1840, used the
same techniques even more successfully, carrying on its
campaign against drink by camp-meetings, songs and stories,
'Cold Water Parades', and travelling lecturers – Timothy
Shay Arthur's *Ten Nights in a Barroom, and What I Saw There*,
was perhaps its best-known product; a novel against liquor
which as a best-seller ranked just behind *Uncle Tom's Cabin*,
and which, in dramatized form, was a favourite tent-show
for another generation. But the societies soon split over the
question of whether drinking was immoral or simply economically wasteful. Nor could they agree on method, some
believing the solution to drinking lay in education, others in
prohibitive legislation. Somewhat ineffectual laws governing
the sale of liquor appeared in thirteen states before 1860,
but not until the twentieth century did the movement
attain its objectives (if temporarily) in the eighteenth
Amendment to the Constitution.

Both the frontier necessity for equal treatment of women
and the eighteenth-century emphasis on the rights of individuals were contributing factors to the movement for
women's rights. It was also apparent to any onlooker that
women in America had but few more legal, political, and
social rights than the Negro slave – as the abolitionists con-
tinually pointed out. The question of female participation
in contemporary religious revivals brought the issue up in
another connexion; could not women testify and be saved
too, thus finding equal status with men in salvation? Strong-

minded women like Catherine Beecher, Emma Willard, Lydia Maria Child and Margaret Fuller, began to agitate in earnest for the recognition of women's legal and personal rights. Lucy Stone spent a lifetime on the lecture platform; Amelia Bloomer campaigned for dress reform and immortalized her name in an unlovely article of feminine apparel; Harriet Hunt and Elizabeth Blackwell graduated from medical schools to become the first women physicians; Sarah Joseph Hale edited *Godey's Lady's Book;* Abby Kelley, Elizabeth Cady Stanton and the Grimkè sisters went into the abolitionist movement. The first victory came in 1848 with the passage of New York's Married Women's Property Law. Their real accomplishments, however, came after the Civil War, culminating in the nineteenth Amendment, which became part of the Constitution in 1920.

In practice, all the reforms of pre-Civil War America, however disparate their aims, merged into a single great attempt – to make America perfect. With political equality seemingly achieved by Jacksonian democracy, and with the dominance of an authoritarian theology threatened by a variety of new faiths, the nation turned its attention to the removal of all possible obstacles from the path of national progress. The democratic and the humanitarian-reform movements melted together, pooling their methods, efforts, objectives. 'Every possible form of intellectual and physical dyspepsia brought forth its gospel,' wrote James Russell Lowell in retrospect. 'No brain but had its private maggot.' But Lowell recognized that there was in them all 'a very solid and serious kernel, full of the most deadly explosiveness. It was simply a struggle for fresh air . . . , this life which the reformers demanded, with more or less clearness of consciousness and expression, life in politics, life in literature, life in religion.' Jackson, Emerson, Cooper, and Garrison were products of the same drive.

Reform was not of course a peculiarly American phenomenon. On both sides of the Atlantic philanthropic men and women were seeking out and striving to cure social and economic ills. The Reform Bill of 1832, the Chartist movement, the Factory Act of 1833, and the repeal of the Corn Laws in 1846 reflected British attempts at reform; in continental Europe there was a general trend towards a recognition of human rights and the reality of human duties, culminating in the widespread revolutions of 1830 and 1848. Americans learned a great deal from European reformers, who for a long time had wrestled with the same problems in a much older society. The reform movement of the earlier nineteenth century in the United States was not an evangelism of the underprivileged, a class bootstrap lifting of the oppressed, but a movement in which rich and poor, cultured and uneducated, radical and conservative joined. Neither was it a mass revival, like the two Awakenings, but a sincere and rational effort (with the eccentric, it is true, showing at the edges) to realize fully for once and all the innate capabilities of man.

Emerson summed up the trend best with the remark that the cause of reform lay in the belief 'that there is an infinite worthiness in man, which will appear at the call of worth, and that all particular reforms are the removing of impediments'. The reformers were all simply interested in removing impediments. They trusted the individual and believed in his ability to better himself. A good digestion, a ten-hour working day, sensible apparel and a vote for women, temperance, better gaols, labour unions, utopian economics, and a state of spiritual communion with God were each of them steps that might advance humanity a few paces farther towards the ideal. But above and beyond all American efforts to secure social and political and economic justice, above all lesser humanitarian reforms, stood the question of slavery, which eventually overshadowed and embraced them all.

The anti-slavery movement began as part of the whole great stirring of nineteenth-century humanitarianism. It was a reform motivated by the same drives that produced Jacksonian democracy, utopian communities, and other humanitarian and social experiments. Until the mid-forties anti-slavery was simply one of many reform enthusiasms, one frowned on, in fact, by the more stable and conservative-minded reformers. Gradually it rose to eclipse the others, because its appeal was wider, its leadership more skilful, its relation to politics more direct, its relevance to the future of American democracy more unmistakable.

In the opinion of many Americans, chattel slavery was a clear violation of and a direct threat to the traditional concept of American democracy. The slavery question became eventually a question of whether the nation would continue to exist, and if so, of whether it would exist as a democratic nation. There was a compelling danger, as Lincoln pointed out, that it might continue as an undemocratic nation, completely given over to slavery. Slavery existed near enough to touch the orbit of every individual's future, yet geographically far enough removed from some to allow it to be judged and evaluated more or less impersonally. It was also confined to a portion of the nation whose political and economic interests differed sharply from those of the non-slave-holding portions. In addition, the slavery system was politically accessible, subject to state and federal law.

Neither slavery nor its abolition became an important issue in America until 1830. Opposition to slavery was common in colonial days, but it was not until after the formation of the Republic and the enunciation of eighteenth-century doctrines of liberty and equality that a serious examination of the institution began. The prohibition of the slave trade in 1808 aroused little real opposition. After that date anti-slavery sentiment grew, especially in the South. In 1827 Benjamin Lundy, the Quaker reformer, listed 130 anti-slavery groups, 106 of them in slave-holding areas. State societies, beginning with Pennsylvania's in 1777, were working in nearly all the states outside the South before 1830. But with the increasing importance of cotton as the basic Southern crop, Southerners perceived that slavery was absolutely essential to their economic and social welfare. Thereafter anti-slavery talk abruptly stopped south of the Mason-Dixon line; in 1837 Lundy could find only a very few of the 106 societies still in existence.

At the same time the temper of Northern anti-slavery sentiment changed. What had once been mild approval of some sort of emancipation, or at best mild disapproval of slavery in principle, became an aggressive, forthright, sometimes intemperate demand for the instant abolition of the entire institution. William Lloyd Garrison, the New England firebrand, struck the keynote of the new crusade in the first number of his abolitionist paper, *The Liberator*. 'I am in earnest,' he wrote. 'I will not equivocate – I will not excuse – I will not retreat a single inch – AND I WILL BE HEARD.' Under the leadership of Garrison and others, newly organized societies carried abolitionist doctrines through the North and Northwest. Garrison and a few friends founded the New England Anti-slavery Society in Boston in 1832. Within the next year similar groups appeared in New York City, Providence, Philadelphia, and Ohio. In 1833 representatives of these societies met in Philadelphia to organize a national body, the American Anti-slavery Society, which remained under Garrisonian control throughout most of its existence. In 1840, however, a large number of moderates withdrew to form the American and Foreign Anti-slavery Society. Both societies sent out speakers and organizers, published newspapers and tons of pamphlets and books, founded state and local branches, and publicized the abolitionist cause with unflagging zeal. By 1840 the entire complexion of the argument had changed; compromise or agreement among anti-slavery, abolitionist, and pro-slavery adherents was no longer possible.

The arguments on both sides of the slavery question were extremely complex, nor were pro- and anti-slavery groups always able to agree among themselves. The anti-slavery societies intended to appeal to the nation by fact and argument, to change public opinion, and thus to build a great body of Northern and Southern anti-slavery sentiment that would eventually (by legal and political means) abolish slavery. Their attack on slavery rested on several principles, any one of which might be stressed to the exclusion of others.

First, said some, slavery was wrong, on moral grounds.

Slave breeding, and the refusal of slave-holders to sanction slave marriage or to recognize the slave family as a unit, struck at the very foundations of morality. Relations between slave and master encouraged immoral behaviour in Negro and white alike. The system was cruel, barbaric, and inhuman; Theodore Weld's study, *American Slavery As It Is* (1839), Mrs Stowe's *Uncle Tom's Cabin* (1852), and countless other studies and novels appeared to document the accusation with stories of whippings, tortures, confinements, bloodhounds, slave marts, and separated families.

Slavery, said others, was unchristian and irreligious, a clear violation of Scripture. Chattel slavery arrogated to one man a power which belonged rightfully only to God; it violated both the Christian ethic of brotherhood and the law of Christian charity. It was impossible, in the Garrisonian view, for a man to be a slave-holder or a slavery sympathizer and a Christian; it was equally impossible for an American church to remain Christian while condoning or supporting slavery. Such views naturally aroused argument within the Protestant Churches, leading the Wesleyan Methodists to withdraw from the Methodist convention of 1843 in protest against its failure to take an official anti-slavery stand. Two years later the Southern Methodists, objecting to anti-slavery talk in the churches, separated from the Methodist organization to found the Methodist Episcopal Church, South. In the same year the Southern Baptist Convention split on the issue. Presbyterians managed to postpone the break until 1857, when their Southern congregations seceded.

Some groups attacked slavery on the grounds that it was undemocratic, irreconcilable with other American institutions and with the American tradition. It produced a small, powerful, minority class of aristocratic landholders who, it was claimed, had entered into a secret 'slave-power conspiracy' to extend slavery everywhere and to impose their rule on the nation at large. After 1850 the progress of this 'conspiracy' was carefully charted by the abolitionists; as some Northerners pointed out after the Dred Scott decision of 1857, it needed but one more favourable Supreme Court decision to make slavery a national rather than a Southern institution. 'Reflecting men,' wrote Henry Wilson, 'saw that there must be some malignant and potent agency at work . . . a commanding power in the land . . . before which all other interests were compelled in greater or lesser degree to bend.' If the Southern 'slaveocracy' joined forces with the Northern industrial capitalists, abolitionists pointed out, the two oligarchies together could and would control the nation. Only the abolition of slavery itself could forestall the combined tyranny of 'The Lords of the Lash and the Lords of the Loom'.

Slavery, it was argued, was economically unsound, wasteful, and inefficient. The poor white man in the South could not compete with unpaid slave labour; neither could he break the political and economic domination of the slaveholding aristocracy over the South. Last of all, some anti-slavery men claimed that slavery was simply illegal. The Declaration of Independence, they said, banned slavery by its enunciation of the natural rights philosophy. If the Declaration were not considered as part of constitutional law, then the Constitution, by outlawing the slave trade, also implicitly outlawed slavery. If the Constitution were neutral on the subject, as some assumed it was, the abolitionists reasoned that since the Declaration had abolished slavery prior to 1787, the framers of the Constitution had not considered it necessary to label as illegal an institution already outlawed. If the Constitution did actually sanction slavery, as certain commentators believed it might under the guaranteed property clause, the Christian must then obey 'a higher law' of morality and reject the authority of the Constitution. Thus William Lloyd Garrison publicly ground a copy of the Constitution under his heel. exclaiming, 'It is an agreement with Death and a covenant with Hell!'

Anti-slavery sympathizers, whatever their reasons, agreed generally that slavery was wrong and that it must be abolished, but they found great difficulty in agreeing on how and when to abolish it. The question of 'when' caused especial trouble. One faction favoured instant emancipation and 'immediate enfranchisement of our slave population', the policy generally approved by the New England societies. The 'gradualist' school of thought favoured piecemeal emancipation, extended over several generations, with gradual absorption of the Negro into the social and political structure – a policy attacked by Garrison as 'gradualism in theory and perpetualism in practice'. The so-called 'New York doctrine', adopted by the New York Society, compromised on 'immediate emancipation, gradually accomplished', a theory difficult to understand and equally hard to publicize. In the West the Lane Seminary group evolved a theory of 'gradual emancipation, immediately begun'. The Garrisonian and Lane factions found most supporters, but never reached agreement.

The 'how' of abolition proved no less troublesome. One group, basing its opposition to slavery on moral and religious grounds, believed that a national campaign for moral regeneration – an evangelical religious crusade – would result in the abolition of slavery by unanimous consent, North and South. Appeals to the national conscience, thought Theodore Weld, would soon convince slave-holder and non-slave-holder alike that the system was against God and Christianity. Another school of thought believed that slavery could best be abolished by legal action within the existing political framework, either through existing parties, which could legislate slavery out of existence, or through a third party, which might gain control of the Federal government to accomplish the same end. For this reason abolitionists founded the Liberty Party and nominated James G. Birney for President in 1840 and 1844. The political phase of the abolition movement, culminating in the Liberty, Free Soil, and Republican parties, rested primarily on the Lane doctrine, though it held Democratic-flavoured ideas on the tariff, bank, and internal improvements issues. A third group, believing that the Constitution legalized slavery and that there were no proper legal means of abolishing it, advocated either abandoning the Constitution for a new one or seceding from any government based on it. If the Constitution sanctioned a system which violated 'higher laws' of morality and natural right, a man must follow his conscience and refuse to remain in the Union. Garrison's *Liberator* carried on its masthead for years the slogan, 'No union with slave-holders!'

The 'colonizationists' proposed to extirpate slavery by transporting the Negro elsewhere, either to Africa or to some unsettled portion of the West. The American Colonization Society, founded in 1816 and counting among its members such men as Bushrod Washington, James Madison, Charles Carroll, and Henry Clay, established the colony of Liberia in West Africa for this purpose in 1822. After 1830 the abolitionists attacked the colonizationists both for their lack of success and for their refusal to face the problem directly; understandably, the colonizationists never found much support in the West. In forty years of activity the Society shipped about eleven thousand Negroes to Africa at a cost of more than a million dollars. Within a month the slave population had made up for this exodus by natural processes. Various other methods received some notice. Quaker groups argued that a boycott of slave-state products would force the South into emancipation. Some recommended paying wages to slaves so that they might buy their own freedom. Others proposed an appropriation of state and federal funds to purchase slaves for expatriation.

Free-soilism, a doctrine developed in the forties in the Northwest, was less a scheme for the abolition of slavery than for its containment within existing Southern boundaries. The Northwest farmer, who could not afford slaves and who found slavery unadaptable to his type of agriculture, did not want the fertile land of the plains states given over to slavery. Frontier egalitarianism mitigated against the system, while Western rural society was formed on a much more fluid and less stratified pattern than Southern slave society. The free-soil farmer had little humanitarian concern for the Negro and great unfamiliarity with slavery, but he definitely did not want the Negro as an economic competitor. Gradually the free-soil position moved closer to the legalistic, humanitarian, natural-rights theories of the abolitionists. By the mid-fifties the Free Soil and Liberty parties, both opposed to slavery but on different grounds, joined with the new Republican party. 'Immediate' abolitionism eventually killed off or engulfed its opponents, until by 1860 the single great issue became – not if, how, and when slavery must be abolished – but one of freedom versus oppression, right versus wrong, Christianity versus evil.

The pro-slavery forces from the outset presented a much more united front than the anti-slavery groups. There were, however, some disaffected areas in the South (western Virginia, western North Carolina, parts of upland Georgia, eastern Tennessee and Kentucky) which refused to co-operate. Anti-slavery thought in the South was in general very well controlled, either by legal intimidation or by social pressure, and the pro-slavery cause was so efficiently propagated that by 1850 the slave-holding states formed a solid bloc of opinion on the issue. In order to obtain solidarity Southern leaders were forced to make clear infringements on freedom of press, speech, thought, and education, to condone and encourage mob action, and to appeal to distinctly anti-democratic political, social, and racist theories.

The pro-slavery argument was both defensive and offensive in nature. In rationalizing the existence of slavery in a democratic nation, its proponents encountered stumbling blocks in the great Virginia liberal tradition and in the Declaration of Independence it had produced. The only alternative was to discredit both the tradition and the document, which Southern writers proceeded to do. Jefferson was ridiculed as an unstable reformer, infected with French radicalism and New England venom; Washington was drawn as a good-intentioned but politically naive man taken in by Northern propaganda. The Declaration of Independence, said Calhoun, represented an admirable theory but no guide for practical life. Of Jefferson's phrase, 'All men are created equal', he remarked, 'Taking the proposition

A History of the United States

literally, there is not a word of truth in it', a view to which many other Southern leaders agreed. 'The universal law of nature is force,' wrote Thomas Cooper. 'By this law the lower animals are subdued to man, and the same law governs the relations between men.' Slavery, from a Southern point of view, had deep roots in natural law, the Declaration notwithstanding.

The attempt to discredit the Declaration of Independence was accompanied by a compensatory effort to exalt the Constitution. At first the pro-slavery group found their sustenance primarily in Article IV, Section II:

No person held to service or labor in one State, under the laws thereof, escaping into another, shall in consequence of any law or regulation therein, be discharged from such service or labor, but shall be delivered up on claims of the party to whom such service or labor may be due.

This, it was argued, provided explicit authority for the return of runaway slaves but it also implied a recognition of the institution of slavery.

Gradually, however, the issue of slavery became for those who favoured the institution irrevocably mixed with the debate over states' rights. The Constitution, they argued, was an instrument which depended upon the consent of the individual states; just as that consent had been granted so could it be withdrawn if central government interfered with the authority of the individual states or the wishes of their citizens.

Replying to Northern critics, the exponents of slavery retorted that men were actually born neither free nor equal. Liberty is not an inheritance granted to every man, they said, but only to those who are equipped to deserve it. *Natural* rights to liberty do not exist. Men possess only such rights as society grants to them; that which society gives it can also take away. As Calhoun summarized the argument, men are born into a political and social state, subject to its laws and institutions. A Negro, being socially, mentally, and anthropologically inferior to white men, has no natural rights, deserves none, and could not make responsible use

426

of them if he had them. 'The Negro,' wrote J. B. D. DeBow, 'cannot be schooled, nor argued, nor driven into a love of freedom.' Southern preachers scrutinized the Bible for arguments justifying slavery as carefully as Northern divines examined scripture for arguments against it. Both Jesus and his apostles exhorted slaves to obedience and fidelity to their masters; the sons of Ham were cursed to eternal servitude by divine decree.

Having once justified slavery on political and religious grounds, its supporters proceeded to prove that its continued existence was both necessary and desirable. Slavery was best for the Negro, since he needed the care and guidance that only some system of servitude could provide. 'Providence has placed him in our hands for his good,' wrote Governor Hammond of North Carolina, 'and has paid us from his labor for our guardianship.' The fact that the Negro failed to appreciate this arrangement simply proved his lack of intelligence. Economically, the pro-slavery writers continued, slavery was absolutely necessary to the South and to the world. The Negro represented a huge investment in property, whose loss would mean financial ruin for one-third of a nation and probably for the nation itself. David Christy, in *Cotton is King* (1860), reasoned that since cotton depended on slavery, and the world economy depended on cotton, therefore the world economy depended on slavery.

Slavery, said the South, was an absolute social necessity. Only by declassing and subduing the Negro could the white race keep itself racially pure; if the black man gained social status, miscegenation inevitably followed. Freeing the Negro meant reprisals on white masters, murder, pillage, rape, and destruction. A slave uprising in 1831, led by a Negro named Nat Turner, costing the lives of sixty-one white men, women, and children, served to emphasize the point. The argument from plain personal safety was a powerful one, and the spectre of the 'Black Terror' hung always over and behind pro-slavery talk.

As time passed the South produced a flood of pro-slavery literature proclaiming slavery not only necessary and justifiable, but the best possible system – a 'positive good' – that should be extended to the North and West, perhaps to white men everywhere. 'Free society', editorialized the Richmond *Enquirer*, 'is in the long run an impracticable form of society.' John C. Calhoun pointed out that inequality is essential to progress, which is possible only when individuals desire to better their condition. A real democracy, like the Athenian, could exist only in a clearly stratified society; slavery therefore was 'the most safe and stable basis for free institutions in the world'. Furthermore, the conservatism of the established master class guaranteed social stability, since its interests lay in maintaining the *status quo*, while the classes that could make revolutions had no power to do so. The 'demoralized, insurrectionary' free society of the North contrasted ill with the 'harmony, union, and stability' of the slave-holding states. In the South there were no starving paupers, no 'wage slaves' to foment strikes, no 'free love' colonies. Senator Downs of Louisiana, echoing Carlyle's sneer at British abolitionism, challenged anyone 'to prove that the white laborers of the North are as happy, as contented, or as comfortable as the slaves of the South'. George Fitzhugh of Virginia, in *Sociology for the South* (1854) and *Cannibals All?* (1856), carried the 'positive good' argument to its ultimate conclusion. One sentence penned by Fitzhugh – 'Slavery is the natural and normal condition of the laboring man, whether black or white' – probably did more damage to the pro-slavery cause in the North than all that Garrison ever did or wrote. When war came Fitzhugh's words were used as concrete evidence of what a Southern victory might mean – white slaves in the North, as well as black ones in the South.

The pro-slavery argument achieved its purpose. One anti-slavery editor printed two quotations side by side in 1855. The first, from the Richmond *Enquirer* for 1832, called slavery 'a dark and growing evil'. The second, from the same paper for 1855, called it 'a natural and necessary and hitherto universal, hub, element, or institution of society'. The contrast, representing more than twenty years of agitation, illustrated the effective work of the Southern pro-slavery forces.

The Whigs elected Tippecanoe in 1840, but they got Tyler too. When Harrison died suddenly, only a month after his inauguration, the succession passed to Vice-President John Tyler, a Democrat who happened to be in the Whig party chiefly because he hated Jackson. Tyler was a pro-slavery Virginian, a strong opponent of federal centralization, the tariff, the Bank, federally-financed internal improvements, and the rest of the Whig programme. A proud, stubborn man, Tyler immediately ran headlong into Henry Clay, the Whig leader. Since he either opposed or vetoed nearly every bill Clay and the Whigs supported, Tyler's entire cabinet (except for Secretary of State Webster) soon resigned in disgust. Clay himself left the Senate and retired to Kentucky to prepare himself for the presidential election of 1844, while Tyler was formally ejected from the Whig party. With the Whigs split, their congressional strength divided, and a President without a party in the White House, legislation on domestic issues came to a dead stop. The only real accomplishments of Tyler's administration were those of Daniel Webster.

Webster became Secretary of State at a time when relations with England were in a delicate state of balance. Lord Palmerston was always difficult for Americans to handle; it was a tribute to Webster and to Lord Ashburton, Palmerston's emissary, that Anglo-American relations remained relatively peaceful. But Webster had his hands full. The northeastern boundary between the United States and Canada had been in dispute since the Treaty of Paris; over it, in 1837, some Maine and Canadian lumberjacks fought the abortive 'Aroostook War', and the entire American-Canadian boundary was still vague in places, especially in the Oregon country. Ashburton came to Washington in 1841 to open negotiations for a settlement, finally fixing a satisfactory boundary as far west as Lake of the Woods.

But there followed immediately another incident. During

the Mackenzie rebellion in Canada many Americans sympathized with the insurrectionists, sending them both volunteers and supplies. In 1837 the British seized and burned a small supply ship, the *Caroline*, and in the process killed a crew member. The *Caroline* affair stayed quiescent for three years, until a drunken Canadian named McLeod boasted in a New York saloon that he had been with the boarding party and had killed a seaman. McLeod was immediately arrested for murder, whereupon Palmerston in his usual forthright fashion informed the United States that since the boarding party had acted under official orders, hanging McLeod meant war. Again Webster spread oil on the waters, while McLeod, fortunately, was acquitted.

Less than a year later Webster was involved in another dispute with Britain. The slave trade had been illegal since 1808, but a good many 'blackbirders' still ran slaves into Southern ports. The British Navy took the lead in attempting to suppress them, stopping and searching suspicious-looking vessels. When some American ships were searched, protests poured into Washington. Though Webster and Ashburton worked out an agreement whereby both British and American squadrons shared the African coast patrol, the United States Navy never fully lived up to its agreement and many slave-runners filtered through. Much more serious was the *Creole* case. When American ships were forced into British West Indian ports by storm, any slaves aboard were usually declared free under British law. In 1841 the *Creole*, carrying slaves from Virginia to the Louisiana canefields, was seized by the slaves and sailed into Nassau, where they became free. Since the *Creole* case involved both mutiny and murder on the high seas, it became a complicated diplomatic issue. Webster and Ashburton could work out only an unofficial solution, but in 1853 the United States was awarded $110,000 in damages.

The Texas problem, however, overshadowed all else on the foreign and domestic fronts. The Texas country had been settled as early as 1821 by Americans attracted by free, fertile lands and by the liberal colonization policies of the

Mexican government to which it belonged. Westward-moving Southerners from Missouri, Kentucky, and Tennessee swarmed into it in the late twenties, carrying cotton-culture and slavery with them; a few Germans, French, and Northerners came too. However, friction between Texans and the Mexican government developed swiftly. Texas was not even a separate Mexican state; it had practically no political representation in Mexico City; it was a Protestant island in Catholic Mexico. In 1830 Mexico stopped immigration from the United States into the Texas area, armed the border, and suspended trade relations with the United States. Several times the American government unsuccessfully attempted to purchase Texas or parts of it.

In 1835 the Texans, smarting under Mexican rule, began a revolution which ended in 1836 with the proclamation of the Texas Republic. Santa Anna, Mexico's dictator, wiped out a small group of Texans at the Alamo, but the main body of the Texas army defeated him decisively at San Jacinto and made good their independence. The Washington government maintained a sympathetic neutrality throughout the revolution, although many Americans, including Andrew Jackson, favoured immediate annexation of the Republic to the United States. After some delicate diplomacy, and since Mexico threatened war if Texas were annexed, Jackson on his last day of office recognized Texas as a Republic. There was a great deal of sentiment, nevertheless, for admitting it to the Union as soon as possible. The prospects of fresh land for cotton and new markets for American products were attractive, and it was assumed that absorbing Texas was simply part of America's 'manifest destiny' to expand to the Pacific.

'Man and woman were not more formed for union, by the hand of God, than Texas and the United States are formed for union by the hand of nature,' wrote one newspaper editor. Since Texans were, after all, Americans by blood and heritage, they belonged under the American flag. There was also fear in official circles that if America did not annex Texas, Great Britain might accept it as a protectorate in defiance of the Monroe doctrine, thus establishing a second outpost on United States borders. On the other hand, some believed that the entry of Texas into the Union meant another step in the extension of slave territory westward, with a corresponding shift in the congressional equilibrium between free and slave states. Texas, an area as large as Germany, might be divided into several states, all of them slave, thereby completely upsetting the balance of power in Congress.

From 1836 to 1838 Texas, constantly threatened by Mexico, repeatedly requested annexation to the United States. In dire need of loans, trade agreements, and military protection, Texas emissaries travelled to Europe, where the British welcomed them, anticipating a lucrative trade in cotton. Tyler, under pressure from both Congress and the State Department, in 1842 again encouraged Texas to apply for admission, and the issue of Texas became important in the 1844 campaign, with the Northern Whigs in general opposing Texas's entry and the Southern Democrats favouring it. Tyler approved the annexation treaty, only to have the Senate reject it, but in his last weeks of office another resolution of annexation was passed. Before the end of 1845 Texas became a state, but troubles with Mexico were only beginning.

The westward march of the 1830s and 1840s brought 'manifest destiny' to other western lands. The Santa Fe Trail, running from Missouri to the Far Southwest, opened in 1822 and soon developed into a lively trade route, though the desert lands of Arizona and New Mexico attracted few permanent settlers. Americans began filtering into Mexican California in 1822, where millions of acres lay open around Sutter's Fort on the Sacramento river. Both Jackson and Tyler, recognizing California as a potential Texas, offered to buy the area from Mexico but met a flat refusal. The British, too, were interested in California, with a fair-sized colony established there by 1840. Although Lord Aberdeen ordered British agents in California to be 'entirely passive' in their conduct, the State Department feared that the

British had designs on the west coast area. In 1842, in fact, Commodore ap Catesby Jones and a naval squadron captured Monterey and claimed California for the United States, under the mistaken impression that a war with Mexico had broken out and that the Royal Navy was about to seize California for Britain. Jones had to give it back, of course, but the fate of California remained closely bound up with United States–Mexican–British relations until after the Mexican War.

The most difficult problem of westward expansion during the forties concerned Oregon. The Oregon Trail was an important trade route early in the century, after Lewis and Clark and the Astors had once opened the area. The United States acquired the Oregon Territory from Spain by the Florida Treaty of 1819, while Britain acquired an adjoining area from Russia in 1825. The United States and British claims overlapped, but since there was no immediate necessity of settling the boundaries, the two countries made provisions for joint occupancy. During the 1830s friction appeared among American and British settlers, fur traders, and missionaries. There was excellent farming land to be had in the Oregon country, and in the early forties thousands of emigrants left Independence, Missouri, for the long trip over the 2,000-mile trail, leaving a plainly marked road of wagon ruts that can still be seen on the prairies. The Conestoga wagon of the Cumberland Road turned into the 'prairie schooner', a huge covered wagon built of three-inch planks, with wheels six feet high, drawn by four to twelve horses. A moving fort, capable of carrying complete households, strong enough to ford rivers, withstand rocks, and deflect Comanche or Kiowa arrows, the covered wagon carried America west.

The growth of population made it necessary to settle the boundary line quickly, for as early as 1843 an Oregon convention petitioned Congress for territorial status. The South favoured the petition, since the North might be placated by admitting Oregon as free territory in exchange for Texas as slave. With the Oregon and Texas questions thus tied directly to both 'manifest destiny' and political sectionalism, one great issue of the campaign of 1844 became, in Democratic phraseology, 'The reoccupation of Oregon and the reannexation of Texas.' Over the Oregon boundary the cry was 'Fifty-four forty or fight!'

While the emigrants were pushing into the Far West the settlement of the Mississippi Valley was nearly completed. Ohio, Indiana, and Illinois, bordering the Ohio river, all entered the Union before 1818. Michigan came in in 1837, and the rest of the Northwest Territory followed rapidly. Iowa beame a state in 1846, Wisconsin in 1848, and Minnesota achieved territorial status in 1849, entering in 1858. Florida, admitted in 1845, and Arkansas, added nine years earlier, filled in the area east of the Mississippi. West of the river the land sloped gradually upwards into a great plateau, ending abruptly at the barrier of the Rockies. This was dry and forbidding country, considered until the 1850s to be uninhabitable and impossible to farm. Iowa, it was generally believed, was the westernmost boundary of tillable land; beyond Iowa the country was good only for Indians.

Westward expansion, of course, met vigorous opposition from the Indian tribes, who saw land, forests, and game disappear before the white man's advance. The frontiersman usually considered the Indian simply something to be pushed aside; a savage, cruel, pagan, unreliable barbarian, the only good Indian was a dead one. The Indian, on the other hand, was often cheated, defrauded, and maltreated by the white man, who had little understanding of his civilization and less respect for his rights. There was constant frontier warfare between Indian and American throughout the nineteenth century, with scalpings, torture, pillage, and massacre common to both sides. The only solution to the Indian problem, as the Eastern tribes were slowly pushed toward the Mississippi, seemed to be to resettle them west of the river on the great plains, a move agreeable neither to the Eastern nor the Plains tribes. Monroe initiated the Indian removal policy, while Jackson continued it more energetically. Congress authorized the exchange of lands west of the Mississippi for Indian lands east of it, and the great resettlement began in the 1820s, not without bloodshed. The Seminole War in the Gulf South, which lasted nearly ten years, ended only when the Seminoles retreated into inaccessible swamps. The Black Hawk War of 1832, culminating in the merciless slaughter by militia of hundreds of defenceless Sacs, Foxes, and Winnebagoes, marked the last serious Indian resistance in the Mississippi Valley. By 1850 nearly all the tribes east of the river had been moved into a vast Indian Territory, created for the purpose and stretching from the Dakotas to Texas. After the Civil War, when the Plains territory beckoned to settlers, the conflict began all over again.

The election of 1844 hinged on the Texas issue. At the outset it seemed certain that Martin Van Buren would be the Democratic candidate and Henry Clay the Whig; neither, however, wished to declare himself unequivocally on Texas. Both issued vague letters on the subject early in the year; both advised against undue agitation of either the Texas or the slavery issues. Clay's refusal to take a stand did him no harm in the North, but Van Buren's caused consternation among Southern Democrats. 'I would to God I had been at Mr V. B.'s elbow when he closed his letter!' exclaimed old Andrew Jackson. A few days after his letter appeared, Clay received the Whig nomination. Later in the month the Democrats, however, rejected Van Buren in favour of James Knox Polk of Tennessee, a 'dark horse' unknown to most Democrats, and adopted a platform calling for the immediate occupation of both Texas and Oregon. The anti-slavery Liberty Party offered James G. Birney for the second time. Ironically, in the election that followed, Birney drew enough Whig votes to throw the victory to Polk, a slave-holder himself and the nominee of the Southern-dominated party.

James K. Polk was a political unknown, but he had served seven terms in the House as Representative from Tennessee, and he knew politics from the inside. He was a conscientious, hard-working man with a definite programme and before he left office his entire programme had been completed. First of all the Walker tariff of 1846 abandoned the protective principle, despite the efforts of the manufacturers to defeat it, and pacified the South. The Oregon boundary settlement of 1846 redeemed another campaign pledge, although the United States accepted the forty-ninth rather than the fifty-fourth parallel, and did not fight. At the same time Polk began negotiations to acquire California from Mexico, a transaction completed by the Mexican War.

As soon as the resolution annexing Texas passed Congress in the closing days of Tyler's administration, the Mexican minister left Washington in protest. Nevertheless, Polk appointed John Slidell of Louisiana as Ambassador to Mexico with orders to adjust the Texas boundary, to settle Texas claims against Mexico, and to purchase both New Mexico and California. Since the Mexican government had virtually broken off relations with the United States, Slidell found no response whatever to his proposals; in fact, anti-American feeling ran high in Mexico City and the Mexican press talked loudly of war. To complicate matters further, Texas and Mexico had never settled an old boundary dispute – Texas claimed the Rio Grande as its southern boundary, while Mexico claimed it lay at the Nueces river. Polk, hoping to precipitate a settlement, ordered General Zachary Taylor and his army to occupy the north bank of the Rio Grande, an action regarded by the Mexicans as an invasion of their territory. On 24 April 1846 American dragoons and Mexican patrols clashed along the Rio Grande. Polk notified Congress that 'Mexico has passed the boundary of the United States, has invaded our territory, and shed American blood on American soil'. Congress immediately declared war.

The war with Mexico was not popular with all Americans. Northern Whigs charged the Democrats with fomenting war to gain popularity for the 1848 elections. Anti-slavery Northerners, bitter over the annexation of Texas, claimed the war was a slave-holders' conspiracy to extend slavery.

Texas, wrote James Russell Lowell, was simply 'a bigger pen to cram slaves in'. Many Southern Whigs supported the war while denouncing Polk for starting it. Western Whigs and Southern Democrats welcomed it: more than half of the army volunteers came from the West, and some Westerners in Congress urged the annexation of Mexico itself when the war was won. Nor was victory easy. The American armies were inexperienced, badly supplied and equipped, and inadequately trained.

Fortunately the Mexican armies were worse, so that General Taylor's little army, advancing into Mexico, defeated the Mexicans in quick and decisive engagements at Palo Alto and Resaca de la Palma. Within five months he occupied the important city of Monterey. Two other armies, under General John Wool and Colonel Doniphan, marched from Texas and New Mexico to join Taylor. Another, under the brilliant Colonel Stephen Kearny, captured Santa Fe in New Mexico and struck across the desert to California, joining the marines who had landed near San Diego. Once there, they found that American settlers under John C. Frémont had already seized control of California and had set up an independent 'Bear Flag Republic', which lasted only until Commodore Sloat and the Navy took formal possession of California for the United States.

The swiftness of his victories made Zachary Taylor a national hero. Taylor had no visible political affiliations, but there was Whig talk that 'Old Rough and Ready' was good presidential timber. Polk therefore decided to shift the plan of attack on Mexico with a drive at Mexico City by way of Vera Cruz. When a new commander was chosen for this expedition, Taylor was passed over, and since there were no really successful Democratic generals available, the choice fell on General Winfield Scott, a Whig but dependable. Scott's forces took Vera Cruz in early 1847. After six months of extremely hard fighting they captured Mexico City and hoisted the American flag over 'the halls of Montezuma'. By the terms of the Treaty of Guadalupe Hidalgo, accepted in February of 1848, Mexico agreed to recognize the Rio Grande boundary and to cede New Mexico and California to the United States, including all lands between. The United States agreed to pay fifteen million dollars for the territory and to assume slightly more than three millions in claims.

California proved an immediate treasure. Before the Treaty of Guadalupe Hidalgo could be ratified, a few flakes of gold were discovered in a mill-race on John Sutter's California ranch. The news spread swiftly, turning California from quiet ranching country into a roaring, crowded, hell-raising paradise for fortune hunters, singing

> Oh, Susanna, don't you cry for me,
> I'm off to California with my washbowl on my knee.

President Polk himself confirmed the reports of gold strikes in his annual message to Congress in 1848, while men raced by land and sea to wash millions out of the gulches and dig more from the hills. By May 1849 there were 5,000 wagons on the California trail; one observer on the Missouri river reported that 12,000 wagons had already passed the fords. Cholera, Indians, starvation, and the freezing cold of the mountain passes killed hundreds, but thousands got through. California grew from 12,000 population to 92,000 by late 1850, when it was admitted as a state, and by 1860 it had grown to 380,000. In the towns hastily thrown up – Poker Flat, Hangtown, Skunk Gulch, Red Dog, and others with unprintable names – eggs cost $10 a dozen, bread $25 a loaf, beds rented for $500 a month, and law meant nothing. Gamblers and prostitutes found easy prey in men who could make $100 a day with a shovel and a pan. The wealth that flowed out of California during the next few decades can be compared only with the flow from South America to sixteenth-century Spain; the Pacific Mail Company alone carried 122 million dollars' worth of gold dust and bullion in its first four years of operation.

Northern anti-slavery men, who had bitterly opposed the Mexican War, determined that slavery must not be allowed to profit by it. As early as 1846, David Wilmot of Pennsylvania, an anti-slavery Democrat, added, to a bill appropriating money for the purchase of Mexican lands, an amendment designed to exclude slavery from any territory so acquired. In effect the 'Wilmot Proviso', even before the war, linked the slavery question with politics and westward expansion. It lost, but the issue was hotly debated for several years. Some, like Polk, suggested extending the old Missouri Compromise line of 36° 30′ to the Pacific Coast. Calhoun, speaking for the slave South, argued that the new West belonged to the federal government; since slavery was constitutionally legal anywhere in federal domain, it could not be banned from any new federal territory. Webster, speaking for New England, claimed that since California and Oregon had never had slavery, they were automatically free territories. Others, like Lewis Cass of Michigan, thought that the new territories themselves should be allowed to decide – a doctrine called 'squatter sovereignty', later dignified by the title 'popular sovereignty' and espoused by Stephen A. Douglas. After long debate, Oregon was admitted as a free state in early 1848; Iowa and Wisconsin, free states admitted in 1846 and 1848, were balanced by Texas and Florida, both slave states admitted in 1845. Southern leaders viewed the future, however, with trepidation. The North was fast outstripping the South in population, Minnesota and California were nearly ready for admission, and the rest of the Mexican cession was approaching territorial status. Would the new states be slave or free?

At the close of the Mexican War the United States experienced a tremendous outburst of national pride. The westward march to the Pacific was over. Within the short space of three years the nation had gained Texas, Oregon, and huge areas from Mexico, a total of more than a million square miles. In foreign affairs, especially after the military triumphs in Mexico, diplomatic relations with Europe were marked by an aggressive self-confidence combined with an ill-concealed contempt for the 'effete monarchies' of the Old World. During the 1850s American ministers abroad were ordered to abandon the gold braid, lace, and other trappings of diplomatic livery and to appear in black evening clothes, 'the simple costume of an American citizen'. Twisting the tail of the British lion, or making sport of the 'perfumed lacqueys of France' became favourite political practice. Bellicose speeches in Congress, breathing defiance of Europe, were commonplace. Europe, it was assumed, was done for; there was a new world power on the scene.

The most important aspect of American foreign affairs during the Mexican War period involved the struggle with Britain for supremacy in South and Central America. The idea of a canal across the Isthmus of Panama was not new, but recent acquisition of great areas of land fronting on the Pacific made a short water route to the West a matter of great importance to the United States. In 1846 New Granada (Colombia) granted the United States transit rights in the Panama region, an agreement viewed with suspicion by the British Colonial Office. Since England had important colonial stakes in Jamaica, Honduras, and elsewhere in the area, American control of a vital canal meant not only American dominance over trade routes but an invitation to further Yankee expansion. British land and naval forces accordingly moved into the region to seize both the Pacific and Atlantic terminals of the proposed canal route. Conversations between the British Foreign Office and the State Department ended nowhere; neither nation would ever consent to a canal controlled by the other. 'These Yankees,' Palmerston remarked, 'are most disagreeable fellows to have to do with about any American question', a feeling heartily reciprocated in Washington.

After protracted discussions the Clayton-Bulwer Treaty of 1850 provided a grudging settlement. The two nations, it was agreed, would cooperate in constructing a canal and would neither fortify nor assume exclusive control over it; in addition, Britain promised (though in somewhat ambiguous terms) to stop its attempts to expand in Central America. Many Americans were dissatisfied with the settlement, since it seemed to block prospects of American expansion as well, but on the other hand, it did place an obstacle in the path of British imperialism and it did imply a tacit recognition of the underlying principles of the Monroe Doctrine. Nevertheless, clashes of interest between Britain and the United States continued to occur in Central America, since both (whatever the implications of the 1850 Treaty) obviously did have imperialistic aims. Eventually Britain's attention was diverted by events in Europe, especially after its declaration of war on Russia in 1854. By 1860 British policy in Central and South America was much more pacific and less expansionist.

But the island of Cuba remained a tender spot. Spain, after the disastrous Central and South American revolutions, retained only Puerto Rico and Cuba among its once great Western possessions. The latter island, because of its wealth and strategic location, Spain was anxious to keep, although the United States had looked at it with interest since Jefferson's time. Not only did Cuba appear to be a highly desirable possession, but its occupation by France or Britain would be a major threat to American security. Spain received several assurances that the United States would assist her in resisting any attempt by another power to take Cuba, as well as several offers of purchase. Southerners were anxious to obtain the island as new slave territory to balance the free territories of the West; Democrats made frequent references to it in various campaign platforms. By the 1850s the Cuban question agitated politics considerably and relations with Spain were somewhat strained. The intervention of the Civil War distracted attention and, for the moment, prevented the possibility of open conflict.

The triple-headed question of slavery, sectionalism, and territorial expansion dominated the elections of 1848. The Democrats who nominated Lewis Cass of Michigan carefully avoided any mention of it in their campagin. The Whigs were even more careful. They adopted no recognizable platform whatever and nominated General Zachary Taylor on the basis of his military record, but as it happened, Taylor lived in Louisiana and owned slaves. For Vice-

President they chose Millard Fillmore of New York State, an old-line Whig. With both major parties silent on the matter of slavery and its extension, a convention representing seventeen states met to found a third party, the Free Soil Party, and to nominate Martin Van Buren. Although the new party was by no means predominantly abolitionist, its chief issue was the prevention of slavery in the new territories, expressed in its slogan, 'Free Soil, Free Speech, Free Labour, Free Men!' The election itself was not an exciting one, since only Free Soil candidates seemed willing to discuss the real issues. As it happened, the Free Soilers polled 300,000 votes, sent thirteen men to the House and two to the Senate, and by robbing Cass of votes in New York, threw that pivotal state into the Whig column and helped give Taylor the Presidency. The results showed no popular mandate on slavery. Cass carried eight free and seven slave states, Taylor seven free and eight slave, although Taylor's popular vote was less than Cass's and Van Buren's combined.

Zachary Taylor, born in Virginia but raised in Kentucky, took over the leadership of a disturbed and troubled nation in 1849. He had spent nearly his entire life in the army, had no real party ties, and little political experience. His cabinet, which contained three Southerners and no abolitionists, satisfied the South, which assumed that he would somehow keep political peace on the slavery question. Taylor, however, did not live up to expectations. The pressing question of whether or not slavery should be admitted into the new territories acquired from Mexico was still unsettled, and the application of California (and later Utah) for admission to the Union as a free state presented his administration with difficult problems. Taylor's answer was simple – allow the new states to decide for themselves – a solution that seemed to the South to be simply the Wilmot Proviso in new form.

The Congress that met in December 1849 to wrestle with these problems was so evenly divided between Whig and Democrat that the handful of Free Soilers actually held the balance of power. It was an able Congress, including such men as Clay, Calhoun, Webster, Douglas, Jefferson Davis, Salmon P. Chase, William H. Seward, and Alexander Stephens. Sectional feeling was intense. Taylor's stand on slavery in the West aroused immediate, bitter opposition from the Southerners. Into the breach stepped aged Henry Clay of Kentucky, 'the Great Compromiser', to attempt once more to adjust the differences between North and South.

In January of 1850 Clay introduced into the Senate a series of eight resolutions (later packaged into an omnibus bill) designed to effect a reasonable solution to the problem of slavery and its extension. Among these resolutions the most important involved admitting California as a free state, placing no restrictions on slavery in the rest of the Mexican cession, assuming the pre-annexation debts of Texas, and instituting a new and more stringent Federal fugitive slave law. It was this, said Clay, or dissolution of the Union, possibly open war, for he believed that the states were 'twenty-odd furnaces in full blast', ready to erupt. Disunion was closer than Congress knew. Everyone should 'conjure at the edge of the precipice before the fearful and disastrous leap'.

In the eight months of debate that followed over Clay's resolutions, the entire problem of slavery – of its continuation and expansion, of sectional versus national interest, of federal versus state power – was thoroughly explored, not without heat. As usual, Calhoun of South Carolina spoke for the South. Too ill to stand and less than a month from his grave, Calhoun sat glowering in the Senate while Mason of Virginia read for him his last great speech, an uncompromising demand for concessions from the North. The only way to mollify the South, he said, was to cease agitating against slavery, allow the Southern states equal rights in territorial expansion, recognize slavery as a permanent, national institution, and enforce the fugitive slave laws to the hilt. Failing this, 'Let the States . . . agree to separate and part in peace.'

Three days later Daniel Webster, the foremost statesman

of New England, rose to defend the North against Calhoun's charges and to plead for union, compromise, concession, sanity, peace – a speech that shocked and angered the abolitionists who had long considered him their champion. William Seward of New York and Salmon Chase of Ohio, representing the anti-slavery forces, quickly replied, answered in turn by Jefferson Davis of Mississippi, whose stand was as bitterly uncompromising as Calhoun's. As the debate wore on, the tide gradually turned toward Clay. Tempers cooled; Calhoun's death removed the leader of the South; Taylor's death (probably from typhoid) in July of 1850 brought Millard Fillmore, who favoured compromise, into the presidency. Clay's bill failed, but the essential issues it contained were finally incorporated in another bill presented by Stephen Douglas of Illinois, passed, and signed by Fillmore. California came in as a free state. The matter of slavery in the Mexican cession was left for the territories themselves to decide. Slavery was abolished in the District of Columbia. A drastic new Federal fugitive slave law was approved. The Compromise of 1850 was over. It settled nothing, satisfied neither North nor South, and widened the sectional breach, but it did delay the 'inevitable conflict'.

Southern leaders found little to cheer about in the settlement. In exchange for an unpopular and unworkable fugitive slave law they lost the West and the balance of power in Congress, for the free states now outnumbered the slave, sixteen to fifteen. Georgia, Alabama, Mississippi, and South Carolina called state conventions to consider the advisability of secession, led by hot-headed men like Davis of Mississippi, Toombs of Georgia, and Yancey of Alabama. In South Carolina the secessionists actually had a majority, but the dispute simmered down without decisive action.

At the same time the new fugitive slave law angered many Northerners who hitherto had been cool to abolitionism, and gave the abolitionists a real propaganda weapon. The law denied jury trial to the escaped slaves, barred their testimony, ordered Federal and state officials to aid in their

capture, and provided stiff fines and imprisonment for those
who aided escaping slaves. The harshness of the law seemed
a taunt and an ultimatum to the North. 'It turns us all into
slave catchers,' cried one Ohio newspaper, and even mild-
mannered Ralph Waldo Emerson was moved to exclaim,
'I will not obey it, by God!' John Ramsdell, a New Hampshire tanner, phrased it in doggerel:

> What, bend the knee to Southern rule?
> What, cringe and crawl to Southern clay?
> And be the base, the simple tool
> Of hell-begotten slavery?

One of the irritations felt most strongly in the South was
Northern aid to those fugitive slaves who successfully escaped
into free territory. Not only was the loss of a slave financially
serious in itself – a good strong slave might be worth $2,000
– but his flight was a direct refutation of the claim that
slaves were happy and contented labourers for kindly masters. Since the Constitution and the Fugitive Slave Law of
1793 both required the return of fugitives, assistance to an
escaped Negro was punishable by law. But Northern abolitionists and anti-slavery sympathizers, appealing to the
'higher laws' of morality, retorted that the violation of
existing state and federal fugitive slave laws was a Christian
duty. Southerners, understandably sensitive about runaway
Negroes, searched constantly for ways of plugging loopholes
in the border-state areas. The 'patrol' system, whereby
organized groups patrolled Southern roads and towns looking for wandering slaves, was only a partial answer to the
problem. The only solution seemed to be more stringent and
carefully-enforced Federal laws.

Northern free Negroes had helped runaway slaves since
the mid eighteenth century, but it was not until after 1830
that Northern white abolitionists joined them. Pennsylvania
Quakers founded the first more or less organized white
group pledged to aid fugitives, and after the formation of
abolitionist societies in the 1830s and 1840s a network of
routes and stations for an 'underground railway' appeared
in Indiana, Illinois, and particularly in Ohio, with Canada

as the terminal. In New England another system centred on Boston, where stowaway slaves arrived on boats from Southern ports. After 1850 abolitionist agents, white and black, worked in the South, organizing slaves into groups and furnishing them with maps and instructions. Josiah Henson, Mrs Stowe's model for Uncle Tom, escaped with his family to Canada in 1830 with just such instructions, and on later forays of his own into the South brought out 118 Negroes through Ohio. Those who were caught assisting runaways and who were prosecuted under the new Federal law were hailed as martyrs in the abolitionist press, while government officials in several Northern states deliberately disobeyed or impeded its operation. Despite the harsh provisions of the 1850 statute, the 'Underground Railroad' expanded swiftly. Abolitionist societies boasted in 1851 that a slave could be run from any Southern border state to Canada in forty-eight hours or less; several newspapers openly published route maps, travel instructions, passwords, and locations of overnight stops. It is impossible to estimate accurately the number of Negroes who escaped by the underground route, but it is clear that while the 'railroad' probably did not materially weaken slavery, it did a great deal to create ill-feeling in both North and South. In the North it made the runaway slave an object of public sympathy and his 'conductor' an heroic fighter for liberty. In the South the existence of a well-organized conspiracy to defeat the Federal Law seemed simply another proof of the North's determination to destroy the South's vitally important labour system.

Yet the Compromise of 1850 represented quite accurately the temper of American public opinion. The nation at large was tired of argument, accusation, and acrimony. Business was good, farming profitable, wages high, industry prosperous, and those who profited from good times wanted no apple carts upset. In the elections of 1852 the air was full of olive branches. Early in 1851, before the party conventions met, fifty-four Congressmen of both major parties signed a pledge to oppose any presidential candidate who refused to accept the Compromise of 1850 as the final statement on the slavery question. At convention time the Democrats, after a deadlock among Cass, Douglas, Marcy of New York, and James Buchanan of Pennsylvania, compromised on Franklin Pierce of New Hampshire, an undistinguished but respectable candidate; not even Nathaniel Hawthorne, who wrote the official campaign biography, could make Pierce a great man. The Democratic platform hopefully promised to 'resist all attempts at renewing in Congress or out of it, the agitation of the slavery question'. The Whigs felt much the same. After pledging the party to a 'discountenancing' of the slavery question, their convention nominated General Winfield Scott, who said that he personally agreed to the Compromise but who was by birth and upbringing a Virginian and yet known to have powerful friends in anti-slavery circles. The Free Soilers, who roundly condemned the Compromise, nominated John P. Hale. The campaign was lethargic and uninteresting, since both Scott and Pierce avoided embarrassing questions. The election, fairly close in terms of the popular vote, gave Pierce a large margin in electoral votes.

The result seemed to show that the nation preferred Pierce and quiet to Scott and uncertainty or to Hale and agitation. The new President, in his inaugural address, put it very well by saying, 'I fervently hope that the question [of slavery] is at rest, and that no sectional or ambitious or fanatical excitement may again threaten the durability of our institutions or obscure the light of our prosperity.' It was a false hope. In 1852 Harriet Beecher Stowe's *Uncle Tom's Cabin* appeared, selling 300,000 copies in ten months. When Anthony Burns, an escaped slave, was captured in Boston and marched to the train in irons, the streets were lined with stony-faced, silent Yankees, flags at half-mast, church bells tolling. Politicians might 'discountenance' the slavery question, but it was there – and the people of the North knew it.

CHAPTER 24

THE EMERGENCE OF LINCOLN

FRANKLIN PIERCE declared in his inaugural address that
the Compromise measures of 1850 were 'strictly constitutional' and 'unhesitatingly to be put into effect'. In an
attempt to divert public attention from the slavery question,
he suggested the 'acquisition of certain possessions not within our jurisdiction', that is, in the Caribbean and South
American regions. Pierce's cabinet, composed chiefly of
Southerners, was as favourable to imperialistic expansion as
it was to slavery, while Pierce apparently wished to make
the purchase of Cuba the outstanding achievement of his
administration. However, the only result of his programme
was the purchase of a small slice of Mexican land south of
the Gila River, the 'Gadsden Purchase', to provide a better
route for a future railroad to California. In the Far East,
American expansionism was more successful. Commodore
Perry visited Japan in 1854 with the largest fleet ever
gathered by the U.S. Navy in the Pacific, and impressed by
the display, the Japanese agreed to open two ports to
American ships, beginning what soon became a highly
lucrative trade.

Despite all the efforts to find a substitute issue, the slavery
problem would not die. Northern abolitionists attacked the
expansionist policies of the Democrats as further evidence
of a Southern plot to add more slavery territory to the
Union. Fugitive slaves, captured under the provisions of the
1850 Compromise, made headlines in Northern newspapers;
churchmen hotly sermonized on the morality of slavery; the
'underground railroad' grew in size and efficiency; several
Northern states passed 'personal liberty laws' designed to
nullify the Federal acts. It was evident too that initiative in
politics was passing to new leaders who had little of the
spirit of compromise that marked the old. Van Buren was
retired, Calhoun dead, Clay and Webster both to die in

448

1852. In the North, men like Seward of New York, Charles Sumner of Massachusetts, Salmon P. Chase and Joshua Giddings of Ohio went to Congress, all uncompromising anti-slavery or free-soil men. From the South came men like Jefferson Davis of Mississippi, Robert Toombs of Georgia, and Barnwell Rhett of South Carolina – pro-slavery, states' rights, anti-Northern firebrands. There were, of course, peacemakers (usually called 'doughfaces') such as Marcy of New York and Cass of Michigan, but their influence was never strong.

The responsibility for reopening the slavery question in Congress must rest on the shoulders of Stephen A. Douglas, the Democratic Senator from Illinois. Douglas, known affectionately in his home state as 'The Little Giant' or 'Steam Engine in Britches', was a New Englander who came West to seek and find his political fortune in Illinois. An ambitious, shrewd, audacious little man, Douglas accurately represented the rough and aggressive democracy of the frontier country. He was especially interested in developing the West; he had already won large land grants for railroad building and had helped to make Chicago the chief Western rail centre. What really appealed to him, however, was the prospect of a railroad linking Chicago with the Pacific coast; but before it could be built the Indian lands west of Iowa had to be organized into territories, surveyed, and put up for sale.

Douglas boldly determined that this should be done. In January 1854, after receiving promises of support from Pierce, Douglas introduced into Congress a bill to organize the area west of the Missouri and Iowa into territories in which 'all questions pertaining to slavery' would be 'left to the decision of the people residing therein' – the old 'squatter sovereignty' principle, now called 'popular sovereignty'. The area, to be divided into Kansas and Nebraska, lay north of the Missouri Compromise line of 1820 and was therefore not open to slavery. Douglas appended to his bill an amendment declaring the Missouri Compromise inoperative, superseded by the principles of the Compromise of 1850. He knew exactly what he was doing. He did not particularly like slavery, nor did he have much sympathy for abolitionists or free-soilers. At the same time he believed sincerely in the people's right to decide matters for themselves, and he believed even more strongly in western expansion. Reopening the slavery question was in his opinion a small price to pay for a transcontinental railroad. What Douglas did not understand was the tremendous emotional charge generated by the issue of slavery and its extension.

The Kansas-Nebraska bill passed Congress in March 1854. Pro-slavery Southerners were overjoyed, seeing in it a magnificent opportunity to add one or possibly two slave states to the Union. Anti-slavery Northerners and Northwest free-soilers regarded it as a deliberate betrayal of the Missouri Compromise and an open attempt to introduce slavery into the Northwest. The bill split the Democratic party sharply into pro- and anti-Nebraskans and left the Whigs hopelessly divided. Douglas was bitterly denounced in Northern pulpits as a modern Judas; angry mass meetings formed in major Northern cities, while Douglas admitted that he could probably travel from Washington to Chicago by the light of fires built to burn him in effigy. The South had won again, and as Horace Greeley wrote in his *Tribune*, Douglas made more abolitionists overnight than Garrison could have made in fifty years. Southern Congressmen in their jubilation paid no attention to old Sam Houston croaking from Texas that the bill was 'the worst thing for the South that has ever transpired since the Union was formed'.

The passage of the bill simply moved the struggle over slavery from Congress to Kansas; nature and the Missouri Compromise might have intended the area to be free, but the pro-slavery men had no intention of allowing it to stay free. Settlers from Missouri, Kentucky, Mississippi and Tennessee poured into Kansas, and by 1854 they had organized it as a territory. In early 1855 they held elections for the territorial legislature, with armed bands stationed at key centres to see that the winning candidates were slavery sympathizers. Although the territorial governor declared many elections fraudulent, no anti-slavery men were elected and the new legislature immediately enacted laws protecting slavery in Kansas.

In the meantime settlers from abolitionist New England arrived, financed by the New England Emigrant Aid Society and church groups. Henry Ward Beecher, the great Massachusetts preacher, urged that all emigrants be equipped with rifles (henceforth known as 'Beecher's Bibles'), and the New Englanders were ready for a fight. Late in 1855 the anti-slavery men called a convention at Topeka, drafted a new state constitution forbidding slavery, and elected a new governor and legislature. A few months later a band of pro-slavery men sacked the town of Lawrence, anti-slavery headquarters. In retaliation John Brown led a raid on the settlement at Ossawatomie, murdering five pro-slavery men in cold blood – a deed which made him a hero in New England. With Kansas teetering on the brink of civil war, Pierce finally appointed a new governor, John Geary, who called in Federal troops to restore order, but not before more than two hundred lives had been lost.

The Topeka constitution was submitted to Congress for ratification in 1855, with a petition for statehood which Pierce angrily rejected. The ensuing debates over the admission of Kansas were perhaps the most rancorous ever heard in Congress. The climax came in 1856, after Senator Charles Sumner of Massachusetts completed a violent tirade against the South, bristling with insults and personal allusions. Two days later Congressman Preston Brooks of South Carolina approached Sumner, who was seated at his Senate desk, and brutally beat him into insensibility with a heavy cane. Sumner's injuries kept him out of the Senate for two years, during which time Massachusetts proudly refused to replace him. Brooks resigned from the House, was promptly re-elected, and was showered with gifts of canes from applauding Southerners. Many Southern moderates immediately disowned him, but to the North he remained 'Bully' Brooks.

Douglas's assertion that his legislation would take the slavery issue out of national politics could hardly have been further from the mark.

After the passage of the Kansas-Nebraska bill the pattern of politics changed with amazing swiftness. With both the Whig and Democratic parties irrevocably split, the way was open for a new anti-slavery party. In February of 1854 an anti-Nebraska meeting at Ripon, Wisconsin, recommended the organization of a party opposed to the extension of slavery, suggesting that the name of Jefferson's old party, 'Republican', be appropriated for it. In July the Republican party actually came into existence at Jackson, Michigan, asking for repeal of the Kansas-Nebraska bill, abolition of slavery in the District of Columbia, and repeal of the federal fugitive slave law. 'Republican', 'Independent', and 'Anti-Nebraska' parties showed considerable strength in the elections of 1854, carrying the state of Ohio and sending forty members to Congress. Old Free Soilers and Liberty men flocked to the new party in the West and Horace Greeley's powerful New York *Tribune* supported it in the East.

This new Republican party was unusual in that it originated almost spontaneously. No single leader or set of politicians formed it, as Jefferson shaped the first Republicans, Jackson the Democrats, or Clay the Whigs. The solution was there, and Douglas's bill chilled it into crystallization. Although abolitionists joined the party in droves, they never constituted a dominant element in its councils; as Woodrow Wilson later observed, the Republican party got 'its radical and aggressive spirit from the abolitionists, whom it received without liking'. Resistance to the extension of slavery, not its abolition, was the Republicans' real issue, based in turn on the deeper problem of the disposition of Western lands. That the party outlived slavery so long is good evidence of the fact that the slavery issue was less important to it than the aim of keeping the 160-acre western homesteads safe for free farmers, not for huge plantations. Republican issues were Free Soil issues, not Whig. At the same time, labour contributed a substantial amount of support to the new party. The fear that the institution of slavery might become nation-wide and the necessity of maintaining a free labour system in the North, attracted many elements from labour's ranks.

Political waters were further muddied by the appearance of the American or 'Knownothing' party, a nativist, anti-Catholic movement originating in Eastern urban centres, strong wherever Irish and German immigrants were numerous. An odd mixture of secret society and political organization, the party got its name from the reply supposedly given by its members to questioners, 'I know nothing.' It drew a great deal of support from Eastern Whigs, and except for its appeals to racial and religious prejudices, looked much like the old Whig party. Knownothingism also had a fair following in the South, where it was assumed that since immigration strengthened the Northern industrialist system, it therefore constituted a secondary threat to slavery.

Whigs and Democrats alike watched the election year of 1856 with interest. The Whig party was split and rapidly dying; the Democratic party, controlled by the South, was steadily losing Northern support; the bigotry of the Know-nothings repelled intelligent men both North and South. The new Republican party seemed to offer a haven for homeless anti-Nebraskans; Seward of New York (an anti-slavery Whig) and Chase of Ohio (a leading Democrat) both swung over to it. With the border warfare in Kansas and Brooks's assault on Sumner fresh in the public mind, the young party met to evolve a platform and choose a candidate for the forthcoming campaign.

They picked John C. Frémont, soldier, explorer, politician, popular hero; a man who possessed, remarked one contemporary, 'all the qualities of genius except ability'. Their platform called for the admission of Kansas as a free state, denounced the Kansas-Nebraska bill, opposed the extension of slavery, advocated a railroad to the Pacific, and asked appropriations for internal improvements – a good Western platform. The Democrats passed over Pierce to choose James Buchanan of Pennsylvania, a conservative

old-line politician who had been absent as Minister to
London during the Kansas-Nebraska argument and therefore was not on record about it. The Knownothings nominated ex-President Fillmore, a choice with which the pitifully
small remnant of the Whigs concurred.

The Republicans campaigned in 1856 almost solely on
the issue of 'Bleeding Kansas' and the extension of slavery.
George Fitzhugh's remark that slavery was the 'natural
condition' of the labouring classes received due emphasis,
and in hundreds of enthusiastic rallies Republicans sang
(to the tune of *The Marseillaise*):

> Arise, arise ye brave
> And let your war-cry be,
> Free speech, free press, free soil, free men –
> Frémont and liberty.

The Democrats stressed the necessity of soft-pedalling
slavery, holding the Union together, preventing a division
of section against section, keeping peace between North and
South. Despite internal dissension, the Democrats won.
With a middle-of-the-road candidate they could still win
an election, but what of the future?

Frémont polled a million votes, carried all but five of
the states north of Mason and Dixon's line, and showed
considerable strength in the five he lost. Actually the
Republicans came closer to uniting Northeast and Northwest than ever before – and this in less than two years of
party activity. The million Frémont votes, in Southern eyes,
posed a direct threat to Southern interests; a Frémont
victory, wrote Rufus Choate, would have meant 'a hostile
government' representing 'a vast region of States organized
on anti-slavery'. 'Almost as a mass,' said one Southern
editor, 'the North has gone for him, and gone for him too
on a platform the carrying out of the principles of which
would inflict immeasurable degradation upon the Southern
people . . .' After 1856 there was real fear in the South and
much talk of secession if the election of 1860 should go
against them.

Neither the doctrine of secession nor its corollary doctrine of states' rights was new to American political history. Their genesis lay in the theory that the states have certain rights preserved to them by the Constitution, which defines the spheres of power belonging to the nation and to the states. The base of the Southern argument rested on the proper construction of the language of the Constitution, particularly that of the Tenth Amendment, which 'reserved to the States respectively or to the people' those powers 'not delegated to the United States by the Constitution, nor prohibited by it to the States'. The problem was, simply, the old political puzzle of aligning unified Federal control with state sovereignty. The Revolutionary War was fought in part because the British government failed to find a satisfactory solution to the same problem; the Articles of Confederation provided only a temporary and unsatisfactory answer; the Constitution attempted to solve it in a different manner, but no more clearly. Leaders of both states' rights and Federalistic schools of thought could (and still can) find evidence in the Constitution to support their opposing views.

The question of states' rights and secession had appeared frequently in American politics before 1861. The Virginia and Kentucky Resolutions of 1798-9, aimed at the Alien and Sedition Acts, affirmed that the Union was a compact of sovereign states whose rights could not be contravened by a federal government that exceeded its constitutional limitations. The Hartford Convention of 1814, as we have seen, in protest against the War with Britain, reaffirmed the states' rights tradition and flavoured it with talk of secession from the Union. The Georgia legislature of 1827, during its dispute with the federal government over Indian policies, ordered state officials to refuse to honour any mandate of the Supreme Court that violated Georgia's 'sovereign rights'. Calhoun refined and developed the doctrine during the nullification troubles of 1832-3, though the result of his tangle with Jackson seemed to indicate that an aggressive federal government would always be able to prevent a state from exercising its sovereignty in conflict with federal law.

But the South Carolina legislature in 1831 uncovered the kernel of the secession idea with its announcement that 'this is a confederacy of sovereign states, and each may withdraw from the confederacy when it chooses'. The next logical step was to substitute secession for nullification as a last-resort answer to Federal 'tyranny'. From 1830 to 1861 justifying this substitution became the primary task of the Southern proponents of the states' rights doctrine. By 1861 the question was clear: is the nation a confederation of states, with certain sovereign rights guaranteed to each; or is it a sovereign union of states, with the central government holding final authority over its disparate units? The Civil War decided by force of arms what the Constitution meant; in a broad sense it was fought between two interpretations of that document.

For twenty-five years before his death in 1850, the chief political philosopher of states' rights was Senator John C. Calhoun of South Carolina. Calhoun, like John Marshall, was a product of the Southern frontier, born in the same county that produced Daniel Boone and Andrew Jackson. He was no planter-aristocrat, but he respected the institution of slavery, considered it an absolute necessity for the South, and was convinced that it could not be abolished without utterly ruining Southern life. After 1830 he watched with apprehension the spread of abolitionism in the North, the rapid growth of Northern wealth and population, and the increasing difficulty by which a balance of political power between slave and free states was maintained. The day might come, and soon, Calhoun prophesied, when Northern and Northwestern free states obtained a congressional majority and destroyed slavery by federal action; indeed, Northern abolitionists frankly admitted that such was their aim. The problem became then, to Calhoun, how to protect the Southern minority against the Northern majority within the framework of the American political system.

Calhoun's *Disquisition on Government*, published in 1850, together with his numerous speeches in Congress, contained his answer. The majority, he reasoned, must inevitably control the minority in any democratic state; the minority, consequently, must have some method of safeguarding its rights and interests. Only by appealing to the states' rights doctrine could the South protect itself against a Federal government controlled by a Northern majority. By conceding the sovereign rights of states, the Federal government therefore lost the power to encroach on these rights; the states' rights doctrine gave the state the power (as it had in the nullification controversy) to declare an act of the Federal government inoperative. But what if the Federal government refused to recognize the state's right to void such an act, as it had in the nullification argument? Then, in Calhoun's view, there remained only the final step of secession from the Union. The parting might be peaceful or not, but it must be a parting. Thus, in 1850, Calhoun addressed the North, 'If you are unwilling we should part in peace, tell us so, and we shall know what to do, when you reduce the question to submission or resistance.'

Calhoun's theories were expanded and augmented after his death by an articulate and militant South, conscious of its minority status and fearful for its rights in a world that seemed to be running against them. As the tempo of the argument over slavery quickened, more and more Southerners were forced to stand with South Carolina and Calhoun. Southern 'fire-eaters' like Rhett of South Carolina, Yancey of Alabama and Ruffin of Virginia hammered at the notion of secession, emphasizing the confederate nature of the Union and the absolute right of any state to secede from it; they envisaged a new Confederacy of seceded states, where they might construct an empire on the pattern of Calhoun's Athenian democracy and Fitzhugh's aristocratic society, founded on cotton and slavery. As early as 1856 Preston Brooks advised the South to 'tear the Constitution of the United States, trample it underfoot, and form a Southern Confederacy'.

The economic and political implications of slavery had much to do with the South's position. There was, however, always a racial factor involved – fear of the Negro as a social, political, and economic competitor; miscegenation, revolt, riot; destruction of a whole traditional pattern of race relations – which partially explains the willingness of a non-slave-holding majority in the South to consider slavery as absolutely essential and to secede from the Union if it were threatened. The South must be kept a white man's country, the Negro kept in his place. Slavery, it must not be forgotten, was among other things a device to guarantee white supremacy.

After 1850 the South held the conviction, true or false, that sooner or later the North and Northwest intended to use the power of the Federal government to destroy its peculiar institution and to ruin its social and economic system, regardless of Southern rights. States' rights and secession were the last shots in the Southern locker, the last defences against Federal authority. By 1861 the South agreed that the time had come to use them; only Kentucky, a border state, chose a neutral course. The Mississippi convention that voted that state out of the Union summarized admirably the Southern position:

We must either submit to degradation and the loss of property worth four billions of money, or we must secede from the Union framed by our fathers to secure this as well as every other species of property. For far less cause than this our fathers separated from the Crown of England.

James Buchanan was ill-equipped to take over the leadership of a confused and divided nation. Sixty-five years old, he was a weak and uncertain man, firmly convinced that the Union must be preserved but that the only way to preserve it was to give the South its way. He spoke optimistically in his Inaugural of a quick settlement of the slavery issue – let the people speak, and the majority will prevail – and evinced vague hopes that a solution might soon be worked out 'speedily and finally'. Two days after his inauguration the Supreme Court provided a solution, but one that threw a whole new light on the controversy.

The Dred Scott decision, finally handed down after years of litigation, gave the Republican party a new issue. In 1833

Dred Scott, a St Louis Negro, had been sold by one Elizabeth Blow to an army surgeon, Dr John Emerson. Emerson took Scott with him during brief residences in Illinois (a free state) and Wisconsin territory(where slavery was forbidden under the Missouri Compromise) and returned to Missouri (slave territory) in 1838. On Emerson's death Scott became Mrs Emerson's property, but she remarried and moved to Massachusetts, whereupon Scott, an apparently shiftless worker, fell back upon the charity of the Blow family. At the insistence of the Blows Scott sued for his freedom on the ground that his residence in free territory ended his status as a slave. He lost the first case and won a second. Meanwhile Mrs Emerson (now Mrs Chaffee) transferred Scott's ownership to her brother, who wanted to use him as a test case. Scott therefore claimed Missouri citizenship and sued his new owner, a citizen of New York, for his freedom. Eventually the case came to the United States Supreme Court.

The majority decision, written by Chief Justice Roger Taney, declared that Scott as a Negro slave was not a citizen of Missouri nor of the United States; hence he could neither sue nor be sued in federal courts. Scott's visits to free territory north of the Missouri Compromise line had not made him free; the Compromise was, in Taney's opinion, unconstitutional in that it denied protection to property (and slaves were property) in that part of the Louisiana Purchase. Though Justices Curtis and McLean dissented, Southerners could hardly have asked more from the Court, for Taney and the majority accepted the Southern position completely. The entire nation was open to slavery; though the decision was denounced as 'wilful perversion', 'an atrocious doctrine' and 'the last victory needed by the Slave Power', still it stood, with a President to enforce it. The Dred Scott decision appalled the North. If the Missouri Compromise, a law of Congress, could not exclude slavery from a territory, how then could it be excluded by a territorial legislature which derived its authority from Congress. What became of 'popular sovereignty'?

Shortly after the Scott decision Buchanan sent a new Governor, Robert Walker of Mississippi, to bring order out of chaos in Kansas. Walker called an election of delegates for a constitutional convention, but the free-state settlements, suspicious of a Mississippian, refused to participate. As a result, the overwhelmingly pro-slave convention at Lecompton drafted a pro-slavery constitution and submitted it to the people for ratification. However, taking no chances, the convention had the ballots marked in such a manner that a vote *yes* meant Kansas would definitely be a slave state and a *no* meant that slavery *as it existed* in Kansas 'would in no manner be interfered with'. Recognizing the ruse, the free-staters refused to vote and the pro-slavery constitution passed. However, the free-state men did vote and win in the following elections for the legislature. This legislature resubmitted the Lecompton constitution to the people, but this time the pro-slave men refused to vote.

Buchanan, convinced that elections and votes solved nothing in Kansas, recalled Walker and submitted the pro-slavery Lecompton constitution to Congress, urging its acceptance. It passed the Senate, but failed in the House. Meanwhile, Buchanan's course of action in the Kansas affair was more than Stephen Douglas could swallow. He believed deeply and sincerely in the principle of popular sovereignty. The mishandling of it in Kansas, added to Buchanan's obvious pro-slavery favouritism, angered him. Breaking with the administration took courage, since it also meant loss of favour in the Democratic South, but Douglas took the step. 'By God,' he said, 'I made James Buchanan, and by God, I will unmake him!' Douglas therefore opposed the Democratic hierarchy with all the vigour he possessed, and for his stand on Kansas, he was promptly read out of the party. Since he was up for re-election in 1858, his entire political future was in jeopardy.

Yet at the same time Douglas found many allies among Northern Democrats and even among Republicans. Horace Greeley in the East, alert for leaders, considered Douglas a potential Republican and advised party leaders in Illinois that it might be wise not to oppose him for re-election; others spoke guardedly of him as Republican presidential candidate in 1860. But Illinois Republicans regarded Douglas as a congenital Democrat and did not like his 'popular sovereignty' principle at all. As one of them said, it was asking too much 'to now surrender to Judge Douglas . . . to quietly let him step foremost in our ranks and make us all take back seats'. So the Illinois Republicans prepared to enter the campaign, choosing Abraham Lincoln of Springfield to run against him. Lincoln was a worthy opponent and Douglas knew it. 'He is the best stump speaker, with his droll ways and dry jokes, in the West,' said Douglas when he heard of Lincoln's candidacy. 'He is as honest as he is shrewd, and if I beat him, my victory will be hard won.'

Abraham Lincoln was well known in Illinois. Born in 1809 in a crude log hut in Kentucky (a few miles from Jefferson Davis's birthplace) as a boy he moved with his improvident father to Indiana and later to Illinois, growing up on the hard, rough, poverty-stricken frontier. Self-educated, primarily by thorough reading of the Bible, Shakespeare, Blackstone, Euclid and the English classics, when he entered politics he had behind him an undistinguished career as farm-hand, storekeeper, flatboatman and clerk. Lincoln's family, like most poor frontier families, favoured Jackson, but young Abraham, an admirer of Henry Clay, came into politics as a Whig. Shortly after his arrival at New Salem, Illinois, he ran for the state legislature and lost, but won at a second attempt and served several terms. At the age of twenty-seven he became Whig floor-leader in the Illinois House. Meanwhile he read law, was called to the bar, and married Mary Todd, an ambitious and moderately wealthy young woman with a strong belief in his talents. In 1847 he was elected to Congress for one term as a Whig.

From 1849 to 1854 Lincoln lived in virtual retirement, practising law, searching unsuccessfully for a way back into politics. For him it was, without doubt, a period of deep frustration, for he had set his mind on a political career and as his law partner Herndon said, 'His ambition was a little engine that knew no rest.' During the debates over slavery Lincoln laboriously threaded his way through the issues and puzzled out his solutions, disentangling the strands of argument with his clear, precise mind. An avid reader of newspapers and an inveterate keeper of scrapbooks, he constantly traced and tested public opinion on the streets, in the press, in the courts, on the law circuit. By the mid fifties Lincoln was probably one of the best-informed men in the nation on political matters.

It took Lincoln a long time to make up his mind on slavery. In the early fifties he adopted a position much like that of the free-soilers. 'The whole nation,' he wrote at the time, 'is interested that the best use shall be made of these Territories. We want them for the homes of white people. This they cannot be, to any considerable extent, if slavery shall be planted within them.' He was not an abolitionist, and took pains to say that he was not; he recognized the constitutional right of slave-holders to hold property, and never advocated the abolition of slavery in areas where it existed. But in his careful analysis of contemporary issues he became convinced that slavery, unless its spread were prevented, would become nation-wide, and, as Calhoun and Fitzhugh prophesied, eventually engulf the white labourer. Not until 1854 did Lincoln publicly denounce slavery on moral grounds, condemning it as 'a monstrous injustice'. Not until then did he decide that the institution threatened the democratic tradition he believed in, that the alliance between cotton capitalism and industrial capitalism was close at hand. For Lincoln the slavery question was tied closely to the questions of Union and democracy. In every recorded speech from 1854 to 1861 he repeated the warning that slavery might become national, and that if it did, free America was doomed. His classic 'House Divided' speech of 1858 expressed this theme most cogently.

I do not expect the Union to be dissolved – I do not expect the house to fall, but I do expect it to cease to be divided. It will become all one thing or all the other. Either the opponents of slavery will arrest the further spread of it, and place it where the public mind shall rest in the belief that it is in the course of ultimate destruction; or its advocates will push it forward, till it shall become alike lawful in all the States, old as well as new, North as well as South. Have we no tendency to the latter condition?

The oft-omitted last sentence, with its implied affirmative answer, is essential to the meaning of the passage.

The acrimonious debates over the Kansas-Nebraska bill brought Lincoln back into politics as a 'Conscience' or 'Anti-Nebraska' Whig, and his first real opportunity came at the Illinois Anti-Nebraska convention in 1856. Here he dominated the proceedings, welded the motley assembly of delegates into something resembling a political unit, and practically created the new Republican party in Illinois. But Lincoln was cautious. He went to the national Republican convention of 1856 as a Whig, and although he made fifty campaign speeches for Frémont, he refused to call himself a Republican. Not until 1858, when he accepted the party's senatorial nomination, did he really affiliate with the party.

The congressional elections of 1858 were fairly quiet throughout the country, except in Illinois where the attention of the nation was focused on Douglas, fighting for his political life. Lincoln knew that he could not hope to battle with Douglas, a powerful orator, on his own level, and as the two men stumped the state it became apparent that of the two, Lincoln seemed to make the more sense. Torchlight processions and rhetorical flourishes meant little in cold newsprint; Lincoln's dry, sharp, informal talks sounded better and better as time wore on. He asked questions, hard ones, and when Douglas answered them, Lincoln asked more. Cleverly shifting tactics, he then challenged Douglas to a series of public debates, a challenge the Little Giant could hardly refuse. The situation was all to the advantage of Lincoln, probably the ablest jury lawyer in the West.

The debates that followed represent a high-water mark in American political history. They also made Abraham

Lincoln a national figure, and killed Douglas's chances for the Presidency. In the second debate at Freeport, Illinois, Lincoln forced Douglas's hand with the question, 'Can the people of a United States Territory, in any lawful way, against the wishes of any citizen of the United States, exclude Slavery from its limits prior to the formation of a state Constitution?' If Douglas answered yes, he repudiated the Dred Scott decision, lost the South, and stood on 'popular sovereignty'. If he answered no, he repudiated his own principle and lost Illinois and the North. Douglas answered yes, won Illinois, and won the Senate seat. But Lincoln's question brought the real issue into the open – might not slavery become the national system?

The 'lame duck' session of Congress that met after the 1858 elections was badly split on sectional lines. Except in Illinois, the elections had gone against the Democrats, and it was clear that the next session would be under Republican control. Southern Congressmen, hoping to accomplish as much as possible before it met, supported but lost a bill to purchase Cuba (as probable slave territory). Congressmen from the Northwest demanded a homestead bill, opening up the western public lands, but Buchanan vetoed it. A Pacific railroad bill, supported by the Northwest, lost to the Southern bloc, and so did the tariff bill much desired by New England manufacturers. Southern congressmen orated bitterly about Northern aid to escaped slaves, while Northern congressmen accused the South of slave-running in violation of the 1808 embargo. It was an unpleasant session, and after its close something happened to make the next one worse.

John Brown of Ossawatomie fame had been travelling freely through the North, though under indictment for murder in Kansas. Deeply religious, by 1859 Brown had developed his abolitionism to a point well beyond fanaticism. In New England he collected money from a number of prominent abolitionists to finance what he outlined vaguely as a scheme to free numbers of slaves. In May of 1859 he met with a handful of followers in Canada, held a 'constitutional convention', adopted a new 'constitution'

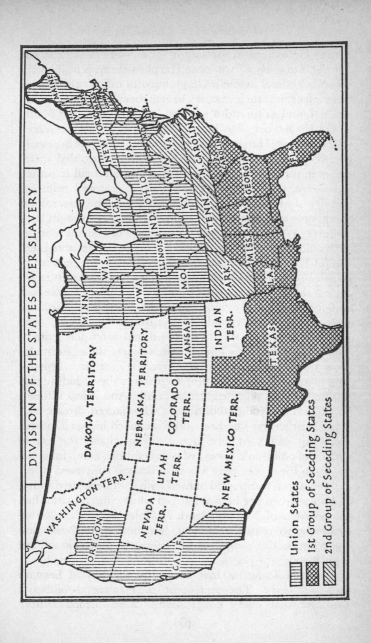

DIVISION OF THE STATES OVER SLAVERY

Union States
1st Group of Seceding States
2nd Group of Seceding States

for the United States (providing for a Negro president) and returned to lease a farm near Harper's Ferry, Virginia, the site of a Federal arsenal. He planned to call on all Negroes to revolt against their masters, to arm them from the captured arsenal, and to spread a wave of terror through the South.

On 16 October 1859 Brown and his band of eighteen men descended on Harper's Ferry, captured thirty prisoners in the sleepy and surprised little town, and barricaded themselves in the arsenal while emissaries went abroad to arouse the slaves. But Harper's Ferry was far removed from the heavily slave-populated plantation area, and his raiders found only a few confused Negroes whom they brought back by force. Within two days a detachment of Federal marines arrived, commanded by Colonel Robert E. Lee and Lieutenant J. E. B. Stuart; after a short, sharp engagement, in which Brown's two sons were killed, his raiders surrendered. In less than a week a grand jury indicted Brown for treason and for waging war against the Commonwealth of Virginia.

News of Brown's raid swept through the South. The 'Black Terror' of slave insurrection had eaten for years at Southern hearts. Was John Brown a sign of things to come? Was this abolitionism in action? The fact that Brown's raid was a senseless failure, engineered by a half-insane zealot, was lost on a frightened South. And it was difficult to explain away the abolitionists who backed Brown, and those Northerners like Emerson who hailed him as a martyr to a just cause, or like Louisa May Alcott, the gentle author of children's books, who called him 'Saint John the Just'. In the weeks that followed Brown, convinced of his righteousness, comported himself with calmness and dignity, but on 2 December he was hanged while church bells tolled in the cities of New England. 'I, John Brown,' he wrote before he went to the gallows, 'am now quite *certain* that the crimes of this *guilty land*: *Will* never be purged *away*; but with Blood.'

The new Congress met under the shadow of Brown's dangling body. The statement of Hammond of South Carolina that every congressman came 'armed with a revolver – some with two – and a bowie knife' was an exaggeration, but it reflected the temper of both houses. Douglas's quarrel with Buchanan had cut the Democrats in half. The balance of party power lay with Buchanan and the Southern wing, controlled by Jefferson Davis, who set about to drive out Douglas and to make of the Democrats a Southern party. At the same time machinery was in motion in the Southern states for the same purpose. In 1858 state Democratic leaders like Yancey, Rhett, and Ruffin organized the League of United Southerners to 'fire the Southern heart, instruct the Southern mind, give courage to each other', and to agitate for Southern political rights. In December 1859, as Congress convened, the South Carolina legislature sent delegates to other Southern states to organize for action; Virginia held back, but Alabama, Louisiana, Mississippi, Florida, Texas, and Arkansas agreed to cooperate.

The wide rift in the Democratic party immediately appeared at its presidential convention, which met in Charleston, South Carolina, the centre of Southern extremism. Douglas, backed by the Northern Democrats, was a logical candidate, but Davis and the South would have none of him. When the Douglas Democrats succeeded in getting through a compromise platform, the Southern delegates stalked from the convention and called for a rump meeting in Richmond. The remaining delegates, after fifty-seven futile ballots, adjourned to meet in Baltimore. There the Northern Democrats nominated Douglas; the Richmond meeting named John Breckenridge of Kentucky. Thus the division of the party into Northern and Southern wings was made complete.

In the meantime two other parties were holding conventions. A sizeable group of Whigs and Knownothings met in May 1860 to form the Constitutional Union party, pledged to recognize 'no political principles other than the Constitution of the country, the Union of the States, and the enforcement of the laws' – meaning the laws governing slavery. To attract unionists and moderates in both sections of the country, they chose John Bell of Tennessee as their candidate and Edward Everett of Massachusetts as his running-mate, both middle-of-the-roaders.

The Republicans, jubilant over the Democratic split, met in Chicago. The practical politicians felt that a good ticket and a good platform stood an excellent chance of winning. The platform they evolved was a masterpiece of multi-group appeal, based on old Free Soil and Whig issues with anti-slavery interpolations. It denounced disunion and secession, which could offend no one outside the South. It opposed the extension of slavery into the territories, but pledged non-interference with the system where it already existed, thus attracting both free-soilers and anti-slavery moderates. For the New England businessman it promised protective tariffs; for the Western farmer it promised a railroad to the Pacific, a quarter-section of land to settlers, and federally-financed internal improvements; for the foreign-born it promised more liberal naturalization laws. It denounced John Brown, and approved the Declaration of Independence. There was, in effect, something in it for everybody. The choice of a candidate was harder. Seward of New York or Chase of Ohio were logical choices, but their records looked too radical. Abraham Lincoln of Illinois – considered a moderate – won on the third ballot.

Nearly every plank in the Republican platform favoured something that the South had fought against for years. The strong nationalism of the party meant that if it won states' rights was dead. Its opposition to the extension of slavery meant that the new Western states would all be free, making the slave-holding states a permanent minority in Congress. Both Lincoln and the party's proclaimed platform promised not to interfere with slavery where it existed; but was this an honest promise, and was Lincoln the real leader of his party? The presence of known abolitionist radicals in the party councils was not reassuring. The Republicans offered everything to the Northeast and Northwest; to the South they promised nothing. Davis's old prediction that the aim of the North was to dominate and vassalize the South seemed about to come true, and Southern leaders in general agreed that the election of Lincoln would constitute cause for secession.

The campaign itself was strange. In the North the contest lay between Lincoln and Douglas; in the South between Breckenridge and Bell. 'Honest Abe, the Railsplitter', 'The Man of the People', polled 1,800,000 votes, all from the North, Douglas and 'popular sovereignty' polled 1,300,000 in both sections. The radical candidate, Breckenridge, received 850,000, practically all from the South. Unionist John Bell polled less than 600,000, from both North and South. Lincoln's popular vote was smaller than the combined total of votes against him, but his majority in the electoral college was decisive, and even if the votes against him had been given to a single candidate, still he would have won. The key to the election lay in the Northwest. As late as 1858 the Democrats had recorded large votes in that area, but in 1860 it swung to the Republicans, completing the alliance of Northeast and Northwest so much feared by the South. Slavery helped to cement it, but it was not that issue alone; the sections were tied together by bonds of economic and political interests – unionism, railroads, water routes, business commitments, markets, migrations – that were stronger than a common aversion to slavery and secession. When Lincoln was elected the whole North was united and the nation finally divided.

'The people are run mad', wrote Alexander Stephens of Georgia. 'They are wild with passion and frenzy. . . . Men will be cutting one another's throats in a little while.' Allowing for hyperbole, there was some truth in his view of the South at the news of Lincoln's victory. Many in the South feared 'Black Republicanism' as deeply as those in the North feared the 'Slave Power', but cool-headed Southerners agreed with the Tennessee editor who counselled that secession was 'no remedy for the South's wrongs, or only a madman's remedy'. Others disliked the turmoil created by hot-heads and believed that the South could best achieve its purposes within the Union, that Lincoln's election

was perfectly legal, and that the democratic process must
be trusted. Economic circumstances, too, favoured patience,
for the South was prosperous. The panic of 1857 had touched
the slave-holding states but lightly; the cotton crop was
good and prices satisfactory.

The secessionists, however, were determined and organized. They set to work quickly in Alabama, Mississippi, and
South Carolina. In South Carolina a convention met a
month after Lincoln's election and on 20 December 1860 it
adopted an Ordinance of Secession, dissolving 'the Union
now subsisting between South Carolina and the other States
under the name of the United States of America'. Commissioners were immediately appointed to visit other Southern
legislatures, to urge secession and propose a new union of
seceded states. Before the close of January 1861 Mississippi,
Florida, Alabama, Georgia, Louisiana and Texas followed
South Carolina out of the Union. The conventions which
voted for secession met quickly and acted speedily; lacking
unity and organization, Southern unionists had little chance
to resist. But still from the list of departed states there were
notable absentees: all the border states of the upper and
western South, where Union sentiment was strong.

While Lincoln waited in Illinois for his Inauguration,
Buchanan followed a do-nothing policy that undoubtedly
encouraged secessionism in the South. In his annual message
to Congress he denied that a state had a right to secede, but
he also admitted that the Federal government had no real
power to force a state to remain in the Union, and to calm
Southern excitement, he recommended a constitutional
amendment recognizing slavery in areas where it already
existed. He allowed the seceded states to take over all
Federal property within their borders, including all arsenals
and forts except Fort Pickens in Florida and Fort Sumter in
Charleston Harbour. On 8 January 1861 a supply ship
approached Sumter, only to be turned back by the shore
batteries, but Buchanan preferred to ignore what was
really an act of war.

Congress at once set about finding a compromise. Committees in both House and Senate discussed several proposals, of which two received special attention. Andrew Johnson of Tennessee submitted a plan for electing Senators directly (instead of by legislative appointment), alternating the Presidency between North and South, dividing Northern and Southern representation on the Supreme Court, and providing for a run-off election in case no future presidential candidate received a majority. Crittenden of Kentucky, another border state, submitted a milder proposal to extend the Missouri Compromise line, define Congressional power over slavery, and provide compensation to owners of runaway slaves. Against solid Republican opposition both suggestions collapsed. In desperation the Virginia legislature called for a 'peace convention' under the chairmanship of ex-President Tyler, and delegates from twenty-one states met at Washington in February 1861 – again to no avail. Neither the seceded states nor the Republican-controlled states of the West bothered to send representatives. As Salmon P. Chase declared, 'Mr Lincoln was the candidate of the people opposed to the extension of slavery . . . Do you think we who represent this majority will throw it away?'

While the 'peace convention' met in Washington, delegates from the six seceded states met in Montgomery, Alabama, to establish a new nation, and on 8 February this meeting adopted a provisional constitution for the Confederate States of America. Next day it chose Jefferson Davis of Mississippi as President of the Confederacy and Alexander Stephens of Georgia as Vice-President. Then it remained in session for several weeks, acting as a national legislature and drawing up a constitution, modelled on the Federal document but differing sharply from it in several respects. The importation of slaves was banned, but slavery was protected in the territories and the Confederate Congress was specifically forbidden to deny or impair the right to hold property in slaves. The President was limited to one term of six years, the rights of states carefully noted, and cabinet members given seats (but not votes) in the House and Senate. The provisional legislature also voted a bond

issue of fifteen million dollars to support the new government, and authorized the creation of an army of 100,000
men.

As Inauguration Day approached, the divided nation
watched Lincoln. He said nothing, spending his time selec-
ting a cabinet chiefly from among the disappointed presidential candidates of his own party. Seward went in as
Secretary of State, Chase as Secretary of the Treasury,
Cameron of Pennsylvania as Secretary of War (soon ousted),
and Bates as Attorney General. While the 'peace convention' floundered and the Confederacy met in Alabama,
Lincoln began a leisurely trip to Washington, stopping for
frequent speeches that were eagerly scanned for intimations
of his policy. For the most part he repeated safe generalities
– the Union must be preserved; he would execute all laws
in all parts of the United States; no force would be used
unless to meet force. But his inaugural address was a calm,
clear statement of policy, cautious, conservative, conciliatory.

The apprehension seems to exist among the people of the Southern
states that by the accession of a Republican administration, their
property and their security are to be endangered. There has never
been any reasonable cause for such apprehension.

No state had the right to secede; therefore none had. The
Union remained whole. 'I hold that in contemplation of
universal law and of the Constitution,' said Lincoln, 'the
union of these states is perpetual.'

It is safe to assert that no government ever had a provision in its
organic law for its termination. No State upon its mere motion can
lawfully get out of the Union. I therefore consider that the Union
is unbroken and shall take care that the laws of the Union are
faithfully executed in all the States.

'The government will not assail you,' he told the South.
'You can have no conflict without being yourselves the
aggressors.' Thus Lincoln shifted responsibility for secession
to the Confederacy, leaving the South no alternatives but
to remain in the Union or make war to stay out.

In all of this there was little satisfaction for the South,

where, even in the border states, the unionists accepted the right to secede, if not its wisdom. Nor were the Republican leaders in the North mollified by Lincoln's statement of principles. Seward, in fact, believing Lincoln confused and incompetent, offered to take over the reins of government, leaving Lincoln a figurehead, an offer that was politely refused. Again Seward came forward with a plan to unify the nation by a quick declaration of war against France and Spain, but with the same result. For nearly a month Lincoln did nothing.

The problem that eventually forced his hand was the question of Federal property in the seceded states. Post offices, mints, customs-houses, arsenals, and forts (except for Pickens and Sumter) belonging to the United States had been occupied without incident by Confederate state officials and forces; and as soon as Lincoln was inaugurated, Confederate commissioners called on Seward to ask for the surrender of Fort Sumter, commanding Charleston harbour. Seward quite properly refused to receive them, but Major Anderson, commanding the Sumter garrison, reported that he was running desperately short of supplies. Feeling that the prestige of the Federal government was at stake, Lincoln, over the objections of most of the Cabinet, determined to send relief expeditions to both Pickens and Sumter. The ship to Fort Pickens arrived safely and the fort remained in Federal hands.

Sumter, however, was a different matter. When news reached Charleston that the fort was to be provisioned, Brigadier General Pierre Gustave Toussaint Beauregard of the new Confederate Army placed batteries along the shore, consulted Governor Pickens of South Carolina, and asked for instructions from the Confederate Secretary of War. The Confederate Cabinet discussed the matter carefully. The issue was perfectly clear. The relief of Sumter would constitute a direct challenge to the Confederate government. On the other hand, while resistance meant open war, it might also serve to tip the balance in the hesitant border states. Beauregard was instructed, therefore, to demand the evacuation and surrender of the Fort.

The cast and setting at Fort Sumter was chosen as if some other-worldly producer had intended to demonstrate for all time the tragedy of civil war: a U.S. Army Commander, Major Robert Anderson, was himself a Southerner and no abolitionist but believed that an oath taken in adult consciousness must outweigh pride in place of birth or political conviction; and, facing him, his friend and one of the most romantic and chivalrous of the military leaders of the Confederacy, General Pierre Beauregard. Muddleheaded administration in Washington and muddleheaded administration in South Carolina; right cancelling right, and right as much with the Presidents as with Governor Pickens. A sense of unreality, of 'this can never happen to us', even while it was happening.

On 11 April 1861, Beauregard formally requested the possession of Sumter. Major Anderson refused, and on the morning of the 12th the first gun fired in the Civil War was touched off. Through the day the shore guns boomed while the Federal relief squadron stood off the harbour. On the 13th, with food and ammunition exhausted, Anderson surrendered 'with colors flying and drums beating . . . , saluting my flag with fifty guns'. One man was killed while firing the final salute, but there would be more before it was over. Lincoln, on the 15th, called for 75,000 militia for ninety days to subjugate rebellion and to restore the authority of the Union.

The first post-war generation of historians almost unanimously agreed that the Southern states seceded because of slavery, and that the North fought secession as treasonable rebellion. Later historians have found the causes of the Civil War much more numerous and complex. Was it caused by slavery? Was it caused by the aggressions of a 'slave power conspiracy', or by a 'Northern plot' to vassalize the South? Was it a constitutional conflict between states' rights and nationalism? Was its cause chiefly economic, the clash of an agrarian with an industrial civilization? Was it a

The Emergence of Lincoln

failure of leadership, the work of hot-headed agitators and irresponsibles on both sides? There is reason to accept some or all of these as factors in the precipitation of the conflict. At any rate, it had been brewing for a long time. Even at the Constitutional Convention of 1787 Madison noted signs of friction between Southern planters and Northern merchants. After the War of 1812, the underlying clash of sectional interests grew sharper, complicated not only by slavery, but by changing economic conditions, the opening of the West, political rivalry, and other points at issue. American history from 1814 to 1861 was a record of constant compromise and concession on sectional issues, all tending toward the final break. Whether the war could have been avoided, or whether it was truly, in Seward's phrase, an 'irrepressible conflict', are insoluble questions.

Despite abolitionist claims, there is no evidence to support the existence of an organized 'slave power plot' to subvert national liberties and make slavery into a nation-wide institution. The South was never so completely unified as the abolitionists assumed, though there was obviously a tacit agreement among slave-holders and non-slave-holders that slavery was a good system, perhaps the best, and one most certainly to be retained and extended. Nor is there evidence to support the Southern accusation that Northern interests were allied in an attempt to crush the South and reduce it to economic and political bondage, despite the warnings of Calhoun, Davis and Rhett.

The cause of the war cannot be laid solely on an economic clash between the sections, though such conflict undoubtedly played a major part in initiating it. It is quite possible that if slavery had not been an issue, secession might have come about from economic rivalry alone. Almost from the beginning of the Republic sectional leaders differed sharply on economic policy, over the tariff, public lands, western settlement, internal improvements, financial measures. According to Toombs, 'The instant the Government was organized . . . the Northern States evinced a general desire and purpose . . . to pervert its powers for sectional advan-

tage, and they have steadily pursued that policy to this day.'
By the 1850s it seemed to Toombs and others that the North
was steadily winning the race for economic advantage. The
Northern states, as successive censuses showed, grew rapidly
in wealth, population, and industry, while the South,
despite the general prosperity of its staple crop system, became more and more dependent on the North. The conflict
between a static, agrarian, cotton-producing, slave-labour
economy and an expanding, commercialized, industrialized
economy was deeply rooted. Secession obviously meant
economic loss for the Northern merchants, manufacturers,
property owners, shippers, middlemen, and creditors, but
it is doubtful if such loss alone would have precipitated a
war to prevent it.

There was also the issue of state sovereignty versus
federalism, at bottom a contest over control of national
policy in regard to such things as banking measures, tariffs,
internal improvements, and especially slavery. If the Union
was a voluntary federation of sovereign states, with the
important powers residing within them, the whole course of
national policy followed the Southern channel. If the Constitution created a perpetual, tightly-bound union with a
strong national government, the Southern cause was lost.
To Alexander Stephens, for example, secession and war
were necessary to prevent the subversion of the rights of
states; the 'constitutional compact', said the South Carolina
legislature, 'has been deliberately broken and disregarded
by the non-slave-holding states . . . and the ends for which
this Government was instituted have been defeated'.

Lincoln's first Inaugural, presenting the other side of the
case, affirmed that 'the Union of these States is perpetual',
and that the power of the whole remained always superior
to the power of the parts. In effect, the war was truly a civil
war, fought to decide which theory of government should
become the basis of future national policy. There was in the
North (and especially in the Northwest) a strong and deep-
seated belief in a strong Union as the best instrument for
maintaining freedom and democracy. This belief was power-

ful enough to tie together abolitionists and non-abolitionists, New Englanders and Westerners, city workers and pioneer farmers in a struggle, as Lincoln called it, 'for maintaining in the world that form and substance of government whose leading object is to elevate the condition of man'. Believing this, men who had never seen a slave were willing to fight a war to preserve a union without which their democratic way of life could not continue.

In both sections the seizure of leadership by agitators and propagandists influenced the final break. The generation of Clay and Calhoun was willing to compromise, to delay, to temporize, but the generation of Davis and Seward and Garrison was not. Both sections had been subjected for nearly thirty years to a thorough propagandizing that oversimplified and distorted the real issues. Northern abolitionists launched vicious attacks on the morals, religions, personal character, and family life of slave-holders. Southern fire-eaters replied with vitriolic abuse of Northern civilization, fanning a hatred of 'damyankees' that struck deep into Southern life. Politicians eager for votes played on popular fears and emotions until a reasonable approach to a solution of the sectional conflict became nearly impossible. A majority of sober Northerners disapproved of the fanaticism of Garrison, Sumner, and John Brown, quite as strongly as intelligent Southerners disagreed with the extravagances of the Fitzhugh–Brooks school of thought. Nevertheless bitterness and misapprehension grew.

And of course there was slavery, heavy with economic, moral, political, social, and emotional connotations. The abolition of slavery, a symbol as well as a system, meant the overthrow of the whole Southern way of life and all that it stood for – the killing of the dream of a chivalric civilization, of Calhoun's vision of a new Greece. Though moderates on both sides held no strong feelings on slavery (Douglas said he did not care if it were 'voted up or down') thousands viewed it as either a national disgrace or the best possible social and economic institution. There was moral idealism on both sides. To the South slavery meant much more than the simple issue of free versus slave labour. It involved the social and economic status of five and a half million white men and three and a half million black. It involved a whole concept of race relationships within a traditionally fixed social system. It involved a legitimate, sincerely-held belief that the minority had rights that must not be subject 'to the tyranny of an unbridled majority'. To many in the North, slavery represented a blot on the national escutcheon, a moral blight. 'No man is free,' wrote one Northern moderate, 'so long as another is held in bondage.' War, then, was to some a terrible and last resort, but nevertheless an act of national purification.

The Confederate government, from the moment of its organization, carried within it the seeds of its own destruction. For nearly four years Jefferson Davis and his cabinet faced the impossible problem of imposing unity upon an area that was by no means a social, political, or economic unit. Only a minority of Southerners held slaves; large segments of the population were lukewarm towards secession. Within the Confederacy the conflict between moderates (such as Stephens, Walker of Alabama, and Mallory of Florida) and sturdy radicals (such as Rhett, Toombs, Yancey, and Howell Cobb) was never completely resolved. The Rhett faction was almost completely overlooked in Davis's government and constantly criticized it.

Southern leaders were divided in their opinion of the nature of the Confederacy. Some thought of it in terms of a Southern nation; others assumed that it was to be a loose confederation of sovereign states. Jefferson Davis was a Southern nationalist. Robert E. Lee, who did not resign his commission in the Federal Army until his own state of Virginia left the Union, was a states' rights man, and was later charged with neglecting the rest of the South in Virginia's favour. Late in the war Davis was soundly berated for his 'despotism' by his state governors (all of whom were states' rights men); Georgia even threatened to recall its troops from the Confederate armies. Born in war, plagued through its existence by the harsh necessities of war, the

Confederacy never had a chance of normal development. Urgent military and diplomatic problems left no time for internal adjustments, no time for discussion and compromise, no time for politics.

Eleven states left the Union, twenty-two remained within it. In the division of population, wealth, and resources the North had far the greater potential. The Confederacy totalled nine million people, one-third of them slaves. Since Southerners were naturally reluctant to place rifles in Negro hands, Davis's armies never had a pool of more than a million men available for military service. The North had a total population of twenty-two million, four and a half million of military age, and a steady stream of immigration pouring into its cities. But at the same time the South possessed a strong military tradition, for Southerners had long dominated West Point and the Federal Army. Almost one-third of all Federal officers resigned their commissions to go with the Confederacy, among them Lee, Jackson, Albert Sidney and Joe Johnston, Bragg, Stuart, and others who represented the cream of the American military. The Southern aristocrat, accustomed to leadership and command, possessed in common with the Southern middle class and lower-class soldier a belief that he could 'lick any five Yankees' singlehanded. The Southerner was used to caste lines and adjusted himself more quickly to military life than did the independent individualists from the Northeast and Northwest. That the outmanned Confederacy held out as long as it did is a tribute to its courage and military skill.

The Confederacy was always harassed by shortages of material, supplies, and transportation facilities. By seizing the Federal arsenals its armies gained 135,000 stands of arms, only a small portion of them modern; the Southern soldier was always poorly armed, often dependent on rifles captured in battle. Only two main railroad lines linked the Eastern and Western halves of the Confederacy, slowing down movements of supplies and men. There was no place in the South to manufacture a locomotive. Since the available supply of iron was needed for munitions, neither rolling stock nor rails could be easily replaced; rails on secondary railroads had to be torn up for use on vital lines. The Confederacy had only a small merchant marine to obtain supplies and arms from abroad, and no navy to protect its shipping. The Federal blockade hurt it badly.

Yet the South had a virtual monopoly of the world's cotton, comprising both tremendous potential wealth and a useful diplomatic weapon. Had the Confederacy been able to export its cotton freely, in exchange for goods manufactured abroad, it might have been a different story; as it was King Cotton figured largely in Confederate foreign relations. The South was a predominantly agricultural area with a substantial supply of slave labour, the great majority of which remained loyal. The Confederacy never really suffered from a shortage of foodstuffs, although both military and civilian populations were consistently bothered by lack of facilities for its transportation.

Jefferson Davis, in his first Inaugural, said that 'our future policy is peace' and that he would appeal to arms only if 'the integrity of our territory and jurisdiction be assailed'. Therefore from the beginning the Confederacy had the psychological and military advantages of a defensive war, believing that it need only fight until the North tired and sued for peace. Except for two or three forays into Northern territory (notably Lee's invasion of Pennsylvania) the Confederacy fought the entire war on its own terrain, in familiar territory where the location of every creek and bush was known, where shorter inside lines of communications and supply gave it a distinct advantage. Furthermore the Southern soldier had the moral stimulus of fighting surrounded by a friendly civilian population and against an invader in defence of his home, his independence, and his right of self-government.

The North possessed by far the greater share of the nation's manpower and resources. Nearly all known American deposits of coal, iron, copper, and other minerals lay within Northern boundaries. Ninety-two per cent of the nation's manufacturing facilities was located in the North;

New York and Pennsylvania alone produced each year more than twice the amount of goods manufactured in the entire South. Lincoln had a Navy, and the bulk of the American merchant marine belonged to Northern owners. The North had 30,000 miles of railroad, connecting all parts of Northeast and Northwest, as well as lake, river, and canal routes. It had raw materials, a good supply of skilled labour, efficient transportation, and growing factories.

The Northern soldier, although more difficult to train and discipline than his Confederate counterpart, was educated, resourceful, and mechanically inclined. He suffered through the early years of the war from indecisive and often downright incompetent leadership, since the North had no established military tradition and no officer caste. McClellan, Burnside, Rosecrans, Pope, Hooker, and even Meade were not the stuff of Lee and his lieutenants, but the Federal armies developed leaders under the stress of war – Grant, Sheridan, Thomas, Sherman – who learned to think in new terms and unorthodox patterns. And always, as Southern ranks thinned, the Federal armies could draw on their tremendous reserve of manpower.

The regular Army of the United States in 1861 numbered about 16,000. Lincoln's first request for 75,000 additional troops was based on an old militia law which required each state to furnish a certain number of militia regiments to the Federal government in time of need. No Northern state, however, had a sufficient number of organized militia units to answer Lincoln's call. Each state governor, therefore, called for volunteers to enlist in the state militia. Companies were recruited and enlisted locally, each town contributing its quota to be formed into regiments and brigades at the state capital. Companies and regiments as a rule elected their own officers, with the governor retaining the right to appoint those of regimental command grade; in practice he often simply ratified the election results. General officers were commissioned by the President.

Theoretically the states were responsible for training and equipping their own militia. Arms and uniforms were sometimes furnished by the men themselves or by the town, for few states had either proper equipment or training facilities to add much to the volunteer's accoutrement or military education. As a result, Northern troops reported to training camps in an astonishing variety of uniforms, with arms ranging from flintlocks to squirrel rifles and in various stages of disciplinary disorder. There were established outfits like the New York Fire Zouaves (wearing red fezzes and baggy trousers); the socialite New York Seventh; the old Philadelphia Light Artillery; New England militia companies whose names appeared on the rolls at Saratoga and Bunker Hill; Wisconsin and Iowa farm-boys in homespun and butternut; the proud Michigan Rifles; Unionist Kentuckians whose grandfathers had fought at New Orleans under Jackson. War Department policy kept volunteer and regular units apart, although regular officers were usually chosen for training purposes and higher command posts.

Lincoln's request for ninety-day men was followed by a second for 42,000 troops on a three-year enlistment, and by a third for a volunteer army of 400,000 three-year men. Liberal cash bounties were offered for enlistment and re-enlistment, but in early 1863, after two years of heavy fighting, Lincoln asked for and received a conscription law which, combined with enlistments, kept the Federal forces at full strenth, though it caused serious riots in New York and a few other cities. The volunteer system had certain military advantages. It kept home-town boys together in units, served to lift morale, and capitalized on local enthusiasms. Soldiers knew their own officers and shared their responsibilities. However, it had its disadvantages too. Soldiers knew their officers sometimes too well and took discipline lightly. The concentration of troops from the same community raised havoc with home-front morale; battles like Shiloh and Antietam swept away at one blow all the young men from some small towns. Democratic election of officers did not necessarily produce the best ones, for popularity and political skill too often overshadowed other and better qualifications.

Shortly after Lincoln's first call for troops, Jefferson Davis sent a similar request to the Confederate states for 100,000 volunteer militia. Many organized and equipped militia companies were ready, and the Confederacy mobilized somewhat faster than the Union. Like the Northerners, the Southern troops reported in all manner of uniforms and states of discipline. Wade Hampton, the wealthy South Carolina planter, brought his Hampton Legion, in which it was rumoured even privates had Negro body-servants; the Louisiana Zouaves came up from New Orleans to join the Richmond Greys and the Life Guards of Virginia, men whose grandfathers had ridden with Marion the Swamp Fox and Light Horse Harry Lee; hundreds of Southern farmers joined line regiments that had fought at Cowpens and Kings Mountain. The Confederacy had, of course, no standing army, but it had a large number of well-trained regular and ex-regular officers who established an excellent system of recruitment and training that quickly produced an efficient fighting force. The manpower shortage, however, forced the Confederate Congress in 1862 to pass a conscription law that was strongly resisted by some states' rights men. Nevertheless, neither resistance to conscription nor desertion was ever a factor in Confederate military affairs, even towards the end of a losing war.

At the outbreak of the war Lincoln seemed to possess neither the skilled political advisers nor the military leadership that Davis had at his side. His cabinet contained several able men, all of whom at the outset considered Lincoln an inexperienced man of mediocre talents. One of his major problems was to impose unity on his party and his cabinet, and to find competent subordinate leaders, both civilian and military.

In the Cabinet, Cameron of Pennsylvania, the Secretary of War, proved to be so untrustworthy that Lincoln removed him within a few months, replacing him with Edwin Stanton of New York. Stanton, an Ohio-born Quaker and a famous lawyer, was an old-line Jacksonian who shifted to Republicanism over the slavery issue. A master of knife-in-the-back politics, he had served briefly in Buchanan's Cabinet, and his appointment to Lincoln's caused considerable comment; a man with a violent temper and an insulting tongue, he held little respect for Lincoln and had already attacked him privately and publicly. Yet he was a brilliant organizer and administrator, and a man of boundless energy. Seward of New York, Lincoln's Secretary of State, still entertained some bitterness over his failure to gain the Republican nomination in 1860. He had little respect for Lincoln's ability, but he gradually acceded to Lincoln's will and became one of the nation's better Secretaries of State, threading his way carefully and expertly through the tangled diplomacy of the war years. Salmon P. Chase of Ohio, Secretary of the Treasury, was the only authentic abolitionist in the cabinet. With Seward and Sumner he led the anti-slavery contingent in Congress during the fifties, and like Seward he was a disappointed presidential hopeful at the 1860 Republican convention. Chase left behind him a good record in wartime finance and later served as a distinguished Supreme Court Justice, but he never really liked or trusted Lincoln.

At the beginning of the war Lincoln had few competent military advisers or officers. The best of the officer crop went South, leaving only a handful of second-grade commanders. Major-General Winfield Scott, although a Virginian, stayed behind as chief of the Union armies, but while his brain was as sharp as ever, he was so old and fat as to be almost completely inactive. Brigadier-General Irvin McDowell, who commanded the armies in the field, was an able organizer but no match whatever for anyone on the Confederate staff; McDowell's highest command before the outbreak of the war had been as lieutenant of artillery. At first Lincoln pinned his hopes on young George McClellan, who replaced Scott in late 1861. McClellan, a West Pointer with a good Mexican War record, had resigned his commission some years before to enter the railroad business in Illinois, where he was eminently successful, but at the outbreak of the war he re-entered the army, took over the training of troops in

Ohio, and performed brilliantly in the early West Virginia campaigns. McClellan, however, suffered from a Napoleonic complex and from political ambition. Cursed by an inherent lack of agressiveness, obnoxiously arrogant, unable to adapt himself to new situations, McClellan eventually clashed once too often with Lincoln and was removed. The real military leaders in the North were buried in the army during the early phases of the war, and emerged only after Lincoln's patient search for someone he could depend on.

William Tecumseh Sherman was an Ohio-born West Pointer who, like McClellan, had retired from the army to enter business. In the West, where he re-entered the service, he held gradually increasing responsibilities under Halleck and Grant until Grant's departure, when he took command of the Western armies and drove to the sea. A short-tempered, nervously energetic man, Sherman recognized war as a violent and unlovely business and never tried to make it anything else. George Thomas, another Virginian who remained loyal to the Union, was placid, dignified, and courtly, a perfectionist in war and an excellent foil for Sherman, with whom he worked well, although his lethargy exasperated both Grant and Sherman. Philip Sheridan, a handsome, volatile Irishman, viewed war much as did Sherman. A fine infantry commander, Sheridan eventually became one of the great cavalry leaders of all time, and with Gregg, Kilpatrick, Buford, Custer and others made the Union cavalry into a powerful weapon.

In 1861 Ulysses (Hiram) Simpson Grant, like Sherman an Ohio-born West Pointer, was an admitted failure both as a soldier and a civilian. After a poor record at West Point and undistinguished service in the Mexican War, Grant served at an Oregon frontier post and drank himself out of the army just ahead of a court-martial. Unsuccessful at farming and real estate, he entered his father's hide and leather business in Illinois, where he was known locally as 'Cap' Grant, a shiftless ne'er-do-well. At the outbreak of the war he offered his services to the War Department and received no reply. Fortunately he was appointed colonel of an Illinois volunteer regiment, and from that point on his star rose steadily. Grant was made for war; war gave him the stimulus that in peace had been provided by alcohol, and, as Henry Adams noted, his cold and emotionless nature exactly suited the business of fighting. He had two qualities lacked by nearly every other commander in the North – he never made the same mistake twice, and he avoided politics like the plague. He was no military genius like Stonewall Jackson, nor a god-like leader of Lee's stamp, yet the stumpy man with the rumpled uniform and the dead cigar had a common sense, a directness of mind, and a tenacity that set him apart as a great military commander. It is significant that Sherman and Sheridan, the two finest combat officers in the North, idolized him, and that Lee held him in highest respect.

Abraham Lincoln remains the greatest enigma of them all. It is clear that he was the most skilful politician in American history; no man ever out-intrigued or out-manoeuvred him, though many tried. Nothing but politics really interested him, and even as a lawyer he was happiest in that kind of practice that most resembled politics. His law partner, Billy Herndon, who knew Lincoln as well as any man could, wrote, 'It was in the world of politics that he lived. Politics were his life . . .' His conduct of the military aspects of the Civil War was not notably effective, but more than anyone else, North or South, Lincoln recognized the importance of the politics of war. In making his moves and counter-moves he faced a cabal within his own party, organized opposition from without it, a constant threat of foreign interference, a divided and arrogant cabinet, and shifting public opinion at home and abroad – all within the framework of a war whose fortunes rose and fell with every report from the field. Yet his mistakes were few, quickly rectified, his political sagacity unquestionably dominant.

But to think of Lincoln only as a skilled politician is to falsify him. He was an extraordinarily complex, compelling figure, of contradictory qualities, the despair of biographers and historians. His political philosophy, an eclectic thing, was drawn from many internal and external sources. The

Union was the central fact of his political life, an almost mystic belief colouring all his ideas and acts. He stated many times his view of the slavery controversy and of the war – his objective was to preserve the Union, to guarantee its continuation on democratic principles, and nothing else. The Union must be saved, he repeated, for he believed it to be the chief instrument of democracy. Without union there could be no democracy; without democracy there could be no union. The spread of slavery doomed democracy; the threat of secession doomed the union. This was the inspiration of Lincoln's mature career, that he saw, as no other man of his time, that slavery and secession struck at nationality and democracy. There was no cheap and easy solution.

His belief in democracy was deep. His frontier background, his contacts with people and events, his political experiences, and most of all his innate admiration for the Jeffersonian tradition, combined to produce in him a profound faith in it. He accepted the Declaration of Independence literally and completely, not as a theory but as a practical manner of life. 'I have never had a feeling politically,' he once said, 'that did not spring from the Declaration of Independence', and his memorable phrase, 'government of the people, by the people, and for the people' is still as much a part of the texture of American political life as Jefferson's preamble. Yet like Jefferson he too faced the old question of centralized versus decentralized political power; in his considerations of practical politics and war he was capable of using strong Hamiltonian measures to preserve Jeffersonian and Unionist ends. As he once wrote, 'Must a government, of necessity, be too strong for the liberties of its own people, or too weak to maintain its own existence?' – a question he tried to answer with his whole political life.

Certainly part of Lincoln's strength sprang from his own feeling of averageness, from an inner awareness of his own commonness. Until 1858 there was nothing about him to lift him above the crowd. He was a good lawyer, but others were better known; he was a fairly successful politician on a small scale, but no success like Douglas; and as his wife and friends pointed out, like his pioneer father he had a lamentable tendency toward laziness. He could laugh at coarse jokes with his friends, call a soldier from the ranks with 'Hey, bub!' and lounge in the Capitol in his shirt-sleeves, all with perfect genuineness and not as a political act. Never happy alone, he had a sense of sharing life with his fellows. Men recognized this. He drew men to him and was drawn to men with some irresistible force. This quality led worldly-wise John Hay to think of him as 'the greatest figure since Christ', and made tough-minded men like Stanton and Seward worship him. The 'man of the people' theme has been strummed too often by his biographers, yet it has in it undeniable truth. His feeling for people enabled Lincoln to understand his times and his contemporaries more clearly than others could. Few men in American history ever had so precise a grasp of the meaning of events, or a clearer sense of the drift of public opinion. It was this, possibly, that helped to make him the supreme politician he was, that led him with an unerring sense to weigh the situation, make up his mind, and do the right thing at the right time. He gambled – in the Douglas debates, at Sumter, on Grant, on emancipation – but it was a calculated risk with the odds on his side.

With all his averageness, Lincoln possessed an uncommon mind and never lost a chance to sharpen and improve it. He was flexible, alert, intelligent. The hours spent with the Bible, Shakespeare and Blackstone were hours of mental training; he used geometry as a sort of mental exercise long after he laid Euclid down. The erudition of Douglas or Everett was far beyond him, but one need only to read Lincoln's speeches – clear, concise, terse, with underlying echoes of the King James version – to realize that Lincoln's was by far the greater and better-trained intellect. His mind cut through the confused welter of ideas and issues like a surgeon's knife. But with this clarity of intellect there was a strain of melancholy that at times almost unfitted him for action. Dreams, forebodings, black moods of depression overcast his life. He had an unmistakable sense of the irony of life, of the operation in human affairs of 'certain irrefragable and irresistible laws . . . that what was to be would be inevitable'. 'I must . . . confess plainly,' he once said, 'that events have controlled me' – yet as Herndon wrote, 'he was always calculating and planning ahead', supremely capable of decisive and perfectly timed action.

The cabinet selected by Jefferson Davis included several able men, but none of the calibre of Stanton or Seward. Alexander Stephens of Georgia, Vice-President, was a unionist with an instinctive mistrust of military men and secessionist politicians. Secretary of Navy Mallory, a Floridian, agreed with Stephens. Christopher Memminger of South Carolina, a strong secessionist, was Secretary of the Treasury, and nowhere near Chase in ability. Regan of Texas, Postmaster General, was a hard-headed realist and no admirer of Davis. Walker of Alabama, Secretary of War, was an aristocratic lawyer who so disbelieved in the possibility of war that he once offered to 'wipe up with his handkerchief every drop of blood spilled by secession'. Judah P. Benjamin, the Jewish lawyer from Louisiana who was Attorney-General (later Secretary of War and Secretary of State) was by all odds the most brilliant man in the cabinet, but he was highly unpopular, a theorist, and an opportunist. Robert Toombs of Georgia, a fire-eating secessionist and a financial expert, was Secretary of State, probably the one post for which he was least fitted. Thus the Confederate Cabinet was filled with men in the wrong positions; half of them were lukewarm towards secession, only one or two depended on slavery for a livelihood, and only one represented the radical point of view. Davis was never able to impose any unity on it or to get complete cooperation from it.

A great deal of the fault lay in Davis himself. A Kentuckian by birth, Davis lifted himself out of the lower middle class to the Mississippi planter aristocracy by his own bootstraps. A West Pointer with a fine Mexican War record, he entered politics during the forties as a friend of Franklin

Pierce and an ardent admirer of Calhoun. From that point on, he became one of the leaders of the militant corps of Southerners in the Senate, and after 1857 was generally acknowledged as the foremost Southern statesman. Davis was really a Southern nationalist who saw the Confederacy not as a loose aggregation of states but as a strong, central-ized, slave-holding nation. A powerful and sincere speaker, a shrewd reasoner, a good administrator, Davis had at the outset of the war the support of both radicals and moderates in the South, but he did not have the political skill to keep it.

Jefferson Davis was an honourable man, but he had more than his share of arrogance and a vain respect for his own opinions. As time passed he identified himself more and more with the Southern cause, refusing advice, losing himself in theory, wishful thinking, and administrative detail. He had no real concept of the human element in politics and little understanding of the common people of the South. In the end, his aloofness and rigidity undid him. He lost touch with reality, and while the Confederacy col-lapsed about him he busied himself with records, orders, and querulous arguments with his advisers. He never fully under-stood the arts of war and politics; after the war he remained a tragic, proud, and puzzled figure, writing his life away explaining a lost cause.

But in military personnel Davis had all the advantages. He himself had a good grasp of military problems and avoided much of the inefficiency and entanglement that plagued Lincoln's War Department in the early years of the war. He created five generals immediately – Cooper, Albert Sidney Johnston, Lee, Joe Johnston, and Beauregard – set up a full army staff of experienced military men, and soon had a functioning military machine. In the two Johnstons, Stuart, Hood, and Longstreet, he had leaders of undoubted talent; in Lee, Jackson, and Nathan Bedford Forrest he had men of genuine military genius. Davis, however, had an ex-profes-sional soldier's propensity for meddling with commands and a strong but misplaced confidence in lesser men like Cooper, Braxton Bragg and Beauregard.

Lee was the South's greatest asset. A scion of the great Virginia dynasty, son of the famous 'Light Horse Harry' Lee, a patrician cast in the perfect mould of the Southern gentleman, he was the embodiment of all that was admirable in the Southern tradition. He had served as Scott's chief of staff in the Mexican War, won three brevets for personal gallantry in the field, and was regarded by Scott as the ablest officer in the service. (Before he chose the Confederacy, Lee had been offered command of the Union forces.) Lee was, above all else, a Virginian, who believed neither in slavery nor secession, yet who, when war came, saw it his duty to serve Virginia. As a military commander he was blessed with brilliant subordinates to whom he allowed considerable latitude; but the overall plan was always Lee's. His tactical skill was unsurpassed (though Longstreet always thought him 'over-combative') and he had an uncanny knack of judging his opponent's weaknesses with devastating accuracy. Five Union generals broke themselves on Lee, who outgeneralled and outmanoeuvred each in turn, until the appearance of Grant – whom Lee could never quite fathom. Under Lee the Army of Northern Virginia emerged as the finest fighting force of the war, possibly matched only by Sherman's Army of the Tennessee; it was 'Marse Robert's' personal army, bound to him by something stronger than a chain of command. Significantly, it was to Lee that the South in its death throes turned for leadership.

Thomas Jonathan Jackson, another Virginian, was something else. Jackson came from a poor back-country family of rigid Scotch-Irish Presbyterians. A silent, grim, godly man, brusque and introverted, Jackson seemed a throwback to the Cromwellian Roundheads, in whose army he would have felt perfectly at home. The romantic appellation of 'Stonewall', attached to him after First Bull Run, never suited him. His infantrymen called him 'Old Tom' or 'Old Jack' and would follow him anywhere he rode on his white horse, with the Bible, Napoleon's *Maxims*, and a lemon in his saddlebags. The Army of Northern Virginia was never the same again after Jackson died at

Chancellorsville at the end of one of his most brilliant movements.

James Ewell Brown Stuart was Jackson's exact opposite. Called 'Beauty' Stuart for his handsome face, tall trim figure, and curling yellow hair, half the women of the South were in love with this *beau ideal* of a soldier, who kept an Irish banjo player named Sweeney on his staff to provide music in the lighter moments of war.

Nathan Bedford Forrest, a bearded giant from Tennessee who entered the Confederate army as a private, later formed and commanded his own battalion of cavalry, or 'critter company' as he called it. A crude, profane, semi-literate slave-trader, Forrest knew nothing of war as West Point taught it, but he developed into perhaps the finest irregular cavalry leader of all time. Eventually he became a lieutenant-general, but the war was already lost and Forrest's untutored military genius was largely wasted. His statement 'I git thar fustest with the mostest' is still the classic definition of the first principle of attack.

Thus the forces gathered for a civil war over issues for which Americans could find no compromise. From the early tentative attempts to gain a foothold on the continental edge of the wilderness, through two wars and all the internal racks attendant to an experimental government, the United States succeeded by concession and adjustment in establishing a nation. Now it was threatened, split in two; possibly (if the breach were not closed) it might be divided again into five, or a dozen, or more. The struggle now was not against Indians, or the wilderness, or foreigners, but between irrevocably divided ideas – to determine whether its government, or any government so conceived and dedicated, could long endure.

CHAPTER 25

YEARS OF BLOOD
1861–5

LINCOLN's call for volunteers, added to his announcement of a blockade of the Confederacy, crystallized opinion in the wavering border states. Kentucky, Arkansas, Maryland and Missouri had close commercial ties with the North, while the mountain counties of Virginia, Tennessee, and North Carolina were anti-slavery and unionist in sympathy. Since Virginia was the pivotal border state, others watched to follow its lead. The planters of the seaboard Virginia counties, where slavery was economically important, favoured secession. The farmers of the western hill country, bordering on Ohio and Pennsylvania, were against it, but the secessionists controlled the state legislature. Two days after Lincoln's call for volunteers, the Virginia state convention passed an ordinance of secession (to be ratified by popular vote) over the protests of the delegates from the forty-six unionist counties, who immediately retaliated by threatening to secede from Virginia. Votes from this area were not counted in the tally on the secession ordinance, which passed. Virginia therefore formally seceded from the Union on 7 May 1861; the unionist counties later applied for admission to the Union as a separate state and were eventually admitted as West Virginia in 1863.

Arkansas preceded Virginia into secession by a few days, but in Tennessee and North Carolina opinion was sharply divided. The secessionists, however, seized the initiative and quickly rushed through bills of secession. Plans for eastern Tennessee to follow western Virginia's course were scotched by the quick entry of Confederate troops into unionist areas. Maryland and Missouri were similarly kept in the Union by the speedy dispatch of Federal militia to secessionist centres. Kentucky proclaimed itself neutral, and, when Confederate troops entered the state, unsuccessfully protested at the violation of its neutrality and declared itself loyal to the Union.

Meanwhile, ninety thousand volunteers poured into the Union training camps. The largest number went to Washington, for Confederate outposts had already appeared across the Potomac and the secession of Maryland, which seemed imminent, would cut the Federal capital off from the North. Other training posts were placed at St Louis, Cincinnati, and Chicago. In the West, the dashing, wavy-haired explorer and ex-presidential candidate, John C. Frémont, took over leadership of the raw troops. At Cincinnati young George B. McClellan drilled the Ohio volunteers. At Washington General Irvin McDowell, in command of the entire Union forces, tried to make an army out of daily trainloads of whooping militia – St Louis Germans, singing songs of '48; Irishmen from Boston and New York; New England and Pennsylvania farm-boys clutching flintlocks. Not far to the South the Confederates faced the same problem. Beauregard, the conqueror of Sumter, commanded one army along the Potomac, threatening Washington, while Joe Johnston gathered his forces in the Shenandoah Valley of Virginia near Harper's Ferry.

While the troops drilled, Lincoln's council planned strategy. It was clear that the North must invade, the South defend. The Appalachian mountains, running north and south, split the Confederacy into two battlefronts, while the Mississippi, Cumberland, and Tennessee rivers, as well as the East–West rail lines converging on Atlanta and Chattanooga, formed the major lines of Confederate supply and communications. Old 'Fuss and Feathers' Winfield Scott still had a keen brain. He advised Lincoln to follow an 'anaconda' policy: first, with the Navy, blockade the entire Southern coast, then drive two armies into the Confederacy, one in the East and one in the West, to capture the river and rail systems that linked it together. Then while the Navy squeezed the Confederacy from without, the armies within might cut it up into smaller and smaller pieces.

First, however, the fighting front had to be stabilized.

After Virginia had threatened to move Lee into the area to hold it in the Confederacy, the loyal West Virginia counties sent appeals for help to Washington. Lee, busy near Richmond, dispatched General Garnett and 8,000 men into the mountains toward Wheeling and the Ohio river, and Scott therefore moved in McClellan's Ohio troops, now fairly well trained. McClellan's campaign was a brilliant success. Partly by skill and partly by luck, he completed a difficult flanking movement that caught the Confederates napping, appropriately at Philippi, and drove them back toward Richmond; then he succeeded in encircling the main Confederate force, cut it off, and captured most of it in July 1861. The Northern newspapers exulted at first blood and 'Little Napoleon' McClellan made headlines.

While McClellan chased Garnett in the mountains, Lincoln called a council of war to discuss a movement against Richmond, the Southern capital city. McDowell thought his troops still too green for an attack in force, but so were the rebels. Ninety-day enlistments were running out, and Congress demanded action; the Confederates, it was pointed out, might move first. Beauregard sat with 23,000 men near Harper's Ferry while in the Shenandoah Valley was Johnston with some 20,000 militia. So McDowell, with some misgivings, agreed to move on Richmond with 28,000 men of his own and 22,000 militia under General Patterson. The Union march was slow, disorganized, and remarkably well publicized; Washington newspapers published McDowell's plans in full, including good maps, before he began to move on 16 July 1861.

McDowell's advance was a weird parade of undisciplined troops, some still in civilian clothes, accompanied by congressmen and their families in buggies and by dozens of newspapermen. Johnston and Beauregard had no intention of waiting for him. Johnston left a force to confuse the timid Patterson and marched double-quick to join Beauregard. On 20 July the Union advance guard pushed in Confederate pickets near Bull Run Creek, twenty-five miles from Washington, and on the next morning McCowell began his attack. It was a good attack, and the Confederate lines wavered, except for those troops under Jackson, who, it was said, 'stood like a stone wall'. By afternoon Johnston's army swung into line after their hard march and the picture changed. Once the raw Union volunteers began to fall back, their retreat turned into a panic-stricken rout. All night the beaten Union army flowed into Washington, leaving behind its artillery, equipment, and even a few frantic Congressmen. In the dark hour of panic Scott and Lincoln called for McClellan, who arrived in a crisp new uniform, exuding confidence. McClellan put regiments of regulars to work reorganizing the shattered commands, and began the long task of rebuilding the Army.

Bull Run had a salutary effect on both sides. No one now believed that the war would be a ninety-day affair. 'On to Richmond' and 'On to Washington' headlines disappeared from the papers while both armies settled down to learn how to fight a war. McClellan marched and countermarched his troops on the Washington flats. Joe Johnston, who replaced Beauregard, drilled his not far to the South. By autumn, McClellan had increased his army to 90,000 troops and had more than doubled his ego. 'By some strange magic,' he wrote to his wife, 'I seem to have become the power of the land.' Old General Scott resigned in November and Lincoln, remarking that he would hold McClellan's horse if he would only win victories, gave complete command to 'Little Mac'.

On the Union side the western theatre of war was divided between General Buell, commanding the department of the Ohio, and General Halleck (Frémont's successor) commanding the Mississippi-Missouri area. Facing them was General Albert Sidney Johnston, commanding the Confederate Army of the West. Buell's first march was across Kentucky to relieve the Unionist sympathizers in eastern Tennessee, a slow and indecisive advance that ended in a stalemate at the battle of Mill Spring in January 1862. Under him in the Department of Missouri Halleck had a

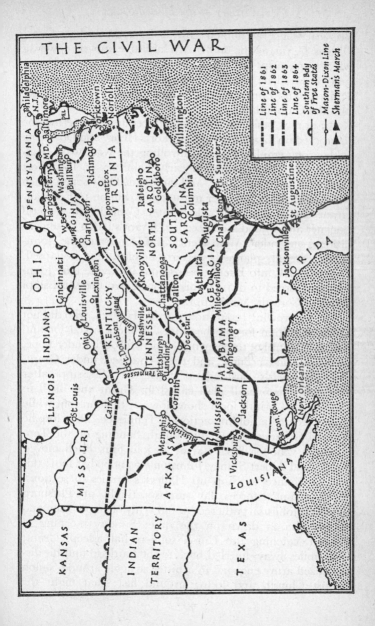

THE CIVIL WAR

Line of 1861
Line of 1862
Line of 1863
Line of 1864
Southern Bdy of Free States
Mason-Dixon Line
Sherman's March

Philadelphia
N.J.
Baltimore
DEL.
MD.
Harper's Ferry
Washington
Yorktown
Norfolk
PENNSYLVANIA
WEST VIRGINIA
Bull Run
Richmond
Appomattox
Charlestown
VIRGINIA
Raleigh
Goldsboro
Wilmington
NORTH CAROLINA
SOUTH CAROLINA
Columbia
Charleston
Ft. Sumter
OHIO
Cincinnati
Louisville
Lexington
Knoxville
Chattanooga
Dalton
Atlanta
Augusta
GEORGIA
INDIANA
Ohio
KENTUCKY
Ft. Donelson
Cumberland
Nashville
TENNESSEE
Decatur
Milledgeville
ALABAMA
Montgomery
St. Jacksonville
St. Augustine
FLORIDA
ILLINOIS
MISSOURI
St. Louis
Cairo
Pittsburgh Landing
Corinth
MISSISSIPPI
Jackson
Memphis
Vicksburg
Baton Rouge
New Orleans
KANSAS
INDIAN TERRITORY
ARKANSAS
Mississippi
LOUISIANA
TEXAS

Brigadier-General named Grant. In command at Cairo, Illinois, Grant, acting on his own initiative, moved down the Mississippi, surprised the Confederate garrison at Belmont, and captured it; next he swung across Kentucky to seize Paducah and Smithfield at the junctions of the Tennessee and the Cumberland.

Grant now besieged Halleck with requests for permission to proceed up these rivers against Forts Henry and Donelson, both strong emplacements controlling the waterways. Halleck finally gave in, and in early February of 1862 Fort Henry fell to Grant's army and gunboats. Donelson, a much stronger fort, was a harder nut to crack, but on 13 February Grant encircled it. Two days later Confederate General Buckner and 17,000 men accepted Grant's terms of 'unconditional surrender'. With Henry and Donelson gone, Johnston's carefully-planned western defence line collapsed. Kentucky fell into Buell's hands, and Nashville too; Johnston was forced to draw in his troops down the Mississippi River to Corinth, Mississippi.

Grant's growing reputation worried Halleck, who did not like competition for the headlines. Halleck asked for and received control of three armies – the Missouri, under Pope, the Ohio, under Buell, and the Tennessee, under Grant, who was swiftly pushing on down the Mississippi after Johnston. His overall plan called for Grant and Buell to combine at Corinth for a show-down with Johnston, while Pope executed a holding action in Tennessee. Therefore he ordered Grant to stop at Pittsburgh Landing on the Tennessee to wait for Buell's army to join him. Buell moved slowly, and Albert Sidney Johnston was nobody's fool; this was his chance to chop up Halleck's armies in sections. While Grant's forces lay unsuspectingly at Pittsburg Landing, Johnston gathered his full army of 40,000 men and fell on him at dawn on the quiet Sunday morning of 6 April, catching the Union soldiers half-asleep. Grant, seven miles away, hurried back to the battle to find his disorganized army engaged in a bitter struggle around Shiloh Baptist Church and losing ground fast; that night the

Confederates camped on the Union lines. But Buell arrived in the dark with 20,000 fresh troops and on the next day pushed the Confederates back toward Corinth, leaving Johnston dead on the field and Beauregard in command. Shiloh was a drawn battle, with a loss of 10,000 on either side; its most decisive feature was that Grant was never surprised again.

Shiloh broke the back of Confederate resistance along the Mississippi. Halleck, who rushed down to take personal command after Grant's fiasco, inched his armies toward Corinth and finally took it, only to find Beauregard gone. At the same time, a joint army-navy expedition under General Ben Butler and Admiral Farragut took New Orleans and closed the river's mouth. The Mississippi was open now from north to south, except for Vicksburg, the last remaining Confederate stronghold. Kentucky and western and middle Tennessee were in Union hands. East Tennessee was still under Confederate control, including Chattanooga, the junction point of three railroads connecting with Memphis, Atlanta, and Richmond.

In contrast to the unsuccessful campaigns in the East, Halleck's western manoeuvres were a welcome relief to the North. He was promoted to Washington, leaving Grant in command of the armies west of mid-Tennessee and Buell of the Army of the Ohio. Halleck did not think well of Grant; his reputation for drinking preceded him; he had acted precipitately in the Henry–Donelson campaign and was likely to do so again; he had been badly surprised at Shiloh. But Lincoln said, 'I can't spare this man; he fights.' Grant stayed.

In April 1862, while Grant rested at Shiloh, McClellan finally responded to Lincoln's urgings and began his long-delayed march towards Richmond. The 'Little Napoleon' did not like Lincoln's plan for an overland attack on Richmond, preferring to circle it and attack from the sea. He also had an inherent tendency to overestimate the strength of his opponent, and what Lincoln wryly called 'the slows'. Nor was the eastern theatre of war unified. Lincoln had moved

Halleck east as supreme commander, placed Pope in command of a new Army of Virginia and McClellan in command of the Army of the Potomac, thus dividing both armies and leadership. Though General Joe Johnston could gather only about 70,000 Confederates to oppose him, McClellan moved cautiously across the tangled swampy terrain, writing ill-tempered notes back to Lincoln, arguing, temporizing, and demanding more men and supplies. Nevertheless some progress was made, and by May 1862 McClellan's main army was encamped only twenty miles from the Southern capital, with another force proceeding toward it up the James river from the sea. On 31 May Johnston's army hit McClellan at Seven Pines, hurt the Union forces severely, and stopped McClellan's careful advance dead in its tracks. When Johnston was wounded, his command passed to Robert E. Lee.

Lee's mastery of battle was at once evident. Realizing that McClellan's slow, siege-like tactics might eventually take Richmond, Lee evolved an audacious counter-attack. Stonewall Jackson had a small army of 19,000 men to the west in the Shenandoah Valley; Lee sent him Ewell's division and turned him loose. This was Jackson's kind of war. Leaving Ewell to hold his bases, he set off with his 'foot cavalry' in an amazing march of fifty miles in three days, struck one Federal force, demolished it, swung back in a three-day sixty-mile march, hit another, and drove it clear back to the Potomac. Halleck, in consternation, began recalling troops from McClellan's army to protect Washington, but Jackson slipped between the Federal forces and hit again at Port Republic and Cross Keys. Then, after having tied down nearly 100,000 Federal troops and frightened Washington half to death, he swung back into Virginia to join Lee.

While the Union troops vainly chased Jackson in the Valley, Lee shook loose J. E. B. Stuart's cavalry. Stuart rode north and then turned east, circled McClellan's army, cut the railroad lines, destroyed seven million dollar's worth of supplies, and returned with a complete map of McClellan's

positions and forces. As the Northern generals reeled, Lee
first consulted with his staff – Jackson, Longstreet, D. H. and
A. P. Hill – and then attacked. In the Seven Days' Battle
that followed, ending at Malvern Hill, Lee lost 16,000 men,
but Richmond was saved and the 20,000 Union casualties
left on the field sent a wave of gloom through the North.
McClellan's campaign had failed. Lincoln left him on the
James with a few troops and called on John Pope to
command a new army to march from Washington to
Richmond.

Pope took over with complete confidence. 'I have come
from the West,' he said, 'where we have always seen the
backs of our enemies.' He scraped together a dispirited
army, while McClellan sat at Fortress Monroe and sent
angry explanations of his failure to Washington. Pope was
not brilliant, but he was stubborn. His orders were to march
on Richmond, and as soon as he had his forces organized he
set out so to do. But Pope was easy for Lee. While Jackson's swift-marching infantry swept around his flank and
Stuart's cavalry slashed across his supply lines, Lee hurried
the Confederate army over the mountains into position near
the old Bull Run battlefield. Hopefully Pope prepared to
attack and on 30 August he sent his men at the Confederate
lines. When this attack was spent Lee released Longstreet
and Hood with the Virginia and Texas infantry. The
Union lines wavered, broke, and fell back, while the Confederates cut isolated regiments to pieces. It was not a rout
like First Bull Run, for McClellan had trained his men well,
but it was a decisive defeat.

Second Bull Run produced bitter disappointment in
Washington. The demoralized Army of Virginia was broken
up, Pope sent back to the West, several staff officers relieved
of duty, and one court-martialled. Halleck, at his wits' end,
seemed able to do nothing, so, much against his better
judgement, Lincoln recalled McClellan to command the
armies based on Washington. McClellan managed to instil
new spirit into the reconstituted Army of the Potomac but,
still cursed with that military under-confidence which

always seemed to deny his personal conceit, McClellan waited for Lee to move first.

After his resounding successes over McClellan and Pope, Lee dominated Southern military thinking. In the North, he knew, there were mutterings of discontent over the string of Union defeats. If he could inflict one great blow, such as the capture of Washington (which the Federal government expected momentarily) the Northern public might tire of the bloody business and force Lincoln to sue for peace. In Lee's opinion it was time to shift to the offensive, and an invasion of Maryland seemed the best move. The Army of Northern Virginia was short of rations and recruits. The barns of Maryland farms bulged invitingly. There were in Maryland a great many Southern sympathizers and they, Lee hoped, would flock to the Stars and Bars.

Lee marched northward through the mountain gaps with 40,000 men, intending to advance toward Hagerstown, Maryland, and then to turn east toward Baltimore and Washington. The Marylanders, unimpressed by his ragged army, neither flocked to the colours nor loaded the Confederates with supplies. At the same time the Federal cavalry probed sharply at Lee's columns, harassing his movements and even capturing a copy of his orders. Armed thus with complete knowledge of his opponent's plans, McClellan marched on him with 70,000 men, reorganizing his army as he came. Since Lee had detached Jackson and 20,000 men to clear the Federals out of Harper's Ferry and Martinsburg to the west, McClellan hoped to catch him with his army divided.

McClellan's move was as always ponderously slow, while Stuart's cavalry brought in periodic reports on the Federal advance. Jackson hurried back on one of his famous forced marches, but even so Lee's army was not at full strength when the Army of the Potomac made contact with it at Sharpsburg, near Antietam Creek on 15 September. Had McClellan attacked at once, he might have crushed Lee with overwhelming numbers, but his desultory tactics betrayed him again. On the 16th Jackson's men arrived and went into the line. And then, at last, McClellan attacked.

At dawn on the 17th, 'Fighting Joe' Hooker's corps hit the Confederate left in the first phase of McClellan's plan; a hard, vicious assault that almost cracked Jackson's defence line, followed by attacks from Mansfield's and Sumner's corps that should have been better coordinated with Hooker's. This bad timing enabled Lee to draw troops from his centre and right to hold on, while Burnside's delayed attack on the Confederate right came too late to do any good. As it was, the Army of Northern Virginia lost 10,000 men; the Army of the Potomac lost 12,000 men, but they had replacements on the way. Lee, knowing he could ill afford further losses, drew back along the mountains to reform his shaken army while McClellan, having bungled a battle, called Lincoln for more men. 'Sending that man reinforcements,' remarked Lincoln, 'is like shovelling flies across a room.' Instead he removed McClellan from command and substituted Ambrose E. Burnside, a man with little to commend him except imposing whiskers and abolitionist sentiments, but a man who knew his own limitations, did not want the command, and took it only after some persuasion.

When Burnside accepted he found 113,000 men on the rolls of the Army of the Potomac, the majority of them seasoned troops with battle experience. Lee, reorganizing his Army of Northern Virginia at Fredericksburg, now had 80,000 (the result of the new Confederate conscription law) commanded by Longstreet, Jackson, D. H. Hill and J. E. B. Stuart. With commendable energy Burnside began the customary overland march toward Richmond, planning first to crush Lee at Fredericksburg and then to sweep into Virginia. His army moved so slowly in the rainy autumn weather that it was not until early November that it reached Fredericksburg. Lee, guessing Burnside's intentions perfectly, had fortified the city to the teeth. In an agony of uncertainty, Burnside waited three weeks before deciding on a direct frontal assault, probably the most insane scheme of the war. His plan meant throwing his men across a river under the direct fire of good artillery, storming a steep, well-fortified hill, and then fighting hand-to-hand with 80,000 well-trained troops. Hooker's men, after receiving their orders on the evening of 12 December 1862, quietly divided up their possessions and wrote farewell letters home. The next morning they charged up Marye's Heights and returned, leaving behind 15,000 dead and wounded.

That night, under cover of the artillery, the Army of the Potomac withdrew while Burnside sobbed in his tent. Not long after, heeding the requests of Burnside's entire staff, Lincoln removed him and gave the command to Joe Hooker. That there was still an Army of the Potomac to command at all was a wonder. Beaten at First Bull Run, decimated in the Seven Days' Battle, mishandled at Second Bull Run and Antietam, slaughtered at Fredericksburg, the army still had fight and spirit, and still hoped for the right leader. Perhaps Joe Hooker was that man.

The first effect of the Civil War was to throw the North and Northwest into a sharp economic depression that shortly gave way to a tremendous boom of prosperity. The demands of a huge army for food and supplies more than compensated Northern merchants and farmers for the loss of Southern markets. The need for increased crops led to the opening of two and a half million new acres in the West, while Congress obligingly passed the Homestead Law of 1862 (long opposed by the South) granting virtually free land to all comers. Loss of manpower to the Services was more than offset by the increased use of farm machinery that enabled the farmer to extend his acreage without requiring more labour. Throughout the war growing conditions were ideal, market prices high and steady, and export demands consistently good. At the close of the conflict the farmer was more prosperous than he had ever been before.

Northern industry, stimulated by military needs and protected by ever-higher tariffs, profited more than agriculture. Old factories expanded and new ones sprang up wherever the new railway lines stretched. Government contracts could be had almost for the asking. Cloth manufacturers profited above all, selling uniforms to the army, while the war changed the clothing habits of the American male by accustoming him to ready-made suits, shoes, hats, caps, and other clothing. Unfortunately, much of the business done with the Union Army was shot through with graft. 'Shoddy' uniforms sometimes dissolved in a hard rain; casks of sugar turned out to be half sand; coffee bags held rye; purchasing agents took bribes and accepted favours. Business in general developed an attitude of 'get-rich-quick' cynicism that carried over undiminished into the post-war period. Yet despite the waste and inefficiency, things somehow got done. Chicago's meat-packing industry expanded swiftly; Pittsburg strengthened its position as a steel-production centre; Pennsylvania's new oil industry (from deposits discovered in 1859) went through the first stages of its development. The North's natural resources were exploited as never before – lumber from the Great Lakes region, gold and silver from the west, copper and iron ore from Michigan and Minnesota, coal from the great Pennsylvania fields. Railroads, the key to Northern industrial expansion, did increasing amounts of business; Erie stock, for example, jumped from 17 to 126 in three years.

War-born industrial activity created a whole new class of *nouveaux riches*, but labour complained that prosperity was not evenly distributed. While the cost of living went to 125 per cent of pre-war levels, real wages rose by only about 20 per cent. Trade union activity increased and there were numerous strikes, nearly a hundred in 1864 alone. Industry, in a favoured position, showed marked tendencies towards centralization. Monopoly was on the way.

The financing of the war had lasting effects on American financial history. The classic method of financing the nation – a higher tariff – proved to be inadequate. To augment the Federal income Secretary Chase resorted to loans, and by 1865 the Treasury had issued 2,000 million dollars' worth of bonds, often sold through private bankers who collected for themselves a comfortable commission. Taxation during the war was the heaviest yet recorded – income taxes, excise taxes, use taxes, every conceivable kind, nearly all of them repealed after 1865. But since neither taxes, bonds, nor tariffs provided sufficient revenues, Congress therefore legalized several issues of paper money, called 'greenbacks'. (About $430,000,000 in greenbacks still remained in circulation in 1865.) Early in the war the Federal government suspended payments in specie, so none of the greenback issues were worth their face value in gold. Their value fluctuated with the fortunes of the Federal armies, reaching their low point of 39 cents in the dollar in early 1864, during Grant's hammering campaigns in the Wilderness.

To the South the war brought nothing but dislocation and adversity. The blockade turned Southern economic life upside down. Before the war the Southerner exported two main crops, tobacco and cotton, importing not only his manufactured goods but also a substantial share of his foodstuffs from the North and abroad. The blockade cut off his exports and imports; he had no market, no credit, and no means of getting either. Blockade runners got through a little cotton and returned with a minimum supply of manufactured goods. Southern farmers substituted wheat and cattle for cotton, but there was never enough. Lack of railroads hampered distribution of the few supplies there were; corn raised in Georgia sold in Virginia for fifteen times its Georgia price and flour cost $300 a barrel in Richmond. The Confederacy was forced to shift almost overnight from a one-crop to a diversified agricultural system, an impossible task in the face of blockade, loss of markets, and inadequate transportation.

For four years the agricultural South kept up a futile struggle to develop an industrial machine capable of supplying its military and civilian needs. Munitions, shoes, clothing, iron and steel, salt, and other necessary industries had to be developed without the aid of technically skilled men and adequately trained labour. Since private capital was hardly equipped to develop huge industries swiftly, the

Confederate government took over the establishment of firms producing salt, guns, powder, and medicines. But while Northern factories mushroomed, the South was forced to turn back to pre-Industrial Revolution methods of hand industry, making clothes, shoes, and other necessities whenever possible in the home. Great as was the effort of the South, it was never enough. In need of nearly everything, Southerners were forced to draw on accumulated wealth or to provide make-shifts. Church bells reappeared as guns; window weights were melted down for bullets; rings and jewellery were needed for currency. Old clothes were remade into 'Sunday best'; burnt corn or rye served for coffee, molasses for sugar, carpets for blankets. Newspapers appeared on wallpaper or wrapping paper, books almost not at all; *Tannhäuser*, wallpaper edition, sold for $7.

Wartime financing in the Confederacy was a tangled maze. Heavily in debt to Northern and European creditors in 1861, the South was unable to obtain sufficient credit from abroad. Both state and Confederate governments floated bond issues at home and in Europe, but they sold only passably well. Like the North, the South soon resorted to direct taxation and levies, though few in the Confederacy had money with which to pay. Early in the war the Confederate government flooded the South with paper money – eventually to the extent of a thousand million dollars – backed only by promises. As the amount of paper increased and military reverses continued after 1863, Confederate money depreciated swiftly – 25 cents to the U.S. dollar in late 1863, 5 cents in early 1864, nothing at the time of Appomattox. 'I used to go to market with money in my pocket and bring back my purchases in a basket,' one Southerner said in 1864, 'now I take my money in a basket and bring home what I buy in my pocket.'

Social life in the North, reflecting the frantic uncertainty of wartime, turned into an extravagant pursuit of pleasure for those who could afford it, and many could. Theatres played to crowded houses, prize-fights and horse-races were jammed. Baseball, a comparatively new game in the army camps, grew in popularity. Tiffany's, the New York gem dealers, reported an unprecedented demand for diamonds and pearls, while urban merchants everywhere were swamped with orders for expensive clothes and furnishings. Wealthy socialites held ostentatious balls and salons. The sale of alcoholic beverages tripled. The stock market spiralled dizzily, while trading on the New York Exchange went from twenty-five to one hundred millions a day and was still rising at the war's end. The majority of Northern citizens remained as steady and hard-working as before, caught in a whirl of wartime inflation, trying to make ends meet; yet it was apparent that a brassy new tone, frenetic and often vulgar, had entered American life.

In the South the picture was different. War tore up the established ways of life by the roots. Cut off from Europe and the North, Southern cultural life came to a dead stop. Schools and colleges closed; students enlisted and teachers followed them, while those scientists, writers, artists, and scholars who were ineligible for service turned to war work. Publishing houses shut their doors and the great Southern magazines, like *De Bow's Review* and *The Southern Literary Messenger*, closed their files forever. Its society and economy disrupted, its manpower depleted, food and supplies short, and money almost non-existent, the culture of the Old South disappeared under the stress of war, never to return.

When Halleck went to Washington he left Grant in charge of the Armies of the Mississippi and the Tennessee, with Don Carlos Buell commanding the Army of the Ohio. Facing Buell was the Confederacy's Braxton Bragg, and Generals Van Dorn and Price held Grant's armies at Corinth, Mississippi. It was Halleck's plan that Grant should capture Vicksburg, thus opening the Mississippi river to the Gulf while Buell drove through Tennessee and beyond, dividing the eastern from the western Confederacy. Bragg, however, confused the plan by slashing northward across Kentucky clear to the Ohio river, and Buell, in hot pursuit, finally caught up with him at Frankfort, Kentucky, in the autumn of 1862. Grant meanwhile set a trap for Van Dorn and Price, sprang it a little too late, and then soundly beat them at the battle of Corinth in October 1862. Disappointed at the defeat, Jefferson Davis sent General John C. Pemberton, a Pennsylvanian gone South, to take over Van Dorn's and Price's combined armies.

As the Confederates retreated from Corinth, Bragg and Buell made contact in Kentucky near Perryville. After an indecisive engagement, distinguished by the brilliant action of young Philip Sheridan, a newly-made general, Buell allowed Bragg to escape to Murfreesboro, in middle Tennessee. Both Halleck and Lincoln were dissatisfied with Buell's performance – he was a good tactician, but unable to handle troops in the mass – and offered his command to his able lieutenant, George Thomas, who turned it down. On the strength of his deportment at Corinth and Iuka, the post went to William Rosecrans of Grant's staff, who took over the Army of the Ohio (soon to be renamed the Army of the Cumberland) in the closing months of 1862. Corinth and Perryville caused similar dissatisfaction in the South. Since some of the Confederate difficulties in the West seemed to arise from divided authority, Davis assigned Joe Johnston to full command of the area, with Bragg and Pemberton under him. But Davis neither liked nor trusted Johnston, argued with him, and occasionally countermanded his orders, making matters if anything worse than before.

Bragg, resting with his army at Murfreesboro, and Rosecrans, in winter quarters at Nashville, pecked at each other for weeks while Richmond and Washington demanded action. In December 1862 both armies finally began movements that brought them together at Stone's River, Tennessee. A bloody two-day battle sent Bragg reeling in retreat to Chattanooga, leaving behind him 14,000 casualties. Rosecrans' Army of the Cumberland, with 11,000 dead and wounded, was too battered to follow, but Bragg's invasion of Kentucky and Tennessee was over. No Confederate army in the West ever marched so far north again.

In early 1863 the war in the West seemed a virtual stalemate. Bragg was beaten back, but he still held Chattanooga,
the key to Tennessee and Alabama. Grant had repelled
Van Dorn and Price, but Vicksburg still blocked the Mississippi. Here was Grant's task, and a hard one. Heavily fortified and garrisoned, the city was protected on the north side
by swamp, on the west or river side it bristled with guns, and
on the east and south the approaches were heavily entrenched and manned. Grant, in the autumn of 1862, hoped
to send Sherman's army down river to try the fortifications
on that side, while he was to march overland from his base
at Memphis to attack from the east and north. Both movements were failures. Snatching at ideas, Grant tried digging
canals so that the river guns could be by-passed, but this
too failed. By April 1863 he was still stuck in the swamp
bottoms and questions were being asked in Washington.
Soldiers died of fever; rations were short; five assaults on
Vicksburg left only fields littered with dead.

But Grant's cold brain was working hard. Capture of
Vicksburg from the river side was impossible, nor could an
army go through the swamps to the north of it. The only
way to capture Vicksburg was from the south and south-
east, on dry ground. To get there meant marching from
Memphis in a great circle to the east, leaving his supply
lines extended and vulnerable to the Confederate cavalry.
But he could march in a circle down the west bank of the
Mississippi past the city, cross to the south of it, and get at
Vicksburg from the rear; a movement that might cut his
army completely from its Memphis base. If it failed it
meant probably complete annihilation of his army and
certainly for him court-martial and dismissal from the
service.

In mid April Grant made his move, crossed the Mississippi, and marched down the west bank with 40,000 men.
'What is your plan now?' asked Sherman. 'Cross here and
reach high ground,' said Grant. 'But your communications?'
asked Sherman. 'You can't get supplies down the river past
the guns.' 'No communications,' replied Grant. 'The troops

can live off the country.' Sherman was thunderstruck. It was impossible. But Grant did it. On the last day of April the Federal troops began to stream across the river and a week later his army was moving on Vicksburg from the south and southeast, travelling fast. Ten days later he had it surrounded – Pemberton and 30,000 Confederates trapped inside — with the right wing of his army touching the river north of the city and his left wing touching the river to the south of it. He tried a few assaults, then settled down to wait. Johnston, rushing north to Pemberton's aid, met Sherman's 40,000 and turned back. In June mule-meat and rats began to appear on Vicksburg menus, and on 3 July Pemberton asked for terms. On 4 July he surrendered, and the Army of the Tennessee, buttons polished and flags flying, marched into the city with its bands playing 'John Brown's Body'. Grant was master of the Mississippi, which, Lincoln said, 'once more flows unvexed to the sea'.

The 'anaconda policy' of slowly strangling the Confederacy called for a complete naval blockade of the South. Early in 1861 Jefferson Davis authorized privateers to prey on Northern commerce, and two days later, on 19 April, Lincoln retaliated by declaring a blockade of all ports in the seceded states. The task of making this effective fell to the new Secretary of the Navy, efficient Gideon Welles of Connecticut.

The problem was by far the most difficult yet faced by the small Federal Navy. The Confederacy had 3,000 miles of coastline dotted with hundreds of good natural harbours. The Union Navy, at the outbreak of war, consisted of some ninety ships, about half of them fit for blockading purposes. On the other hand, since the Confederacy possessed no navy and no evident facilities for building one, almost any vessel that could carry a gun was useful. Before the end of 1861 about one hundred auxiliary ships were in blockade service with more building in Northern shipyards. Furthermore, ninety per cent of the American merchant marine was in Northern hands, providing a pool of trained seamen and officers to man the new ships.

The blockade was almost immediately effective, and was in the long run a prime factor in the defeat of the Confederacy. By the close of 1861 the Navy had sealed off most of the South Atlantic coast and the big Southern ports of Savannah and Charleston. In early 1862 it extended the blockade to the Gulf Coast, capturing New Orleans in May and gradually closing off lesser ports by 1863. After the first few months of war, shortages of tea, coffee, sugar, cloth, soap, manufactured goods, and particularly medical supplies were obvious in the South, and remained throughout the course of the conflict. The Confederacy had plenty of cotton and foodstuffs, but neither the facilities nor the technical skills to produce much else.

The Confederacy quickly improvised blockade-runners to pierce the Federal naval line with cargoes from foreign ports. These swift ships successfully eluded the Navy for four years, bringing in minimum supplies needed to keep the Southern armies in the field. The Confederacy also commissioned raiders to attack Northern commerce, swift, heavily-armed ships built and outfitted chiefly in British ports. Nineteen of these *Alabama*-class raiders were built; they raised havoc with the Northern merchant marine, sinking more than 200 vessels during the war. To engage the Federal Navy directly, the Confederacy planned a fleet of powerful rams, remaking the captured *Merrimac* into an ironclad that in 1862 struck a unit of the Navy at Hampton Roads and nearly destroyed it – until it was stopped by the famous *Monitor*, the 'cheese-box on a raft', in the first major naval battle between ironclads. The Northern blockade was never again seriously threatened.

Inland, particularly in the West, the Federal Navy also played an important role. In May 1861 Captain John Rodgers armed three river steamers and sheathed them with heavy timbers for use in river war. Shortly afterwards James B. Eads, a famous ship designer, built nine flat-bottomed paddle-wheel gunboats, plated with iron, which were placed under the command of Flag Officer Foote. The 'Eads gunboats' and the 'timberclads' provided the West-

ern armies with effective floating artillery. Wisely and
bravely used, the 'webfoot navy' performed an essential
function in the capture of fortifications on the Mississippi,
Tennessee, Cumberland, Red, and other rivers in the
Western campaigns. 'Wherever the ground was a little
damp,' said Lincoln, 'they left their tracks.'

Hooker wintered the Army of the Potomac along the
Rappahannock River in Northern Virginia. He had a
reputation as a hard fighter (and, like Grant, as a hard
drinker) and his soldiers responded to him well. In April
1863, when Lincoln came to review the troops, Hooker
could show him an army of 110,000 infantry and 11,000
cavalry, organized into eight well-drilled corps. Lee had
only about 65,000 effectives at Fredericksburg, and when
Hooker heard that Lee had sent Longstreet's forces to worry
the Union garrison at Fortress Monroe, he believed it time
to act. He planned to send the Union cavalry sweeping to
the west around Lee to divert his attention, while he
pushed around Lee's left to block his path to Richmond.
Late in April Hooker crossed the Rappahannock toward
Fredericksburg.

His flanking manoeuvre fooled Lee for the moment, but
the tangled wilderness country made Hooker's march difficult. His army slowly gathered itself near Chancellorsville,
a few miles east of Fredericksburg, where Lee moved his
forces to intercept it. By the evening of 1 May 1863, Lee
and Jackson held strong positions between Chancellorsville
and Fredericksburg, while Hooker's huge army thrashed
about in the forest, forming battle lines. That night Lee and
Jackson discussed the next day's plans. Their position was
not wholly favourable, but while they talked in the firelight,
Stuart's cavalry rode in to report that Howard's division, on
the right flank of Hooker's army, lay exposed west of
Chancellorsville. Lee and Jackson talked excitedly, drawing
diagrams in the dirt with a stick. Then Jackson, his face set,
walked away.

Lee's plan was as dangerous as it was brilliant. Jackson

was to take his whole wing, nearly half of Lee's army, and in a swift night march swing in a wide eight-mile circuit to Hooker's right, cutting in on the exposed right flank. This left Lee with the other half of the army facing Hooker's centre and left. When Jackson hit the right, Lee was to attack and hold. The manoeuvring meant dividing the smaller army directly in the face of the enemy; it required perfect timing and depended on swift, secret movement. If Hooker attacked while Jackson was on the march, the Army of the Potomac could easily crush Lee and then turn on Jackson.

It worked like a charm. Jackson's men were on the march at midnight on 2 May and into position early the next morning. Von Gilsa's Germans of Howard's corps were quietly cooking their noon meal when 30,000 yelling rebels swept out of the woods. In half an hour Howard's corps was in complete rout, the Union right disintegrating fast. Only tough artillery resistance kept the whole Union from front collapse, and by nightfall the Army of the Potomac was bent double like a horseshoe. Jackson extended his lines, made contact with Lee, and pulled A. P. Hill's division into line, ready to close the open end of the horseshoe and spring the trap. Eagerly Jackson rode forward into the dusk, looking for a weak spot to hit the next morning. The 33rd North Carolina, firing at shadows in the darkness, shot him down.

Joe Hooker was a brave man, but the first day of Chancellorsville required more than bravery. Helplessly tangled in the maze of a nearly disorganized army, Hooker struck back the next morning as best he could. He tried to move his army towards Fredericksburg, but Lee and Stuart (A. P. Hill was wounded) beat him back. Soon the Army of the Potomac held nothing but the river ford behind it, the only way of retreat. Hooker, dazed by the concussion of a cannonball that struck near him, in great pain and in complete confusion, ordered the retreat. Sickles's and Slocum's men held off the Confederate army for hours until the beaten Federals were safely disengaged. Lee's masterpiece was complete. He had outgeneralled and outfought a superior army, had very nearly closed a trap that would have annihilated it, and had inflicted 16,000 casualties to his own 12,000. If Jackson had been there on 3 May it might have happened as Lee planned it. But Jackson, lingering on his death bed, fought out in his delirium some old action, muttering, 'Tell Hill to bring up the guns, bring up the guns!' On 10 May he spoke again: 'Let us cross the river and rest under the shade of the trees.' So died Thomas Jonathan Jackson, the long right arm of Lee.

The news of Chancellorsville brought despair to Washington and jubilation to Richmond. Hooker, it seemed clear, must go, but Lincoln could find no one to replace him. To the South, the Confederate government felt sure that one more such battle should bring peace feelers from Lincoln. Both Davis and Lee believed it absolutely necessary to continue aggressive action in the East, though General Longstreet wisely argued for sending reinforcements at once to the West, where Grant gnawed at Vicksburg. Longstreet was overruled. Lee needed rations – let him get them in Pennsylvania. Lord Russell in London wrote to Lord Palmerston; in view of the string of Union defeats, would it not be wise to offer Britain's services as peace mediator?

On 3 June 1863 Lee's army began to move northward, reinforced to 75,000, a sharp-honed fighting force that had never been defeated. By 12 June Confederate cavalry was reported in the upper Shenandoah Valley, while Hooker (shades of McClellan!) called on Lincoln for reinforcements. There was no doubt about it; Lee was coming north, swinging in a wide circle west of Washington, sending Longstreet's infantry and Stuart's cavalry ahead of him, ranging through the valleys of Maryland and southern Pennsylvania. Hooker moved the Army of the Potomac in a smaller inner circle, keeping between Lee and Washington. Panic hit Philadelphia; business suffered in New York; Pittsburgh organized home guards and dug trenches; the papers called for McClellan again. 'Old Jubilee' Early's Confederates captured York, Pennsylvania, then ransomed it for $100,000 and a thousand pairs of shoes. Stuart's cavalry appeared on the outskirts of Washington, then again near Harrisburg; Ewell turned up in Chambersburg, Pennsylvania, then left to join Lee. Meanwhile, with the Confederate forces approaching mid-Pennsylvania, Hooker called for more men, threatening to resign unless he got them. Lincoln surprised him. He accepted the resignation, and in Hooker's place put George Gordon Meade, untried in battle but a brilliant engineer and a good tactician.

Hooker's proposed counter to Lee was sound enough, but he never had a chance to put it into execution. His idea was to concentrate somewhere between the head and tail of Lee's advancing army, strike it in the middle, divide it, and defeat it by halves. The concentration had barely begun when Meade, aroused from sleep, took command. Lee remained uncertain as to the location of the main body of Meade's army, and when he discovered the Union forces massing south-east of Chambersburg, he begun to pull back his advance units and to concentrate his own army. A fight was in prospect, and after winning it, Lee intended to move straight on to Washington. On 1 July 1863 General Heth's division of A. P. Hill's Corps ran into resistance at Gettysburg, Pennsylvania. 'Don't worry,' said Heth, 'it's only Pennsylvania militia.' He was wrong, for this was Buford's cavalry and the famous Iron Brigade of the Army of the Potomac, sweeping out of the woods in a bayonet charge. The battle of Gettysburg had begun.

At Gettysburg the two armies, both at nearly full strength, suddenly stumbled together. Lee's main force lay somewhat to the north and west of the sleepy little farming town, Meade's to the east and south. When the news came of contact at Gettysburg, both men knew instantly what had happened, but Meade was fortunate in having General Reynolds on the scene. Reynolds quickly surveyed the terrain, chose a long low hill, called Cemetery Ridge, south of the town as suitable ground, and fell dead from a sniper's bullet. Ewell's Confederate II Corps came rushing in from the north, while the Federals, fighting fiercely against three to one odds, slowly fell back towards Cemetery Ridge.

By the evening of 1 July Lee had two thirds of his army at Gettysburg, and Longstreet on the way. The union army was still outnumbered on the field, but Meade was hurrying his main force toward the town. Lee arrived at midnight, talked to Hill and Ewell, and laid his plans. Longstreet was to hit the Union left, entrenched along the Ridge; then Hill was to attack the centre, while Ewell circled the Union right and cut in behind it. Meade arrived that night too, exhausted and sleepless. He knew Lee's favourite trick of breaking down a wing and poured troops into line until dawn.

Cemetery Ridge is shaped like a fish-hook, two miles long, the curved end on the north, the shank on the south. On the morning of 2 July Longstreet sent McLaws's Carolinians and Hood's Texans at the south end of the Union line, while Ewell struck at the north end of the hook. But Sykes's and Sedgwick's Corps came rushing up to stave off McLaws and Hood, while Gregg's cavalry beat back Ewell. Hood noted something that no one else had seen: at the south end of Cemetery Ridge stood two small hills, Big Round Top and Little Round Top. If the Confederates controlled those, artillery could enfilade the entire Union line. At the same time Meade's Chief of Engineers, Warren, saw them too. Acting without authority he called up the 20th Maine and a New York regiment, in time to meet the first wave of Hood's assault. Outnumbered two to one, the Federals fought hand-to-hand with clubbed rifles and held the hills.

That night Lee believed he had victory firmly in his hands. Two days of fighting, he was sure, had badly shaken his enemy, and he proposed on the third day to drive straight through the centre of the Union Line, a plan Longstreet did not like. Meade, during the night, shifted his troops about, sending Gregg and Custer with the cavalry to hold off Stuart, whose tired men had just ridden in. Hancock's II Corps Meade placed in the centre to relieve the battered XII and III. For the assault at the Union centre, Lee chose Pickett's fresh Virginians, prepared a tremendous concentration of artillery to support it, and waited for morning.

On the morning of 3 July Stuart's attack failed; Custer and Gregg soundly whipped his cavalry for the first time in his career. Noon came. Pickett's division formed ranks, bayonets in line. Artillery opened thunderously against the Union centre. Federal artillery fire slackened, then stopped – to let the guns cool, though Lee thought otherwise. Then, at Lee's word, Pickett's division burst out of the woods into the rolling fields, lines dressed, flags waving, the flower of the Army of Northern Virginia.

Longstreet was right and Lee was wrong. Meade had simply out-thought Lee. Guessing that Lee's assault would strike the centre, he reinforced it with fresh troops, concentrations of artillery backed by cavalry in case of a breakthrough. Hancock's II Corps, lying behind a low stone wall, was the best in the Union army, and Pickett's charge headed straight at it. The Union artillery opened up again, tearing huge holes in the advancing line, but Pickett's men came on while the Federal artillerymen pulled their guns up with the infantry, switched to canister, and then to grape at point-blank range. The Confederates came up to the wall and over it, into the guns, and for one brief moment the Union line was pierced. Then Hancock, lying wounded, saw two Pennsylvania and Maine regiments sweep by, bayonets low, to plug the hole. That was the end. Pickett's column, torn to bits, fell back, fell back further, and finally reached the Confederate lines. Fifteen thousand of them went out. Five thousand came back. Lee watched them come, and broke into a sob. 'It's all my fault,' he said. Gettysburg was over.

The Army of Northern Virginia lost 22,000 men at Gettysburg, the Army of the Potomac 18,000. On 4 and 5 July Lee's men took up the long weary retreat southward into Virginia, a defeated army but by no means a broken one. Meade's army was too badly hurt to follow. The battle proved nothing, except perhaps that Lee could not successfully invade the North. It did not establish that Meade was a better general than Lee; it did prove that Meade was

capable of excellent staff work and knew how to use efficient subordinates, whereas Lee no longer had a Jackson to
help him carry out his plans. The fall of Vicksburg on 4 July
and of Chattanooga in November had much more to do
with the final outcome of the war. Yet Gettysburg was for
Lee the turning point. From then on it was all downhill.

They gathered the dead from Gettysburg field, Union and
Confederate, and buried them near Cemetery Ridge under
row on row of white stones. It was designated a national
cemetery, and on a cool November morning in 1863 the
officials held the dedication ceremonies. Edward Everett,
the great New England orator, spoke for two hours. Then
Lincoln walked awkwardly forward on the platform to read
in a high, thin voice the sentences he had scribbled on a sheet
of paper the night before. 'Fourscore and seven years ago
our fathers brought forth upon this continent a new nation,
conceived in liberty, and dedicated to the proposition that
all men are created equal . . . ' It lasted less than five
minutes, followed by a spatter of applause. Seward whis-
pered to Everett, seated beside him, 'He has failed, and I
am sorry for it.'

War or not, politics went on as before. Within the Republican party one group (of which Lincoln stood as representative) believed that the war was being waged to preserve the
Union, with slavery but a secondary issue. Another group of
Republicans, the so-called Radicals, insisted that the
emancipation of slaves was the chief objective of the conflict.
The Joint Committee on the Conduct of the War, formed by
Congress in April 1862, and controlled by the Radicals,
hampered Lincoln's war efforts, tampered with military
policy, favoured Radical Republican army commanders,
and in general attempted to seize control of the party and
the war. Meanwhile men like Ben Wade of Ohio, Zach
Chandler of Michigan, and Thaddeus Stevens of Pennsylvania – Radicals all – loudly criticized Lincoln for his
failure to free the slaves. Lincoln, however, in his reply to
Horace Greeley of the New York *Tribune*, stated his position
in clear language:

My paramount object in this struggle *is* to save the Union, and is *not* either to save or destroy slavery. If I could save the Union without freeing *any* slave, I would do it; and if I could save it by freeing *all* the slaves, I would do it; and if I could do it by freeing some and leaving others alone, I would also do that.

Eventually Lincoln's hand was forced. Convinced that freeing the slaves would help to prevent foreign intervention in the war, would relieve abolitionist political pressure, unify his party, and clarify Northern war aims by injecting the issue of freedom into the war, he issued the Emancipation Proclamation on 22 September 1862, not long after his letter to Greeley.

The Northern Democratic party was also sharply divided over support of what seemed to some purely a Republican war. 'War Democrats' like Douglas (who died in 1861) and Stanton cooperated to the full with Lincoln and the Republicans, but the 'Peace Democrats' (or 'copperheads') attacked Lincoln's war policies and clamoured, after every military defeat, for a negotiated peace. Extremist 'copperheads' formed secret societies, such as the Sons of Liberty or the Knights of the Golden Circle, which attacked conscription laws, discouraged enlistments, and covertly shipped supplies to the Confederacy. When the 'copperhead' movement reached its peak Lincoln moved swiftly to suppress it. He suspended the writ of *habeas corpus* (actually illegally, since only Congress could so act) and arrested the 'copperhead' leaders, many of whom were summarily tried in military courts and quickly imprisoned. Ohio Congressman Clement Vallandigham, leader of the western 'Peace Democrats', was banished to the Confederacy as a traitor. Lincoln's course aroused widespread criticism in the North. Defections from Republican ranks in the congressional elections of 1862, when six normally Republican states went Democratic, can be laid in part to dissatisfaction with Lincoln's handling of the 'copperhead' cases.

The proclamation of emancipation helped to bring some harmony to the Republican party, although the Radicals never ceased their criticism of Lincoln's conduct of the war.

Meanwhile Lincoln attempted to formulate a workable policy whereby the seceded states might return to the Union. As soon as the Federal armies established control over some portion of a Confederate state, Lincoln appointed a provisional military governor for the area and prepared for the re-institution of civil government. In late 1863 he presented a more elaborate plan, one that he hoped might prove attractive to unionist elements in the South. Under this plan pardons were promised to all those citizens of seceded states (with some exceptions) who would take an oath to support the Constitution of the United States and all executive acts and presidential proclamations governing slavery. When 10 per cent of the voting population of 1860 subscribed to this oath, the state might then organize a civil government which would be recognized as the legal government of that state within the Union. Under this system minority governments in Arkansas, Louisiana, and Tennessee (all chiefly under control of the Federal armies) were organized and recognized in 1864. Such an attractive and convenient scheme for reconstructing the Union, however, failed to satisfy many Northern Republicans. It did not guarantee, obviously, that the reorganized governments would be Republican; the Radicals claimed that Lincoln's method would simply allow ex-secessionists, Democrats, or conservative Republicans to gain control within the returned states and in Congress. The Radical-sponsored Wade-Davis bill, which Lincoln killed by pocket veto in 1864, provided a much harsher substitute plan.

The 1864 election provided a serious test of Lincoln's strength. He faced the Radicals within his party and the 'Peace Democrats' without, as well as growing pessimism throughout the North over the long lists of casualties and defeats. Certain that his chances were slim, he prepared a memorandum promising to cooperate with his successor during the period between election and inauguration. Indeed, there was reason for his uncertainty, for a group of Radical Republicans met in May, condemned Lincoln and his war as failures, and declared themselves for John C.

Frémont. Cooler Republican heads, however, thought the renomination of Lincoln better strategy. Frémont withdrew, and the Republican convention chose Lincoln and Andrew Johnson of Tennessee (a War Democrat) as its ticket; deciding, as Lincoln aptly phrased it, 'not to swap horses in the middle of a stream'. The Democratic convention ended in confusion. The 'Peace Democrats' pushed through resolutions declaring the war a failure and demanding an immediate peace. For President they chose General Mc-Clellan, who at once denounced the peace resolution on the ground that 'no peace can be permanent without Union'. Before the election Sherman captured Atlanta, and Sheridan ravaged the Shenandoah Valley, effectively refuting the Democratic platform. The result was a clear endorsement of Lincoln, 212 electoral votes to 21 for McClellan.

Jefferson Davis did not fare so well. In November of 1861 the Confederacy held its first elections, confirming Davis and Stephens in office for six-year terms and returning the majority of members of the provisional Congress. Yet there was growing dissatisfaction, despite the election returns. The blockade was beginning to hurt Southern economy, and Davis's government was soundly berated for shortages, high prices, and profiteering. The Confederate Congress passed a series of price-fixing and anti-profiteering laws, satisfying no one, and as prices rose and supplies dwindled criticism became sharper. The conscription law of 1862, filled with loopholes and exemptions, aroused resentment in certain states, especially in Georgia and South Carolina, which protested against it as an invasion of states' rights and counselled open resistance. At the same time Congress passed a number of acts suspending *habeas corpus* with much the same reaction that Lincoln met in the North.

The old political conflict between unionist and secessionist, small farmer and planter, states' rights man and nationalist continued unabated in the Confederacy. Davis suffered from his inability to conciliate men or to effect compromise between opposing views. Southern newspapers, operating under heavy censorship, failed to provide a clear picture of events and policies, so that rumours floated freely and misunderstandings multiplied. Furthermore, the Confederacy was committed to a defensive war, the military victories – of which there were many – seemed to accomplish nothing as the war continued and casualties mounted. The bloody record of 1862 caused an upsurge of peace talk in the South. Davis, it was said, failed to take advantage of opportunities to end the war honourably; Vice-President Stephens openly accused him of refusing to send out peace feelers to Washington, and in 1863 Stephens went so far as to attempt to arrange a talk with Lincoln. In the same year the long-concealed opposition to Davis came to light in the election, which sent an anti-Davis majority to the Confederate Congress. After 1863 Davis was forced to deal with a hostile Congress and an increasingly hostile public. As the armies in the field won disastrous victories and later suffered equally disastrous defeats his leadership swiftly faded.

In the closing months of 1863 and the winter of 1863–4 both the Army of the Potomac and the Army of Northern Virginia remained inactive. The centre of action shifted to the West, where the Confederacy was in serious trouble: Bragg holed up near Chattanooga, the Mississippi open, Louisiana, Texas, and Arkansas split away from the rest of the South. Rosecrans held the Army of the Cumberland at Nashville and Murfreesboro, facing Bragg. Neither man had any especial taste for aggressive action, though both were under strong political pressure to do something quickly. In June 1863 Rosecrans began a slow advance towards Chattanooga, flanking Bragg out of his advanced positions in a series of minor actions. Rosecrans simply had more men, and by August he had cleared the Confederates out of eastern Tennessee, leaving Bragg holding only Chattanooga. Located at a gap in the Cumberland mountains made by the Tennessee river, Chattanooga was the control point for railroads radiating north, east, west and south, and a city as important to the western Confederacy as Richmond was to the eastern. It was heavily fortified, but Rosecrans cleverly deceived Bragg by feinting an attack from the north

and east while sending Thomas's corps to the south and
southeast. Bragg suddenly woke up to find the major portion of Rosecrans' army marching behind him and Chattanooga almost cut off. Rosecrans occupied the city unre-
sisted, and Bragg retreated into northern Georgia.

Success made Rosecrans over-confident. He assumed
that Bragg was in full retreat toward Atlanta. But Bragg
was gathering his army for a stand, with reinforcements
on the way from Mississippi and Longstreet's division
en route from Lee's Army of Northern Virginia. By early
September Bragg had 66,000 troops to Rosecrans' 57,000,
and Rosecrans, realizing Bragg's intentions, began to pull
his scattered corps together near Chickamauga Creek, a
few miles south of Chattanooga. On 19 September, a foggy,
wet morning, Bragg sent Polk's troops into the attack,
followed by Hood's Texans, but the Federals under Thomas
and Crittenden staved them off. On the 20th Bragg tried
again with no greater success. Late in the morning, however,
the break came when a muddled order left a huge hole in
the Union line. Longstreet poured his 12,000 Virginians
through it, swept down the line right and left, and shattered
the Federal front. The Army of the Cumberland broke in
panic, while Rosecrans fled to Chattanooga, wiring Louisville and Cincinnati to prepare defences immediately. Only
slow-moving George Thomas and the Federal 14th Corps
remained on the field, planted on the Union left, holding a
low ridge called Snodgrass Hill.

Thomas knew nothing of what had happened. At noon
he saw a cloud of dust on his right, looked with binoculars,
and turned away, his face white. The approaching troops
wore Confederate grey. He realized that somehow the rest
of the Army of the Cumberland had been smashed, and that
his 14th Corps covered the only escape route back to Chattanooga. He had three divisions, about 22,000 men; in front
of him, and to his right and left, were 57,000 Confederates.
A few minutes later the Confederates came boiling up the
ridge. The 14th Corps threw them back, and a second and
third time. They beat back Hood's Texans, and Longstreet's

Virginians, later Longstreet again, and two more desperate charges. Water was gone; ammunition was gone; men crawled down the ridge to rob the canteens and cartridge boxes of the dead. Thomas's men soberly fixed bayonets in the deepening twilight; and the last charge they beat off with bayonets and rocks. Longstreet, after this last unsuccessful attack, asked Bragg for reinforcements. 'I have none to give,' said Bragg. Chickamauga, the most murderous battle of the war, was over, with 23,000 casualties. By nightfall Thomas and the remnants of the 14th were on the way back to Chattanooga, where Rosecrans, dazed and weeping, watched the stragglers come in. George Thomas, 'The Rock of Chickamauga', had earned his name.

Bragg immediately surrounded Chattanooga and closed the Army of the Cumberland in a trap. There were repercussions in both armies. Bragg dismissed Polk and Nathan Bedford Forrest for 'insubordination' (Forrest wanted to pursue Thomas and cursed Bragg when permission was refused) and Rosecrans, a broken man, was removed from the Army of the Cumberland. Thomas took over for the moment, until Lincoln, recognizing the need for a unified command, called Grant to take charge of the entire West. There was no doubt about the fact that Chickamauga was a shattering Union defeat, but the tide was turning. Bragg had all the advantages – superior numbers, the muddled order, fine troops – yet the Army of the Cumberland still existed as a fighting force, its morale high though its rations were short. And Grant was there.

Grant rode into Chattanooga in the dripping cold autumn rain, spattered with mud, 'an ordinary, scrubby-looking man with a slightly seedy look', wrote the New York newspaperman, R. H. Dana. The situation was bad indeed. Behind Chattanooga lay a mountain chain, fine hunting grounds for the Confederate cavalry, which had already cut the single railroad supply line; 10,000 horses and mules died of starvation while the troops ate acorns and parched corn. In front of the city Bragg's troops held all the strong points, waiting for the Army of the Cumberland to starve out.

Hooker came from the Army of the Potomac with two corps, raising Grant's numbers to 40,000. Supply, reasoned Grant, was the important thing, so he and Thomas set about opening a 'cracker line' on the Tennessee river. This was done with almost ridiculous ease – Hooker's men slipped out of the city, down a narrow valley, and in a surprise attack crossed the river and captured a bridgehead. Within a week wagonloads of food rumbled in and the army felt better. Next Grant called in Sherman with the Army of the Tennessee, raising his force to 60,000. Then he began to think about battle.

Chattanooga lies on the south-east bank of the Tennessee river, which curves in a narrow bight around it. To the south, southwest, and southeast of the city Lookout Mountain, Orchard Knob, and Missionary Ridge enclose it in a box. Bragg held them all, and the lines between. Grant planned to strike at the tip of Missionary Ridge, which protected Bragg's line of supply southward. On 23 November Sherman crossed the river and headed for the ridge, while Hooker was sent to demonstrate against Lookout to cover Sherman's movement. Sherman's maps were inaccurate: his men struck an unmapped ravine at the base of the ridge, and the Confederates had time to assemble defence. When Sherman requested aid, Grant sent Thomas's troops to him to help him hold on. Thomas's men paused at the foot of the ridge, above them three lines of rifle pits and sixty field guns. Then, without orders – no one yet knows why – they started up the steep cliff in the strangest charge of the war, straight into the guns, past the rifle pits, on over the ridge and down into Bragg's headquarters, yelling like demons. The centre of the Confederate line melted away, the right wing collapsed, and Bragg himself narrowly escaped capture; only a quick-thinking Confederate officer managed to hold his division in place long enough to cover the disorganized retreat. It was an absurd ending to a well-planned battle. Missionary Ridge was militarily impregnable to direct assault, and neither Grant nor Thomas would have dreamed of ordering a charge up its rocky sides. Yet it happened.

Chattanooga finished Bragg. He had beaten Rosecrans at Chickamauga, trapped an entire Union army in Chattanooga, and yet somehow he was now in full retreat. His friendship with Davis failed to save him. Joe Johnston took over command of the West and the fighting stopped for the winter, the Confederates resting in northern Georgia. Congress revived the grade of lieutenant-general, vacant since Washington's day, and at Lincoln's request gave it gratefully to Grant. So Grant went to Washington in March 1864 to take full command of all Union armies. Sherman replaced him in the West, while Halleck remained as chief of staff with nothing to do but fuss over reports. Lincoln's seach for a general was finished. From now on Grant and Sherman would work together, stolid bulldog and wiry gun-dog, closing the ring about the Confederacy.

Grant, on his arrival in Washington, submitted to Lincoln his plan for the final defeat of the Confederacy. With the Armies of the Potomac, the James, and two smaller forces, he intended to advance on Richmond, pinning down Lee. At the same time Sherman, with the Armies of the Cumberland and Tennessee, was to move on Joe Johnston with Atlanta as his goal. Meanwhile, Grant brought Sheridan east to command the Federal cavalry, with orders to 'keep Stuart out of trouble'. Grant's plan was neither new nor brilliant, but it coordinated and concentrated the superior Union forces and settled on definite objectives in both eastern and western theatres, something that his predecessors had never managed. Lincoln approved, and with a sigh of relief turned the war over to Grant, rarely interfering again in military affairs.

On 4 May 1864, Grant, travelling with Meade and the Army of the Potomac, crossed the Rapidan River in the first step of his hammering campaign at Richmond. The Union armies moved blindly and slowly in the tangled underbrush of the wilderness country, while Lee, watching his cavalry reports, kept track of their progress. On 6 and 7 May, Lee hit the Federals a few miles west of the old Chancellorsville field while Stuart and Sheridan clashed in a sharp cavalry duel to the south in the hills. Caught in thick woods, with artillery useless, Grant's army lost 18,000 men in the two-day engagement. This was to Lee an old story: let them come on, strike hard, and send them reeling back toward Washington, another Union general broken. The Army of the Potomac knew the script too. That night the Union troops waited for the familiar retreat order, but this time the general was U. S. Grant; the order came for a sliding advance to Lee's right, aiming at Spotsylvania Court House.

It was Lee's turn to be surprised. By all the rules Grant should have been backing away, but instead he acted as if he had won a battle. By the time Grant's armies arrived at Spotsylvania, the Confederates were there, dug in across the roads to Richmond. The result was as before – a field covered with dead, the Confederate lines intact. Again Lee waited for Grant to retreat, but Grant wired Lincoln, 'I propose to fight it out on this line if it takes all summer,' and began his flanking advance once more. Thunderstruck, Lee hit the Federals again at North Anna; tremendous losses, the same inexorable flanking movement toward Richmond. Lee was worried, especially since Sheridan's cavalry was loose behind him, cutting at the Confederate supply lines. Nothing like this had ever happened before. Stuart, rushing back toward Richmond, caught Sheridan at Yellow Tavern only a few miles from Richmond and fought it out, but 'Beauty' Stuart fell with a bullet through his chest and the Confederate cavalry was leaderless.

On 26 May, in a swift march covered by wide-ranging cavalry, Grant swung in a wide arc to Lee's right, straight at Richmond. By 2 June Lee had the move blocked at Cold Harbor, only six miles from the Confederate capital. The strain on both armies was heavy, almost a month of ceaseless movement, fighting, and slaughter. After a wrangle with Meade, Grant ordered a direct assault on the Confederate positions, a decision that he regretted for the rest of his life. In less than twenty minutes the Army of the Potomac lost 7,000 men. 'All day long,' wrote General Warner, 'a perpetual funeral procession goes by my headquarters.' No

army could stand such constant hammering, 55,000 casualties in three weeks to Lee's 19,000. People in the Northern
towns read the daily death lists in silence and began to talk
about 'Butcher' Grant. But Grant and Lee both knew that
the end was not far off. Union losses could be replaced;
Confederate could not. Boys of fifteen began to appear in
the Confederate lines.

After Cold Harbor Grant shifted to McClellan's old plan
of attacking the city from the rear, up the James River.
Moving his army in a circle to the east of Richmond, he
threw his forces about Petersburg, twenty miles south of the
city on the Appomattox river, cutting off three of the five
railroads into Richmond. After one unsuccessful attempt on
Petersburg he settled down for a siege, Vicksburg-fashion,
the kind of war he knew best. The fall of Richmond, in Lee's
opinion, would be only a matter of time if Grant were
allowed to hover on the city's outskirts, slowly closing in.
The only answer was a diversion, a movement toward
Washington that, Lee hoped, might so frighten the North
that Lincoln would hastily pull Grant back to protect the
capital. It had worked before, and should again. Therefore,
Lee detached Jubal Early, gave him 30,000 men, and orders
to swing up the Shenandoah Valley toward Washington.
This was the type of action that needed Stuart, but Stuart
was gone.

On 5 July Early crossed the Potomac and cut the Balti-
more and Ohio railroad at Hagerstown, Maryland. Three
days later he occupied Frederick, and Washington quaked.
A motley force of 7,000 men met him at the Monocacy
River and Early promptly engulfed them. On the 11th
Early looked into Washington streets through his binoculars.
But at that moment a corps of regulars from the Army of
the Potomac disembarked from the ships; a few days later
it was joined by a division from Sherman's army in the West.
Early hesitated, turned away, and swung north to demand a
ransom from Chambersburg, Pennsylvania, burning it to
the ground when the half-million dollars he asked was not
forthcoming.

Early's raid northward from the Valley had to be stopped. A new army was created, the Army of the Shenandoah, with more than 10,000 cavalry. For its commander Grant chose Sheridan, turning him loose with instructions to smash Early and sweep the Valley clean. 'I will leave them nothing but their eyes to weep with,' said Sheridan, and made his word good. He struck Early at Frederick, Winchester, Fisher's Hill, and Cedar Creek, defeated him decisively, and sent his army retreating rapidly toward Richmond. Then for three leisurely weeks Sheridan laid waste to the Shenandoah Valley, leaving it so barren, his soldiers said, that 'a crow flying across it had better carry his own rations'. His army burned 2,000 farms, took every horse, cow, mule and sheep for seventy-five miles, and Lee got no more food for his army from the rich farms of northern Virginia.

The 'municipal theory' on which Lincoln chose to fight the war had certain advantages for the North, but it soon proved unworkable in foreign affairs. The President could, by the Constitution, suppress insurrection, but he could not make war without the vote of Congress except in case of actual invasion by a foreign power. Lincoln's position that the seceded states had never left the Union placed the Confederacy in the position of an insurrectionary government but did not recognize it as either belligerent, foreign, or independent. However, in issuing his blockade order, Lincoln ran foul of a delicate technicality in international law. Asserting on the one hand that there was no war, but rather a rebellion, he yet proposed to seize ships of any nation attempting to break the blockade. Instead of proclaiming a blockade, which might be construed as recognizing the legal belligerency of the Confederacy, Lincoln might well have followed Jackson's lead and issued an order closing rebellious ports, as 'Old Hickory' had shut up Charleston during the nullification troubles. In the first case to appear in the prize courts, involving a captured British blockade runner, the Supreme Court decided that the conflict with the Confederacy must be a war with a foreign government, since only such a war could justify blockade and search. Queen Victoria, taking advantage of the legal point, immediately recognized the Confederacy as a belligerent and accorded Confederate ships the same status as Federal ships in British ports, against the protests of the newly-arrived Minister, Charles Francis Adams, John Quincy's son.

Confederate diplomacy depended on 'King Cotton'. 'No, you dare not make war on cotton,' remarked Senator Hammond of South Carolina. 'No power on earth dares make war upon it.' Southern leaders like Hammond were convinced that lack of raw cotton would soon force Britain and France to recognize the Confederacy as an independent nation and break the blockade, thereby precipitating war with the North. *Punch* pointed out in early 1861 that

> Though with the North we sympathize,
> It must not be forgotten,
> That with the South we've stronger ties,
> Which are composed of cotton.

The Charleston *Mercury* predicted that recognition of the Confederacy would come the day after British and French mills closed for lack of cotton; some Southerners, in fact, restricted cotton acreage and burned existing stores in order to hurry the shortage abroad. But there were large supplies of raw cotton in British and French warehouses, and although shortages in 1862 forced some British mills to suspend operations, the English working classes had great sympathy for the Union and for Lincoln – particularly when the Emancipation Proclamation placed the war on an abolitionist basis. New sources of supply, especially from India and Egypt, eased the scarcity in Britain, while Northern merchants shipped large amounts of captured Southern cotton abroad. Furthermore, Britain, suffering from crop shortages, began large importations of Northern wheat, and 'King Wheat' proved to be as diplomatically potent as 'King Cotton'.

In May 1861 Davis sent three commissioners to London to attempt to secure recognition of the Confederacy as an independent nation. Lord Russell, the Foreign Minister, gave them no promises, but two months later Victoria's proclamation recognized the Confederacy's belligerent status. It was followed by similar proclamations from other European nations. Regardless of the slavery issue, the attitude of the British ruling class was markedly pro-Southern, and Minister Adams faced the constant animosity of Lord Palmerston, the Foreign Secretary, who, he wrote, 'indulged in derogatory and insulting language rather than in conciliation'. Lord Russell, more flexible and astute than Palmerston, was less of a problem for Adams. Both mature, skilful, and brilliant diplomats, Adams and Russell staged a four-year duel that ended slightly to Adams's advantage: Britain did proclaim its neutrality and recognize the Confederacy as a belligerent, but it never recognized Confederate independence, the prize most coveted by the Southern emissaries. At the same time Adams found it necessary to check Secretary of State Seward, whose hot temper often led him into rash statements and dangerous policies. To add to his labours, Adams had also to watch Confederate agents in England, both diplomatic and commercial, to prevent if he could their purchase of war materials, ships, and manufactured goods.

Lord Russell at first received the Southern agents informally, but after Adams's protestations he closed his doors to them. In September 1861 the Confederacy decided to send formally accredited agents to both Britain and France, in the hope that they might gain an official audience. John Slidell of Louisiana, the commissioner for France, was an able diplomat and politician; James Mason of Virginia, the commissioner for England, was a skilful speaker and a personable man. After running the Federal blockade to Cuba both men took passage for Southampton on the British mail packet *Trent* on 7 November. But on 8 November the *Trent* was stopped by the Federal gunboat *San Jacinto*, (Captain Charles Wilkes commanding), the ship searched, the commissioners removed, and both commissioners and their families carried to Boston for confinement.

The '*Trent* affair' gave Adams a new headache. The

Northern public was enthusiastic; Wilkes was hailed as a hero, flooded with dinners and presents, and congratulated by Secretary of the Navy Welles, though Lincoln doubted the wisdom of his act. Inevitably resentment ran high in Britain. Palmerston, in a towering rage, demanded an apology and immediate release of the prisoners. Seward, who originally applauded Wilkes, soon began to have misgivings; a Northern war with Britain was exactly what the South desired, and furthermore there were obvious irregularities in Wilkes's conduct. Fortunately Prince Albert wisely toned down the ministry's angry note to the Queen, while Seward and Lincoln evolved a reply to the British that mollified public opinion at home. Mason and Slidell were released, sent to Europe on a British vessel, and everyone breathed a sigh of relief. As Adams remarked, 'The *Trent* affair . . . has proved somewhat in the nature of a sharp thunderstorm which has burst without doing any harm, and the consequence has been a decided improvement in the state of the atmosphere.'

In England Mason found considerable sympathy for the Confederate cause, especially among the upper classes who felt more kinship with Lee and the Southern aristocracy than with Lincoln and the class from which he sprang. After First Bull Run portions of the British press jibed at the 'drunken scum' put to rout by the Southern heroes, and even cool-headed Englishmen held the conviction that the South could not be conquered. The North's case was never fully clear to a large segment of the British public, which tended (at least until emancipation) to view the war less as an attempt to free slaves than to coerce a sovereign people into a Union they had already rejected. In 1862 when Confederate military successes followed quickly one after another, British sentiment for recognizing the Confederacy as an independent nation was at its highest. Gladstone declared in October that 'We may anticipate with certainty the success of the Southern States . . .', and pointed out that 'Jefferson Davis and the leaders of the South . . . have made a nation.' Russell, however, held Mason off politely, never committing himself, and after Antietam, in September of 1862, the Federal armies began to turn the tide. Lincoln's proclamation of emancipation enlisted the support of the British working classes to the Union cause, strengthening the hands of pro-Northern liberals like Cobden and Bright. With the freeing of the slaves, Adams held a strong moral weapon that he used to good diplomatic advantage.

The most delicate of Adams's continuing problems had to do with the South's attempts to build a navy in British shipyards. Lacking both designers and construction facilities, the Confederacy sent Captain James Bullock to England in 1861 to organize contracts for ships, the most important of which were to be a series of commerce-raiders built by Laird Brothers at Birkenhead. In the spring of 1862 the first, *Number 290*, was launched while Adams protested to the Foreign Office over the delivery to the Confederacy of a ship obviously designed to attack American commerce. International law did not prevent a neutral nation from trading in war materials with belligerents, said Adams, but it did bar direct intervention or the use of the neutral country as a military or naval base. The Laird ships, claimed Adams, violated this latter rule. While British officials combed the books for an answer, *Number 290* went to sea, was armed and equipped in the Azores with material sent from British ports, and, renamed the *Alabama*, began its depredations on Union shipping. The *Florida* followed shortly, under the same circumstances. However, Adams's violent protests stopped further construction of raiders. Years later, at the *Alabama* tribunal of Geneva in 1871, the British government officially expressed regret over the 'escape' of the raiders and paid fifteen and a half millions in damages.

The 'Laird rams', powerful ironclads built by the same Birkenhead firm in late 1862 and equipped with nine-inch rifles, provoked a similar crisis. At first Lairds declared that the ships had been ordered by France and then by Egypt, both claims officially denied by the governments concerned. Confederate agents actually did have ownership of the vessels transferred to a French firm, a ruse that deceived no one. Though legally the Confederacy was on safe ground, Adams kept up such a volley of protests that Lord Russell ordered the rams to be held in the yards. They were never released, and with them went the last Southern chance to break the blockade.

John Slidell found considerably greater encouragement at the court of Napoleon III, who was quite willing to penetrate the blockade with French ships and to recognize Confederate independence, if only Britain would agree to co-operate with him. During 1862 Slidell and Mason held hopes of consolidating a Southern alliance with both France and England. In April 1862 Napoleon proposed a joint naval expedition up the Mississippi, a plan that Russell refused to consider; and in July, at Slidell's insistence, Napoleon sent another proposal to Russell for recognition of the Confederacy; again Russell refused. In January 1863, after Fredericksburg, Napoleon offered his services to Lincoln as a mediator, which Lincoln politely declined. Union victories at Gettysburg and Vicksburg in mid-1863 cooled British and French enthusiasm for intervention considerably, and Adams afterwards found his path much easier.

Napoleon, however, had a deeper game to play. The key to his diplomatic manoeuvrings during the Civil War lay in his desire to establish a puppet Mexican empire, a venture made possible when Britain, France, and Spain decided that the Civil War gave them a chance to challenge the validity of the Monroe Doctrine. Frequent and bloody revolutions in Mexico, resulting in defalcation on debts and extensive destruction of foreign-owned property, led the three nations to agree in October 1861 on a joint military expedition into Mexico to protect investments and collect debts. Seeing little advantage in the scheme, Britain and Spain shortly withdrew, but not Napoleon.

In 1861 and 1862, with its hands full and military reverses following in quick succession, the Washington government could do little to thwart him. French troops entered Mexico, scattered Juárez's native army, and easily occupied Mexico

City in June 1863. By that time, however, Union military prospects were considerably brighter, and Secretary of State Seward could turn his attention toward Mexico. He had no desire to push France, already friendly to the Confederacy, into an outright alliance. At first he contented himself with carefully worded notes defining the American position and reaffirming the Monroe Doctrine, but never by name. In 1864, when Napoleon's nominee Maximilian, the brother of the Emperor Franz Joseph of Austria, accepted the throne of Mexico, the tone of Seward's notes became sharper; after Appomattox, with the Confederacy no longer a factor in diplomacy, he strengthened his demands that French military forces leave Mexico. The North had 900,000 men under arms, and Grant had already ordered Sheridan with 50,000 veterans to the Texas border. In 1866 Napoleon abandoned Maximilian to his fate before a Mexican firing squad, and the French dream of a new American empire vanished.

After Gettysburg the sands of Confederate diplomacy began to run out. Crises in Italy, Poland, and Schleswig-Holstein turned Europe's attention away from the American conflict; Adams wrote that 'America is not much talked of here, never so little since I first came.'

Early in the war Lincoln resolved to send prominent unionists abroad as unofficial ambassadors – men such as Thurlow Weed the politician, the Catholic bishops of Ohio and New York, and Robert Walker of Mississippi – who had strong influence on public opinion in Europe. Northern appeals to British workers proved extremely effective; though Lincoln's insistence on the preservation of the Union as his chief war aim meant little to the working man, the emancipation of the slaves completely changed his picture of the war. The war brought unemployment to 400,000 cotton mill workers, but Bright and others urged them to support 'the holy war' against slavery, and mass meetings of workers responded by passing resolutions favouring the North. The mill-hands of Manchester, among others, vowed to support the Union cause and congratulated Lincoln on his 'erasure of that foul blot on civilization and Christianity –

chattel slavery'. White Southern propagandists vainly attempted to enlist British support and hoped that un-employment would force the British working classes into acquiescence, their hopes were shattered both by the deter-mination of John Bright and by the shrewdness of the Federal Congress which mitigated the worst horrors of idle-ness in the mills by sending to Britain shiploads of wheat.

By 1864 the Confederate agents had lost the battle for Britain. Sherman marched to the sea, Grant penned Lee in Richmond, and Davis observed that the French and British both treated his emissaries with cold formality. Davis's last desperate manoeuvre – an offer to abolish slavery in the Confederacy in exchange for British recognition – fell on deaf ears, and Lee's surrender closed the books. At the news of Lincoln's assassination the British press excelled itself in praise of the man it had once bitterly reviled. Adams's work was done. As James Russell Lowell said, 'None did more for the North than he in his forlorn outpost at London.'

When Grant moved on Richmond in May of 1864, Sherman, the other arm of the pincers, left Tennessee. He had nearly 100,000 men; between him and Atlanta, the stronghold of the western South, stood Joe Johnston with 72,000. Johnston and Sherman were closely matched anta-gonists; in Thomas and Hood both had able lieutenants; both armies were experienced, disciplined, confident. There was only one feasible route to Atlanta – a city filled with heavy industry, iron-works, and storehouses – straight down the railroad from Chattanooga, and both Sherman and Johnston knew it.

An expertly executed series of flanking movements, begin-ning in the spring of 1864, took Sherman's army into middle Georgia, and by early July he was only fifteen miles from Atlanta. Mutterings in the Southern press grew louder as he came closer, and there were angry debates in the Congress at Richmond. Joe Johnston's Fabian tactics – draw Sherman farther and farther away from his base in Chattanooga, and then strike him one shattering blow – were not popular in a

South accustomed to Lee's victories. The Georgia delegation in Congress railed at Davis; he in turn railed at Johnston, who quietly told him that there was no way of stopping Sherman short of Atlanta itself. On 11 July Davis removed Johnston and gave the command to John B. Hood, a giant one-armed Texan with a flair for attack. Sherman, who respected and feared Joe Johnston, highly approved of the change.

Atlanta, built on a plateau surrounded by hills, ravines, and creeks, was expertly fortified with a ring of entrenchments. There Johnston felt he could have held Sherman off indefinitely. Hood, however, was no defensive warrior. He promised action, and on 2 July he attacked Sherman at Peachtree Creek north of the city. The brunt of the blow fell on Thomas's Army of the Cumberland, veterans of Snodgrass Hill and Missionary Ridge, and Hood lost 4,000 men in less than two hours. To make matters worse, Sherman sent McPherson and the Army of the Tennessee slipping around Hood's right, threatening Atlanta and cutting two of the four railroads into the city. The Texan pulled back his army, and the next day hit McPherson east of the city, losing 10,000 more men. Sherman immediately drew the ring tighter. Facing Atlanta from the northwest, north, and southeast, he slowly pushed the right wing of his army around Atlanta to the west. Hood struck at the circle again on the 28th – 5,000 casualties. 'They no longer come on so boldly as before,' noted a Union commander, and shells from Sherman's artillery began to drop in the city streets.

For nearly a month Sherman held on, shelling the city, testing its defences, probing for a weak spot. Meanwhile, Wheeler's Confederate cavalry cut at Sherman's long supply lines, stretching north along the railroad to Chattanooga. Election time was approaching in the North, and after Grant's bloody Wilderness campaigns, the anti-Lincoln politicians shouted that the war was a failure. Finally, on 27 August, Hood's cavalry brought in reports that Sherman's army was abandoning its positions north of Atlanta, obviously preparing to fall back along the railroad lines toward northern Georgia. Hood was overjoyed, but while Atlanta's church bells rang in jubilation, the wind brought the sound of heavy artillery from the south. It was Sherman, who had cut loose from his supply lines, swung his main army around Atlanta, and at the moment was hammering at Jonesboro, fifteen miles to the south of the city. The next day he took Jonesboro, severed the last rail lines into Atlanta, and turned on Hood with his full force. Two nights later, sitting on a stump in the dark, Sherman heard guns to the north: Slocum's artillery booming salutes as his men marched into Atlanta's deserted streets; and he ordered a dispatch to Lincoln, 'Atlanta is ours, and fairly won.' Atlanta's fall, said Seward, 'knocked the planks out of the Democratic platform' and practically assured Lincoln's re-election.

Hood, after escaping from Atlanta, reformed his army at Macon. Sherman's position, despite his successful capture of Atlanta, was precarious. He was deep in enemy territory, dependent on a single railroad line connecting him with his bases; Confederate cavalry cut it so often that the Union army was almost constantly on short rations. Hood's army was intact, though weakened, and Hood still perfectly able to mount a strong offensive. Hood, furthermore, had plans of his own to slip behind Sherman, march on Tennessee, and force Sherman to rush back from Georgia to defend his bases. With this in mind, Hood began to edge his way north and west, aiming at Tennessee.

Sherman, having come thus far, refused to be forced back. He detached Thomas and two corps, and sent them back to Nashville with orders to hold Hood at all costs. This was hardly enough to defeat Hood, but Sherman trusted Thomas to weld an army that could, out of the replacements and minor forces scattered through Tennessee and Mississippi. Let Hood move on Tennessee, Thomas could hold him. As for Sherman, he had an audacious plan of his own. Why not break away from Atlanta, live off the country, and head straight across Georgia to the sea, thus severing what remained of the Confederacy and isolating Georgia, Alabama, and Florida? Dangerous the plan might be. Lincoln was fearful and even Grant uncertain. Against it stood so many chances of misadventure. If Hood defeated Thomas and took Tennessee, then the war in the West had to be fought over again. Suppose Sherman's army could not live off the country, or met such resistance that it never reached the sea and the naval supply ships? Grant temporized, but Sherman prepared for his march with complete confidence. All sick, convalescent, and older troops he sent back to Thomas, stripping his own army down to young, battle-seasoned veterans. He reorganized his 60,000 remaining troops into two big wings, with a powerful cavalry force to sweep along at their sides. Then, in early November, he received from Washington grudging permission to begin what the newspapers immediately labelled 'the wild adventure of a crazy fool'. On 12 November, after the last train left the city, Sherman tore up the railroad and headed for Savannah and the sea, while Atlanta, a useless hulk, burned fiercely behind him. 'I will make Georgia howl,' he said.

For three weeks neither Lincoln nor Grant had news of Sherman except from Southern newspapers. There was nothing in front of him except Wilson's cavalry and a motley collection of militia and home guards who scattered before 'Uncle Billy's bummers'. His troops ripped up railroads, twisting the rails into 'Sherman hairpins'; they pillaged stores and barns, burned towns, and left blackened chimneys where plantation houses once stood. They swept through Milledgeville, the state capital, and pressed on to the sea, leaving behind them a swath of destruction fifty miles wide. Negroes, convinced that 'de day ob Jubilo' had come, marched happily behind them, while cavalry raiders cleared plantation smokehouses of hams and filled their knapsacks with the family silver. It was almost a picnic; sixty years later old men vividly remembered that march in the cool Southern autumn as they sang exuberantly,

> How the darkies shouted when they heard the joyful sound!
> How the turkeys gobbled which our commissary found!
> How the sweet potatoes even started from the ground —
> While we were marching through Georgia!

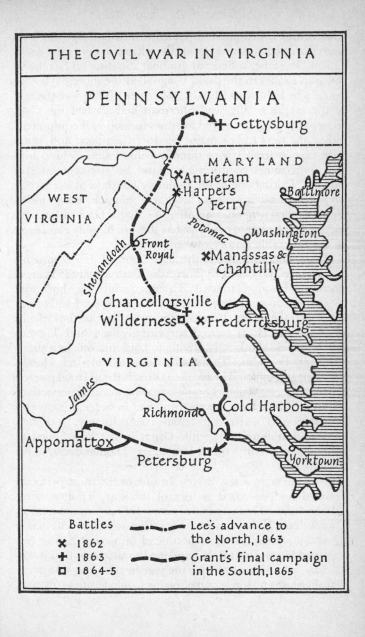

THE CIVIL WAR IN VIRGINIA

PENNSYLVANIA

+ Gettysburg

MARYLAND

× Antietam
× Harper's
Ferry

○ Baltimore

WEST
VIRGINIA

Potomac

○ Washington

Front
Royal

× Manassas &
Chantilly

Shenandoah

Chancellorsville
Wilderness ☐ × Fredericksburg

VIRGINIA

James

Richmond ○

☐ Cold Harbor

Appomattox ☐

☐ Petersburg

○ Yorktown

Battles
× 1862
+ 1863
☐ 1864-5

—·—·— Lee's advance to
the North, 1863

— — — Grant's final campaign
in the South, 1865

Meanwhile, at Richmond, trains from the deep South no longer arrived, and one by one the telegraph lines went dead. On 10 December a Federal gunboat standing off Savannah saw gun-flashes in the dusk. It signalled the shore, 'Who are you?' The light winked back, 'Sherman'. That was the end of the march to the sea. Sherman had slashed the Confederacy in two, destroyed fortunes in food and equipment, closed the next to last major Southern sea-port, and stood with 60,000 fresh troops directly behind Lee. Behind him too, in the ruined Southern heartland, he left anger that still rankles. 'During one of the intensely hot days of last week', an Atlanta citizen wrote in his diary, '300 sick and wounded Yankees died at Andersonville. We thank Heaven for such blessings.' Comments as brutal as this are happily rare, even in the miserable history of wars.

While Sherman sliced through Georgia, Hood and his 50,000 men, preceded by Forrest's cavalry, marched across northern Georgia toward Thomas, who was hurriedly moulding an army from the casuals, sick, and unfit that (added to the 22,000 from Sherman) he had for the defence of Nashville. Hood moved surprisingly fast, and Thomas sent Schofield south of Nashville to hold him off. In a sharp clash at Franklin, Tennessee, Schofield slowed Hood's advance and inflicted heavy casualties, but still Hood pressed on toward Nashville. Thomas, a slow-moving perfectionist, refused to act until everything was in order; his cavalry lacked mounts, an ice-storm made roads slippery, he needed arms and ammunition; while Grant in the East fumed at his inaction. Finally, on 15 December, Thomas declared his army ready.

It was over in a few hours. In one of the most perfectly planned and executed battles of the war, Thomas completely smashed Hood's entire army. Of his original 55,000, a week later Hood was able to gather together only 9,000 men; 13,000 captured, 10,000 dead or wounded, the rest scattered beyond recall. It happened so suddenly that it was hard for men to realize that the war in the West was over; that there was no longer an effective Confederate army west of Richmond. Jefferson Davis now governed only three states, Virginia, North Carolina, and South Carolina, and only Lee was left to defend them. A month later a group of Confederate Congressmen called on Lee to offer him the Presidency. He refused, but Jefferson Davis never again had any real power in the Confederacy.

The loss of Savannah and the annihilation of Hood's army brought affairs in the South to a crisis. Lee, placed in complete command of all Confederate forces, called on Joe Johnston to stop Sherman, who turned north from Savannah and swept into South Carolina. Johnston was able to muster only 34,000 troops, drawn from the South's last reserve of manpower and no match for Sherman's veterans. Pushing the Confederates before him, Sherman lashed across South Carolina ('Here secession began,' said one Union soldier, 'and here, by God, it will end') into Columbia, the capital, while the Navy closed off the South's last seaport at Charleston. By March Johnston's position was desperate. Retreating slowly into North Carolina, losing heavily at every engagement, outnumbered two to one, he asked Lee for reinforcements.

Lee had none to give. Grant waited near Petersburg, never attacking in force, wearing down Lee's army. The Confederate lines were dangerously thin; replacements were non-existent; no more supplies came in from the Shenandoah Valley or the deep South, no more arms or medicines from the blockade-runners. In March Lee gathered all his forces for a single desperate blow at Grant's centre, hoping to break out of Richmond and join Johnston for an attack on Sherman. The Union army beat it back, and Grant kept pounding at Richmond, hitting here and there, keeping Lee's tired and hungry divisions running back and forth within the circle to ward them off. It was a magnificent defence, ably and bravely done, but it was 60,000 against 120,000 and there was not enough to eat. Wherever Lee turned Grant was there, double in numbers. Richmond and Petersburg had only two rail lines running to the west; if Grant circled the city and cut these, Richmond and Lee's army were lost. On 1 April Lee attacked Sheridan's forces at Five Forks south of Petersburg in an attempt to break out of the circle. Sheridan beat him back, but Grant reasoned that if Lee could mount an attack at Petersburg, his lines must be dangerously thin somewhere else. He ordered an immediate attack on all fronts.

On Sunday, 2 April, Jefferson Davis went to church. In the middle of the service a man tiptoed down the aisle and handed Davis a note. He read it, flushed, and left. Lee was evacuating Richmond, dropping back along the railroads to the west. Richmond refused to believe it; but the next afternoon there was a sound of bugles and the Union cavalry rode into the city, followed by a crack Negro infantry regiment, its flags flying, band playing, uniforms creased and brass shining. The President came too, and Lincoln, walking in the quiet Virginia dusk, knocked at a door and asked for his old friend George Pickett. He was not at home.

Lee's troops marched westward along the rail lines to Danville, the Union army moving parallel, knifing into the tired columns. At Danville Lee found nothing but Federal blue. He turned toward Lynchburg. Sheridan's cavalry, a cloud of superbly mounted horsemen carrying repeating rifles, barred the way. The Army of Northern Virginia wearily prepared to attack, but almost with contempt the cavalry lines parted to show massed behind them the solid blue mass of Ord's infantry, spread out in battle order, artillery in place. On 7 April Grant called on Lee to surrender, shifting to him 'the responsibility of any further effusion of blood'. 'Then there is nothing left for me to do but to go see General Grant,' said Lee, 'and I would rather die a thousand deaths.' On 9 April he sent for Grant and met him near Appomattox Courthouse; Lee, dignified and impassive in a handsome gold-braided full-dress uniform; Grant, with the inevitable cigar stump, in a faded blue private's uniform with three tarnished gold stars on the shoulder straps. The two men talked for half an hour of old friends and Mexican War days, until Lee, recognizing Grant's diffidence, reminded him of the purpose of their meeting. The terms were easy and honourable: surrender of all men and equipment, but the Confederates could keep their horses and the Army of the Potomac would provide immediately full rations for 28,000 men. So the Army of Northern Virginia surrendered.

The events at Appomattox were among the most dramatic in history: a moment of tragedy that is still recognized even by those who see in it the triumph of right. Such tragedy is drawn of contrast: it is the memory of Lee victorious which makes his final defeat more bitter, and extra poignancy comes from the knowledge that Ulysses Grant had so nearly been left to rot in the West. The contrast is accentuated by the future of the two men, Lee still serving his country (Virginia or the reunited States) in the comparatively humble position of President of Washington College, firm and clear-minded even when surrounded by the consequence of other men's follies, and Grant, elevated beyond his understanding, bumbling in the White House.

Five days after Appomattox, tragedy struck once more. At Ford's Theatre in Washington, Lincoln watched *Our American Cousin*, a broad satire on British society. A half-mad Southerner shot him in the head, mouthed the motto of Virginia, *Sic Semper Tyrannis* – a most inappropriate quotation – and was gone.

With that insane act, Booth removed the one man who could have given a happy ending to the violence. It is the custom of the average American to see the horror of the Civil War in comparatively simple terms: brother against brother, colleague fighting colleague, and then reunion. Between 1861 and 1865, American nationhood was fired and in that process completed. Yet it can be seen as the end of the American dream. American fought American and both sides took up causes which were antithetical to the principles upon which American nationhood had been founded. The South had taken up arms to defend slavery although not even the most rabid Southerner could reconcile slavery with the self-evident truth 'that all men are created equal'; the North had preserved union by force as if unable to recognize that there would have been no United States had not earlier generations of Americans fought for the right to secede from the established political entity. Lincoln might have removed the paradox. Without him there could only be uncertainty and paradox upon paradox in American political behaviour.

News of Appomattox reached Johnston and Sherman by 18 April and on 26 April Johnston surrendered. On 4 May, the small Confederate forces isolated in the deep South gave up, followed in a few days by the scattered troops west of the Mississippi. Fleeing southward, Jefferson Davis joined Johnston, but Johnston refused to continue the hopeless struggle and Davis left for Mexico. Federal troops captured him in southern Georgia on 10 May and sent him to Fortress Monroe, where Vice-President Stephens and other Confederate officials were already imprisoned.

The long dying was over.

CHAPTER 26

THE GILDED AGE
1865–96

THE issues of post-war reconstruction were both sectional and national, so interlocked as to make them virtually inseparable. The Southerner's problem was threefold: to adjust to a new set of social and economic conditions; recreate a new political society; and pick up the pieces (if he could) of a life shattered by war. The North meanwhile was concerned with consolidating victory, retaining control of the Federal government, and establishing economic and political authority over the conquered Confederacy.

No period of American history saw such a drastic revision of the character of American life as the decades 1860–90. War and reconstruction, first of all, settled the old controversy between nationalism and states' rights. Even in the South the nationalizing process continued in wartime; the Confederate government laid taxes, conscripted troops, seized private supplies and facilities, ran industries – or in other words displayed all the qualities of a centralized state. Particularly in the Northwest, where provincial loyalties were never strong, wartime nationalism continued undiminished. Proud of having survived its first test, more conscious than ever of its 'destiny', post-war America possessed, as one editor said, 'a new sense of free, quickened, national existence'.

The Civil War resolved the conflict over slavery, but in doing so created new conflicts. By eliminating chattel slavery, the war cut away the whole underpinning of Southern life. When slavery went the aristocratic leader-class went too; not for a generation could the South develop another set of leaders to replace them. Political power in the South had been vested since the founding of the Republic in a relatively small group of planter-aristocrats whose authority rested on slavery. The war swept them out of power

547

and left the majority of Southern white men without leadership, side by side with four million new Negro voters.
Without slavery the South's whole labour system required
revision. Ex-slaves, almost all of them unskilled agricultural
workers who owned no land, dreamed of owning 'forty
acres and a mule'. Planters no longer had a supply of chattel
labour nor money to hire their former slaves. 'Share-
cropping' provided a substitute. Instead of wages the worker
accepted a share of the crop, or (in the case of a tenant
farmer) the landowner furnished tools, land, horses or mules,
and the farmer furnished the toil. The system, at first a
device to attract Negro labour, was shortly extended to
whites, creating labour problems as difficult as any that ever
existed under slavery.

The abolition of slavery upset the traditional system of
race relations carefully worked out in the South over the
space of a century. Readjustment was hard for both white
and Negro. Deep-rooted prejudices simply carried over into
post-war Southern life without noticeable change. Slavery
may have ended, but not racism. By the war the North had
eliminated slavery as a social and economic institution, and
in reconstruction it did not provide any substitute. The
Negro had his freedom, but with it he gained precious few
rights. This was perhaps the most tragic aftermath of the
Civil War.

His sudden freedom confused and bewildered the Negro,
and for a year and more after the war thousands of ex-
slaves wandered over the South while the Freedman's
Bureau tried to make some order out of reconstruction. The
freedman's first hope was for economic equality, either as a
wage worker or as a farmer, but since slaves were taught few
skills or trades, his prime usefulness was as a simple labourer.
His 'forty acres and a mule' never came, and Thaddeus
Stevens's suggestion that large plantations be confiscated
and the land distributed to Negroes was quickly quashed.
Congress instead left the matter in the hands of states or
private agencies, with the result that the majority of Negroes
went into share-cropping, which served as an effective way

of keeping them under social and political as well as economic control.

The place of the Negro in American life was fixed during Reconstruction by Northerners as well as by Southerners. Opposition to slavery as a labour system did not always imply acceptance of the ex-slave as a social, economic, or political equal. Prejudice against the Negro was strong in the post-war North; the main body of Northern opinion believed as the South did, that the Negro was an inferior being, that he could never be fully assimilated into the American system, that he was best kept subordinate to the white man. Segregation, discrimination and 'jim crow' customs received the tacit approval even of such Northern liberals as Godkin of the *Nation*.

Negro leaders were cruelly disappointed at the failure of Northern reconstruction to keep its promises. Frederick Douglass commented bluntly that the Civil War simply changed the form of slavery. Booker T. Washington, who built Tuskegee Institute into a leading American Negro educational institution, developed a policy, however, that became the pattern for Negro life until well into the twentieth century. The Negro, said Washington, must not attempt to become a white man. He should learn to be a skilled workman and businessman, avoid conflict with white men over civil or social rights, and earn the respect of the nation through thrift, industry, courtesy, and morality. Not all Negroes agreed. Some of Washington's contemporaries and many of the leaders of the next generation believed that a more aggressive struggle for Negro rights might hasten their acquisition. Shortly after the turn of the century the National Association for the Advancement of Coloured People organized to press for the observance of all Negro social and civil rights as guaranteed by the Constitution and its amendments. Both philosophies of action still exist within the ranks of Negro leaders.

War had an incalculable effect on American economic life. The Civil War put the finishing touches to the Industrial Revolution, and when it closed, industrialism was firmly fixed as the primary fact of the national economy. This would have happened had there been no war, but the military conflict speeded up the process and hastened the shift from agriculture to business as the nation's principal concern. Industrial interests took full advantage of the magnificent opportunities provided by the war to gain almost everything they could possibly desire: protective tariffs, easy access to natural resources, lowered taxes, government subsidies, near-monopoly of certain economic areas. After 1865 'captains of industry' replaced farmers as the sovereign political class. The philosophy of business – the ideal of self-help, business leadership, beneficent industrialism – became the dominant ideal of American life. The agricultural interests of the Northwest were neither strong nor well organized enough to challenge the leadership of business; Southern agrarians, defeated and discredited, could no longer offer the resistance they had maintained for fifty years. So 'big business' arrived. 'The leading capitalists,' wrote John Sherman to his brother the General, ' . . . talk of millions as confidently as formerly of thousands.'

Devastated though it was by war, the recovery of the South was noticeable by the eighties. Railroad tracks twisted by Sherman's armies were relaid and new lines built into the Southwest; the old harbours of Norfolk, Charleston, Savannah, Mobile, and New Orleans hummed with trade. Where credit could be had a few enterprising manufacturers opened old factories or built new ones. Instead of shipping cotton north, Southerners began to develop their own textile industry. Coal and iron deposits in Alabama and Tennessee, neglected since the eighteenth century, were soon producing one-fifth of the nation's iron and coal, while the soft pine forests of the hill country became the basis of a new lumber industry. Tobacco crops flourished; twenty years after Appomattox North Carolina alone produced ten million pounds of tobacco a year.

Yet the South, despite its industrial advance, remained a predominantly rural and agricultural section; only one city in the South, New Orleans, exceeded 100,000 population.

Its tobacco, lumber, and textile industries were closely linked to its farms. Small farmers, poor whites, ex-slaves, and city-dwellers, shut out from the land by the planters for generations, bought up farm-plots when the cotton kings were forced to sell, eliminating the old-style thousand-acre plantation. In pre-war Mississippi few farms were less than ten acres in size; in 1870 there were 11,000 of ten acres and less, carved out of the feudal holdings of the great planters. Out of all this emerged a Southern class of merchants, farmers, artisans, businessmen, bankers, and small industrialists, the middle class the South lacked under slavery.

War stimulated Northern economy into wild activity. Congress and the states financed the construction of railroads to the tune of nearly a hundred million dollars; ten years after the war 20,000 miles of new track stretched through the West and the South. In the same ten years the number of Northern manufacturing firms increased 80 per cent. More coal was dug, more iron produced, more steel made, more metals mined, more cotton milled, more of everything manufactured than in any previous period in American history. Names like Vanderbilt, Stanford, and Gould in railroading; McCormick in farm machinery; Carnegie, Hewitt, Frick and Morgan in steel; and Rockefeller in oil, filled the headlines. The rewards of such industrial enterprise (and of plain luck) were fantastically large. Wealth influenced state and Federal legislation, founded colleges and universities, financed churches and foundations, bought art collections and filled museums. Wealth was the key to almost any kind of success, and wealth came from business and industry.

The farmer profited by the war, though never so much as the businessman. The Republican-sponsored Homestead Act opened up new land areas to the small farmer, though some of it was virtually stolen by land companies and speculators. Wartime demands for wheat and corn and beef pushed farm production to new heights; millions of acres of virgin soil made it possible; thousands of miles of new railroads brought it to market. Agricultural production doubled between 1865 and 1875, most of the increase coming from the Northwest, where Nebraska, Iowa, Kansas, Minnesota, and the Dakotas became the centre of grain and corn production. The post-war boom introduced into the national economy new and extremely complex agricultural problems of markets, credit, over-production, and tariffs that led directly to the agrarian uprisings of the nineties. But in the immediate post-war years the outlook for the farmer was rosy.

The working man probably gained least from the war. Wages rose, but prices rose faster. The return of a million veterans, added to the millions of immigrants admitted during wartime, upset the post-war labour market. As corporations grew in size and wealth the bargaining power of the individual worker (and of his union, if he had one) decreased. During the war a few skilled groups, such as shoemakers, printers, and bricklayers, organized into unions to protect themselves, without much success, against cheap labour, new machinery, and falling wages. The Republican party, anxious to pass legislation for business and industry, neglected the needs and wishes of the labouring man for the next twenty years, but not until near the turn of the century did labour become a real political force.

Post-war chaos carried within it the seeds of moral laxity and public dishonesty. Wartime spending encouraged speculation, lavish expenditure, and a consequent loosening of political morality. Money greased the ways while those profiteers and shady politicians who reaped harvests from wartime graft had no intention of going poor in peace-time. Political fortune-hunters ('carpetbaggers', because they came with a few spare clothes packed in a carpet-bag) rushed southward to take advantage of new opportunities for pocket-lining. Uneducated, without political experience, dazzled and puzzled by his new responsibilities, the Negro was ridiculously easy prey for the grafter. There were also millions of Southern poor whites who, long before the Civil War, had been virtually disenfranchised; added to these were millions of Europeans who poured into the country under loosened immigration laws. Unaccustomed to political processes and with little understanding of governmental administration, the Negro, poor white, and immigrant provided during reconstruction perfect tools for unscrupulous politicians, North and South.

The war temporarily destroyed the two-party system in American politics. The Republican Party emerged from it strong and triumphant; the Democrats ended it discredited as 'rebels', divided in the North, suppressed in the South. When the war closed and some of the seceded states began to prepare to return to the Union, the Republicans faced the prospect of losing control of state and Federal governments. Reconstruction, therefore, had to be undertaken in such a manner as to ensure Republican party supremacy for years to come. At stake were all the gains the Republicans had made during the war – policies of tariff, subsidy, taxes, currency, disposal of land and natural resources – and Republican leaders had no desire to see Southern and Northern Democrats allied with the Northwest farmer, in a position to oppose them on any of these policies in Congress. The post-war plan of the Radical Republicans, therefore, was to delay the return to the Union of any Southern state under anything but Republican control.

To accomplish this it was first necessary to disenfranchise Southern Democrats and to enfranchise the only group that could be so controlled as to guarantee a Republican vote, that is, the Negro and the poor white. The Republican plan failed to consider the explosive nature of the racial issue in the South. The poor white (like his middle-class brother) so feared the Negro that a political coalition of the two was impossible. As soon as Union military forces withdrew from the South, its whole political pattern was rearranged. The white political leaders never completely lost their vote or their influence; Democrats quickly found effective ways of disenfranchising the Negro; the poor and middle-class white man simply followed his old leaders and voted with them. The Republican party, built on Negro votes and supported by Northern armies, virtually disappeared from the South after 1876.

The Republican organization itself was less unified than appeared at first sight. Under stress of war the abolitionists, War Democrats, old-line Whigs, and Northwest free-soilers who made up the party evolved an unstable unity on one principle only, opposition to slavery. Lincoln attempted to bind it together on the issue of union, but even his consummate political skill could not keep his party entirely unified: fissures had appeared in its structure long before Appomattox. By 1863 it was clear that within the Republican party there existed a deep cleavage between Radical and Conservative Republicans, between the Wade–Stevens–Sumner group and the faction led by Lincoln. The Radicals angrily resented Lincoln's attempts to interfere with the process of wartime reconstruction and scoffed at the hope he expressed in his Second Inaugural that the Union be restored 'with malice toward none and charity for all'.

After Lincoln's death Republican leadership quickly passed to his opponents. The Radical Republicans in Congress, representing Northern industrialism, took charge of the party and of reconstruction, remaining in almost absolute control of the national government for twenty years. Meanwhile the Democratic party slowly and painfully developed into an opposition party of non-industrial, agrarian, and labour interests. Then and only then did the two-party system re-establish itself.

The scars of war healed very slowly, and encouraged intensely emotional political partisanships – 'the Solid South', and 'rock-ribbed Republican New England', among others. Sherman's march to the sea and Sheridan's ravages in the Valley are remembered to this day in parts of the South; the horrors of Libby Prison and Andersonville stockade stuck in Northern minds for years. Veterans of both armies formed solid voting blocs that influenced the strategy of politics for at least two more generations. The Union veterans' organization, the Grand Army of the Republic, became a sort of unofficial wing to the Republican party. In the South, candidates wooing the Confederate vote needed only to refer to Lee, or Jackson, or Stuart, and wave the bloody shirt of the gallant dead. There was little hope of solving intersectional political problems so long as politicians fostered animosity and bitterness. It was twenty years after the war before a Democrat entered the White House, almost fifty years before a Southern-born candidate could be elected President, nearly seventy years before a Southern state gave its electoral vote to a Republican.

The real political meaning of the Civil War is that it was a war between governments representing sections. It was not a 'rebellion' nor 'a war between the states', but a war between the United States of America, a *de jure* government, and the Confederate States of America, a *de facto* government representing eleven states of the Federal Union. The result of that conflict determined that one set of sectional interests would dominate another, that one sectional political group would direct the national policy according to its own particular theories. The Northern victory meant that Northern industrial and business interests, long held in check by a coalition of South and Northwest, were free to run the nation as they wished. Questions of land, taxes, internal improvements, industrial expansion, finances, tariffs, and the like, which had been hotly debated in Congress for years, were quickly settled as the Northerner wanted them settled. For a decade the South simply ceased to exist as a political force. The Northwest, not yet organized as a political unit, was for the time being allied with the Northeast. But in combining with the Northeast to crush the South the Northwest lost its old agrarian ally. When the South was rebuilt, and the Northwest emerged as a sectional unit with its own set of political and economic interests, the sectional conflict resumed.

When Grant and Lee met at Appomattox the trans-Mississippi West was still an empty wilderness of mountain and plain covering almost half the total area of the United States; California, of course, was a full-fledged state, and in the Pacific Northwest a hundred thousand settlers clustered on the rich coastal lands of Washington and Oregon; but between the Pacific and the eastern rim of settlement in Iowa, Kansas, Nebraska, and Minnesota there was only an immense expanse of rolling plain, the land of Sioux and Crow, Cheyenne, Arapahoe, Ute, Kiowa, Blackfoot, and Apache. By 1890 all this was changed. In that year the Census Bureau declared that the 'frontier of settlement . . . cannot any longer have a place in the census reports'. After three hundred years of westering, the frontier line was gone.

The opening of the last West was delayed by problems of climate and geography as well as by war. The farming line stopped at the 98th meridian, beyond which lay a high, arid plateau of sparse grassland reaching to the Rockies. There was little rainfall and long droughts, rivers were shallow, muddy, and unpredictable, there were no forests for timber, and the climate (from 110° in summer to 30° below zero in winter) was among the most inhumane known to man.

The most important factor in the settlement of the trans-Mississippi West was the railroad. A transcontinental rail-road had been discussed in Congress since the fifties, but was blocked annually by the Southern delegates. When secession removed their opponents, Congressional supporters of a cross-continent rail line passed an act giving the Union Pacific a charter to build westward from Iowa, and the Central Pacific a charter to build eastward from California, the two to meet at some unspecified point between. By the terms of the act the construction companies received land and timber grants and Federal loans to cover costs; in 1864 a new act increased the grants and eased the credit terms. In all the railroads received twenty-four million acres of land and sixty-five millions in loans.

Construction began in 1863, although the major portion of the work had to wait until the end of the war. The Union Pacific imported thousands of Irish labourers; the Central Pacific used Chinese coolies, hence the remark that the eastern half of the line was built on whisky, the western half on tea. The labourers lived in shanties and tents, going to work each morning on 'track trains'. When the track was down for sixty miles the crews moved to 'end of track' and set up again, with a central 'Big Tent' (100 feet by 40 feet) housing a bar, dance floor, and gambling equipment. Each new 'set-up' was surrounded by tents and shacks housing more bars, more dance-halls, more gambling quarters, and 'houses' for the women who followed the crews – some 3,000 people who formed a movable Gomorrah designed to separate the labourer from his wages every Saturday night. Today, a string of towns spaced roughly sixty miles apart still marks the path of the Union Pacific.

But the men laid track, four rails a minute. Racing with time, the crews battled over desert and mountain, dredged rivers, built bridges, fought off Indians, weathered forty-foot snows, and blasted through mountains; in one stretch of sixty miles the Central Pacific bored fifteen tunnels. On 10 May 1869 the two tracks met in Utah and the continent was spanned. Chicago celebrated with a procession seven miles long, Philadelphia rang the Liberty Bell, and the New York City Council ordered a 100-gun salute. Other lines soon pushed across the plains, the Santa Fe, the Southern Pacific, the Northern Pacific, the Great Northern.

The presence of the railroad, which sometimes preceded the settler, changed the character of the last frontier. For the pioneer there was no longer the painful, lonely period of isolation before settlement caught up with him, for the rails linked him with civilization, with markets, newspapers, magazines, politics, ideas. The whole process of evolution from empty land to territory to state was hastened by decades. The roll of states admitted to the Union after the war illustrated the speed with which this was accomplished. Nevada was first, admitted in 1864 when the Republicans believed its electoral vote might be needed. Nebraska followed in 1867, Colorado in 1876; in 1889 and 1890 North Dakota, South Dakota, Wyoming, Montana, Idaho, and

Washington entered, followed by Utah, Oklahoma, Arizona and New Mexico, the last three after 1900.

The first break into the Southwest came with the cattle-man's invasion of the plains. The Spanish had raised cattle there for centuries, but Texas ranchers after the Civil War built an empire on beef. Selective breeding produced a tall, tough animal with enormous twisting horns; there were five million such longhorns in Texas by 1865. The ranchers' biggest problem was transportation, since rail lines had not yet reached the area, but Texas cattlemen solved it in 1866 by simply driving the hardy stock across the dry lands to the Kansas railheads. By 1872 a half million cattle, destined for the stockyards of Chicago and Omaha, had made the trip via one of four trails, the Western (to Dodge City, Kansas), the Chisholm (to Abilene, Kansas), the Sedalia (to Missouri), or the Goodnight-Loving (to Cheyenne, Wyoming Territory). By the eighties the cattle kingdom reached into Colorado, Montana, Idaho and the Dakotas, but the spread of railroads, the fenced range, and industrialized methods of stockfarming changed the character of the old-style 'cow country'. The beef boom collapsed.

The golden era of the rancher and the cowboy lasted only twenty years, though it left behind a legend that still remains in American mythology – the old romantic West of tumbleweed and cowtowns, hard-shooting punchers and rascally rustlers, chuck-wagon camp-fires and sad songs of the cowboy's lonely lot. Cattle driving was a profession much followed by veterans of the Civil War. A *Tribune* correspondent, a veteran of the Union Army, wrote from Abilene, Kansas, that many of the cowboys were 'the identical chaps I first saw at Fair Oaks and last saw at Gettysburg. Some had not yet worn out all their distinctive grey clothing'. Refighting the Civil War was not the least of their pleasures, especially when they were in their cups. There were also a surprisingly large number of Negro cowboys, some of them veterans of the war and others who followed their fortunes westward after emancipation.

While longhorns roamed the plains the farmer pushed his

way into the last undeveloped areas of cheap land in the West. The invention of barbed wire in 1873 and the widespread use of the windmill helped to solve some of the problems of plains agriculture; in the mid-seventies the Federal government broke the land monopoly of the cattlemen and threw open the arable grasslands to homesteaders. Railroads, with millions of acres of land to dispose of, flooded the East and Europe with propaganda for the West, promising easy credit, reduced rail rates, good land, and every possible form of assistance. (In 1859 Horace Greeley had reported in his *New York Tribune* that the desert was swallowing rivers and eating grassland. In 1865, within weeks of Appomattox, he was urging the nation to turn from mourning and take up the free land offered to veterans by the Homestead Act. 'Go west, young man,' he wrote. The phrase was not his own, but he made it the catchphrase of westward expansion.) Land speculators, steamship companies, banks, and state and territorial governments advertised relentlessly for settlers. The Union Pacific described the Platte Valley as 'a flowery meadow of great fertility clothed in nutritious grasses and watered by numerous streams'. Minnesota bought space in Irish newspapers, hired agents in Germany, and printed pamphlets in six languages. Germans, Irish, Scots, Scandinavians, and Russians responded in droves. In less than twenty years the population of the plains states leaped from one to four millions.

A second factor in the settlement of the plains West was the post-war mining boom. Gold was discovered in Colorado before the war, though the veins ran out fairly soon and those adventurers who stayed settled into farming. In 1859 prospectors located the great Comstock lode in Nevada, which produced 340 million dollars' worth of gold and silver before 1890; the Tonopah and Goldfield strikes brought another rush, immortalized by Mark Twain, who was there, in *Roughing It*. Deposits in these areas, and in Idaho and Montana, gave out quickly, but the huge copper mines of Montana, opened shortly afterwards, kept the mining boom alive. The year 1876 saw the last real gold rush, to the Black Hills of South Dakota. Yet the mining frontier, like the cattle frontier, left its stamp on the American past. Mining camps like Hangtown Gulch, Red Dog, Silver City, and Deadwood attracted the most adventurous and desperate elements in society:

> Oh, what was your name in the States?
> Was it Thompson or Johnson or Bates?
> Did you murder your wife, or fly for your life?
> Say, what was your name in the States?

Wide-open, lawless, spilling over with riches, drunkenness, and violence, the mines created a West of dance-halls and stud games, hurdy-gurdy girls and cheap whisky, stage-coach robbers and sudden hangings, a West that still lives in the legends of 'Wild Bill' Hickok and 'Calamity Jane' Canary.

The pioneer farmer, the rancher, and the miner intruded into the last major area left to the Indian, transferring to the plains the same Indian–white conflict that marked the settlement of the East a half-century earlier. Originally intended to serve as a huge reservation belonging to the Indian tribes alone, the plains-land, the Department of the Interior decided, must be opened to settlers and the Indians herded into smaller, separate reservations, one for each tribe or family of tribes. Friction immediately developed. Sioux uprisings in Minnesota in 1862 and Arapahoe and Cheyenne massacres in 1864 brought the problem to the attention of Congress, which appointed an investigating committee in 1865. Indian affairs had been handled since 1849 by the Bureau of Indian Affairs in the Department of the Interior, but as a result of the investigation, which revealed a shocking amount of inefficiency and graft, Congress in 1869 created a Board of Indian Commissioners to advise the Department. In succeeding years the Department assumed greater and greater responsibility for the Indian, though his treatment was often far from merciful. The Dawes Act of 1887, intended to break tribal ties, teach the Indian agriculture, and educate him in the white man's culture, inaugurated the modern policy of merging him into American society.

The major points of contention between Indian and white were land and buffalo. The prospect of nomadic tribes holding thousands of tillable acres was too much for land-hungry settlers to bear; successive treaties, purchases, and grants gradually stripped the red man of his land, pushing him into desolate, sub-marginal areas. The buffalo was the staple of plains-Indian economy, providing the tribes with food, shelter, clothing, and fuel. But fifteen million buffalo were a constant menace to farmers and ranchers. The spread of railroads restricted the buffalo grazing grounds, while professional hunters like Buffalo Bill Cody killed thousands for meat, hides, and fertilizer. After 1872 hunters killed two million buffalo a year, and by 1885 the Western herds were almost completely gone.

It was not easy to make peaceful, reservation-dwelling farmers out of a savage race of hunters. Detachments of army regulars, charged with pacifying the tribes, found them formidable opponents, poorly armed though they were. Mounted on tough Spanish ponies and led by such expert warriors as Sitting Bull, Crazy Horse, Chief Joseph, Black Kettle, Red Cloud, and Geronimo, the Indians were a match for any cavalry in the world. The last serious fighting followed the Black Hills gold rush which sent thousands of miners and settlers into Dacotah Sioux territory. Here Custer, lured into ambush by Sitting Bull, lost his life and his command at the Little Big Horn. Sporadic outbreaks occurred until the eighties, when Geronimo, the Apache, was captured and exiled to Florida. Few Americans, reviewing the history of American–Indian relations, could disagree with President Hayes's statement of 1877: 'Many, if not most, of our Indian wars have had their origin in broken promises and acts of injustice on our part.'

The lot of the Indian in the United States has been hard. Some six thousand Indians were killed by the United States Army between the Civil War and the closing of the Frontier.

Tragic enough, but insignificant when compared with another statistic: in 1960 there were half a million Indians in America, only half as many as at the time of the landing at Jamestown. Three centuries of war played its part; disease and liquor did more. Epidemics in the seventeenth and eighteenth centuries, when diseases new to the New World were introduced into a tragically vulnerable population, decimated the tribes of the East and South. The passing of the buffalo, his source of food and clothing, broke the power of the Plains Indian and drove him into the white man's reservations. Just before the Civil War there were something like thirteen million buffalo on the Great Plains; a quarter of a century later the hunter's rifle had destroyed all but two thousand. Full legal rights and citizenship were not granted to him until 1924, and his assimilation into the pattern of American culture is still a problem. Some tribes, clinging to the old customs, remain alien islands in a white sea; others have adopted white ways and have achieved full equality. It is encouraging to note that of all racial groups in the United States, the Indian is now increasing in number fastest of all.

The settlement of the last West left permanent marks on American life. The pioneer plainsmen, reinforced by tradition of ranch and mining camp, were and are men of an individualistic turn of mind. Their rowdy politics, noted by every foreign observer since Bryce, was the source of every major radical or liberal movement up to 1924. Life on the prairie was a hard and challenging experience, with no place for the faint-hearted. The fertile soil could make a man rich in a few years, if all went well, but grasshoppers, drought, Indians, storms, and a murderous climate tried the soul. Like all pioneers, the plainsman had an eagerness for change, an unshakable faith in himself, and great hopes for his future. This was the heritage of the farmer's frontier. There was another West that left another heritage, the West of action and adventure, of violence and romance. This West too has become firmly established in American folklore as a native tradition of the Round Table, in which the Lone Ranger, Hopalong Cassidy, and Roy Rogers (before them 'Deadwood Dick', Tom Mix, and William S. Hart) perform as gallantly as Lancelot or Robin Hood.

'I shall do nothing in malice,' wrote Lincoln. 'What I deal with is too vast for malicious dealing.' Lincoln's plan for Southern reconstruction was based on his contention that since the Confederate states had never really left the Union, reconstruction was simply a matter of readjustment rather than re-entrance. His Amnesty Proclamation of 1863 and his handling of the loyal West Virginia and Tennessee governments revealed that the general principles of his policy were to make the readjustment as rapid and easy as possible, and to reconstitute the Union as it was before secession. If one may judge from Lincoln's acts and speeches during the war, his notion of reconstruction involved three basic ideas: the Southern states themselves should make their own rules for re-entering the Union, within reason; re-establishment of the Union should be accomplished as swiftly as possible; there should be a minimum of disenfranchisement of the Southern white man and a slow, gradual extension of suffrage to the freed Negro, who was, however, to have other civil rights at once. This programme should be Presidentially directed, cautiously, conservatively and humanely administered. 'We must extinguish our resentments,' said Lincoln, 'if we expect harmony and union.'

The Radical Republicans had a wholly different concept of reconstruction. In contrast to 'Mr Lincoln's policy of tenderness', men such as Thaddeus Stevens of Pennsylvania, Zach Chandler of Michigan, Charles Sumner and Ben Butler of Massachusetts, Boutwell and Wade of Ohio, Davis of Maryland, Colfax and Julian of Indiana, and Stanton, Secretary of War, favoured a more sharply punitive programme for the seceded states. Their aim was threefold: destroy the political power of the old Confederate leaders; place reconstruction under the control of Congress; devise the machinery of reconstruction so that Republican dominance of the South might be maintained. The Radicals protested that the Confederate states had 'committed suicide' by secession and had lost all rights as states; they were to be treated, as Stevens said, simply as 'conquered provinces'. Thus a Massachusetts abolitionist meeting resolved in 1866, 'The true doctrine of reconstruction is, that defeated rebels have no civil or political rights, which loyal men are bound to respect . . .' Harsher by far than Lincoln's Amnesty Proclamation, the Radically-sponsored Wade–Davis bill of 1864 provided that fifty per cent of a seceded state's inhabitants must take a loyalty oath before a civil government could be established within it. When this figure was reached the state's constitution must then be amended to repudiate any Confederate debts, abolish slavery, and refuse the vote to any Confederate official or officer of colonel's rank or above. Lincoln's pocket veto of this bill called forth Congressional cries of 'studied outrage' and 'insult'. With the death of Lincoln, the last barrier to complete Radical control of reconstruction was removed, or so they believed.

For more than half a century, historians tended to explain Reconstruction as an effort by vindictive men to humiliate a gallant, beaten opponent, leading to the view of the period as a 'tragic era' of retaliation upon the Confederacy by a victorious North. True, the South's slaves were freed; some of its leaders were briefly imprisoned and deprived equally briefly of political rights; attempts were made to extend the franchise and other rights of citizenship to improperly qualified freedmen. There were injustices and hard feelings and mistakes, to be expected in the light of postwar emotions, but the 'tragic era' myth has been highly overstated. It should not be forgotten that Southerners who had borne arms against the United States were serving in Congress and in the Cabinet ten years after Appomattox, and that Confederate officers who fought against the United States Army not many years later held high command posts in that same army. 'Rarely in history,' writes historian Kenneth Stampp of the Reconstruction years, 'have the participants in an unsuccessful rebellion endured penalties as mild as those

Congress imposed upon the people of the South, and particularly upon their leaders.'

Nor is it accurate to interpret Reconstruction as an attempt by the Radical Republicans to give over their governments to irresponsible and corrupt Negro and white leaders for their own exploitation and gain. Yet in retrospect it is reasonable to suppose that the Radicals and their supporters were moved by something more than desire for revenge or political power. Some may have been so motivated, but to generalize thus is to forget the blazing fervour of the anti-slavery crusade and the deep faith in freedom that buttressed it. Some Northerners thought, not without reason, that the war had been fought to abolish slavery and that the terms of peace must be such that the old slaveholding master class could never again dominate the South. Fortune-hunters with graft in their hearts went South after 1865, but there were also schoolteachers, lawyers, doctors, ministers and plain people who went with an earnest desire to help make the Negro a man. Ostracized, hated by the Southern white, faced with real physical danger, these Northern idealists are all too often lumped with the carpetbagger or promoter. Reconstruction was a time of moral idealism and conviction as well as self-seeking. Out of its travail came the Fourteenth Amendment, which gave the Negro citizenship, and the Fifteenth, which gave him the right to vote, and with them the ultimate promise of his equal civil and political rights which, in the twentieth century, may well come to fruition.

Andrew Johnson, Lincoln's successor, came from a poor North Carolina family and grew up in Tennessee as a Democrat. A tailor by trade, Johnson was almost illiterate at twenty. His wife taught him to read and write, and by his own vigour and drive he hammered out a political career in Tennessee as Congressman, Senator, Governor, and Vice-President. A rough, obstinate, choleric man, the South he knew was the poor man's South and he hated the cotton aristocrats with undying venom. Although he considered himself a states' rights man in the tradition of Calhoun, he was also a strict constructionist who could find no Constitutional justification for secession, which he condemned as treason. Throughout the war Johnson breathed fire against the Confederate leaders, and the Radicals called on him a few hours after Lincoln's death to assure him of their support. 'By the gods,' said Ben Wade, 'there will be no trouble now in running the government.'

But Johnson soon made it very clear that he intended to follow his own personal plan of reconstruction and not that of Congress. His Proclamation of Amnesty of May 1865 was a blow to Radical hopes. Johnson called for the abolition of slavery in the South, the repudiation of Confederate debts, nullification of ordinances of secession, and disenfranchisement of certain classes of Confederate supporters including – significantly – all those worth $20,000 or more. Though he was as bitter as the Radicals in his denunciation of the Southern planter, Johnson envisaged a wholly different rearrangement of Southern society. The Radicals hoped to build on Negro votes a South under Republican control. Johnson hoped to destroy the power of the old aristocracy and raise instead a middle-class agrarian South controlled by the small farmer, merchant, and artisan. War Democrat though he was, Johnson disliked Northern industrialists as much as he loathed slave-holding aristocrats. The Civil War, thought Johnson, gave men of his own kind a chance to take control of the South. He had no objection to Negro suffrage, but as a states' rights man believed that only the states could bestow the vote on the freed slave. His programme, therefore, was immediately attacked by the Radicals in Congress, who demanded that the Negro be enfranchised by Federal decree and that harsher punishment be inflicted on the seceded states.

Johnson's hot temper and obstinacy worked against him. He slowly lost public and political support until it seemed clear that the Radicals could put through their own plan against his opposition. The Joint Committee of Congress on Reconstruction, controlled by Radicals, in 1866 proposed the fourteenth Amendment to the Constitution, rolled it through Congress, and sent it to the states for ratification. This amendment, conferring citizenship on Negroes and disenfranchising Rebel leaders, satisfied all Radical demands except immediate votes for the freedmen. When the elections of 1866 returned a Radical majority to Congress Johnson was doomed. Not only the fourteenth Amendment, but also the fifteenth (which gave the Negro the ballot) were passed and with them a new plan of reconstruction. The South was divided into military districts, each governed by a Federal general. In each district the military authorities registered eligible voters. Ex-Confederates and others of doubtful politics were rigidly excluded from the registration lists while Negroes were enrolled by day and tutored in Republican politics at night. In all the ex-Confederate states (except Georgia, where the numbers of each race registered were about equal) registered Negro voters outnumbered white.

By giving votes to obedient Negroes and withholding them from influential white men the Radical Republicans, supported by the Federal armies, exercised complete control of the new Southern state governments. Not only did they succeed in beating Johnson, but they very nearly threw him out of the Presidency. In 1867 Congress passed the Tenure of Office Act, making it a misdemeanour for a President to remove civil office-holders without Senate consent – a slap at Johnson's authority. Johnson put the law to the test by dismissing from the Cabinet Edwin Stanton, one of his most vicious critics, whereupon the Radicals in the House voted to impeach Johnson for 'high crimes and misdemeanours'. He was tried before the Senate, sitting as a court as prescribed by the Constitution. Conviction failed by one vote.

The 'carpet-bag' legislatures of the reconstructed Southern states were among the most corrupt that American history has ever known. Yet their corruption must be placed in focus with the general decline of political morality that followed the war, for what happened in the South was but one phase of what happened elsewhere. Carpetbaggers' graft paled into insignificance beside the thefts perpetrated by their Northern brethren. The Tweed Ring stole six million dollars in six years in New York City; similar political machines in Pennsylvania, Massachusetts, and elsewhere lagged not far behind. Political corruption was neither new not confined to carpetbaggers or Negro legislatures.

The newly-enfranchised ex-slaves elected both Negroes and white men to Congress, filled the state offices, wrote and passed reams of new legislation. Some of them were intelligent and able men; others were ignorant, unaware of their responsibilities and lacking in any concept of public morality. The so-called 'black legislatures' passed vengeful laws against former Confederates, forbade racial segregation, organized and controlled state militia, legalized exorbitant taxes, and authorized fantastically wasteful expenditures. In these things the Negroes were skilfully guided by renegade Southerners ('scalawags') and Northern carpetbaggers who reserved for themselves the choicest plums. From seven Southern states four Governors, ten Senators, and twenty Representatives were Northerners.

Yet these 'reconstructed' state governments put some good laws on the books. When the newly-enfranchised Negroes were given capable leadership and the cooperation of intelligent and sympathetic Southerners, the state governments they formed were good. They abolished property qualifications for voters and widened the basis of suffrage; they established better free schools, provided new penal codes, and opened up new areas of social and educational legislation. The constitutions developed by the 'black legislators' remained unchanged for nearly twenty-five years after their adoption, and subsequent revisions amplified and expanded rather than changed their principles. A majority of Southern white men, of course, regarded Radical policies as a 'barbarization of the South' and found the Negro vote a bitter pill to swallow. Appeals to Congress and to the North fell on deaf ears, and meanwhile the Republican party, depending on its Negro vote, wrote and ratified the new state constitutions and petitioned Congress for the reentry of the seceded states. By mid 1868 seven of the ex-

Confederate states were back in the Union. Only Virginia, Mississippi and Texas remained outside.

After the effort to impeach Johnson the Radical Congressmen ran the nation without much regard for 'the dead dog in the White House', as Thad Stevens gleefully called him. In preparing for the presidential campaign of 1868 the Republicans made a deliberate appeal to the veterans' vote, denouncing Johnson as a traitor and the Democrats as the party of secession. Their convention unanimously chose U. S. Grant as its nominee, with Schuyler Colfax, a dependable Radical, as his running mate. Grant was a wise political choice. His name and record were on every tongue, his popularity with veterans was obvious; he had never touched nor had he been touched by politics, he was a man of simplicity, directness, and common sense. The phrase 'Let us have peace' in his letter of acceptance was platform enough for a nation weary of bickering. The Democrats endorsed Johnson's programme of reconstruction but not Johnson. For President they chose Horatio Seymour of New York, an able conservative, and keyed their campaign to an attack on Republican corruption.

In spite of Grant's popularity his margin of victory was much smaller than the Republican leaders had anticipated – a popular majority of only 300,000 – but the success of the radical reconstruction programme lay in the fact that the Negro vote in the South contributed 600,000 to Grant's total. Radicals remained in control of both houses of Congress by small majorities, though the death of Thad Stevens robbed them of their most capable leader. With Congress and the Presidency firmly under control, the Radical Republicans in 1868 set out to establish their supremacy so completely that it could never again be challenged.

Grant was utterly unaccustomed to civil responsibility and temperamentally incapable of providing the nation with the leadership it needed during a critical period. The army had taught him that loyalty to subordinates was to be highly valued; in politics, party loyalty made Grant dependent on second-rate men and often he found himself defending crooks and thieves. He left office as he entered it, a silent, unassuming man who never understood that he had been the instrument of the worst elements ever to appear in American government. After his first year in office he relied almost exclusively on the advice of his Radical Republican friends who ran the party and the nation much as they pleased.

Not long after his inauguration Grant approved the re-entry into the Union of Texas, Virginia, and Mississippi, once they had endorsed the fifteenth Amendment and the Negro ballot, but it is hard to find any other positive accomplishment in his first administration. The Republican party, committed to the support of industry and business, passed all the legislation it wanted. Investors who had purchased war bonds with depreciated wartime currency saw Congress vote to pay them off in hard money. The wealthy were happy to see the income tax disappear. Railroad and land corporations took the pick of available public lands. Congress repealed all wartime taxes on industry but kept the high wartime tariffs. Financial legislation, written at the behest of Eastern banking groups, favoured a hard-money policy over the protests of debtor and agrarian interests. Business and industry, seeking favourable legislation on local, state, and national levels, spent millions for lobbies, gifts, bribes, and 'influence'. Grant's administration was shot through with corruption. The Navy Department accepted bribes from crooked contractors; speculators bribed Department of Interior officials out of millions of acres of public lands; Treasury department officers overlooked tax bills for a fee and took gifts from tax delinquents; customs-houses were full of shady characters. 'The Republican party,' said one Republican with a conscience, '. . . is today the most corrupt and debauched political party that ever existed.'

The carnival of corruption that marked Grant's first term disgusted many Republicans, who grouped together in 1871 as 'Liberal Republicans' to fight against 'Grantism'. When it became clear that the Radicals intended to nominate Grant for a second term so that they could continue as before, these Liberals decided to split the party. At their own convention in Cincinnati the Liberals disavowed Grant and his cohorts and nominated Horace Greeley. Although Greeley had been one of the most energetic pre-war anti-slavery editors and was a strong believer in high tariffs, the Democrats at their Baltimore convention, realizing that only a coalition of Southern and Northern Democrats with the dissident Republicans could beat Grant, endorsed Greeley and the whole Liberal programme. But their plans foundered. After a violent campaign, Grant remained in the White House with a large electoral majority.

When Grant took the oath of office in 1872 it seemed that the Radical Republicans had accomplished what they had set out to do. They had complete control of the executive and legislative branches of the national government, absolute mastery of about twenty states, and a closely-held bloc of a half-million Negro votes in the South. Even the coalition of Liberals and Democrats had failed to unseat them; Grant carried all but two states in the lower South and swept the Northwest. But the Liberal revolt was a sign that Grant and his friends misread. The American electorate could stand only a little more.

The second Grant régime gave the public more than enough. In rapid succession a series of scandals broke in Washington. A small group of stockholders in the Union Pacific railroad (including some Congressmen) organized a construction company called the Credit Mobilier, which systematically milked the railroad of huge sums. Exposed by the New York *Sun*, the 'Credit Mobilier affair' ruined a good many Republican reputations. Other exposures followed with unpalatable regularity. Congress voted itself a fifty per cent salary increase, retroactive for two years, that caused so much public indignation that it was hastily repealed. Grant's Secretary of the Treasury resigned after irregularities in his department were disclosed. The new Secretary uncovered a 'Whisky Ring' of distillers who had defrauded the government of millions in taxes, and the trail of graft led to Grant's own private secretary. No sooner had the 'Whisky Ring' been exposed than the Secretary of War resigned to escape prosecution for selling posts in the Indian Service. Grant himself was never touched by suspicion, although he accepted favours a more circumspect President would have refused. To the end Grant considered the disclosures of graft within his administration as political propaganda and attempts to persecute his friends.

The exposure of corruption in Washington and the returning strength of the Democratic party combined to undercut Radical power in the Congressional elections of 1874. A serious depression, beginning in 1873 and lasting nearly five years, convinced Republicans and Democrats alike of the danger of playing fast and loose with fiscal policy and did a great deal to undermine public confidence in business leadership. Using depression and corruption as their issues, Democrats captured a majority of seats in the House and control of the more important committees. The truth was that the Northern voter at large was beginning to understand that the Radical Republican policy of favouring business and punishing the South was costing the nation more than it was worth. Many Northerners hoped, after 1865, that the Reconstruction governments would open the South to economic and industrial development. Instead the Radicals seemed interested only in exploiting the South for political purposes. So long as organized corruption, supported by military force, existed in the South, the area remained a very poor risk for Northern investment.

Reports of the excesses of the carpet-bag legislatures crept into the Northern press, and Horace Greeley, after a Southern tour, wrote that the area was plagued with 'decayed aristocracy and imported rascality'. Pressure on Congress forced the passage of the Amnesty Act of 1872, which in effect restored political rights to all but a few of the Southern white leaders, on whom Northern investors relied for economic reconstruction. Southern politicians slowly reorganized the Democratic party, took over control of state after state, threw out carpetbaggers and scalawags, and passed laws to prevent or discourage the Negro vote. By 1876 only three states (Louisiana, Florida, and South Carolina) remained in the hands of carpet-bag legislatures, kept in power by Federal troops.

The Amnesty Act was one sign of the approaching end of Radical Reconstruction. Negroes themselves, now learning to play politics, after 1870 showed increasing dissatisfaction with their Republican guardians, for it was noticeable that white carpetbaggers and scalawags took the better offices and the larger share of the loot. And both Democratic and Republican leaders realized that they were playing with fire in balancing white against Negro in politics. One alarmed politician observed that if this 'vast mass of ignorance' ever 'combined for any political purpose, it would sweep away all opposition the intelligent class might make'. Thoughtful men, he added, feared that 'the ignorant voters will in the future form a political party by themselves as dangerous to the interests of society as the communists of France'. Labour unions were on the upswing in the Northeast, and dissatisfied Northwestern farmers were busily organizing the Grange. If these 'ignorant masses' combined, the political consequences would indeed be disastrous to 'the intelligent class'. Faced by this prospect, Northern leaders were willing to modify the methods of Radical Reconstruction.

Despite the shift of Northern public opinion, the dissolution of Radical dominance would have been impossible without a revolt within the South. While the Negro showed restlessness, the Southern middle class and poor white showed more. Johnsonian reconstruction promised to turn over the South to them, but instead the Radicals based reconstruction on their traditional enemy, the Negro. Corruption in carpet-bag legislatures and rising taxes hurt the small property holder as well as the large; political offices and power went not to the native white farmer but to the scalawag or carpetbagger. In desperation this large Southern group turned for leadership to the old aristocracy, not because it wished to re-establish pre-war class alignments in politics, but because it could combine neither with the Republicans on the one hand nor the Negro on the other.

Southern conservatives and ex-Confederate leaders learned their political lessons swiftly. They feared both Negro and poor white rule, and hoped to control the vote of both groups. Meanwhile the cost of Radical rule drove them to desperation. Virginia's state debt rose from sixteen to forty million dollars in five years; South Carolina's from six to twenty-five millions; Texas, from nothing to four millions. Tax-burdened and disenfranchised planters therefore adopted extra-legal means to defeat Radical aims, control the Negro, and effect an alliance with the poor white and small farmer by appealing to his anti-Negro prejudice.

The instrument at hand was the Ku Klux Klan, a secret order formed in Tennessee in 1866 by a small group of Confederate veterans. Dressed in ghostly white costumes, Ku Kluxers frightened Negroes by appearing to them as the 'spirits of dead soldiers'. When the political advantages of the order were recognized, it quickly spread throughout the South, encouraged by planters and small farmers alike. General Nathan Bedford Forrest was appointed 'Grand Wizard' of the Klan 'Empire', while in each community armed Klansmen, riding at night, whipped unruly or 'uppity' Negroes, beat Union soldiers, and threatened carpet-bag politicians. By 1870 several similar organizations appeared, with the result that the pro-Republican white man or Negro risked real danger if he refused to 'keep his place'. Armed bands patrolled parts of the South day and night; the more violent elements of the organizations did not hesitate at torture, arson, and murder.

Far from being the 'holy crusade' drawn by later Southern novelists and historians, the Klan was a vicious and despicable organization. In using it to deprive the Negro of his rights and to regain political dominance of the South, Southern leaders deliberately set poor and middle class white man against Negro by appealing to the lowest form of race prejudice. Congress struck back at the Klan with drastic laws and Federal troops. After some eighty-two convic-

The Gilded Age 1865–96

tions in South Carolina much of the violence stopped, but the Klan itself continued to exist as a deadly means of controlling the Negro under the same banner of 'white supremacy' that had been the chief stock-in-trade of the old pro-slavery aristocracy. By supporting the Klan, conservative upper-class leaders were able to drive a political wedge between the Negro and the white man, but its legacy has been violence, race prejudice, and the development of intimidation as a fine art in parts of the South.

The Republicans prepared for the campaign of 1876 with some misgivings. At their Cincinnati convention they constructed a platform pledging the party to a thorough housecleaning and a sweeping reform of the Federal Civil Service. For its candidate the party chose Rutherford B. Hayes, Governor of Ohio, an honest though pedestrian politician who had given his state clean government for three terms. The Democrats, meeting at St Louis, attacked the Republicans at their most vulnerable points – corruption and carpetbag reconstruction. To oppose Hayes they chose wealthy Samuel Tilden, governor of New York, the very arch-priest of reformers. With Tilden the Democrats hoped to carry a majority of the large Northern states as well as most of the South.

Early returns indicated that Tilden had won, since he took New York, New Jersey, Connecticut, and Indiana in the North in addition to much of the South, although results in South Carolina, Florida, and Louisiana remained in doubt. Without these three states, Tilden had 184 electoral votes, one short of the number needed for election. But with the nineteen electoral votes of the questionable states, Hayes would have 185 or exactly enough for victory. Since Republicans controlled the canvassing boards in these three states, it was not difficult to change Tilden majorities into Hayes majorities. Senator Zach Chandler of Michigan, the Republican national chairman, therefore announced that Hayes had won.

The Constitution, however, provides that the electoral vote shall be counted before a joint assembly of Congress.

Democrats held a majority in the House, Republicans in the
Senate. Both voted investigations that came to nothing.
Democrats, convinced that Tilden had been legally elected
President, threatened to filibuster and delay the electoral
count if the matter were not settled by Inauguration on
4 March 1877. Many citizens, North and South, expected
fighting to break out if Hayes were declared the winner.
Some Congressmen carried sidearms, and Abram Hewitt,
the Democratic national chairman, wrote later that Democratic war veterans in fifteen states were ready to march on
Washington to install Tilden by force. A Congressional commission, however, heard the arguments of contesting counsel
in late February 1877, accepted the Republican electoral
votes from the three doubtful states, and made Hayes the
nineteenth President of the United States.

There was no violence. A compromise had been arranged.
Republican leaders agreed to withdraw troops from the
South, to allow the two remaining carpet-bag governments
(South Carolina and Louisiana) to expire, and to give up
control of the Negro, all in return for Hayes's election. The
Southern Democrats in turn agreed to abandon Tilden and
the Northern wing of the party, to accept Hayes, and to
open the South to Northern economic penetration, in return
for complete political control of the South. This was not a
quick bargain, hurriedly arrived at, but the result of negotiations started months before the election. Railroad and
industrial interests in the North had already conferred with
Southern political leaders on the substance of the compromise; the disputed election simply crystallized it. The
truth was that the North was weary of the old crusade. The
old leaders, Stevens, Garrison, Sumner, Weld, and the rest
were dead or silent. The new leaders, men like Hayes,
Blaine, Conkling, Garfield, in fact the whole continuity of
Republican leaders down to McKinley, were more interested in profitable, practical politics than in reconstructing a new South on the foundation of the Negro and poor
white.

The result of the Compromise of 1876 was a 'Solid South'

under conservative Democratic rule, and the re-establishment of white supremacy as the dominant principle of Southern life. Henceforth the South was to be under 'Bourbon' domination; 'niggers' and 'woolhat boys' were back in their ante-bellum place within the Southern system.

President Hayes was as good as his word. In April 1877 Federal troops left South Carolina and Louisiana. Their carpet-bag governments collapsed and Radical reconstruction was ended.

The Radicals were successful in doing what they set out to do, to keep the Republican party in control of the Federal government for as long as possible after the close of the war. But they were successful in nothing else. In the long run Radical reconstruction solved none of the problems it had posed and created several new ones. It failed to provide a way for Negro and white man to live peacefully together as equals. The politically-motivated 'Negro policy' of the Radicals and the sincere but hasty activities of the abolitionists made racial antagonisms in the South if anything stronger than before. Some of the bitterness was an inevitable consequence of emancipation, to be sure, but much of it was the product of Radical reconstruction policy. The white Southerner found it impossible to plan constructively for the future so long as the Negro remained outside his control, and after reconstruction he spent so much energy on the task of permanently subjugating the Negro that he neglected the South's most pressing problems.

The industrialization of the South, blocked for years by the planters, was accomplished under Northern direction by Northern capital, reducing the South to colonial status and fastening on it a colonial psychology. The activities of the Klan and other organizations made the South tolerant of rule by force and of disrespect for law. Respectable, intelligent Southerners for generations since have often found it difficult, in the face of this tradition, to discourage and punish violence. And no matter what agreements or gestures were made, the hard fact remained that antagonism between North and South was stronger in 1877 than it had been at Appomattox. Radical reconstruction accentuated the after-effects of war and delayed serious consideration of important national issues. For years Northern politicians found it more profitable to quote Lincoln and cry 'Rebel!' than to face issues squarely and honestly. Southern politicians found it equally useful to shout 'Damyankee!' and 'nigger!' at election time. Solutions to fundamental national and sectional problems had to wait until the wounds left by war and reconstruction healed.

'The world after 1865,' wrote Henry Adams, 'became a banker's world.' The American continent offered more natural resources than any country except Russia, and for the man of ability and energy, the rewards for exploiting them were so huge as to stagger the imagination. Carnegie's annual income exceeded twelve and a half million dollars; his total fortune reached 1,000 million; the cheque that he received for the sale of his share of United States Steel totalled more than the entire value of the United States in Washington's day. Rockefeller amassed slightly more than fifteen hundred million dollars. The Guggenheim interests took 2,000 million from the Montana copper ranges. Vanderbilt II inherited a hundred million dollars and added ninety million to it in six years. Morgan's fortune equalled Carnegie's, while those of Gould, Harriman, Stanford, and Huntington (railroads), Stewart (real estate and stores), Swift and Armour (meat-packing), and Duke (tobacco) were not far behind. In 1890 an economist calculated that about 125,000 men controlled between them at least half the national wealth.

The most significant and far-reaching development in American business during the late nineteenth century, and the greatest factor in the amassing of huge personal fortunes, was the development of monopoly. Businessmen soon found, in the intense competition of business life, that the best way to treat a dangerous competitor was to combine with him, thus cutting production costs, controlling prices, fixing profits and suppressing rivals. 'To say that competition is the life of trade,' remarked one businessman in 1880, 'is to repeat a mouldy old proverb.' Manufacturers accordingly formed associations by gentlemen's agreement, but as one industrialist remarked, the participants were not always gentlemen. The 'pool', a popular device in the seventies, was especially well adapted to railroads. By the time the Interstate Commerce Act of 1887 banned agreements and pools, they were already being replaced by the more efficient trust, a device by which the stockholders of competing or related firms agreed to deposit controlling portions of their stocks with a board of trustees in return for trust certificates. The Sherman Anti-Trust Act of 1890, despite the vigour of its language, was difficult to enforce and easily beaten in the courts. The trust reached its highest development in Rockefeller's Standard Oil Company, which eventually controlled four-fifths of the national oil output, while the combined Morgan and Rockefeller interests held control of 341 major firms. By 1904 there were 319 trusts capitalized at 7,000 million dollars or more.

To compete and survive in businesses of such imperial magnitude required a man's entire time, energy, and brains. Thus the 'captain of industry' emerged, a peculiarly American type, ruthless and savage in his business dealings, a daring, imaginative, aggressive entrepreneur. To him business made its own law. He felt no particular social responsibility, recognized no obligations inherent in his possession of tremendous economic power, yet to indict him by hindsight is to indict his age, for his aims and ethics were merely those of contemporary society.

By 1865 no code had been developed for business enterprise on a grand scale, since no necessity for one had ever existed. The sudden appearance of the transcontinental corporation with its huge maze of intricate relationships caught both business and the public unawares. The possibilities of reward were so great, the struggle for survival so intense, that traditional concepts of ethics were lost in the chase. Nor were there laws on the statute books to establish legal control over the industrial juggernauts. When such laws were written business itself, allied with politics, for a long time wrote them to its own advantage. The age itself not only condoned but admired the 'cuteness' and 'slickness' of the shrewd operator, as in earlier days buccaneering and piracy were considered semi-respectable and enviable occupations. What one might object to in the behaviour of the millionaire was equally a part of the *ethos* of the poor clerk, who dreamed that one day he himself would be a millionaire.

The general public, while condemning its methods and decrying its ethics, admitted big business's accomplishments. Whatever the transgressions of the 'robber barons' (and they were many) some of them vastly improved the American standard of living by providing masses of goods at a reasonable price – if at enormous profit. Giant industries, by introducing what they called 'scientific management', effected great savings in manufacturing processes. The substitution of exact knowledge for trial-and-error, of intelligent planning for traditional know-how, of calipers for rule-of-thumb, changed the face of industry the world over. To the mass-production technology of Eli Whitney and his contemporaries, post-war industry added the last ingredient – organization and integration of factory methods – and put into the hands of the ordinary man the tools of better and more leisurely living. Along with the sins of nineteenth-century business this must be counted on the side of virtue.

Nor was there any reason in the light of contemporary opinion why wealth and economic power should not be concentrated in the hands of a few. *Laissez-faire* was engrained in the American way of life, inherited not only from eighteenth-century economics but from pioneer experience. Franklin's 'Poor Richard' maxims expressed an indigenous American tradition. Resourcefulness, self-reliance, the ability to stand on your own two feet and carve out a fortune with nothing but your hands and brain, these things Americans admired. Emersonian self-reliance was never meant to produce captains of industry, but it helped to justify them.

The wealthy men of the period did not consider themselves to be bad men or 'robber barons'. They believed that if individuals of exceptional ability were encouraged to develop the national economic resources the whole of society would benefit, even though a few did enrich themselves enormously in the process – otherwise, where was the incentive? They assumed that it was the function of government to aid and protect business, to guarantee an industrial prosperity that inevitably percolated down to all the people and to some degree enriched them all. Great wealth was a divine gift, a mark that God had chosen the recipient as a steward for his worldly goods, to be used for the benefit of less capable men – an echo of the Calvinist justification of wealth a century earlier. 'Great private fortunes,' remarked Senator Ingalls of Kansas, 'are inseparable from high civilizations. All the great enterprises that exalt and embellish existence and ameliorate the conditions of human life, come from the conception of money in the hands of the few'.

Thus justified by Calvinist theology, frontier tradition, and eighteenth-century individualism, the prevailing ideology of business found additional support from the popular acceptance of Darwinism, especially as worked out by Darwin's disciple Herbert Spencer, who exerted a tremendous influence on American thought. The struggle for existence, said Spencer, was natural and good; social or legislative action limiting or preventing it was unnatural and bad. The theory of the survival of the fittest, operative in nature, applied in the same way to economic life. The rich man got his fortune because he had the abilities required for success in the competition for wealth; the poor man was simply less well adapted, less fit. Both deserved what they got. The millionaire, said William Graham Sumner, the Yale sociologist, was 'the finest flower of a competitive society'.

The Darwinian point of view seeped into the thinking of people who had never heard of Darwin, but who found in the popular conception of his theory a satisfactory justification of current practices. It was very clear, said Francis Walker in 1890, that competition was 'the force to which it is mainly due that mankind has risen from stage to stage of intellectual, moral, and physical power'. The Spencerian philosophy of competition and survival was taught in the colleges, explained in the journals by respectable writers, accepted by the responsible and educated members of society. It was, in effect, the *raison d'être* of the age.

The mass of Americans accepted this attitude toward business, yet with a certain uneasiness. Social Darwinism, particularly in its economic manifestations, seemed to deny the basic tenets both of Christianity and the natural rights tradition of the Declaration. A good many citizens, looking at 'Diamond Jim' Brady or Jay Gould, doubted if they were really the 'flowers of society' that Sumner called them. It was hard to think of J. P. Morgan as a divinely chosen custodian of cash. 'Mister Dooley', Finley Peter Dunne's fictitious Irish commentator, pointed out in the Chicago papers that John D. Rockefeller was 'a kind iv society f'r the prevention of croolty to money. He looks afther his own money and the money iv other people. He takes it and puts it where it won't hurt thim and they won't spoil it.' The billionaires who constituted the 'fit' – had they won in an open, fair 'struggle for survival', or had the rules been rigged? Some of those who were 'eliminated' in the struggle for survival were unwilling to give up without a protest. Since they had votes, they might win politically the victory they had failed to win economically. Others, like Henry Adams, viewing the shameless buying and selling of democracy in the market-place, thought that big business was digging its own grave. The 'Gilded Age' philosophy of business had its sceptics from the time of its inception.

Criticism of the prevailing pattern of business centred about two main arguments. First, its critics claimed, the captains of industry often failed to recognize their responsibilities to society and to assume definite obligations for its progress. Although a few, like Carnegie and Rockefeller, offered socially-conscious theories of wealth, their policies seemed to have little influence on the actual operation of business. Second, there was a growing fear that the divorce of wealth from responsibility might create industrial feudalism, a 'plutocracy' that could finally dominate American life. Thus Henry Ward Beecher wrote in 1871, 'We are today in more danger from overgrown pecuniary interests – from organized money – than we ever were from slavery.'

The influence of wealth on politics provided an illustration. Businessmen of the period asserted that the role of government in economic life was that of umpire, charged with enforcing the minimum rules of fair play to prevent embezzlement, thievery, and abrogations of contract. Price-fixing, minimum wage or maximum hour laws, or laws governing working conditions or labour relations, were unnatural interferences with the operation of *laissez-faire* forces. Yet at the same time business understood that it needed favourable legislation to operate as it wished: tariffs to reduce foreign competition, subsidies for railroads, franchises and contracts to control markets. In order to obtain the right kind of government, businessmen were forced into politics. They needed an ally who could handle affairs for them on the political front, while they gave undivided attention to economic warfare, and the political boss was their man.

The 'boss' was not new to American politics. He had appeared before the large corporations and will probably outlast them, but in the late nineteenth century he found in the businessman the perfect natural alliance. The boss needed funds and patronage for his machine; the businessman needed expert political assistance and was willing to pay for it. Both profited by the exchange. The great bosses served as middlemen who collected contributions from business to see that the right laws were passed (and the wrong ones were not) by placing sympathetic legislators in office. As a matter of insurance, businessmen often contributed to both parties, although by most the Republican was considered to be the safer investment. The real danger lay, as critics pointed out, in the fact that both the boss and the businessman were working for personal rather than for public interest. 'Our political system,' wrote Charles Francis

Adams in 1870, 'cannot much longer sustain the conflict with corporations. Modern civilization has created a class of powers which are too strong for the control of our government. How long can they develop together?'

The businessman needed not only the assistance of the politician, but also the help of the courts. Interpretation of the law was as important to him as the law itself. During the late nineteenth century, and after, the fourteenth Amendment to the Constitution proved to be an invaluable aid. 'No State,' the wording of the Amendment runs, 'shall make or enforce any law which shall abridge the privileges or immunities of citizens of the United States; nor shall any State deprive any person of life, liberty, and property, without due process of law . . .' In the minds of one portion of the committee that wrote the amendment the purpose was to protect the rights of the freed Negro. Others saw in it also a means of protecting business from attacks by hostile state legislatures. The definition of the term 'person' was left to the courts to decide. Over a period of some twenty years the courts determined that the term included corporations and any person connected with them; any state law that deprived a corporation or stockholder therein of property – that is, wealth or profit – was in conflict with the fourteenth Amendment. With both government and law firmly on its side, business by the nineties had entrenched itself into a seemingly impregnable position in American life.

The pre-Civil War national labour movement, never strong, had disintegrated in the depression of the 1830s. A few craft unions, chiefly printers, bricklayers, and train-men, were formed in the fifties, and in 1866 representatives of a number of craft unions organized the National Labor Union, which opened its membership to anyone except 'gamblers, saloon-keepers, bankers, lawyers, and stockbrokers'. The N.L.U. scattered its energies in a diffuse programme, and failed to weather the depression of 1873. Of the thirty unions it represented, only eight or nine survived. Despite the collapse of the N.L.U., labourleaders were convinced that some kind of national labour organization was inevitable. As industry spread, labour spread with it, so that low wages or poor working conditions were no longer local but national problems.

Prospects for a successful national union were not bright, for labour was confused and split, uncertain of programmes or principles. Under mass production labour had lost much of its class-consciousness and pride. The production line made the old craftsman obsolete, killed pride of workmanship, and fixed the workman himself as simply a step in an operation. Every labourer was sure that his job was only temporary, that he would soon make his pile and go into business for himself – and it happened just often enough to convince the workman of the truth of the 'shirt-sleeves to millionaire' myth fostered by Horatio Alger and Andrew Carnegie. With the development of the transcontinental corporation the worker, organized or not, found no one to whom he could carry his problems. He no longer knew his employer by his first name – or perhaps by any name – and had no bargaining power as an individual.

The need for a collective bargaining instrument that the N.L.U. failed to provide was immediately filled by a new organization, the Knights of Labor. Founded in 1869 as a semi-secret society, the Knights, under the skilful leadership of Terence V. Powderly, hoped to establish 'one big union for all'. But like the N.L.U. the Knights diverted their energies into a battle for public ownership of public utilities, cooperatives, and other popular reforms. In the mid eighties they won one strike against the railroads, lost another, and in 1886 struck the McCormick Harvester Works in Chicago. A bomb, exploded by persons unknown, killed seven policemen at a mass meeting in Haymarket Square, Chicago. Seven suspects, all anarchists, were quickly apprehended and tried by the courts in an atmosphere of blind anger. Four were executed, one committed suicide, and two received life sentences, to be pardoned later by Governor Altgeld of Illinois. The Knights never recovered from the after-effects of the Haymarket riot and thereafter slowly declined in membership and influence.

The American Federation of Labor, founded in the year of the Haymarket troubles and still in existence, followed a much more conservative policy than either of its predecessors. Rejecting the 'one big union' idea of the Knights, the A.F.L. built a federation of separate, semi-autonomous craft unions, leaving the mass of unskilled workers unorganized. Samuel Gompers, a London-born cigar-maker who served as its president from 1886 to 1924, saw it grow to half a million members by 1900. Gompers knew the work of British and German labour reformers by heart, believed strongly in the capitalist system, and was convinced that labour could make its greatest gains within its framework. Avoiding third-party politics, he committed the organization to the principle of 'Reward your friends and punish your enemies, regardless of party', a position that with a few exceptions the A.F.L. has steadily maintained to the present day, 'We have,' said one Federation leader, 'no ultimate ends, but only immediate ends.' Using collective bargaining techniques with the strike as a last resort, the A.F.L. pressed for an eight-hour day, higher wages, health and sanitation regulations, and child-labour laws.

The decades 1870 to 1900 were turbulent, restless years, marked by violent conflicts between capital and labour. The working-man's attempt to organize on a national scale naturally aroused tremendous opposition from industry. The right of business to operate without hindrance on its own terms, to form its own protective associations, and to organize lobbies to influence government went unquestioned; if labour organized for similar purpose it was considered 'unAmerican, illegal, and indecent', in the words of one industrialist. Corporations therefore proposed to 'pull up root and branch the unAmerican institution of organized labor as it is at present conducted', a movement culminating in the founding of the National Associations of Manufacturers in 1895.

Organized labour had other problems besides the unremitting hostility of business leaders. The twenty million immigrants who poured into the United States between

1870 and 1900 provided industry with a backlog of unskilled, tractable labour, while at the same time thousands of freed Negroes filtered North to the factory towns. The immigrant and the Negro labourer were difficult to organize, poorly educated, and usually happy to accept low pay, long hours, and unstisfactory conditions. The general effect was to vitiate labour unions and depress working standards. Labour problems were also inevitably tied to politics and law. The power to regulate such things as wages and hours was, until recent years, chiefly lodged in the states. With the legal aspects of most labour disputes lying within the jurisdiction of local and state courts, labour unions might gain significant victories in one section of the country while losing in another. Until the Federal government found ways to establish control over nation-wide industry, the labour union had to fight the same battles over and over in the states against a powerful coalition of legislative, judicial, and industrial forces and their whole arsenal of weapons – the lock-out, the injunction, the strike-breaker, the blacklist, the 'yellow dog' contract. It is ironic that the Sherman Anti-Trust Act was used first by the courts to break labour unions.

The farmer too had his troubles. Between 1860 and 1900 four million acres of new land went under the plough, tripling farm acreage. Agricultural production boomed. The yield of wheat, for example, went from 173 million bushels in 1860 to a spectacular 522 million bushels in 1900, a rate of increase matched by corn, pork, beef, and other products. There were several reasons for this post-war agricultural revolution. The push of population West opened up vast areas of fertile plain, linked to the East by the railroads. As the production of cotton, corn, wheat, and cattle increased, the centre of agricultural production swiftly shifted westward, leaving behind in the East a dislocated farm economy. Farm boys and girls streamed to the cities, leaving many rural communities stripped of young people. One song of the period, protesting against the urban movement, went plaintively:

The city has many attractions,
But think of its vices and sins;
When once in the vortex of fashion,
How soon the course downward begins!
Stay on the farm, stay on the farm,
Though profits come in rather slow.
Stay on the farm, stay on the farm,
Don't be in a hurry to go.

The new Western farms had all the advantages of mechanization. New ploughs and harrows, reapers, twine-binders, corn-planters and huskers, threshing machines, cream separators, and other devices made it possible for fewer men to produce more on larger farms. The labour required to produce one bushel of corn, for example, declined from four hours to less than fifty minutes; one corn-sheller replaced fifty men; four men and a threshing machine did the work of four hundred. The introduction of the steam tractor and, later, the gasoline motor, simply carried mechanization further.

The agricultural revolution drastically changed the position of the farmer within the national economic structure. Though farm production expanded, industrial production increased faster, and agriculture, once the mainstay of the American economy, found itself rapidly pushed into second place. Expansion brought new problems, many with political implications. Farming became a commercial venture involving a large investment in land and machinery and a staple crop to sell in a competitive market. The self-sufficient yeoman, who raised everything he needed, disappeared; in his place came the agricultural capitalist, fitted into a complex national and international economic pattern, tied to banks, railroads, industry, markets, credit, money. After Britain repealed the Corn Laws in 1846 and Western Europe followed, the American farmer became an exporter of food for the world, swiftly affected not only by Eastern market fluctuations but by crop failures in India or a drought in Egypt.

The changing face of American society was reflected in the increased activity of urban life after the war. The expansion of industry, the flood of immigration, and the dislocation of rural society in the Eastern states accelerated the growth of cities. Mechanized farming released workers for the factories; factories tended to locate in populated centres; railroads encouraged the growth of factories and made distant markets accessible; consolidation of industry encouraged railroads, factories and cities. The trend toward the city was not a uniquely American phenomenon, but a result of the Industrial Revolution; both London and Paris grew after 1850, but the growth of American cities was more spectacular. New York quadrupled its size before 1900, Philadelphia tripled, and the rate of increase in midwestern urban centres eclipsed theirs. Chicago, the western rail centre, was twenty times larger in 1910 than in 1860. Cleveland, Detroit, St Louis, Minneapolis, Toledo, and other cities in the Lake area grew almost as swiftly. Smaller towns grew too, until by 1910 thirty per cent of the nation lived in towns of 8,000 or more. Urbanism introduced a new and sophisticated attitude into American culture and marked a sharp departure from the moral and social patterns of rural life. It produced, among other things, a change in the temper of American society, emphasizing the widening rift between classes, placing extremes of poverty and wealth, power and weakness, side by side; mirroring all the racial, social, economic, religious, and political conflicts that beset a new and complex industrialized society.

The surge of population to the cities strained the fabric of urban government. Successive waves of immigration, each larger than the last, threw into the cities large blocs of foreign peoples of widely varying national, racial, and social backgrounds and traditions. Uneducated, innocent, confused, the immigrant was often shamefully used. He provided easily controlled blocs of votes that gave the city boss a heaven-sent opportunity. Subjected to both economic and social discrimination, the new arrivals huddled in slums, until by the eighties New York City housed more than 200,000 people in sub-standard tenements. Diseases like cholera, smallpox, and typhus periodically struck terror into city society, and crime increased alarmingly.

The problems of the cities were not entirely insoluble. The humanitarian impulse, always strong in Americans, prompted a great many efforts at reform: clinics, orphanages, playgrounds, almshouses, settlement houses, social service agencies. Boards of charities in the populous Eastern cities attempted to coordinate charitable work for greater efficiency, and state boards of health, established after 1870, helped to control standards of food and housing. And there were certain profits to be gained from social concentration and cooperation: better schools, museums, art galleries, libraries and theatres than small towns could afford. Most of all, the city provided an opportunity for women to escape some of the rules imposed on them by nineteenth century *mores*. The number of women gainfully employed in cities more than doubled between 1870 and 1900.

From the first founding of the colonies Americans had believed, with Jefferson, that education is the foundation of 'a happy and prosperous people'. New Englanders established Harvard almost as soon as they landed; Franklin and Jefferson founded universities; and in the early nineteenth century the United States committed itself firmly to free public education for children of any race, sex or creed. The traditional faith of the American in education was nowhere better illustrated than in the tremendous educational expansion of the post-Civil War years. The number of schoolchildren rose from five million in 1865 to seven million in 1870 to fifteen million in 1900, illiteracy meanwhile declining from 17 per cent to 11 per cent. The advance was qualitative as well as quantitative. States established teacher-training institutions and certification requirements for teachers. The older private academy was rapidly replaced by the public high school, offering a wider variety of subjects and attracting more students. By the close of the century the pattern of public school systems, still customary in the United States, was established at eight years of elementary school beginning at the age of five or six, plus four years of secondary or high school.

There were also changes in higher education. Both state and private institutions underwent remarkable developments under the direction of a particularly able group of university presidents, among them Eliot of Harvard, White of Cornell, McCosh of Princeton, Porter of Yale, Angell of Michigan, Gilman of Johns Hopkins, and Bascom of Wisconsin. If universities were to be opened to the masses, then a university education must be chartered in terms of its meaning to the masses. The rigid 'classical curriculum' gave way to a broader elective system that included 'bread and butter' as well as cultural courses. State universities, notably that of Wisconsin, stressed education for intelligent citizenship and emphasized service to the state. Technical and professional schools of mining, forestry, agriculture, metallurgy, and engineering appeared in profusion. The proliferation of courses in American universities and the willingness of those institutions to consider almost any skill as fair game stems directly from the ingrained American idea that education is a mass process.

Since the Civil War the United States has developed an elaborate and expensive system of public education, ranging from one-room country school to city high school of 10,000, and from tiny church college to urban university of 40,000 students. The influence of the public school at least equals that of the church in American society, and in some communities surpasses it. Rich men have given millions to the schools; states have poured tax moneys into them; the most imposing public buildings in the United States are those of the urban high schools and the great universities. While the American system of public education has not always lived up to the expectations of its most sanguine adherents, neither has it failed to attain some of its more important objectives.

The influence of the schools in the period was augmented by other means of education, notably libraries and the lyceum and Chautauqua systems. By 1900 eighteen states and many large cities had authorized the use of taxes for the support of libraries, while philanthropists such as Carnegie spent millions in building libraries in small towns and remote communities. The lyceum, a popular New England institution, sent lecturers into every state, where for a small sum an isolated community might hear the nation's best lecturers. The Chautauqua, a Methodist version of the lyceum, replaced it before the turn of the century and lasted until the twenties, when it was killed by the movies and radio.

Late nineteenth-century American religious thought was much affected by developments in the physical and biological sciences. Spencer's volumes found a relatively wide reading public in America; Tyndall and Huxley made lecture tours of the United States in 1872, 1873, and 1876, and Spencer himself arrived in 1882. The new scientific concepts, especially Darwinism, all tended to cast doubt on the validity of established religious beliefs. Theologians of every sect met them with determined resistance, until one by one, as the dispute continued, liberal ministers found a compromise between science and religion. Henry Ward Beecher of New York, a preacher of national reputation, summarized the liberal position by declaring that the Darwinian hypothesis was nothing more than 'the deciphering of God's thought as revealed in the structure of the world'. Nevertheless, despite general adoption of Beecher's point of view, some sects in rural and isolated areas refused to compromise. Within Methodist and Baptist ranks there were many who disliked the new trend. A sizeable number of 'fundamentalist' or 'holiness' groups, determined to keep the old faith pure, split off from the parent churches. Several states passed laws (still existent but inoperative) to prevent the teaching of evolution as fact in the public schools, and as late as 1925 the famous Scopes trial in Tennessee upheld the legality of such legislation.

The contest between science and religion was only one aspect of the unrest, uncertainty, and doubt that disturbed the spiritual equanimity of the age. The effects of a long war, of rapid shifts in social patterns, and of revolutions in industry and agriculture, unsettled the times. 'The props of society,' wrote one commentator in 1889, 'all seem to be coming loose', while people searched for some pillar of emotional and spiritual stability. The number of churches increased at a rate far exceeding the growth of population; a Methodist hymn boasted

> All hail the power of Jesus' name!
> We're building two a day!

The Baptists, who did particularly energetic missionary work among Negroes, spread even faster than the Methodists. Presbyterians made steady gains, while in the cities large and wealthy churches housed famous preachers; Beecher drew three thousand every Sunday to his Plymouth Congregational Church in Brooklyn, Phillips Brooks of Boston's Trinity was known the nation over.

Yet the figures concerning the growth of church membership during the late nineteenth century were deceptive. Organized churches, some believed, did not meet real social and spiritual needs, and failed to provide a positive Christian philosophy of life for a materialistic, industrial age. They were 'affected with moral astigmatism', said one critic; they 'are social clubs pure and simple', said another, 'preaching a faith wholly unrelated to the problems of contemporary life'. One reaction against the established churches took the form of an evangelical revival (in reality a third Great Awakening) which swept the American middle and lower classes. Of the many evangelists of the period the most successful was undoubtedly Dwight L. Moody, who with his choir leader Ira Sankey left a trail of fire across the country in the seventies and eighties. Moody preached an old-fashioned theology applied directly to daily life, filling a popular need unsatisfied by either Beecher's fashionable theology or the hellfire preaching of the 'holiness' sects. Others followed Moody, notably Billy Sunday, an ex-base-ball-player whose career was brief but brilliant, and by 1914 the wave of emotionalism in religion had receded. The touring evangelist with his tent is still a familiar part of the American religious pattern, but no fourth Great Awakening has yet appeared.

There were, of course, other indications that the orthodox churches did not meet contemporary religious needs. Spiritualism, which had enjoyed some popularity in the pre-war years, revived in the seventies. Madame Helena Blavatsky organized the Theosophical Society in 1875, merging spiritualism with East Indian philosophy. The most powerful of the supernaturalist churches founded at this time was the Church of Christ (Scientist) established by Mary Baker Eddy in 1879, attracting thousands of converts from the urban upper middle class, where its strength still lies. An opposite reaction was represented by Colonel Robert Green Ingersoll, who in the tradition of Tom Paine declared himself a free-thinking agnostic. Known as 'Royal Bob' to his friends and 'Devil Bob' to his enemies, he preached a socialized Christianity, independent of churches, applied directly to contemporary problems. His speeches and writings, distributed widely in Haldeman-Julius's 'Little Blue Books' (priced at ten cents), profoundly affected the thinking of his and the next generation.

The most important religious movement of all, however, was the trend towards 'socialized Christianity'. Floods of young men and women coming to the cities needed spiritual guidance. The Y.M.C.A., imported from England in 1851, expanded from 200 chapters in 1861 to 2,000 by 1900. Its sister, the Y.W.C.A., grew almost as fast. The Salvation Army, another British import, began work among the urban poor in 1879, while settlement houses appeared in the cities. In fashionable churches ministers leaned more and more toward what they called 'applied Christianity', later named the Social Gospel. Believing that the church must meet the problems of an urban, industrialized age squarely, Social Gospellers hoped to 'substitute the law of Christian love in the sphere of social and industrial relations for Spencerian competition'. Christianity, as the Reverend Charles Sheldon phrased it, 'is simply putting the teaching of Christ to work in everyday life'. The Social Gospel movement was not confined to any particular sect, although a majority of its adherents were probably Congregationalists and Methodists. Meanwhile, the American Catholic hierarchy, after offering resistance during the eighties, gradually swung toward the leadership of liberal Cardinal Gibbons, while Pope Leo's encyclical of 1891 gave official support to Catholic social reformers.

The shift of emphasis from theology to society that characterized religious thought from 1870 to 1900 had a lasting effect on American church life. It reactivated many Protestant sects, providing them with new energy with which to withstand the assaults of science, industrialism, doubt, and lethargy. The Social Gospel was both an effective counter to the businessman's 'gospel of wealth' and an antidote to the popularity of Social Darwinism. Socialized Christianity, with its demand for immediate Christian solutions to social problems, led ultimately to parallel demands for social legislation, and in turn to politics. Thus it was entirely appropriate that the supporters of Theodore Roosevelt's Progressive party in 1912 should choose 'Onward Christian Soldiers' as their campaign song and that prominent ministers should lobby for minimum wage laws. The character of the American churches themselves was also radically altered. Many large urban churches today, and some in smaller towns, are social as well as religious institutions, with bowling alleys, gymnasia, concert series, group discussion rooms, athletic and social programmes, nursery schools, and vocational classes.

The postwar years marked a period of rather swift transition in American culture. By the eighties the great thinkers of the pre-war Golden Day were dead or scattered; many of those who survived were perplexed by a new industrialized, urbanized America they could not understand. An ageing Walt Whitman believed that America had failed to realize its promises; an embittered Mark Twain, who was victimized by it, called his a 'Gilded Age' of sham; a gloomy Ambrose Bierce wrote, in 1881, 'We are a nation of benighted and boasting vulgarians'. Henry Adams, a disappointed and disillusioned man for whom his society could find no place, pilloried it in his *Education*, which was not in fact published until 1917, in time for the critics of the sophisticated twenties – Charles Beard, Lewis Mumford, Thomas Beer, Vernon Parrington, and others – to build their interpretation of their fathers' generation upon it.

There was some truth, of course, in the indictment; there was much that was brassy and tactless and crude in the latter decades of the nineteenth century, yet it was not all that way. The era had tremendous vitality, as yet unharnessed to ideals, and a great store of rough, creative power. Its heroes were often the doers and fighters, men who did things in a big way – Buffalo Bill, 'Diamond Jim' Brady, John L. Sullivan the 'Boston Strong Boy', J. P. Morgan Sr, – not the thinkers and artists of a fading New England. But the last two decades of the passing century were by no means sterile and unproductive. That they were years of tumultuous social and economic change has tended to obscure the fact that they were also years of extraordinary cultural accomplishment – in painting Winslow Homer, Thomas Eakins, and Albert Ryder, for example; in architecture Louis Sullivan, Stanford White, H. H. Richardson, and young Frank Lloyd Wright. The so-called 'gilded age' saw the founding of the New York, Philadelphia, Boston and Chicago symphony orchestras, of the Metropolitan Opera, of great art collections, museums and libraries. An age that produced philosophers such as William James, Josiah Royce, and John Dewey, or social theorists of the calibre of Lewis Morgan, William Graham Sumner or Lester F. Ward, or novelists such as Henry James, Stephen Crane, William Dean Howells, and Mark Twain himself, could not be called sterile. There was more true metal beneath the gilt than its assayers knew. The beginnings of modern American culture, and the first recognition of some of its problems, lie here.

The period's most vital poet, its only one of stature, was Walt Whitman, whose *Leaves of Grass* exploded on the literary scene in 1855. An astonishing book, it was filled with contradictions, audacities, exhortations, sermons, and some of the most sensitive lyric verse ever written in America. He wanted, Whitman said, 'to put a *Person*, a human being (myself, in the latter half of the Nineteenth Century) in America freely, fully, and truly on record'. In it was his vision of science, industrialism, love and democracy all linked into one mystic circle of poetry, reflecting what he considered to be the 'oceanic, variegated, intense practical energy' of his era; in *Leaves*, too, Whitman evolved his own personalized form of bardic free verse, drawn with eclectic carelessness from everywhere past and present. In the long introductory poem, 'Song of Myself', he struck a pose for the public to see – Walt (not Walter) Whitman, rebellious, egocentric, aggressive, unrestrained, embracing the whole of life like a lover and identifying with all mankind, claiming the individual as the centre of reference for all things, shouting his message forth with a 'barbaric yawp'.

Whitman seemed to be the prophet-poet America had long called for, the native genius who would give reality to the declaration of independence from 'the courtly muses of Europe' which Emerson and Longfellow had both proclaimed. Emerson wrote to him, 'I greet you at the beginning of a great career', and Thoreau likened him to a young buffalo crashing through the thickets of tradition. In his manners and in his poetic manner Whitman drew himself as frank to the point of uncouthness, virile, adventurous, eager and self-confident, the kind of personality that every American not tainted with Europeanism imagined as his own. Yet Whitman was not all the defiant, purely original American rebel he claimed to be. He took from all that had gone before him and as he pleased – from the King James Bible, Shakespeare, Italian opera, sentimental balladry, Homer, even from the sound of the sea he heard as a boy on Long Island. His trumpet-calls for the priority of the individual, his extravagant claims for the importance of 'I', were simply climatic expressions of the older Romantic egoism. And Whitman the nationalist, who wished to exalt the common man as a creation finer than any creator, could not hold himself to political boundaries in his search for the wonders of ordinariness:

My spirit has pass'd in compassion and determination
   around the whole earth,
I have look'd for equals and lovers and found them ready
   for me in all lands,
I think some divine rapport has equalized me with them

he wrote, early in his career as a poet, and, on his deathbed,
'More and more it comes to the fore that the only theory
worthy our modern times for great literature, politics and
sociology must combine all the best people of all lands, the
women not forgetting'.

The freedom of his verse, the vastness of his projects, his
zest for physical expression and, not least, his delight in the
inventory, the loving pleasure which he found in rolling out
American names, like a Grand Central announcer turned
suddenly rhapsodical: 'Otherways there atwixt the banks of
the Arkansaw, the Rio Grande, the Neuces, the Brazos, the
Tombigbee, the Red River, the Saskatchewan or the Osage,
I with the spring waters laughing and skipping and running.'

In all these things Whitman could persuade himself that
he was essentially American. He was close to the truth when
he wrote, 'I know very well that my *Leaves* could not possibly
have emerged or been fashion'd or completed, for any other
era than the latter half of the Nineteenth Century or any
land than democratic America.' He believed that Europe
was feudal and, therefore, damned, and in this shared the
convictions of so many of his countrymen. He, like most of
his countrymen, was an incurable individualist who yet
believed in the virtues of community and cooperation. He
was of his time and his country in his fervent patriotism and
his unshakeable optimism – for America – though in this his
work has been much misunderstood, for it was not only the
achievement of America but also the great American
promise which inspired Whitman's faith, and he tried to
instil into his countrymen a sense of the tragedy of unful-
filled expectations:

Long, too long America,
Travelling roads all even and peaceful you learn'd from
   joys or prosperity only,

But now, ah now, to learn from crises of anguish, advancing,
    grappling with direst fate and recoiling not,
And now to conceive and show to the world what your
    children en-masse really are,
(For who except myself has yet conceiv'd what your
    children en-masse really are?)

Whitman's task, as he saw it, was 'to articulate and faith-fully express . . . my own physical, emotional, moral, intellectual and aesthetic Personality in the midst of the momentous spirit and facts of current America', that is, to be an American man of his times, and a representative man as well. As his poetry matured it lost some of its earlier aggressive nationalism and self-centredness, moving from the arrogant self-confidence of *Song of Myself*, through the quieter mysticism of 'When Lilacs Last in the Dooryard Bloom'd' and 'Out of the Cradle Endlessly Rocking', to the maturity of 'Passage to India'. Whitman worked out of the old poetic tradition into the new. He transformed some of the optimism and vitality of Emersonian transcendentalism into a credo he hoped to fit to a machine age, which paid him little homage for doing it. The critics liked better the traditional sterilities of Bayard Taylor and Richard Watson Gilder; the crowd read the folksy rhymes of Will Carleton and James Whitcomb Riley.

The prospect in prose was different. A variety of good novelists appeared after the Civil War, many of them willing to strike off in new directions. The 'nay sayers', discouraged at the trend of the times, turned back toward a genteel tradition in poetry, prose and criticism, tacitly admitting the failure of the intellectual democracy that Whitman celebrated. The land of Thoreau and Hawthorne could pro-duce nothing more than a succession of minor poets and a few writers of gentle prose like Sarah Orne Jewett and Mary Wilkins Freeman, though it did contribute a distinguished body of critics like Barrett Wendell, C. E. Norton, and later Irving Babbitt and Paul Elmer More. But fiction elsewhere showed surprising energy. The war focused authors' eyes on the variety and richness of the materials available in the newly unified nation, leading to the exciting discovery of 'local color' regionalism. Bret Harte's stories of California opened the Far West to exploitation, Mary Murfree discovered the mountaineers, Edward Eggleston wrote of rural Indiana, George Washington Cable of Louisiana Creoles, Harriet Beecher Stowe of the 'Old Town Folks' of Maine, Hamlin Garland, until he became lost in reminiscence, wrote powerfully realistic stories of Midwestern farm life, and Mark Twain spun the finest local colour stories of them all in *Roughing It, Life on the Mississippi,* and the classics *Huckleberry Finn* and *Tom Sawyer.*

The great literary argument of the period centred about 'realism' in the novel. The frontier 'tall tale' and the humorous, crude folk literature it produced were in themselves forerunners of a native realistic tradition, while the influence of science, industrialism, and urbanism turned artists more directly to fiction dealing with 'actuality' or 'real life', both of them terms hotly debated by critics. Garland, an early convert to realism, proclaimed himself a 'veritist' dealing with truthful pictures of life, and Twain himself, as early as 1868, hoped to be regarded as an 'authentic' writer. Harold Frederick and Joseph Kirkland called for realistic exactness in the novel, but it was William Dean Howells who made realism respectable and who, from his vantage point as editor of the *Atlantic,* defined and encouraged it. Howells, an early admirer of Tolstoy, drew back from the less pleasant implications of realism, preferring what he called 'the realism of the commonplace', of the normal and decent, in his own numerous novels.

Another group of novelists, however, took their cues from contemporary science and industrialism as well as from Darwin, Spencer, Nietzsche, Zola, Hardy and Haeckel. The 'naturalistic' novels they wrote portrayed a deterministic, fatalistic, pessimistic world in which brute Nature controlled the destinies of helpless men. Frank Norris seized on the epic of wheat and its interrelations with railroads, big business, and politics, and left behind him at his early death a truncated trilogy of *The Octopus* and *The Pit.* Stephen Crane, declaring that 'sentiment is the devil', shocked the nineties with *Maggie: A Girl of the Streets*, following with the superb *The Red Badge of Courage* and a collection of lean, terse, beautifully-plotted short stories. Theodore Dreiser, the youngest of the group, published *Sister Carrie* in 1900 only to have it immediately suppressed. Perhaps the purest naturalist of all, Dreiser kept the tradition alive until it was picked up nearly thirty years later by Hemingway and others.

The fundamental cleavage in the American literary tradition was most aptly illustrated by the two major novelists of the post-war period. Samuel Langhorne Clemens, 'Mark Twain', owed not only his literary theory but his entire attitude toward life to the American West. He was born in Hannibal, Missouri, on the Mississippi river, one generation removed from raw frontier, and as printer, soldier, miner, reporter, unlucky businessman, steamboat pilot, and traveller, he sampled almost every aspect of the raucous life of his era. His early work, done in the 'tall tale' tradition of frontier humour, blossomed into the magnificent local colour novels of his middle years; then, shifting to satire in the nineties, he moved late in life toward Swiftian strictures such as *The Mysterious Stranger*. An uneven artist, with a strong sense of the poetic and the melodramatic, Mark Twain created in Tom, Huck, Huck's pappy, Colonel Sellers, the Connecticut Yankee, and others a galaxy of characters whose place is secure in the native tradition. He was strongly nationalistic, reflecting his Western backgrounds; Europe he rejected as effete and feudalistic, lashing out at priests, kings, remnants of tradition, and anti-democratic tendencies wherever he saw them. The savagery of *Joan of Arc*, the bitter passages of *A Connecticut Yankee at King Arthur's Court*, and the aggressive Americanism of *Innocents Abroad* are items in a long tradition of anti-European bias in American culture.

Yet in American culture there has always existed a counter force, a strong pull back toward Europe, a retracing of steps towards the society just left. Mather, Byrd, and Edwards felt it in colonial times; Irving, Longfellow, Emerson, and the rest were drawn toward England and Europe in the nineteenth century; the magnet of the old countries drew Howells and others after the Civil War. Henry James represented the late nineteenth-century version of this return to an older civilization in search of values and codes not quite lost in the departure from the old and not quite established in the new. James was born into a wealthy New England family, his father a philosopher-friend of Emerson, his brother William a psychologist and philosopher. After the age of twelve Henry James made his home in Europe; he travelled and studied abroad, returning to the United States at ever longer intervals for ever briefer stays. In 1876, at thirty-three, he settled abroad, first in Paris, then in London, where he remained to become a British subject in 1914.

James felt the pull of Europe powerfully; it took 'an old civilization', he said, 'to set the novelist in motion'. His early work was concerned with an analysis of the contrasting cultures of Europe and America, as in *Daisy Miller* and *The American*. As time passed he became less and less American and more the conscious artist, ultimately perhaps the most consciously artistic novelist who ever wrote. Vitally interested in providing a sensitive and complete impression of life, he rejected contemporary naturalistic and realistic generalizations about literature and art. His later work was increasingly delicate and intricate, reaching its height in *The Ambassadors*, *The Wings of the Dove*, and *The Golden Bowl*.

The fluidity of post-war America's concept of civilization was apparent in other cultural areas besides literature. American philosophers, educated in the idealism of Emerson, stumbled like the theologians on the hard block of Spencerian naturalism, and like them attempted to find an epistemology suited to the world and society around them. William James typified the struggle of the new philosophy to bridge the gap between the old idealism and the new science. Working outward from an idea expressed by C. S. Peirce of Harvard, James evolved a philosophical system called 'pragmatism', whose sole aim was to provide a guide for action in an age that sorely needed guides. Active, practical, confident, pragmatism represented a distinctively American point of view. An intellectual position, said James, is true if it will work, and if it will work, it will be consistent with other workable theories. The philosopher therefore tests old or new theories against the standard of workability, retaining or rejecting them in a sort of naturally selective process. John Dewey of Columbia University extended pragmatism into 'instrumentalism', which he defined as converting ideas into useful tools by which men can achieve a practical end in life. The effect of pragmatism and instrumentalism, popularized by James's and Dewey's followers, was to drive philosophy out of a corner into a direct preoccupation with contemporary differences and antagonisms. The so-called 'practical cash-value' test of ideas fitted a materialistic age. Its pervasive influence on American thought and institutions is attested by thousands of instinctive pragmatists in contemporary business, law, education and social affairs who found in James and Dewey the guides they searched for.

As realism was to literature and pragmatism to philosophy, so functionalism was to architecture. From the popular Greek Revival buildings of ante-bellum America architecture turned to a confused eclecticism. H. H. Richardson's Renaissance style briefly dominated the scene, while Richard Hunt's French chateaux, built for millionaires, appeared in the cities. McKim, Mead, and White, who designed more public buildings than any other firm in America, favoured massive classicism; libraries, railroad stations, university and government buildings the breadth of the United States reflected their influence for two generations. The functional trend developed when Louis Sullivan proclaimed in the eighties that a building should represent its purpose, that a structure was organic, adapted to its use and environment. Sullivan's ideas (themselves an adaptation of Darwinism) found numerous followers as time passed, among them Frank Lloyd Wright, and the classic, Gothic, baroque, and Byzantine structure began to disappear. One obvious result was the 'skyscraper', an exclusively functional structure necessitated by the rising cost of urban property and the need for office space in the cities.

Art and sculpture displayed no consistent trends during the period. Post-war painters moved away from the Germanized 'Hudson River' school popular in the fifties, strongly influenced by French impressionism on the one hand and by realism on the other. Whistler and Sargent, both expatriates, carried on the French tradition; Homer, Eakins, and others pointed toward the 'revolt' led after 1900 by John Sloan, George Luks, and George Bellows. The Civil War placed hundreds of statues in city parks, done in the popular sentimentalized classic style of the fifties. Not until the appearance of St Gaudens and French, late in the century (both influenced by Rodin) could American sculpture be said to have come of age. In neither art nor sculpture was there evidence of a native tradition or of an 'American school'.

The pattern of American politics after 1865 was profoundly influenced by three factors. First, the idea of evolution and development changed the concept of politics from static to dynamic. Government, it came to be assumed, was not a fixed but a shifting, ever-adapting institution. The Constitution and frame of American government had been shaped according to the eighteenth-century Newtonian concept of order, stability, and permanence, but the later nineteenth century reshaped it according to Darwinian ideas of evolutionary development. This was a violent and revolutionary change of emphasis that outmoded much of earlier American political theory and made politics a thing developed, rather than contrived. Woodrow Wilson, writing in the eighties, expressed the new concept clearly:

Government is not a machine, but a living thing. It falls, not under the theory of the universe, but under the theory of organic life. It is accountable to Darwin, not to Newton. . . Living political constitutions must be Darwinian in structure and practice.

Secondly, Americans adopted a pragmatic approach to

politics. The point of politics, it was assumed, was to understand the actual operation of government, to study unwritten as well as written laws, to recognize the political importance of men and pressures and opinions. The results of this pragmatic approach are evident in the appearance of analytical bureaux, such as the reorganized Census Bureau, the Bureau of Labor Statistics, the Departments of Labor, Commerce, Agriculture, and others. Thirdly, the late nineteenth century began to recognize more fully the functions of power groups. This was not new. Hamilton, Jefferson, Madison, and others had long before considered the importance of 'factions' in government, but political thinkers of the post-war period saw more clearly than they the importance of special interest groups in deciding political questions. Politics, no matter the campaign name or party label, was no longer considered a battle between 'good' and 'bad' but a conflict of interests – private and public, have and have-not, agriculture and industry, East and West.

From 1776 to 1865 the term *democracy* connoted opposition to absolutism, personal power, personal privilege, institutionalized political inequality, suppression of free speech and thought. After 1865 the problem became how to define and interpret the formulas and ideals of an historical eighteenth-century democracy in terms of a new social and industrial order. Though it might be assumed that *democracy* still meant what it always had, what did it also mean in terms of the factory, the 'captain of industry', the labour union, the farmer, the trust? Answers to the question involved recognition of certain new trends in American life, of the entrance of social issues into politics, of the contest among capital and labour and agriculture for political control, and of all those changes wrought in America by urbanism, industrialism, prosperity, increased population, immigration, and the settlement of the West. Politics of the later nineteenth century, therefore (and of the early twentieth as well) settled down into a conflict among differing interpretations of the word *democracy*. It was a contest between a conservative theory of *laissez-faire* and closely restricted government powers, and a liberal theory of stronger government under broader control with a wider social programme. The contest involved certain tangential issues, including, obviously, an attempt to use Hamiltonian means to attain Jeffersonian ends. It involved a complete re-thinking of hallowed concepts of individualism and *laissez-faire*, and it meant, of course, reconsideration of the goals of American democracy.

From 1860 to 1912 the Republican Party was almost continuously in control of the executive and legislative branches of the government. To maintain its position it formed close alliances with industry and business, identifying itself with high tariffs, hard money, stable currency and credit, and aid to industry by subsidy. The Republican Party became, in effect, the political instrument of an expanding industrial capitalism. Moreover, it was the 'respectable' party of the North, supported by the farmer who gained his land under Republican-sponsored Homestead acts, by the veteran who fought the war under Republican leadership and who received his pension from a Republican administration, by the manufacturer who liked Republican tariffs. Republicanism to many in the North was a fundamental and self-evident thing, like the flag, or the Union; how could one disown the party of the martyred Lincoln? Republican leaders of the period traded on the party's *esprit de corps*, developing it into a highly-organized, tightly-disciplined political machine. At the same time the party always had within it an independent element, a 'mugwump' or 'progressive' group that battled constantly with the party leaders and occasionally forced concessions from them. The Democratic Party, despite its minority position, was far from weak or ineffective. It elected Presidents in 1884 and 1890, and for twenty years held intermittent control of one House of Congress.

Hayes's victory in 1876 marked the beginning of the closest balance of party strength in American history. The fact was that the voter found little to choose between the parties. The colourless platforms of the years 1876 to 1896 showed that both parties existed in a vacuum, unaware of the vast economic and social changes that had taken place in the nation after the Civil War. In a sense, parties became ends in themselves, with Democrats existing to battle Republicans, Republicans existing to oppose Democrats. Lord Bryce, in his shrewd analysis of the American political scene, concluded that 'neither party has any clear-cut principles, any distinct tenets. Both have traditions. Both claim to have tendencies. Both have certainly war cries, organization, interests, enlisted in their support. But those interests are in the main the interests of getting or keeping the patronage of government.' The basic issues of the period's politics are discoverable chiefly in the platforms of the multitudes of third parties that dotted the times: the Greenback, Independent, Reform, and labour parties in the states, which culminated in the Populist Revolt in the nineties.

The dynamics of the two major parties from 1876 to 1896 were provided by men, not issues, by organizations, not principles. This was the heyday of the boss and the machine, both of which operated best at the city level, where governmental processes were close at hand, and control easiest to establish. William Marcy Tweed of New York and his Tammany organization were almost the prototypes of bosses and machines, but dozens like them existed in Pittsburgh, Cleveland, Chicago, St Louis, and other cities. The organization of both parties rested on such local bosses. The national committee of each party interlocked with a party committee in Congress, so that congressional politics might be directly coordinated with political strategy; national committees also worked directly with state and city bosses, who delivered votes on demand. The boss himself was an interesting character – never quite socially respectable, shrewd, expert at his business, true to his own peculiar code of ethics. He stood at the centre of a web that was connected with vice (gambling, liquor, prostitution) on one side and special interest groups (utilities, labour, corporations, manufacturing) on the other, serving as intermediary between both and government. For delivering his votes he received fees from both, keeping a percentage himself and passing the rest down to lower levels of the organization. The machine was kept together by jobs passed out through political patronage; by direct contributions from special interests, big and little; by graft legislation allowing access to public moneys; and by a crude but powerful sense of party loyalty.

Surveying the succession of Presidents from 1868 to 1900 Henry Adams remarked, 'No period so thoroughly ordinary has been known in American politics since Christopher Columbus first disturbed the balance of American society.' The Republicans who occupied the White House during those years were respectable mediocrities, dedicated to party service, with little understanding of the vital forces transforming the nation. Hayes, a conscientious man, quickly fell out with his own party leaders because of his insistence on reforming the civil service. The Democrats, who called Hayes 'His Fraudulency, The President', harassed him at every opportunity, and since they had a majority in the House (in the Senate, too, after the elections of 1878) they made his administrative position almost untenable.

Before the presidential conventions of 1880 Hayes announced he was not a candidate, a wise decision since few Republican leaders wanted him. Some of the older party men talked of running Grant again, but more leaned to James G. Blaine, the 'Plumed Knight' from Maine. Neither Blaine nor Grant could gather sufficient support at the convention, which eventually picked James Garfield of Ohio, a young and undistinguished party regular. As a concession to the Grant backers the Garfield men chose Chester A. Arthur of New York as vice-president. The Democrats nominated General Winfield Hancock, a fine soldier but with no political experience. Garfield won by an extremely narrow margin, fewer than nine thousand votes out of nine million. Garfield, however, was shot in July 1881 by a disappointed, and probably insane, office-seeker. Since Arthur was known as a machine politician, the public feared a swift return to 'Grantism'. Arthur surprised everyone by carrying on Hayes's struggle for clean and efficient government and forcing the passage of a good civil service bill. Ironically, it was Chester A. Arthur, from whom no one expected much, who put the first real dent in the old Jacksonian spoils system.

In 1884 the Republicans jettisoned Arthur in favour of Blaine, who had a strong personal following in the party and a none-too-savoury reputation outside it. The liberal Republicans had no use for him, threatening to bolt the party if the Democrats chose a better man. The Democrats did: Grover Cleveland, Governor of New York. In a vicious campaign Blaine's past was thoroughly raked, and several shady but profitable deals with railroads were uncovered. Cleveland, accused of fathering an illegitimate child in his youth, did not deny it, while his supporters pointed out that he had honestly assumed proper responsibility for his by-blow. Democrats chanted

> Blaine, Blaine, James G. Blaine,
> The con-ti-nent-al liar from the State of Maine!

while Republicans shouted in reply

> Ma! Ma! Where's my pa?
> Gone to the White House – ha, ha, ha!

The campaign seemed about even until a New York clergyman, speaking on Blaine's behalf, assailed the Democrats as the party of 'Rum, Romanism, and Rebellion', alienating many Irish Catholic voters in New York. Cleveland won by 23,000 votes in a total of ten million cast. The first Democratic President to hold office since 1856, he also took in with him a Democratic House.

Cleveland fought a courageous battle against the influence of special interests in government, and guarded the Treasury well. The Grand Army of the Republic lobbied numerous pension bills through Congress only to have Cleveland veto most of them. In direct conflict with the advice of his party leaders he attacked the high tariffs beloved by manufacturers and demanded a reduction in rates that was blocked by the Republican Senate. He also increased the effectiveness of the civil service system and ordered an investigation of railroad land grants. By the end of his term Cleveland had offended the Union veterans, industrialists, businessmen, and a great many of his own party leaders, including Tammany. But his concern for doing the right thing earned him the respect of the public, and the party somewhat reluctantly nominated him for a second term.

The Republicans chose Benjamin Harrison, grandson of William Henry Harrison and an Indiana lawyer of no particular distinction. The campaign revolved chiefly about the tariff issue, Cleveland basing his on a demand for a lowered tariff, Harrison supporting a high tariff to protect manufacturing. Business interests contributed heavily to Harrison's support; election-day activities of both parties, in fact, were so scandalous that the movement to adopt the Australian ballot-system gained great headway. Cleveland had the larger popular vote by nearly 100,000, but lost the electoral vote and the election. The Republicans also gained control of both Houses of Congress.

The Republican party, in the light of Cleveland's popular vote, could hardly assume a mandate from the people. Harrison therefore proceeded cautiously. He left party policy mostly to Blaine, his Secretary of State, and for a time the Republicans had things their own way. The G.A.R. pension bills passed. The McKinley tariff went through, with the highest and most peculiarly distributed duties yet recorded in tariff history. Civil service suffered when the Republicans went to work on it; the system probably would have been wrecked had it not been for the resistance offered by Theodore Roosevelt, a young New York Republican on the Civil Service Commission. The congressional election of 1890, in which the Republicans lost control of both Houses of Congress, reflected the prevailing opinion of the Republican record. But in 1892 the Republicans, standing on that record, nominated Harrison once more, while the Democrats countered with Grover Cleveland again, with Adlai Stevenson of Illinois as his running mate. Cleveland won by a respectable majority, carrying both Houses of Congress.

In the election General James Baird Weaver of Iowa,

running on the third-party Populist ticket, polled a million popular and twenty-two electoral votes, all from the agrarian West. The political game of Tweedledum versus Tweedledee, played by Republican and Democrat alike for twenty years, was over and signs of revolt were almost visible in the West.

From Appomattox to the Spanish War American diplomacy faced no serious crises, nor did it have any consistent pattern. National interest centred on westward expansion, on rebuilding the shattered South, on consolidating the gains of industry, and on exploiting the nation's vast natural resources. The 'manifest destiny' of the pre-war years settled into a mild expansionism, tempered by strong public disapproval of imperialism. The most delicate diplomatic problems were those left over from the Civil War, especially those involving Britain, against which the United States had some long-standing grievances. The retirement of Palmerston and Russell from British foreign affairs and the substitution of Clarendon smoothed the path of diplomacy considerably. The American Secretaries of State during the period were less pugnacious than some of their predecessors, and Seward (under Johnson), Hamilton Fish (under Grant), William G. Evarts (under Hayes), and Blaine (under Garfield and Harrison) were exceptionally able men.

Fish's handling of British-American relations during Grant's administration was one of the few accomplishments to its credit. His most difficult problem concerned Canada, the traditional subject of a great deal of spreadeagle annexationist talk by American politicians. There was, to be sure, some anti-British sentiment in Canada, and Britain countered with the North America Act of 1867, creating the Dominion of Canada partly to unify Canadians against American penetration. At the same time the Fenian Brotherhood, an Irish-American society, evolved a wild plan of invading Canada, hoping to precipitate a war with Britain that by some obscure reasoning might end in freeing Ireland. In 1866 and 1870 Fenian bands crossed the border to clash with Canadian volunteers, but in both instances the Washington government swiftly arrested the leaders and seized Fenian supplies. Such energetic action won applause from both British and Canadians and encouraged good feeling toward the United States. Fish's real triumph came in 1871, however, with the signing of the Treaty of Washington, which provided for settlement by arbitration of all remaining points of friction with Britain: the Oregon boundary dispute, the *Alabama* affair, and the Newfoundland fishing claims. For the first time since the outbreak of the American Revolution the British-American agenda was not only swept clean, but negotiation and arbitration were firmly fixed into the pattern of Anglo-American policy.

After the Civil War, Seward, an ardent expansionist, set about establishing control over the Caribbean, Latin America, and the Pacific, but found Congress and the public lukewarm toward his ambitions. When Russia appeared willing to sell Alaska, Seward persuaded Congress to snap it up in 1867 for a little more than seven million dollars; however the isolationist Senate balked at his efforts to acquire Santo Domingo and the Danish West Indies. People paid little attention to the purchase of 'Seward's Icebox', nor did the American occupation of uninhabited Midway Island in the Pacific excite much interest.

Most of American diplomatic activity was concentrated on the Pacific and Latin America. The United States had enjoyed excellent trade relations with China since the forties, but the importation of Chinese labourers in the seventies raised a serious immigration problem. Plagued by recurrent depressions and unemployment, American workmen bitterly resented the presence of 'the heathen Chinee' (as Bret Harte called him) as a cheap labour pool. Pressure on Congress during Arthur's administration brought an 'exclusion bill' preventing the entry of Chinese, the first of a long series of immigration laws directed at specific groups of particular racial or geographical origins. With Japan, opened by Perry in 1854, American merchants had similar good relations. After the United States, Holland, Britain and France joined in 1865 to put down internal dissension in Japan, Japanese-American commerce steadily increased.

The Hawaiian Islands in the South Pacific had long been a port of call for Yankee ships, and the United States a fine market for Hawaiian sugar. American entrepreneurs controlled three fourths of the sugar plantations; in 1875 Fish engineered a trade treaty that markedly improved their position. Queen Liliuokalani, who ascended to the Hawaiian throne in 1891, had a strong anti-American bias, whereupon a revolutionary group overthrew her government with the help of United States Marines and proclaimed a Republic which Washington soon recognized. There was, however, strong public and Congressional opposition to outright annexation, which was not finally accomplished until 1898 during the imperialist enthusiasm of the Spanish War period. Samoa, complicated by the presence of German and British interests in the islands, was much the same story. In 1899 Germany obtained most of the islands, Britain withdrew, and the United States took possession of Tutuila.

With the Southern agricultural imperialists gone from Congress, American interest in Latin America and the Caribbean waned. Cuba seemed no longer a lure, though Cuban revolutionaries, engaged in perennial uprising against Spain, severely strained Spanish-American relations by using the United States as a base of operations. Segments of public opinion sympathized with the revolutionary leaders and there was some sentiment in Congress favouring interference in their behalf, but Washington remained doggedly neutral.

The seizure of power by Dictator Diaz in 1876 opened a period of good relations between the United States and Mexico. Diaz encouraged American investments, settled old claims, and welcomed American counsel. James G. Blaine further cemented relations with Latin America by founding the Pan-American Congress (later the Pan-American Union) to facilitate commerce, improve understanding, and encourage cultural interchange. The one disharmonious note was struck by Richard Olney, Cleveland's Secretary of State.

Venezuela, after long argument with Britain over its boundary with British Guiana, appealed to the United States for arbitration. Olney sent an aggressive and almost insulting note to Britain charging violation of the Monroe Doctrine and claiming complete authority not only over the dispute but over all Latin American affairs. Lord Salisbury at first refused to arbitrate but later agreed, with the result that British Guiana won most of the disputed territory. While American willingness to protect Venezuela pleased the Latin American republics, its calm assumption of hemispheric authority was less happily received.

In total effect, American diplomacy during the period displayed tact and common sense: France quickly cleared from Mexico, the war claims settled with dispatch, the Monroe Doctrine reaffirmed without undue muscle-flexing. The close of the Civil War seemed to mark the beginning of a period of greater self-confidence and maturity in American foreign relations.

The American farmer gained from the Civil War, but did not believe that he gained enough. For a time he was prosperous, but the bubble of prosperity, blown large by the war, collapsed shortly after it. Farm prices wobbled crazily year after year, gradually sliding downward. Wheat, rye, corn, and cotton dropped 20 to 50 per cent twenty years after Lee's surrender, which meant foreclosed mortgages, increased debt, poverty and distress in the West and South. At the same time that the bottom dropped out of the farmer's market, prices on the manufactured goods he bought stayed up, protected by tariffs and trusts, and even went higher. During the same lean years the national currency underwent a gradual contraction (the aftermath of wartime currency inflation) that depressed market prices even more. All this the farmer could not understand. During the Civil War, when 'greenbacks' were plentiful, prices for farm products were high. Why not, then, increase the amount of currency simply by passing the necessary Federal laws? In the same way Congress might settle such other agricultural problems as freight rates, taxes, and interest on mortgages.

Neither major party paid much attention to the farmer's demands. Over a period of years his resentment mounted against the Eastern banker (who tampered with the currency), the city loan shark (who charged high interest), 'Wall Street' (which in some subtle way rigged markets and caused depressions), railroad kings (who collected exorbitant freight rates), trusts (which engineered high tariffs and prices), and politicians (Republican and Democrat alike) who connived to keep the farmer poor. The farmer was angry, very angry, at 'the system that clothed rascals in robes and honesty in rags'.

The seventies and eighties were alive with dissident farm groups. Some, purely social, tried to break down the isolation of life on the empty western prairies – what farm women called 'the lones'. Some were educational, since rural schools lagged far behind urban. Some, by consolidating buying and borrowing power, turned into cooperatives; the great American mail order houses, such as Montgomery Ward and Company, were first founded to deal directly with farmers and to eliminate the middleman. But wherever farmers met in the South and West the talk eventually turned to politics, to government control of monopolies (especially railroads), easier credit with lower interest, cheaper money and more of it, a lowered tariff, better tax distribution with an income tax for the rich man, the elimination of corruption and privilege in government. All these issues boiled down to three general demands that ran consistently through late nineteenth-century agrarian thinking; remove special interest from politics, make government more responsive to the needs of more people, broaden its concepts to include economic and social welfare.

The most comprehensive of the early farm organizations was the Grange, or Patrons of Husbandry, a semi-secret society founded in 1867. Especially strong in the South and Oest, the Grange claimed 750,000 members by the mid seventies. It was avowedly non-political, but since it was virtually impossible to keep farmers out of politics the

Grange became a party in everything but name. When neither major party seemed responsive to Granger demands, farmers in several midwestern states formed Independent, Reform, or Anti-Monopoly parties and put a good deal of legislation, aimed primarily at the railroads, into the statute books. The dominant Republican party stood off the Granger threat, however, and most of the third parties were dead by the late seventies, absorbed into the Greenback party. Since the cheap money of the Civil War years suited the farmer and debtor very well, the Greenbackers framed their organization on the currency issue. They ran a few state tickets with moderate success and in 1876, with Peter Cooper running as presidential candidate, polled a million votes and sent fifteen men to Congress. After 1876 the Greenback party declined rapidly, merged with the Anti-Monopolists, and finally died.

The Farmers' Alliance replaced the Grange and the Greenbackers as an outlet for rural discontent. The Alliance split into two branches, the Southern and the Northwestern (or Northern). It was modelled after the Grange with an important exception – it was an admittedly political organization, since there was no point, as one Alliance organizer said, 'in making a gun that wouldn't shoot'. The Southern Alliance, the larger of the two, excluded Negroes and preferred to work within the framework of the Democratic party. The Northwestern admitted Negroes and labourers, was much more politically aggressive, and hoped to establish a third party. Attempts were made in the eighties to join with the Knights of Labor to form a Union Labor party, but without much success. Nothing daunted, the Northwestern Alliance announced in 1889 that it intended to create a party dedicated to the task of 'obtaining for the farmer and laborer equal privileges with the manufacturing and commercial classes'.

Hard times helped the Alliance cause. There were several successive drought years; wheat dropped to fifty cents a bushel, cotton to six cents a pound, corn was cheaper to burn as fuel than to sell. Meanwhile Congress raised tariffs, voted millions in pork-barrel bills, and paid no attention to the cries of distress from the farms. What the farmer needed to do, said Alliance organizer Mary Ellen Lease (the Kansas Pythoness) was 'to raise less corn and more hell'. Nurtured on falling prices, Alliance-sponsored third parties made strong showings in the state elections of 1890 in Georgia, South Carolina, Kansas, Nebraska, Minnesota, and the Dakotas. The parties varied from state to state, but the People's Party of Kansas, one of the more successful ones, lent its name to the protest movement: 'Populist' and 'Populism' were its hardy derivatives. With a going organization and good leadership provided by Ignatius Donnelly of Minnesota, James Weaver (the old Greenbacker) of Iowa, 'Sockless Jerry' Simpson of Kansas, 'Pitchfork Ben' Tillman of South Carolina, Tom Watson of Georgia, and others, the Alliance believed it was time to strike a nation-wide blow.

Southern Alliance leaders opposed political action on a national scale, since the Democratic party meant white rule in the South and if the white vote were split by a third party the Negro might gain ground. Northwestern leaders went ahead, nevertheless, to call a series of conventions in 1891, ending with the creation of the National People's Party at St Louis. For its presidential nominee the Populists chose Weaver of Iowa, an experienced campaigner, and a Union veteran, and for vice-president James Field of Virginia, a courtly ex-Confederate general. Designed to attract any dissatisfied voter – Greenbacker, Union Labor, Granger, Anti-Monopolist, or anyone else – the Populist platform denounced Republican and Democrat impartially. 'We meet,' it said, 'in the midst of a nation brought to the verge of moral, political, and material ruin.'

The fruits of the toil of millions are boldly stolen to build up colossal fortunes for the few, unprecedented in the history of mankind; and the possessors of these, in turn despise the Republic and endanger liberty. From the same prolific womb of governmental injustice we breed the two great classes – tramps and millionaires.

'Populism,' said the New York *Herald*, 'spread like flame on a dry prairie.' Though Weaver's campaign was a good one, his million votes were not much compared to the combined total cast for Harrison and Cleveland.

Behind the Populist party lay the built-up resentment of years of hard times. It expressed the suspicion of the rural dweller toward an expanding urban America, toward banks and trusts, toward the two major parties which seemed to disregard his interests. Populist thinking on these issues was strongly conditioned by the work of three influential reformers – Henry George of California, Edward Bellamy of Massachusetts, and Henry Demarest Lloyd of Chicago. The paradox of poverty in the midst of plenty puzzled George, until the answer came to him, he said, 'in an ecstatic vision'. The cause of poverty was a land monopoly which deprived the majority of free use of the land and enabled the few to attach the earnings of the many in the form of rent. The remedy, he believed, was a 'single tax' on the unearned increment that accrued to the owner of land or natural resources from the simple fact of ownership. His ideas, first stated in *Progress and Poverty* (1879) and expanded in later books, attracted a large following among Southern and Western farmers. By 1900 five million copies of his book had been sold, Single Tax Leagues founded by his supporters appeared in the cities, and George himself was nearly elected Mayor of New York. He travelled and lectured in Ireland and England, where he had some influence on the Webbs, Shaw, and the early Fabians.

The same problem of monopoly interested Lloyd and Bellamy. Lloyd, a Chicago journalist, studied Rockefeller's oil empire and wrote a series of articles on it in the early eighties. Finally he published *Wealth Against Commonwealth* (1894), the most careful and complete indictment of monopoly ever written. Edward Bellamy tried to solve the problem of centralized industry in terms of state socialism, explained in his utopian novel *Looking Backward* (1888). Monopolies, wrote Bellamy, undermined liberty by destroying competition; to give security and equality to all its citizens, the state should assume control of economic life, substituting cooperation for competition as its motivating principle. Bellamy, George, and Lloyd were best sellers in Granger and Alliance circles and had much to do with the political education of the Populists.

Grover Cleveland entered the White House at an unlucky time. Depression struck almost as soon as he was inaugurated. Before 1894 169 railroads went into bankruptcy, and in late 1893 the banks began to go, national, state, and private, 600 in all before it was over. Cleveland was not equipped to handle the crisis. Business recessions, he believed, were matters for business and not for government to solve; if let alone, depressions wore themselves out. But little by little the national economy slowed down, factories closed, machines stood idle, unemployed flocked the streets, and farm prices plummeted downward, until a Kansas farmer, speaking for the Populist states, summed their situation up by saying, 'We have reached the bottom, we cannot further reduce our rations and live.'

A more flexible politician might have tempered the winds of depression, but Cleveland could not. Serious labour troubles broke out, culminating in the bloody Pullman strike of 1894 in Illinois, led by Eugene Debs of the new American Railway Union. Cleveland's answer was to send in Federal troops and to encourage the courts to use injunctions against the strikers, putting Debs in gaol. In Ohio, 'General' Jacob Coxey, a Greenbacker and Populist, organized and led to Washington an 'army' of unemployed to demand relief. Coxey's arrest for walking on the Capitol lawn simply served to underline the Populist accusation that Cleveland's whole administration was part of an 'unholy alliance with monopoly'. In the offyear Congressional election of 1894 thousands of farmers and labourers deserted the old parties to send a bloc of Populists and Independents to Congress.

The sudden emergence of the issue of 'free silver' muddied political waters considerably. There was nothing new about currency-reform schemes in American politics, but 'free silver' gave a new twist to the old Greenback principle. Though United States finances were set on a gold standard, in the seventies some argued that the lavish issue of government notes backed by silver would improve the nation's finances and smother depressions in an avalanche of money. So 'free' or unlimited coinage of silver took on, for the farmer and labourer, the attributes of a cure-all for economic ills. Few understood exactly how free silver might settle everything, but many were convinced that it would. By tying it to the Eastern banker, to Wall Street, to the 'money power' of monopoly, politicians developed a highly emotional charge from a dry-as-dust, complex currency issue.

'Silver wings' appeared in both Democratic and Republican parties, while pressure increased on the Populists to accept a free silver plank. Silver was not a legitimate Populist issue except as it related to monopoly and hard times – both Populist rallying points – but a good many agrarian leaders who had run the gamut from Grangerism to Greenbackism to Populism were willing to accept it as a means of drawing votes from the major parties and from labour. Others, like Lloyd, were suspicious of it as 'the cowbird of the reform movement, likely to push the other eggs out of the nest'.

The nominating conventions for the presidential election of 1896 met in an atmosphere of tension. The Republicans nominated Governor William McKinley of Ohio and announced a gold-standard policy, the signal for the 'Silver Republicans' to bolt. The Democrats, three weeks later, found the silverites extremely well organized, and after a brief battle, the Western 'free silver' men won control of the meeting. There was no favourite for president until William Jennings Bryan of Nebraska, a comparative unknown, exploded the convention. Rising to speak on a hot afternoon in Chicago, Bryan stampeded the meeting into one of the greatest demonstrations in American political history. Tracing the background of the silver question, recalling all the bitternesses and hatreds of discontent for twenty years past, crying out to labour for support, he climaxed his speech with an inspired image saved for the occasion: 'You shall not press down upon the brow of labour this crown of thorns, you shallnot crucify mankind upon a cross of gold!' When the last phrase of the 'Cross of Gold' speech died in the air, no one else stood a chance. This was the West speaking, the Granger, the Greenbacker, the Populist, the farmer with a mortgage and the jobless worker in the street. The shout of 'Bryan, Bryan, Bryan' began to beat across the land. The great crusade had begun, the 'Great Commoner' at its head. The Populist party, meeting in the shadow of Bryan's cross of gold, succumbed and nominated Bryan too.

Bryan represented the protest of an old agrarian class against the new urban-industrial America. And Bryan himself fired the imagination with his massive, barrel-like body, leonine head with coal black hair, flashing eyes, voice of almost hypnotic power. His mind was not deep and his principles were the simple ones of the rural West – equal rights, popular rule, hatred of monopoly, a life of Christian virtue. Of all he said, only the closing peroration of the Cross of Gold speech remains, yet he was one of the most powerful political influences of his time, a man who captured and held for nearly fifteen years two parties and six million voters.

Bryan faced two opponents in the 1896 campaign, William McKinley and his Republican campaign manager, Mark Hanna. Hanna, a millionaire from Cleveland, was a shrewd, intelligent machine politician who firmly believed that good government was Republican government, instituted for the benefit of business. McKinley, the last Civil War veteran to fill the Presidency, was a smooth, handsome party regular of more than average ability as a politician. The two made a team, each supplying what the other lacked – McKinley the speeches and personality, Hanna the organization. Bryan travelled the length and breadth of the nation, speaking sometimes a dozen times a day, but Hanna quietly collected funds and set the Republican organization to work. The party coffers held nearly twelve million dollars, which Hanna poured out lavishly; in the state of Iowa alone the Republicans mailed out six million pieces of campaign literature and put 6,000 workers in the field. McKinley won by a safe margin in electoral votes, although by only a half-million popular votes. Free silver and Populism vanished in the defeat.

So far as immediate results were concerned, the great agrarian revolt of 1896 accomplished nothing. The political party that had been in power remained in power, its branches shaken by the wind of rebellion but its roots still firmly set. After McKinley's victory the Republican organization seemed more thoroughly in control than it had even in Grant's time. But the spirit of the Populists remained alive. Twenty years of agitation laid the groundwork for what was to come under Theodore Roosevelt, Woodrow Wilson, Robert La Follette, Franklin Roosevelt, and others of lesser stature who followed. Even in defeat Bryan's campaign showed the alterations that had taken place in America and the fundamental changes in the problems of democracy. Only thirteen months after McKinley's inauguration the United States was to engage Spain in war and emerge from it a world power, its traditional isolation ended. There would be a shift, a marked shift, from the old frontier philosophy of individualism toward a new concept of the positive role of the state and social cooperation – a shift, as the historian Turner phrased it, 'from the ideal of individualism to the ideal of social control through regulation by law'. Modern America was about to arrive.

CHAPTER 27

PROGRESSIVISM AND REACTION
1896–1932

WAR, industrial and agricultural revolution, changes in production and transportation, new social groupings and patterns – these shaped the structure of twentieth-century America. The rapid industrialization of the national economy effected a new kind of division of labour, hastened the growth of the factory system, opened up transportation, and altered the nation's financial framework. Agriculture found itself part of a different economic scheme. The chief fact about twentieth-century America was that its developing social complexity changed the relationship of individual to individual and of section to section. American life after 1900 was interdependent, not independent. It took some time for Americans to adjust to this fact.

The most significant development in American politics from 1900 to 1920 was the Progressive movement. Surveying contemporary life, liberal thinkers were dissatisfied with what they saw. The Federal government appeared to some of them to be controlled by a privileged few who ran it for the benefit of the railroads, the banks, and the manufacturing and mining corporations. The subsequent revolt against such 'government by privilege' was the culmination of a protest long brewing, from the Grangers through the Populist agitation of the nineties. The Social Gospellers, too, contributed their share, and the ideas of social planners such as Bellamy, Lloyd, Lester Ward, George, and others did much to undermine the foundations of the old individualistic, *laissez-faire* philosophy. The 'muckrakers', a group of crusading journalists and novelists who specialized in exposure of graft and corruption, played a part: men and women such as Ida Tarbell, Lincoln Steffens, Ray Stannard Baker, and Upton Sinclair.

The reformers of the progressive era approached contemporary problems with pragmatic confidence. The imbalances and injustices of politics and society could be solved, they believed, sensibly and practically, by returning economic, political, and social institutions to a larger degree of popular control. Their aim, therefore, was to formulate new social and political doctrines for a nation whose wealth and political power had apparently outstripped its ability to cope with the problems these things brought. Old theories were scrutinized and rejected, the machinery of government inspected and repaired, traditional political and economic patterns broken and rearranged, the better to square with democracy. For thirty years before 1900 the underprivileged and repressed raised voices of protest from city and farm. All that was needed in 1900 was a set of leaders.

The first signs of progressivism came from the cities, where urban reformers locked in conflict with local political machines. In the states, at almost the same time, 'progressives' fought 'stalwart' conservatives for control of state legislatures, and inevitably the same impulse of reform was transferred to national politics. The progressive movement advanced regardless of party lines; both Republican and Democratic organizations were sharply divided between 'insurgents' or 'progressives', and 'conservatives' or 'stalwarts' by 1908. The liberal wing of the Republican party failed to capture party control, but the Democratic progressives succeeded in 1912.

Progressive programmes varied with leaders and sections. Some stressed economic and social objectives – trust regulation, control of public utilities, tax reforms, prohibition of child labour, public health programmes, educational reforms, conservation of natural resources. Others emphasized the need of democratizing political machinery, proposing the initiative and referendum, direct primary elections, secret ballots, home rule for cities, corrupt practices acts, and better election laws. But all held the same objective, the advancement of the welfare of the majority of the people by the extension of the power and purpose of the state. Both held the same basic philosophy, in no way different from that of other reform movements that preceded them, that the cure for the ills of democracy was more democracy.

Lord Bryce observed in 1888 that city government was 'the one conspicuous failure of the United States'. The facts bore him out. The swift growth of the city after 1870 made it especially vulnerable to machine rule, and the great bosses – Magee in Pittsburgh, Croker in New York, Lomasny in Boston, Butler in St Louis, and others – took full advantage of antiquated, unwieldy city governments to consolidate their power. Beginning in the nineties, reform groups sprang up in nearly all of the large cities. By 1905 the movement reached the proportions of a crusade, and by 1910 some of the bosses were gone and more were in temporary retreat.

City reformers, however, soon found that the city machine was in many cases merely an extension of a larger state organization. Under the American constitutional system, most important matters of a social and political character were under the jurisdiction of state legislatures, such as the terms and conditions of labour, education, suffrage, election machinery, municipal government, and corporation charters. The states, then, became the next battlegrounds. In the East the reform movement was largely urban-directed. In the West the progressive leaders built on the foundations left by the agrarian revolt of the eighties and nineties. Young Theodore Roosevelt, before he went to Washington, cut his teeth on the reform movement in New York City. Woodrow Wilson made his early political reputation as reform governor of New Jersey. Albert Cummins and Jonathan Dolliver of Iowa, George Norris of Nebraska, John A. Johnson of Minnesota, Edward Costigan of Colorado, William Allen White of Kansas, Hiram Johnson of California, and Jonathan Bourne of Oregon, all led progressive movements in the states before they became national political figures. The greatest of them all was undoubtedly Governor Robert M. La Follette of Wisconsin, a Republican who made his home state into a veritable laboratory of progressive reform, intended 'to reconstruct our institutions to meet the requirements of a new age'. His 'Wisconsin Idea' was a practical experiment in progressivism that served as a model for others on both state and national levels, and in 1933 Franklin Roosevelt's 'New Deal' found much worth copying in La Follette's thirty-year-old programme.

While progressives asked for an extension of the power of the state into new areas of responsibility, they demanded no essential changes in the traditional political system. Socialists carried collectivism much further. American Socialism in its various manifestations had a long history, dating from the utopian societies of the eighteenth and nineteenth centuries, from Social Gospellers and Bellamyites, from Christian Socialists and Georgists. Marxian socialism came with the Germans, who in 1869 formed an American section of the First International. In 1874 the International founded the Social Democratic Workingmen's Party, which a year later became the Socialist Labor Party. Socialist Labor and Populist leaders made unsuccessful overtures to each other in the nineties, but were never able to find an acceptable arrangement for cooperation. The rigidity and revolutionism of Marxism repelled many American socialists, until in 1898 they accomplished a successful revolt against Daniel De Leon, the Marxist leader, to create the Social Democratic (Socialist) Party under the direction of Eugene Debs of Indiana, Victor Berger of Wisconsin, and later Norman Thomas of New York.

Socialists and progressives were often willing to combine in support of certain measures, but their alliance was an unsteady one. Socialism, Marxian and non-Marxian, represented an offensive movement for the eventual overthrow of capitalism. Progressivism, like its predecessor Populism, represented a defensive movement offering, for specific capitalistic ills, specific remedies which occasionally might involve collectivistic control or ownership of certain facilities of production and distribution, but never its complete domination over national social and economic life.

The progressive movement was, in effect, simply an

attempt to adjust an older democratic tradition, with its belief in individual freedom and equal opportunity, to the needs of an urban, industrial economy, 'a movement' (as La Follette called it) 'of a new generation toward more democracy in human relationships'. The progressive philosophy was not radical, but liberal, not revolutionary, but evolutionary. Its leaders assumed that their goals could be reached by internal adjustment, through political means, within the existing framework, and they hoped to regulate political and economic life in such a manner as to retain eighteenth- and nineteenth-century values in a twentieth-century society. Progressivism's most conspicuous result was to prepare the way for an extension under Wilson and Franklin D. Roosevelt of the responsibilities of government, local, state, and federal, into new areas of social and economic endeavour.

The results of the election of 1896 were generally viewed as a triumph of intelligent conservatism over ignorant demagoguery. 'God's in His Heaven,' said Mark Hanna when the voters' decision was known. McKinley lived up to his billing as the 'Advance Agent of Prosperity', for almost as soon as he was inaugurated the nation's business boomed – dollar wheat, rising wages, higher corporate profits. Congress passed a Gold Standard Act, putting a final quietus on free silver, and approved a high protective tariff. The most striking development of McKinley's first administration, however, was a tremendous increase in the consolidation of business and finance.

'A carnival of trusts is now in progress,' wrote Henry D. Lloyd, and economist John Moody in 1904 cited 318 trusts, most of them formed after 1898, as evidence that control of business and capital was rapidly concentrating in fewer and fewer hands. The Republican administration encouraged the trend, since the party had long been committed to a policy of non-interference with business. Prosecutions of combinations ran into judicial road-blocks while the Sherman Act languished.

To meet the growth of financial and industrial consolidation, labour began to concentrate its strength. The A.F.L, which had 278,000 members in 1898, doubled its size in

1900 and passed the million mark in 1904, but the old problem of political action still plagued union leaders. A strong minority, thinking in terms of a third party, hoped to convert either the Socialist Labor or the Socialist party into a labour instrument, in contrast to Gompers's policy of nonpartisan politics. Furthermore, Gompers's concept of a loose, federated union of craft workers failed to satisfy those who still adhered to the old Knights of Labor idea of 'one big union for all'. In 1905 Debs, De Leon, 'Big Bill' Haywood, and other labour leaders organized the Industrial Workers of the World, 'one great industrial union, embracing all industries . . . founded on the class struggle'. Though never large, the I.W.W was vocal, aggressive, and ably led. Its violent tactics and revolutionary methods alienated public support and gave its opponents a chance to crush it during the First World War, but during its brief existence the I.W.W convinced the older unions of the values of militancy.

The war with Spain overshadowed all other issues during McKinley's administration. Insurrections against corrupt and inefficient Spanish rule in Cuba had been almost annual occurrences for years. Washington's policy was carefully neutral, but by the 1890s American stakes in Cuban sugar, tobacco, and iron were large enough to cause concern to investors. The revolutionists of 1895, more successful than usual, captured the Cuban capital and a fairly large amount of surrounding territory. The Spanish occupation forces, commanded by General Weyler, suffered from guerrilla depredations and took stern measures to control suspected rebels. Atrocity stories, given wide circulation by the Pulitzer and Hearst presses, excited American sympathies, and President McKinley himself protested to Madrid over Weyler's 'uncivilized and inhuman methods'.

The Madrid government, fearful of American intervention, proceeded with great care in Cuba, but two incidents in rapid succession brought Spanish-American relations to a breaking point. The Spanish minister in Washington, writing to a friend in Cuba, made uncomplimentary remarks about McKinley; the letter leaked, the minister was recalled, but the damage was done. Then on 15 February 1898 the United States battleship *Maine*, moored in Havana harbour to protect American interests, blew up with the loss of 200 lives. Blame for the explosion was never fixed, although the American press and public immediately assumed that the Spanish might be responsible. 'Remember the *Maine*!' became the battle-cry of the moment. McKinley, who did not want war, vacillated while the press screamed for revenge. 'Stop the nonsense!' headlined the New York *World*. 'Stop the trifling!' Madrid, with abject apologies, indicated it would go to almost any length to avoid war, but on 19 April Congress voted to recognize the independence of the people of Cuba and authorized the use of armed force to support it. After that war was inevitable.

The Spanish War, which lasted only 115 days, was a highly popular war, long enough to prove the superiority of American arms, brief enough so that the tragedy could be ignored. The public, finding it a gloriously emotional experience, made war heroes by the dozen. Bryan served as a Colonel of a Nebraska regiment, though without the publicity that followed young Theodore Roosevelt, who organized a 'Rough Riders' regiment of cowboys and society horsemen. Northern and Southern recruits trained together, erasing some of the old bitternesses, and Joe Wheeler of Confederate cavalry fame donned Federal blue to serve in Cuba.

The United States Navy was at peak strength. The Army, sadly undermanned and badly equipped, was hardly more than a token force. Campaign strategy called first for the destruction of the Spanish Navy. Admiral Dewey found the Spanish Pacific Fleet in Manila Bay in the Philippines, and on 30 April 1898 smashed it in a swift engagement that cost the American fleet only seven wounded. An expeditionary force landed soon afterwards and in cooperation with Philippine insurgents took possession of the capital, while Spanish Admiral Cervera, commanding the Atlantic Fleet, eluded the American Atlantic Squadron and slipped into Santiago, Cuba, where Admiral Sampson blockaded him. When Cervera, somewhat against his better judgement, attempted to escape on 3 July 1898, Sampson's force sank or beached every Spanish vessel.

The Army stood at 18,000 when war was declared. Congress voted to expand it to 60,000 and to call up 125,000 volunteers. Amid great confusion some 17,000 troops under General Shafter landed in Cuba in late June to engage in sharp fighting at San Juan Hill, Kettle Hill, and El Caney. After the destruction of Cervera's fleet the Spanish defenders of Santiago surrendered and General Miles, who replaced Shafter, moved on to take Puerto Rico without incident. With its fleet gone and its armies cut off, the Spanish government asked for an armistice. At the peace negotiations in Paris the American representatives drove a hard bargain, demanding that Spain withdraw from the western hemisphere, that Cuba be recognized as an independent nation, and that the Philippines and Puerto Rico become American territories. Since the United States controlled only a very small portion of the Philippine archipelago, Spain balked at ceding her entire claim but gave in; later the United States gave her twenty million dollars in payment. The treaty was signed on 10 December 1898, and though it met strong opposition in Congress from anti-imperialist elements who found colonial possessions undesirable, it was ratified. The United States, having defeated a European nation in war, acquired an overseas empire in the Pacific, established control of most of the Caribbean, and became an imperial power.

The war with Spain could have been avoided. American diplomats handled their affairs with great skill, and Spain for its part went to unusual lengths to avoid hostilities. But America looked at its progress since Appomattox, felt a deep pride in its accomplishments, and hoped to prove itself a great international power, able to smash an arrogant, decadent European monarchy. The decisive factor in precipitating the Spanish War was neither political manoeuvring nor diplomatic failure, but popular mood. 'It wasn't much of a war', said Roosevelt, 'but it was the best we had.' At the same time it marked a definite turning point in

United States foreign policy. For the first time America deliberately extended its sovereignty beyond the North American continent. For the first time America accepted control of territories to which it had no intention of granting eventual statehood. And for the first time the United States, in establishing a colonial system, assumed full responsibility for the future welfare of an alien people.

The debates in Congress over the Spanish peace brought the argument over imperialism out into the open. Nineteenth-century Americans, enthusiastic over expansion, had long assumed it to be their 'manifest destiny' to occupy the entire continent, while agrarian slave-holders had once cast covetous glances at Central and South America. But after the Civil War a new kind of 'manifest destiny' took shape – economically, not agriculturally, motivated – concerned with investments, raw materials, and markets. In 1898 the United States had reached a stage of economic development in which a search for foreign markets seemed vital for the future. It was producing a surplus of nearly everything, had heavy financial stakes abroad, and needed a favourable balance of trade. In its attempt to make one, it found itself in direct competition with Europe. Nor was the United States alone in its economic imperialism, for China lay prostrate under European domination, and Africa was in the process of being split up among the European powers.

Stronger arguments than economic necessity supported American imperialism, the same arguments once employed to justify the Louisiana Purchase, the Monroe Doctrine, and the Mexican War. Americans believed, as they had since the days of Jefferson and Paine, that it was their mission to spread democracy, to bring American civilization to benighted people and backward areas. 'Americanizing the world,' said Theodore Roosevelt, was the nation's destiny. The acquisition of colonies therefore meant that 'little brown brothers' in the Philippines and repressed Cuban colonials were to be christianized and civilized as part of the white man's burden. Current European racist theories of Gobineau, Cuno, and Houston Chamberlain found eager support in the United States, which was, wrote Josiah Strong, the future home of the Anglo-Saxon race, 'the principal seat of its power and the centre of its influence'. Senator Albert Beveridge of Indiana tied economic and racist imperialism neatly into one package by remarking, 'We are Anglo-Saxons, and must obey our blood and occupy new markets, and if necessary, new lands.' Social Darwinism also lent its weight to the imperialists; superior, strong peoples must absorb the weak and inferior. 'Small states,' said Senator Henry Cabot Lodge, 'are of the past and have no future.' And then there was the simple argument from strategic necessity. Captain (later Admiral) A. T. Mahan pointed out that since the United States needed naval bases for its own protection, 'Whether they will or no, Americans must now begin to look outward.'

Opposed to imperialism was a long isolationist tradition and a deep American belief in the self-determination of peoples. The mission of America, some believed, was to construct in the New World a peaceful, open society, free from entangling alliances with the contentious nations of the Old. Domestic issues, not foreign, were the pressing problems, and the progressives in particular urged abstention from foreign entanglements lest the whole reform movement lose its impetus at home. Increased territory abroad merely meant increased expense without profit. It meant, said Bryan, 'heavier taxes, Asiatic emigration, and an opportunity to furnish more sons for the army'. Furthermore, acquiring a colonial empire by undemocratic means endangered democracy itself. 'This nation,' wrote Bryan, 'cannot endure half republic and half colony, half free and half vassal.'

The expansionists won. Congress announced that it had no desire to annex Cuba (annexation also meant assumption of the Cuban debt) but American troops stayed there until 1902, leaving behind them the brilliant work of Walter Reed of the Medical Corps, who freed the tropics from the scourge of yellow fever. The Cubans framed a constitution in 1901, but before they could attain self-rule Congress established Cuban bases for the United States fleet and retained the right (exercised in 1906 and 1917) to intervene in Cuban affairs when American interests seemed to be in danger. American investments in tobacco, sugar, utilities, and mines secured American control over the island economy and Cuba became largely a United States dependency. Puerto Rico, which was annexed, has had a history much like Cuba's. Its two-crop system of sugar and tobacco attached it immediately to the United States economy and it is still almost wholly dependent on American markets. The island attained a measure of home rule in 1900, and in 1917 Puerto Ricans were granted United States citizenship.

By annexing the Philippines the United States inherited the thorniest problem of them all. Disappointed at not gaining independence, the Filipino insurrectionists who had plagued the Lpanish for generations turned on the Americans, involving a 60,000-man expeditionary force in a brisk three-year war. In 1902 the islands were granted the status of an unorganized territory, and in 1907 they received partial self-government. The Philippines, it was hoped, might become the chief channel of United States Far Eastern trade; the hope never materialized, but Washington nevertheless assumed at heavy expense the task of sanitation, education, and economic development. In 1916 the United States announced that it would withdraw completely from the Philippines as soon as they established a stable, democratic government. In 1934 Congress granted Filipino independence, effective in 1945. The conduct of the Filipino people in World War II and the emergence of high-calibre native leadership soon afterwards proved the wisdom of the decision.

The colonial commitments of the Treaty of Paris accurately forecast the drift of American foreign policy. Since it dominated Caribbean and Latin American affairs. the United States turned towards the idea of a 'Pax Americana', based on a reaffirmation of the Monroe Doctrine. Santo Domingo, a country of perpetual revolution and heavy American investment, became a protectorate in 1905; in

1916 United States Marines entered to put down insurrection and ran the country under military rule for eight more years. Haiti consistently refused the offer of a protectorate, but in 1915, again with the aid of the Marines, the Haitian government signed a trade treaty giving the United States control of the island's economy – the last American troops did not depart until 1934. The Virgin Islands, purchased from Denmark in 1917, served chiefly as naval bases. Governed by the Navy until 1931, they were finally transferred to the Department of the Interior. In Nicaragua the Marines put down a revolution in 1912 and remained in virtual control of Nicaraguan policies until 1933.

Colombia became an object of interest to the United States because it owned the Isthmus of Panama, the best route for an inter-oceanic canal. A French company had already tried to construct such a canal, and in 1903 Congress voted to buy its title to the canal route. The Colombian government refused to sell. The State Department assisted a group of Panamanian revolutionists in setting up an independent state under American protection. The new government immediately granted a lease for the canal route for an initial payment of ten million dollars – a Rooseveltian operation of great efficiency if of questionable ethics, as evidenced by an apologetic payment of twenty-five million dollars to Colombia in 1912. A Canal Zone government was established in 1904, and the Canal itself, a monumental engineering project, was completed by the United States Army.

Strong and wealthy Mexico was a different matter. Diaz, who became dictator in 1877, encouraged American investments and punctiliously cooperated with the United States government. By 1910 American interests controlled huge slices of Mexico's resources, including 80 per cent of its railroads and 70 per cent of its oil, while Diaz's regime had begun to totter. Taft gave immediate recognition to the government of Madero, who drove out Diaz in 1911, but two years later Madero fell to Huerta, whom the United States refused to support. Wilson, who respected Madero, was determined to overthrow his tyrannical successor. American troops landed at Vera Curz and Huerta fled, leaving the government to Carranza, whose regime Wilson was willing to recognize. The bandit chieftain Francisco Villa, however, kept up a constant war against both Mexican and American troops, finally invading New Mexico and killing several American citizens. Pershing's Army Regulars pursued Villa fruitlessly until the outbreak of hostilities in Europe and American entry into World War I turned attention elsewhere.

There were other indications that the traditional American aversion to foreign entanglements was rapidly fading. Russian, French, and German penetration of China after its defeat by Japan in 1895 caused considerable alarm in London and Washington. In 1899 Secretary of State John Hay proposed an 'open door' policy, asking that those nations with Chinese interests allow other nations access to the China trade, and succeeded in obtaining the approval of the major European governments. Again in 1900 the United States contributed to the international force that put down the anti-foreign Boxer rebellion.

From the Spanish War to the mid thirties the United States followed an imperialistic policy of intervention and annexation, with more and more emphasis on trade expansion and financial penetration into South and Latin American areas. Theodore Roosevelt in particular reaffirmed and extended the Monroe Doctrine, writing that the United States must shape its foreign policy 'with the view to the ultimate removal of all European powers from the colonies they hold in the Western hemisphere'. Taft followed the Rooseveltian line, while Woodrow Wilson, though less aggressive, followed it in part.

Increasing resentment against American domination of Caribbean and Latin American countries after World War I forced the United States to adopt a more temperate course. In 1928 the State Department formally repudiated Theodore Roosevelt's extremist interpretation of the Monroe Doctrine, and in 1936 it relinquished its long-held right to intervene in Latin America. Since 1930 the trend of United States foreign ploicy has been generally away from overt influence on hemispheric affairs, with reliance instead on 'dollar diplomacy' to maintain American leadership.

Early twentieth-century imperialism has had its good and bad effects. It brought colonies, some of which proved to be unprofitable headaches. It created tremendous administrative problems, obvious injustices, pervasive national guilt-feelings, and increasing involvement in European politics. Most of all the period of imperialistic expansion broke down, for better or worse, the old isolationist tradition. Theodore Roosevelt, Taft, and Wilson all made strong pleas for the establishment of an international court of justice, and by 1914 the United States had negotiated arbitration treaties with most European nations except Germany and Austria. When the United States acquired the beginnings of an empire, it acquired with it certain commitments and responsibilities in global affairs, as it had reason to realize in 1917 and 1941.

Victory and prosperity made McKinley's re-election in 1900 almost a certainty. For vice-president the Republicans chose Theodore Roosevelt, Governor of New York, whose record as a reformer and military hero made him a nationally known figure. The Democrats countered with Bryan again, but good times and Mark Hanna's efficient organization defeated him easily. McKinley's assassination, barely six months after his inauguration, threw the Republican party into confusion.

Theodore Roosevelt, McKinley's successor, was only forty-three years old when an assassin's bullet elevated him to the Presidency. Young, energetic, and independent, already committed to progressive politics, he seemed to be the leader the reformers prayed for. He was an excellent administrator, a genius at political organization and public relations, and a man of devastating personal charm. His rise had been spectacular – assistant secretary of the Navy, Spanish War colonel, Governor of New York, Vice-President–all within the space of five years. His liberal tend-

encies bothered Hanna, who opposed his nomination at
the convention, and his sudden translation to the White
House worried Republican leaders. Yet on his record
Roosevelt was less a radical than an enlightened conservative; his political programme was remedial rather than
revolutionary. He was, to his credit, the first President since
the Civil War to comprehend the changes taking place in
American life, and he approached contemporary problems
with energy and intelligence. Considering himself an 'accidental President', he soon reassured the party leaders that
he intended to carry out McKinley's policies to the letter.

Roosevelt's first term produced nothing sensational. He
raised progressives' hopes by frequent sallies against 'male-
factors of great wealth' and by his promise of a 'square
deal' for capital and labour, but he was willing to work
with the Republican bosses. His foreign policy was decidedly
imperialistic and aggressive. 'Speak softly and carry a big
stick,' he said; enforce and extend the Monroe Doctrine;
expand America's hemispheric influence and keep Europe
out.

On domestic issues Roosevelt proceeded carefully. Promising swift action against the trusts, he ordered his Attorney-General to institute suit against the Northern
Securities Company, a Hill-Morgan combination, and
cracked it in 1904. At the same time he argued against
indiscriminate attacks on monopoly; there were, he said,
'good' and 'bad' trusts, and only the 'bad' deserved prosecution. His forays against big business slowed down considerably after 1902, leading La Follette to comment causti-
cally that after the smoke of Roosevelt's battles died away,
it was astonishing to find how little ground had been won.
He did, however, intervene in the violent coal strike of
1902, brought by the United Mine Workers against the
Pennsylvania operators. His programme for the conservation of national resources was a solid achievement. Progressives of both parties, though disappointed, nevertheless
supported him in 1904 in the hope that in another four
years he could show real results.

Some conservative Republican leaders would have preferred to drop Roosevelt in 1904, but his popularity was too great. Hanna's death left him in virtual control of the party organization, which nominated him by acclamation at the convention. The Democrats rejected Bryan in favour of Judge Alton Parker of New York, a conservative, colourless candidate, hoping thereby to attract anti-Roosevelt Republicans. The result was an overwhelming victory for Roosevelt.

Reactions to Roosevelt's second term were mixed. He attacked trusts, bosses, and reactionaries; he advocated income and inheritance taxes, pushed conservation programmes, speeded up the construction of the Panama Canal, and pursued an aggressive foreign policy. He broke the tobacco, beef, and fertilizer trusts, but somehow there were more trusts when he left office in 1908 than there were in 1904. At the end of his term progressive leaders criticized his record, admitting at the same time that he had faced powerful conservative opposition in Congress. Still, after seven years in the Presidency, Theodore Roosevelt left no ineradicable mark on the pattern of American political, social, or economic life. He had undoubtedly tried hard to be a liberal, but as Lincoln Steffens thought, he was 'a politician much more than he was a reformer'.

Roosevelt announced that he would not be a candidate in 1908, and though he could easily have had the nomination, he kept his word. He chose as his successor William Howard Taft, a large, affable, indeterminate man with an excellent record as judge, governor of the Philippines, and Secretary of War in Roosevelt's cabinet. The Democrats returned to Bryan for the third time, but the Republicans were too strong. Taft, campaigning on the promise that he would devote himself to 'the constructive work of suggesting to Congress the means by which the Roosevelt policies shall be clinched', won an easy victory.

After receiving congratulations, Roosevelt went to Africa to hunt big game. Taft inherited a bundle of problems. The 1908 Republican platform contained a number of vague

promises which it was Taft's business to carry out; a strong
body of conservative Republicans in Congress were determined to prevent him from doing so. There was also in
Congress a block of Republican senators and representatives
from the Mid-western states (old Granger-Populist territory)
equally determined to force Taft and the party itself to
adopt a progressive programme. These Republican 'insurgents', led by La Follette of Wisconsin in the Senate and
by Norris of Nebraska in the House, harried Taft at every
turn until he found himself listening more and more to the
conservative wing of his party. By 1910 the Republican
organization was seriously split. In early 1911 La Follette
and others founded the National Progressive Republican
League, hoping to wrest control of the party from Taft, and
the Republican newspapers called for Roosevelt's return.
'Teddy, Teddy, come blow your horn', a popular parody
ran,

> The cow's in the meadow, the sheep's in the corn;
> The boy you left to tend the sheep
> Is under the haystack, fast asleep.

Roosevelt came back to the sound of trumpets. He was
not the same Roosevelt who had left fifteen months earlier,
for his African trip had given him time to think and to
arrange his scattered political impulses into a more coherent philosophy. Particularly strong on him was the
influence of Herbert Croly, whose book, *The Promise of
American Life*, he read carefully in Africa. When he
landed, Roosevelt had developed a rationale of progressivism called 'The New Nationalism', which in effect involved
a stronger national government for the attainment of
constructive social and economic ends. The aim of the New
Nationalism was to combine 'the Hamiltonian principle of
national political responsibility and efficiency with a frank
democratic purpose'.

Roosevelt accepted a post as editor of *Outlook* magazine
and began to publicize his programme, while jockeying for
position in the presidential race of 1912 continued within
the Republican party. Insurgent elements rallied behind La

Follette. Conservatives, who doubted Roosevelt's reliability, backed Taft, while Roosevelt refused to commit himself but left the way open for a draft. A good many progressive Republicans, however, feeling that La Follette was too far to the left to win if nominated, quietly withdrew support from him while covertly building a Roosevelt boom. Finally, in early 1912, they jettisoned La Follette, asked Roosevelt to run, and received his acceptance.

The 1912 pre-convention campaign was a violent three-way fight. La Follette attacked both Roosevelt and Taft as 'fake progressives'; Taft denounced Roosevelt and his aides as 'neurotics' out for revenge; Roosevelt called Taft a 'traitor to the progressive cause'. At the convention the Republican National Committee, making short shrift of the Roosevelt organization, quickly nominated Taft. Roosevelt had come too far to turn back, so a call went out for a meeting in Chicago to choose a 'progressive' Republican candidate. In an atmosphere of hysterical enthusiasm reminiscent of 1896, the Chicago rump convention nominated Roosevelt. The 'Bull Moose' party (Roosevelt told a reporter, 'I feel like a bull moose') was under way.

Democrats watched the Republican civil war with interest. Bryan, three times a loser, decided not to run, and the party itself was divided between a more-or-less liberal western wing and an eastern conservative wing. The conservatives favoured Champ Clark of Missouri, while the liberals favoured Woodrow Wilson, Governor of New Jersey. Although Bryan threw his weight behind Wilson, a comparative newcomer to politics, he did not thereby guarantee his nomination. Indeed, although Bryan supported Wilson from the fourteenth ballot it was not until the forty-sixth that Wilson got home.

An unusual campaign followed. Wilson stayed out of the bickering between Taft and Roosevelt while La Follette and dozens of Republican progressives refused to endorse either one. As a result Wilson won with 345 electoral votes to Roosevelt's eighty-eight and Taft's eight. So Woodrow Wilson, some-time Johns Hopkins student, political scientist of note, President of Princeton University, and reform Governor of New Jersey, became the twenty-eighth President, carrying with him to the White House the hopes of liberals and progressives everywhere.

Wilson, a Virginia-born Scotch Presbyterian scholar, was exactly what he looked, a cold and austere professor of history. Until he was fifty-four his only experience in practical politics was one term as a governor, and he possessed neither commitment to nor strong ties with the party that elected him. What he knew of government he knew from books – from Bagehot, Gladstone, Burke, and Bryce – and not from the hurly-burly of ward politics. Until 1910 his political thinking seemed strongly conservative, though his writings showed a slow trend toward the progressive politics of La Follette and the insurgents. Like Jackson, he believed deeply in the rule of the people and in the duty of the chief executive to provide strong, positive party leadership. Educated in the tradition of British nineteenth-century liberalism, he conceived of himself as a sort of prime minister, directing his party and nation as he believed best.

Wilson's political philosophy was built about what he called 'The New Freedom'. 'There is one basic fact,' he said, 'which underlies all the questions that are discussed in the political platforms of the present moment. That singular fact is that nothing is done in this country as it was done twenty years ago.' A government constructed on the theory that men live best when let alone, he believed, did not suit the economic and social organization of the twentieth century. To develop a 'new freedom', the nation must evolve a new concept of democratic individualism, with the government serving as coordinator and protector of the individual's rights. The things that Wilson feared most were the trust and its companions, special privilege and concentration of power. Government must remove that 'hindrance of hindrances', the stifling of competition, so that the old days of individual enterprise might come again. The New Freedom was therefore a rebirth of the old freedom, a restoration of individual competition – freedom for small business against the trust, for farmer against banker and manufacturer, for labourer against employer. The New Freedom meant 'a revival of the power of the people, the beginning of an age of thoughtful reconstruction'.

Wilson's choice of a cabinet encouraged his supporters. None of his appointees came from the inner circle of Democratic bosses, and all were considered able men. His most important appointment was that of Bryan as Secretary of State; William McAdoo of California became Secretary of the Treasury; Secretary of Commerce Redfield was a tariff reformer; Attorney General McReynolds was a known 'trust-buster' from Taft's administration. Wilson's Inaugural Address, one of the finest of presidential documents, launched his first term on a high level. 'Our duty', he said,

is to cleanse, to reconsider, to restore, to correct the evil without impairing the good, to purify and humanize every process of our common life without weakening or sentimentalizing it. There has been something crude and heartless and unfeeling in our haste to succeed and be great. . . . We have come now to sober second thought. The scales of heedlessness have fallen from our eyes. We have made up our minds to square every process of our national life with the standards we so proudly set up at the beginning and have always carried in our hearts.

Thus Woodrow Wilson hoped to bring traditional democracy into tune with an urban-industrial America.

His victory, said Wilson, was not simply a change of drivers in the same wagon going down the old road. The Democratic triumph, he believed, represented an indictment of the whole course of recent politics and a mandate for a thorough reorganization and redirection of American political life. There was little in his programme that had not already been suggested by numerous progressive, liberal, and reform leaders who had preceded him. He pledged his administration to a revision of the tariff, a revision of banking and currency laws, a programme of agricultural aid, effective anti-trust laws, and constructive social legislation. Redemption of those promises meant extending Federal authority over ever-widening social and economic areas, creating the powerful government urged by the Populists and Theodore Roosevelt.

With the aid of a Democratic majority in Congress Wilson redeemed nearly all his pledges within two years. His first message to Congress, asking for a revision of the tariff, was answered by the Underwood Tariff. The ink was hardly dry on the Underwood bill when Wilson was back in Congress with the question of banking and money, the traditional Jacksonian–Granger–Populist issue. Congress responded with the Federal Reserve Act of 1913, creating a system of regional reserve banks, recognizing paper as the country's money, and providing for a contracting–expanding currency.

'I am for big business,' Wilson said, 'and I am against trusts.' The argument was not between big and small business, in his opinion, but between business and unfair monopoly. Legislate against unfair business methods, bar illicit practices, keep competition open and free – this was Wilson's principle, not Roosevelt's of allowing the trust to exist and then controlling it, nor Bryan's of splitting big businesses into little ones. In 1914 Congress approved the Federal Trade Commission Act endowing the Commission with investigative and regulative powers, outlawed 'unfair methods of competition', and supplemented the Sherman Act by establishing evidence on which anti-trust prosecutions might be based; the Clayton Anti-Trust Act, enacted the same year, reinforced and clarified the Sherman Act. Other bills, rolling through Congress, extended his programme. The seventeenth Amendment to the Constitution, ratified in 1913, established direct election of Senators, an old progressive issue. The La Follette and Adamson Acts improved working conditions and shortened hours for seamen and train-men. A child labour bill became law in 1916.

America's involvement in the First World War ended Wilson's schedule for domestic reform, yet the record shows that during his administrations more legislation of a progressive nature was passed, and the foundations for more laid, than under any previous administration since Jackson's. In the post-war years the dominant trend of government moved far away from the principles of the 'New Freedom', until the 'New Deal' resurrected portions of its rusty programme.

The period 1900–14 saw the emergence of modern American society. One of the major factors in its development was the current revolution in transportation and communication. The period of uninhibited railroad building was past, but the application of the gasoline engine to transportation opened up an entirely new area of expansion. Duryea, Haynes, Old, Ford, and others experimented with 'horseless carriages' at the turn of the century, and in 1909 Ford began production of his famous and durable Model T. General Motors, formed in 1908 by W. C. Durant, soon rivalled Ford. By 1914 the automobile was well within the price range of the middle income class, and a million cars were on the roads. The Wright brothers' tentative flights at Kitty Hawk dunes in 1903 were to have their effects before very long.

By 1900 telegraph systems spanned every section of the country. The Bell Telephone Company controlled telephonic communication almost as completely as Western Union controlled the telegraph. Marconi's wireless, perfected in 1901, became standard equipment on ships, but proved to be less useful on land. The demand for electricity created by Edison's incandescent electric lamp and by the introduction of trolley cars in the cities led to giant hydroelectric developments, while the manufacture and sale of electric equipment encouraged the rise of giant electrical supply firms such as General Electric and Westinghouse.

These new means of communication directly affected manufacturing and marketing. They broke down isolation and sectionalism, binding the nation more closely together than ever before, accelerating the trend toward urbanism, stimulating the growth of suburban settlements. The great new industrial firms created by the automobile, the electric light, the telephone (and later the aeroplane) opened up completely fresh fields of business enterprise and made new uses for a variety of raw materials – the automobile alone helped to establish a whole new empire based on gasoline and oil. As transportation and communication facilities improved, so the nation's living habits changed. The automobile created new problems of crime, education, morals, traffic, markets; the United States became a nation on wheels.

Perhaps the most obvious shift in the social pattern after 1900 was reflected in the changed status of women. The Industrial Revolution put women into factories and business; the growth of the city gave them vocational opportunities as clerks, stenographers, social workers, and teachers, all of which became almost exclusively female professions. Economic independence gave women a greater degree of domestic independence (especially after the introduction of machinery into the home) and consequent freedom from much of the drudgery of household tasks. With time for economic, social, and political activity, women used it. Women's clubs sprang up in profusion, until by 1914 the Federation of Women's Clubs counted more than a million members. By the opening of World War I women were a significant force in American social and economic affairs.

The chief woman-inspired reform of the period was the prohibition of alcoholic liquors. The nineteenth-century temperance movements faded before the Civil War, but after it the rate of liquor consumption (and of poverty and crime) increased alarmingly in the cities. In 1873 a group of Ohio women founded the Women's Christian Temperance Union to work with the churches in prohibiting the sale of liquor by law. Both Protestant and Catholic groups supported the W.C.T.U. which obtained prohibition legislation in six states and hundreds of localities. Carrie Nation, a Kansas lady who hacked up saloons with a hatchet, was possibly the most spectacular crusader against alcohol, but the organizational skill of Frances Willard, Dean of Women at Northwestern University, had more effective results. The Anti-Saloon League, founded in 1893 as a logical outgrowth

of the W.C.T.U., merged the major prohibition societies into
a powerful lobby that eventually succeeded in passing the
eighteenth Amendment in 1920. The importance of these
groups, however, lay not so much in their battle against
alcohol, but more in the fact that they initiated a nation-
wide network of women's organizations and developed a set
of leaders with useful political experience.

Their real struggle came with the attempt to establish
votes for women. The question of female suffrage harked
back to the reform movements of the early nineteenth
century, but by 1890 its objectives broadened to include
equal pay for equal work, liberalized divorce laws, elimination of the 'double standard' of morality, and legal
recognition of women's rights. The National Woman Suffrage Association followed the aggressive leadership of Susan
B. Anthony; the American Woman Suffrage Association
adopted the more conservative tactics of Lucy Stone. After
1890, when the rival organizations merged to present a
solid front, male opposition rapidly crumbled. By 1914
eleven states had granted the vote to women, and the nineteenth or 'Susan Anthony' Amendment to the Constitution
was ratified in 1920.

The trend toward liberalism traced by politics and reform marked other aspects of American life. By the turn of
the century the battle between modernism and fundamen-
talism in religion was nearly over. Discouraged at the
inroads of Social Gospellers and modernists, representatives
of the fundamentalist sects met at Niagara in 1895 to adopt
a body of conservative doctrine and to found new theological training schools such as the Moody Bible Institute of
Chicago. Theirs was a rearguard action, however, for most
Protestant churches readily accepted the socialized, modern-
ist point of view. The Federal Council of the Churches of
Christ in 1905 and the Methodist Council in 1908 both
adopted creeds aimed at 'making the influence of Christ
effective in *all* human relations'. Episcopal, Congregational,
Baptist, and Unitarian bodies declared themselves favourably disposed to 'useful activity' on progressive, liberal lines.

The greatest single change in the American religious pattern was the result of increased immigration from Southern Europe. Catholic Church membership in the United States grew from nine million in 1807 to eighteen million by 1920, chiefly concentrated in Eastern cities, where Catholics gained an economic and political position comparable to that of the Baptists and Methodists in the South. Catholicism's foreign origins and its monolithic church structure caused fear and hostility among Protestant sects, but under the leadership of Cardinal Gibbons the Catholic Church quickly became Americanized. Protestant-Catholic clashes, particularly over the relation between church and state, have since frequently developed, but rarely to serious proportions.

Social reformers, political progressives, and labour leaders in the late nineteenth and early twentieth centuries all demanded legislation embodying various reforms. Since the majority of jurists tended to favour a conservative interpretation of the law, reform legislation constantly ran into judicial road-blocks. Prevailing legal opinion considered the law an inflexible, axiomatic body of precedents, the Constitution a fixed and absolute legal standard; therefore the courts, state and federal, struck down dozens of bills, particularly on the ground that they interfered with the fourteenth Amendment. Supreme Court Justices Fields and Sutherland and others in lesser courts erased laws governing child labour, working hours, industrial safety and health regulations, workmen's compensation, minimum wages, pensions for the blind, and the like. Before reforms could succeed, the basis of legal decisions had to shift from the positivist concept that the law and the Constitution expressed eternal and unchanging truths, to a relativist concept that both must accommodate themselves to changing social needs and conditions.

In this shift both evolution and pragmatism played a major part. The leaders of the new relativist interpretation were Roscoe Pound and Oliver Wendell Holmes, Jr. Pound, who became dean of Harvard Law School in 1910,

used the term 'social jurisprudence' to describe his concept
of law as an ever-adapting, dynamic social institution.
Dozens of young lawyers who received training under him
became key figures in the New Deal reforms of the thirties.
Holmes, 'the great dissenter', left an even deeper impress on
American legal tradition. After a brilliant career on the
Massachusetts Supreme Court he was raised to the Federal
Bench by Roosevelt in 1902. The law, to Holmes, settled no
disputes; judges settled them by interpreting the law in
terms of the majority experience, the necessities of the times,
public policy and welfare, and prevalent moral and political
facts. The real test of truth, he wrote, is 'the power to get
itself accepted in the competition of the market'. Holmes
was joined later by Louis Brandeis, a Wilson appointee to
the Court, who believed even more strongly than Pound or
Holmes in weighing public needs against private values in
making legal decisions. More or less alone at first, Holmes,
Brandeis, and the relativists gained ground. In the twenties,
driven by social and economic pressures, the courts finally
surrendered to the trend toward 'social jurisprudence'.

Another American institution, the press, underwent drastic modifications after the turn of the century. Though the
old magazines still existed – *Harper's*, *The Century*, *The
Atlantic*, *The North American Review* – the lion's share of the
market went to cheaper, more sensational newcomers such
as *McClure's*, *Munsey's*, *Collier's*, and *The Saturday Evening
Post*, under shrewd editors like S. S. McClure, Frank
Munsey, Edward Bok, and Cyrus Curtis. The development
of the linotype machine, the typewriter, the high-speed press,
and telegraph wire service changed the content of newspapers as well as of magazines. While the nineteenth-century
newspaper had been chiefly an organ for the dissemination of
news and editorial opinion, its twentieth-century descendant
became less an editorial instrument than a profit-making
business. Daily newspapers took on the appearance of magazines, with comic strips, sports pages, bed-time stories, advice
to cooks and lovers, syndicated columns, and serialized
novels.

Like other ventures of the period, the press suffered from consolidation. Chains absorbed smaller papers into empires, Hearst's, Pulitzer's, and others. 'Yellow journalism' increased circulation and profits with sensationalism, emotionalism, sex, 'sobsister' reporting, crime news. Though the accuracy and excellence of reporting might vary with the paper, the fact that news and features were usually gathered and distributed by wire-service syndicates tended to standardize content. The growth of chains and press associations closed the door on the era of personal journalism represented by Greeley, Bennett, Godkin, Bryant, and the great nineteenth-century editors.

Contemporary American painting reflected the prevailing war between traditionalists and moderns, between classical academicians and rebels. Building on the work of Winslow Homer and Thomas Eakins, a New York group founded the 'ashcan' school of native realism; the work of John Sloan, George Luks, Everett Shinn, George Bellows, and their followers caused hot arguments among critics. French impressionism influenced others. The famous 'Armory Show' of 1913 introduced Picasso, Van Gogh, Cézanne, and other 'moderns' to painters and public, leaving behind an army of imitators. In general the gulf between American and European art narrowed considerably after 1900. Architecture, sculpture, and design reacted swiftly to European trends, and Americans themselves began to develop a more mature, sophisticated, international frame of mind.

Music lagged somewhat behind the visual arts as a field of creative activity. Until the establishment of urban cultural centres, interest in musical performance and composition remained on a popular, folk level. The most vital musical force in the late nineteenth century was the Negro, whose cake-walks, fiddle songs, spirituals, and blues were the nearest to a native music that the nation possessed. Minstrel shows (based on Negro music though performed by black-faced white men) became popular in the seventies and eighties; with them the songs of Dan Emmett and

Stephen Foster travelled the country. After the Civil War, Confederate military band instruments fell into the hands of Negroes who began to improvise music of their own, based on religious and folk tunes of Irish, Spanish, British and African origins. In New Orleans Negro bands played in dance halls and brothels, at funerals and weddings, evolving a singular type of two-beat and later four-beat music called 'ragtime' and 'jazz'. After 1900 jazz entered its so-called 'classical period', with the appearance of great Negro musicians like Buddy Bolden, King Oliver, Bunk Johnson, Jelly-Roll Morton and Louis Armstrong. When the river-boats carried jazz up the Mississippi to Memphis, St Louis, Kansas City, and finally to Chicago, it shook off its local and racial origins.

Interest in serious music came with the growth of cities, increased immigration, and the perfection of Edison's phonograph. German, Scandinavian, and Bohemian groups often organized their own orchestral and choral societies almost as soon as they arrived in America. The New York Philharmonic Society, founded in 1842, struggled hard until after the Civil War, when Theodore Thomas made it into a stable and much-improved organization. Thomas, a German immigrant, carried his musical enthus:asm to other cities, helped to found the Boston Symphony and the Chicago Symphony, serving intermittently as conductor of both. New York's Metropolitan Opera Society was established in 1883 with the assistance of several millionaires and by 1914 the 'Met', with Toscanini as conductor and Enrico Caruso as its main attraction, was almost a national institution. Both the symphony and the opera, until after the turn of the century, however, depended on imported music and talent. Only a few native composers or performers, such as Edward McDowell and Emma Eames, gained any prominence.

After 1865 there was a boom in the theatre which it enjoyed until 1914 – probably the greatest period of prosperity and popularity in its history. It was an age of great producers – Frohman, Belasco, Hammerstein – and of polished actors – Edwin Booth, E. H. Sothern, Richard Mansfield, Maude Adams, Otis Skinner and Maurice Barrymore. But the theatre suffered from mediocre playwriting and from the trend towards consolidation. The introduction of the 'star' system, the competition of the cinema, the concentration of theatres in a few major cities, and the tightening control of chain ownership killed off the travelling stock company and closed many smaller theatres. On a popular level melodrama remained a perennial favourite. Plays of common life with a villain, a hero, and a persecuted heroine (*Nellie the Beautiful Cloak Model*), thrillers (*Chinatown Charlie the Opium Fiend*), and old stand-bys (*Uncle Tom's Cabin*) drew large audiences year in and year out. Vaudeville, the American version of the British variety show, had its heyday after 1885, when Keith's in Boston and Tony Pastor's in New York started the first continuous performances. It developed great popular stars like Lillian Russell and Weber and Fields, as well as a host of actors and comedians who moved later into movies and radio. For the rougher trade it developed burlesque, with double-entendre jokes, undraped girls, and eventually the strip-tease. But vaudeville and burlesque, like the legitimate theatre, soon fell under centralized control and became big city entertainment.

Every form of entertainment after 1900 felt the impact of the motion picture, which eventually became the largest single influence on the American cultural pattern. In 1903 E. S. Porter, Edison's cameraman, by producing *The Great Train Robbery*, the first continuous-story feature, changed the motion picture from an amusing toy to large-scale entertainment. An attempted corner of the industry in 1914 was defeated by invoking the Sherman Act, and the movie business turned into a fiercely competitive struggle among several huge companies. After 1916, profiting from the wartime closing of European studios, American movie-makers seized control of the major share of the world market. Bold and imaginative directors such as David Wark Griffiths and talented stars of the calibre of Chaplin sensed the possibilities of the new medium and raised the level of cinematic

651

production. Movie stars set national fashions (good and bad) in speech, dress, action, and ideas, but in general the predominantly middle-class virtues portrayed by the movies for mass audiences tended to reinforce established cultural patterns. Since New York (and later Hollywood) produced standardized products for all sections and classes, the movies exerted a strong nationalizing, standardizing influence. Since movie-making is a profit-making business, American producers have rarely troubled with experimentation in the European manner, nor have they considered the cinema primarily an art form.

Pre-Civil War foreign observers unanimously observed the American passion for sports, especially horse-racing, foot-racing, rowing, and prize-fighting. After the war baseball began to eclipse all other pastimes in popularity. Hundreds of amateur teams were formed by veterans who had learned the game in army camps, and the first professionals, the Cincinnati Red Stockings, scheduled games in 1869. In 1876 eight professional teams founded the National League, which dominated the sport until the appearance of the rival American League in the nineties. The two leagues declared peace in 1903, justifying the first 'world's series' championship play-offs. Football, adapted from rugby in the sixties, took its present form during the eighties. By 1900 it was especially popular in Eastern colleges and universities, but deaths and injuries among players mounted so high that many institutions banned it until rule changes were made in 1906 by the National Collegiate Athletic Association. Basket-ball, invented in 1891 by a Canadian, James Naismith, had a slow start, yet by 1930 it drew the largest attendance of any American amateur sport. Boxing was legally barred in many states and communities until it attained respectability (Theodore Roosevelt was an enthusiastic amateur) at the time of World War I. Hore-racing's connexions with gambling caused every state to pass anti-betting laws; patronage of the wealthy, legalized betting, and construction of public tracks revived interest in it after the First World War.

The First World War was the most decisive event in the history of American foreign relations. Although the State Department suspected that Europe was a powder-keg, the sudden explosion of June 1914 caught both the public and the government off guard. The United States was a world power, irrevocably involved in global events, though neither its government nor people fully realized the fact and those who did were often unwilling to accept it. The outbreak of war in Europe made American isolationism the major issue of the generation.

The first American reaction to European declarations of war after August 1914, was an almost unanimous desire for neautrality. Wilson's proclamation of August stressed the need to be 'impartial in thought as well as in action'. This was Europe's war, not America's, and neither Wilson nor Bryan, his Secretary of State, wished to repeat the mistakes of 1812.

But, as in the Napoleonic era, the path of the neutral proved to be strewn with obstacles. At first the United States refused to allow American loans to the warring nations, lest financial commitments grow too large, while Wilson declared an 'open trade' policy to maintain American rights of trade with any participant. Both decisions benefited the Allies far more than Germany. England and France held large assets in the United States which they liquidated to purchase American goods; since Britain controlled the seas, few but Allied ships reached American ports. When Allied credit seemed exhausted, Wilson's government found itself in an impossible position. The United States economy, geared to wartime demands, would be seriously damaged if its export trade were cut off; on the other hand, both Wilson and Bryan recognized that foreign loans threatened American neutrality. Under pressure from industry, agriculture, and banking, Wilson gave in, until by 1917 loans to the Allies reached 2,000 million dollars while those to Germany totalled only twenty-seven millions. The American financial stake in an Allied victory was high.

Wilson's 'open trade' policy was not wholly satisfactory. Britain blockaded the Central Powers, published a list of trade restrictions, and black-listed American firms suspected of trading with Germany. In each case British proclamations followed recognized international law, but in their observance the Royal Navy sometimes stepped on American toes and State Department protests of minor violations of United States rights on the seas received cavalier treatment, yet American public opinion remained friendly. England's acts cost no lives; American shipping firms were compensated (sometimes over-generously) for their losses.

German violations provoked a different reaction. As Winston Churchill predicted, Germany's announcement in 1915 of a submarine blockade of England brought immediate protests from the United States. The Imperial Government of Germany, Wilson informed the Kaiser, would be held 'to a strict accountability for property endangered or lives lost'. The torpedoing of the British liner *Lusitania* on 7 May 1915, with a loss of 128 American lives, put United States–German relations under severe strain. Wilson's note of 9 June again demanding 'strict accountability', brought Bryan's resignation, since Bryan believed it meant war, and the sinking of the *Arabic* in August, with two American lives lost, brought the break closer. Though the German ambassador promised that his government would stop indiscriminate torpedoings, Germany in February 1916 resumed unrestricted submarine warfare. Another note from the United States elicited a vague reaffirmation of the 1915 pledge, but by this time American opinion was thoroughly aroused.

Nevertheless, a hard kernel of isolationist resistance remained in the United States. Arbitration as a means of settling international disputes was firmly ingrained in American foreign policy. The World Peace Foundation established a million dollar fund in 1910; that same year Andrew Carnegie built a 'peace palace' at The Hague and gave ten million dollars to the Carnegie Foundation for International Peace. Norman Angell's *The Great Illusion* and William James's *Moral Equivalent of War* (both published in 1910) impressed thoughtful Americans with war's futility. In Congress La Follette, Norris, Lindbergh, and other Mid-

westerners opposed any act that might lead to war, and in
1916 Wilson's supporters barely over-rode a bill to forbid
American travel on armed ships.

Isolationist sentiment was strong, but interventionist feeling was stronger. Theodore Roosevelt, a bitter critic of
Wilson's 'soft' policy, was perhaps the most bellicose of the
interventionists. More thoughtful and temperate minds,
however, after wrestling with the problem, came to the conclusion that 'self-complacent isolationism' was impossible in
a twentieth-century world. The war, wrote Herbert Croly in
the *New Republic*, was 'a challenge to the United States to
justify its independence. The nation cannot be independent
in the sense of being isolated' – an echo of Wilson's statement that 'We did not set this Government up in order that
we might have a selfish and separate liberty.'

America's moral dilemma was best illustrated by Wilson's
personal struggle. He realized that war meant the end of his
programme of domestic reform, so bravely and successfully
begun; as a student of history (and a member of the
American Peace Society) he knew war to be a grim and inconclusive settlement of differences. He knew something of
the imperialist beginnings of war and something of the ways
of power politics; he disliked and distrusted armed force.
Yet at the same time he rejected everything that Imperial
Germany represented, and was so steeped in the Anglo-
American tradition that it was manifestly impossible for
him, or for others like him, to maintain absolute neutrality.
Britain and France held the right cause, he believed, and in
a struggle between right and wrong, he found it difficult to
follow an isolationist line if it seemed to favour the wrong.
The internationalist in Wilson triumphed over the isolationist, as it did in the mind of the American public at large.
The war was to Wilson a holy crusade to 'make the world
safe for democracy', with a vision beyond it of a peace
'planted upon the tested foundations of political liberty'.

The election of 1916 cut in half the heated debate over
America's relation to the war. Though some prominent
Democrats disagreed with Wilson's foreign policy, the party

nominated him for a second term almost without dissent, choosing Tom Marshall of Indiana as his vice-president. The Republicans hoped to unify anti-Wilson feeling by choosing a 'safe' candidate rather than the unpredictable and strident Roosevelt. Their convention picked Charles Evans Hughes, a Supreme Court Justice more or less uncommitted on the prevailing issues and a man whose dignity and probity were designed to appeal to liberal and conservative alike. The remnants of the 'Bull Moose' organization hoped to nominate Roosevelt and continue the revolt of 1912, but Roosevelt, who wanted to defeat Wilson even more than he wanted to be President, refused and advised his followers to vote for Hughes.

The Democrats based their campaign on the domestic achievements of the 'New Freedom' and the slogan, 'He kept us out of war', though Wilson, realizing the narrow margin by which America remained at peace, explained that involvement might come sooner than his supporters knew. Hughes conducted a conservative and dignified campaign. Roosevelt attacked Wilson violently up and down the land, warned that his re-election would be 'a damage to the moral fibre of the American people'. The Republican and 'Bull Moose' vote combined could have defeated Wilson, but a large segment of the Progressive vote swung to him. As it happened, his margin of victory was slim. Only late returns from California clinched his election, 277 electoral votes to 254.

Wilson firmly believed that the United States wanted peace, and as soon as the election was over he asked the warring powers to clarify their war aims so that a basis for ending the conflict might be found. The Allies, having suffered huge losses and a succession of disasters, resented his request but complied; Germany refused. Nevertheless Wilson had hopes of a 'peace without victory', a hope shattered by Germany's announcement in January of 1917 of unrestricted submarine warfare. In the light of his previous commitments there was little Wilson could do but sever diplomatic relations, an act Congress approved at once. Speaking optimistically of 'an armed neutrality', the President and Congress created a Council of National Defence, increased the strength of the National Guard, and authorized the construction of four new battleships. In February and March German submarines sank eight American ships. On 2 April Wilson asked Congress for a declaration of war.

The President based his war message on four major points: unrestricted submarine sinkings, German sabotage in American industry, the failure of armed neutrality, and the German threat to the security of American and global democracy. 'It is a fearful thing', he said, 'to lead this great and powerful people into war . . . , but the right is more precious than peace, and we shall fight for the things which we have always carried nearest our hearts.' The Senate responded with a declaration of war two days later, and on Good Friday 1917 the House concurred.

The United States entered World War I on the Allied side for a variety of reasons, but one is clear: America could not afford to do otherwise without risking a German victory in Europe. It is true that American loans to the wartime trade with the Allies gave the nation a heavy financial interest in an Allied victory. Yet American bankers and manufacturers, however important they considered overseas loans, consistently favoured neutrality, where the profits lay, rather than war, which meant mounting taxes and government regulation of industry. It was also true that British propaganda was singularly good and German bad, British diplomacy excellent and German inept. Yet neither loans nor propaganda nor diplomacy put the United States into war. Although it now appears to many Americans that the United States could not afford the risk of allowing Germany to supplant Britain as the dominant force in Europe, in 1917 only a small proportion of the advocates of war were either aware of or willing to express this fear as the reason for United States intervention. For nearly one hundred years Britain had contributed to American security by maintaining control of the seas and a European balance of power. Britain and France were known quantities; Germany, a new strange power, was both unknown and unfriendly. Secretary of State Lansing observed in 1916, 'On no account must we range ourselves even indirectly on the side of Germany . . . German imperialistic ambitions threaten free institutions everywhere.' Wilson's determination that the world must be made safe for democracy stated the real reason for America's entry. So long as military autocracy existed in Europe American democracy was in danger.

The United States Army was not prepared for war. Many Americans at first believed that ships and loans constituted the most effective assistance the United States could give the Allies, but German victories and Allied losses in 1917 made it imperative that an expeditionary force be created at once. Though volunteering was good, Congress passed a Selective Service Act in May 1917 to make more efficient use of American manpower. Eventually twenty-four million men registered for the draft, of whom almost five million entered some branch of military service. Thirty-two training camps were established to receive the draftees, and as they had in 1861, raw recruits poured in from Kansas farms and Eastern cities, from Louisiana swamps and Tennessee mountains. Equipment was scarce and training elementary. Six months of drill and firing practice fitted a draftee for battle, while Officer Training Camps graduated combat leaders in ninety days. Meanwhile General Pershing, commander of the Expeditionary Force, landed in France with a small contingent of soldiers in June 1917. About 200,000 more made the Atlantic crossing before 1918, and the pace increased after March 1918.

The Navy, with several new ships nearly completed, was much better prepared than the Army. By mid-1917 eighteen destroyers were operating in the North Atlantic and within a year five American battleships joined the British fleet. The great American contribution to the sea war was its anti-submarine and convoy work. Britain in 1917 was losing one of every four merchant ships leaving its ports; the addition of American destroyers to convoy duty aided materially in lowering the rate. American minelayers also laid a major share of the North Sea minefield that bottled up the main body of the German fleet.

Pershing from the first insisted on the maintenance of a separate American Army in France, though Foch and Haig hoped to brigade American troops with British and French units. He won his point, and in late 1917 the Americans took over a quiet sector on the Western front. At that moment prospects for victory looked bright to the Germans and Austrians. The Italian defeat at Caporetto had virtually knocked Italy out of the war, and in early 1918 the Soviets overthrew the Kerensky government in Russia, signed an armistice with the Central Powers, and thus released a half-million seasoned German soldiers for the Western Front. Germany immediately launched a heavy offensive against the British, and later in the spring struck along the Marne. Whatever his feelings about a separate command, Pershing did not hesitate to place his troops at Foch's disposal. The First Division fought at Cantigny, the Second at Belleau Wood, and the Third at Château-Thierry.

When the Allied lines held the initiative passed to Foch, who acceded to Pershing's wish. The First and Second Armies, aided by French colonials, participated in the counter-offensive of 1918, while in September the Americans in force attacked at Saint-Mihiel salient, taking 16,000 prisoners with light losses. Later in the year Pershing's men mounted an attack in the Meuse-Argonne offensive for forty-seven consecutive days, cracking the Hindenburg Line. The 'big push' in the autumn of 1918 broke the back of German resistance. On 3 October the German government communicated with Wilson, asking for an armistice, followed by a similar request from Austria-Hungary. When Wilson refused to deal independently with the Central Powers, Allied commissioners met with German representatives in early November, and on 11 November 1918 an armistice ended the war.

Direct American military contributions to the First World War were much smaller than those of Britain and France;

nevertheless they were decisively timed. The American army suffered 125,000 casualties (half of them battle deaths), inconsiderable losses compared to those of the Allies, though sustained in only six months' action. But the United States had a million men in France at the end of the war, and the prospect of facing an ever-growing American army had obvious effects on German morale. The United States' entry into the conflict brought confidence to battle-weary nations who had endured three years of bloody stalemate. With the industrial might of the United States on their side, and with the daily arrival of thousands of self-assured, fresh troops, the Allies felt an immediate lift.

The greatest American contribution, however, was the high-minded idealism of Woodrow Wilson. His famous 'Fourteen Points' of a just peace, embodied in his speech to Congress in January of 1918, gave the Allied cause its most potent ideological weapon. If the world could have 'open covenants openly arrived at', freedom of the seas, autonomy and liberty for people, redress of ancient wrongs, and a 'general association of nations for mutual guarantees of political independence and territorial integrity' – then the end of 'the war to end war' promised hope to victor and vanquished alike. 'Meester Veelson's' vision, which unfortunately others may not have shared, seemed to offer a basis for a just and enduring peace. Germany's claim that it never received at Versailles what Wilson promised made it easier for Adolf Hitler, a generation later, to convince the German people that they had been tricked into an unnecessary surrender.

The war had tremendous internal effects on the United States. Far more so than the Spanish or Civil Wars, World War I provoked an intense nationalism that almost completely obliterated sectional feeling. With twenty-four million men at the call of the Federal government, five million of them under military regulations, the force of Federal power was felt by American citizens as never before. Wartime life was strictly regimented by Federal decree, with industry, food, fuel, housing, even news controlled by

Federal boards and bureaux. In later years during the New Deal attack on the depression, and mobilization for World War II, the experience of World War I provided both pattern and personnel for similar extensions of Federal control.

Congress at the beginning of the war gave Wilson sweeping authority, much of which he delegated to Boards or Commissions, for the most part appointed by him and responsible to him alone. The problem of total mobilization lay with the Council of National Defense, composed of cabinet officers and an advisory planning board. The War Industries Board, headed by Bernard Baruch (later an adviser to Franklin Roosevelt in World War II), was responsible for coordinating industrial effort, regulating production, shifting factories to a wartime basis, and planning use of raw materials. The Shipping Board took over the merchant marine and built new ships to replace submarine losses. The Railroad Administration put the rail lines under federal control, paying rent to the rail companies, while other boards took over grain elevators, warehouses, telegraph lines, and telephone services. The Department of Labor assumed responsibility for housing workers in mushrooming industrial cities. Herbert Hoover, head of the Food Administration, fixed prices, regulated production and distribution, and designated 'wheatless' and 'meatless' days to conserve foodstuffs. The Fuel Administration controlled consumption of coal and oil; the War Trade Board licensed exports so that American goods did not fall into enemy hands; the War Finance Corporation lent capital to expanding industries. The task of mobilizing public opinion fell to the Committee on Public Information, whose executive secretary, George Creel, worked tirelessly to 'sell the war' with the latest advertising methods. To finance the war Congress raised income, corporation, and excess profit taxes, imposed a variety of new taxes, and authorized the sale of government bonds. Using methods pioneered by Jay Cooke in the Civil War, the Treasury sold $21,000 million in 'Liberty Bonds' to small investors.

Labour gained a great deal from the war. Gompers's appointment to the Council of National Defense meant the recognition of organized labour as capital's equal and lifted union morale. To avoid crippling strikes and indiscriminate use of the injunction Wilson created the National War Labor Board to hear disputes between labour and management. The Board handled more than a thousand cases, fixing the principle of collective bargaining firmly in the public mind. With a flood of new workers into war plants union membership jumped 37 per cent. The demands of war production created new opportunities for Negroes, who moved by thousands into Northern industrial cities. At the close of the war labour enjoyed full employment, high wages, a shorter working week, arbitration and collective bargaining, and, above all, general public respect. The War also provided the setting for America's most ambitious attempt at social reform through legislation, the famous Eighteenth or 'prohibition' amendment to the Constitution. The old crusade against alcohol carried on by the temperance societies lost no force over the preceding century; by 1915 fourteen states prohibited the manufacture and sale of alcoholic beverages, and America's entry into the war afforded the Anti-Saloon League, the most powerful of the societies, an opportunity to equate prohibition with patriotism. After a shrewd and well-organized campaign by the League and other groups, Congress in December 1917, passed and submitted to the states for ratification, the Eighteenth Amendment, approved by all except Connecticut and Rhode Island by 1919. Congress, under the powers bestowed on it by the amendment, then passed the Volstead Act (named after Congressman Andrew Volstead of Minnesota, alcohol's implacable congressional foe) which forbade the manufacture, transportation and sale of beverages containing more than 0.5 per cent alcohol. Thus began America's 'noble experiment', as it was later known, in accomplishing social change by law, conceived in idealism and disastrous in effect. Whatever its aims, prohibition brought with it so much 'bootlegging', gangsterism, racketeering and public disregard for law that during the twenties even some of its most sincere supporters began to lose faith in its enforcement, if not its principle.

The most conspicuous failure of the United States during the War lay in the field of civil liberties. War propaganda played on its 'hate the enemy' theme so effectively that tolerance, free speech, and freedom of thought and opinion suffered. Congress, in response to demands for internal security legislation, passed the Espionage Act of 1917 and the Sedition Act of 1918, both more far-reaching in effect than any previous laws in American history. State laws against subversion and disloyalty were even more drastic. Federal authorities arrested and gaoled 1,500 persons, among them Eugene Debs, who had polled a million votes as Socialist candidate for President in 1912. The worst offenders were private patriotic groups and individuals who tracked down 'slackers', 'yellowbacks', and 'pro-Germans' with hysterical intensity. German-Americans suffered especially; German music was banned, universities dropped courses in Goethe and revoked honorary degrees granted to German scholars – even sauerkraut became 'Liberty cabbage'. A few sensible men, such as Holmes and Brandeis, who counselled against stifling democracy during a war to preserve it, went largely unheard. Wilson's prediction that war meant that 'the spirit of ruthless brutality will enter into every fiber of our national life' came true very soon.

The real test of American leadership came with the peace. The Peace Conference met in Paris on 18 January 1919, after slightly more than four years of war, thirteen million casualties, and incalculable expenditure of money and materials. The plenary sessions of the Conference mattered less than the 'Big Four' meetings which set the actual terms of settlement. Lloyd George, representing the world's largest empire and one-quarter of its population, had been elected on the slogan 'Make Germany Pay!' Clemenceau, France's 'Tiger', was so intent on weakening Germany that he appeared to be a narrow, vindictive old man with little interest in anything except France's immediate future. Orlando, Italy's delegate, wanted new territory and sat out much of the conference in a huff. All four representatives were keenly aware of aroused public opinion at home, and in the end, after much bickering, Wilson was forced to make many concessions to conflicting interests and old hatred. Not even the victors were satisfied with the Treaty of Versailles, but Wilson pinned his faith to the League of Nations Covenant it created, believing that the League might settle peaceably the disputes and wrangles bound to arise from the Treaty itself. That his dream of a peaceful and orderly world community did not materialize was not wholly his fault.

The Treaty found a rough road ahead when it was submitted to the Senate for ratification in July of 1919. The question at issue, said Wilson, 'is whether we can refuse the moral leadership that is offered us, whether we shall accept or reject the confidence of the world'. There were few serious objections to most of its terms, but many to the League of Nations idea, particularly to Article X of the League Covenant, by which members were pledged 'to respect and preserve as against external aggression the territorial integrity and existing political independence' of all other members. Some were based on partisan political considerations, some on Wilson's allegedly high-handed methods in framing it without proper consultation with Congress, some on fears of entanglement in foreign wars.

In the Senate the Republicans held a majority as a consequence of the 1918 elections, while control of the Senate Committee on Foreign Relations was firmly in Republican hands. Nearly all Senate Democrats favoured the Treaty. A small group of Republicans was willing to support it with mild reservations, a larger number was willing to pass it with major changes (especially without Article X), and an 'irreconcilable' group of Republicans and a few Democrats refused to approve it in any form. There was also powerful opposition to the League outside of Congress. Theodore Roosevelt attacked it violently, and wealthy isolationists such as Frick and Mellon contributed to a huge campaign against 'The Evil Thing with a Holy Name'. Yet the League had powerful support too. The American Federation of

Labor, the American Bar Association, the Federal Council of Churches, and thirty-two state legislatures endorsed it; ex-President Taft and ex-candidate Charles Evans Hughes supported the League.

The key to the League's defeat lay ultimately in the hands of Senator Henry Cabot Lodge of Massachusetts, chairman of the Senate Committee on Foreign Relations. In 1915 and 1916 Lodge had favoured an association of nations, but his personal antagonism to Wilson and his adherence to party politics were stronger than his internationalist leanings. The Republicans hung amendments on the Treaty, fought Wilson on each one, and wrangled over them on the Senate floor for four months. Wilson himself set out on a nation-wide tour to carry the argument directly to the people, but weary, ill, and worn, he suffered a paralytic stroke in September 1919 and thereafter could put up only a wavering resistance. In March 1920 the Senate voted an end to the war with Germany without ratifying the Treaty, but Wilson vetoed the resolution. Not until the Republican victory of that year did the resolution pass and the war with Germany actually end.

By its refusal to accept membership in the League of Nations the United States implicitly refused to accept world leadership in the peace. Had it entered the League with its full weight, there is a bare possibility that the mistakes of Versailles might have been mitigated and World War II at least delayed, if not prevented. The rejection of the League by the most powerful nation to emerge from the war made international cooperation both difficult and hazardous, and had much to do with the League's failure to meet its challenges a decade later. Wilson's warning that if the League were defeated the United States might have to fight World War I all over again, came back to haunt America.

Though the American people never had a chance to vote directly on the League, congressional opposition to it was obviously based on a large segment of public opinion. American thinking after 1919 was prevailingly disillusioned, nationalistic, and isolationist. The nation had just completed its first great adventure in global politics and did not like it. Few lamented the League's demise during the twenties, and Wilson's lonely death in 1924 brought few twinges to the national conscience. As late as 1937 with another world war about to break, a poll showed that 70 per cent of those who had an opinion on the matter believed that the United States' entry into World War I had been an error. War propaganda backfired badly; the Allies seemed to be human after all, and the squabblings at Paris were not pretty. It became popular to claim that America had been tricked into war by slick British propaganda, by bankers and munitions makers, by clever politicking. It was all over, the nation rolled in wealth, business boomed, and the war was long ago and far away. The American people would not be easily fooled again.

Throughout the twenties revisionist historians, ably aided by politicians and the press, proved not only that World War I but also the Civil War and perhaps the American Revolution need not have happened. The terms of Versailles were carefully analysed and the manoeuvrings of 1900–14 scanned to show that Britain, France, and Russia were not blameless and that Germany possibly had a case. It was fashionable to be objective, sceptical of men and motives, rigidly neutral toward moral issues, emphatic about economic ones. Thus World War I became 'Wilson's War', brought on by an impractical college professor; his aim of 'making the world safe for democracy' was twisted into an impossible dream and his vision of a peaceful world commonwealth derided as unrealistic idealism.

During the twenties foreign relations were chiefly concerned with problems left over from war. The Washington government lent more than 10,000 million dollars to the Allies, usually at 5 per cent interest, and as soon as hostilities ended the debtor nations clamoured for cancellation, or at best, adjustments in both interest and principal. Most of the money, it was argued, had been used to purchase war materials in the United States and never left the country; furthermore, the loans might well be considered as America's contribution to a cause for which Europe had suffered much more heavily in men and materials. American tariff barriers prevented liquidation of the debts by trade, while payment in gold would wreck European currencies.

American opinion, however, regarded a debt as a debt; Coolidge's classic remark, 'They hired the money, didn't they?' reflected the attitude of those who understood neither the intricacies of international finance nor the prostration of post-war Europe. Arguments over war debts embittered feelings on both sides, creating the myths of 'Uncle Shylock' abroad and 'dishonest ingrates' at home. The British settlement of 1923 somewhat mollified American opinion, but negotiations with France, Italy, and Belgium were long and unsatisfactory. Though Hoover announced a moratorium on war debts in 1932 a moratorium was hardly enough. In 1932 six debtor nations defaulted. In 1934 others followed, convincing many Americans that it was useless to do business with 'faithless foreigners' and reinforcing the isolationist trend of the early thirties.

Ironically, the Republican party that had held America out of the League made long strides toward international cooperation under Coolidge and Hoover. By calling the Washington Conference on Limitation of Armaments in 1921, Harding hoped to end the frantic naval rivalry among Britain, Japan, and the United States. Secretary of State Hughes proposed a plan of armament reduction which was adopted in revised form by most of the major powers, though Japan in 1934 renounced all such agreements. In 1927 Coolidge suggested another conference which turned out less successfully. At the same time the 1921 Conference paved the way for a four-power pact (Britain, France, Japan, and the United States) to keep peace in the Pacific, and for a nine-power pact for control of Chinese affairs.

Plans for a World Court of International Justice under the League Covenant found the Republican leaders favourably disposed to American participation. Coolidge gave the Court his personal support, and in 1925 the House declared in favour of joining the tribunal. However, there were still those who feared a recurrence of Wilsonism, and after long debate the Senate crippled the resolution with cautious reservations. While the Senate worked over a compromise, the United States began a programme of careful cooperation with the League, sending observers and advisers to 'non-political' League conferences until by 1930 the United States had five permanent representatives in Geneva and a record of attendance at more than four hundred League meetings. Secretary of State Frank Kellogg, with Coolidge's approval, negotiated a series of arbitration treaties, culminating in the signing of the Kellogg-Briand pact in Paris in 1928. Ultimately sixty-two nations approved the agreement in principle and renounced war as an instrument of national policy. Although the American public was enormously cheered by Kellogg's achievements, less optimistic observers pointed out that the pact made no provisions for its enforcement and could hardly be construed as a broad step away from isolationism. Japan's attack on China in 1931 illustrated their point.

Herbert Hoover, a man of cosmopolitan views and international experience, approved and expanded Coolidge's foreign policy. As a Quaker and as an engineer Hoover hated war's immorality and waste. Although he announced himself opposed to the League of Nations, he urged adherence to the World Court and after careful preparation submitted the necessary legislation for American participation to Congress. Again the 'irreconcilables', aided by the press, rallied enough isolationist sentiment to defeat it, one of the great disappointments of Hoover's life. At his suggestion Ramsay MacDonald called the London Conference of 1930 to discuss naval disarmament, and although the final agreement was only a partial victory for disarmament, it passed the Senate without hampering amendments. In 1932 Hoover electrified the World Disarmament Conference at Geneva by proposing that all existing armaments be slashed by one third, an idea that was enthusiastically buried with oratory. Hoover's sincere, statesmanlike, somewhat visionary plan simply did not fit the temper of a world already coming apart at the seams.

In the period 1920–32 American public opinion was about equally divided between isolationist and internationalist thinking. America's entrance into the First World War emphasized Wilson's idea that 'We are participants, whether we would or not, in the life of the world', and Republican administration of the next decade (particularly under the enlightened leadership of Hoover) went far beyond any previous policies of international cooperation. At the same time American statesmen always faced at home a strong determination to avoid foreign entanglements, keep up trade barriers, and emphasize domestic progress – just as they faced abroad the hostility of a ravaged Europe, sinking into fascism, toward a rich and expanding America. The United States, remarked Coolidge, needed no importations, 'industrial, intellectual, or political'. The sharp division of opinion forced American foreign policy into a middle path. The United States was willing to participate in internationally-flavoured pacts and agreements, but unwilling to bind itself either by machinery or promises to actual involvement in European or Asian affairs. With the onslaught of World War II the United States reluctantly faced again, as it did in 1917, the problem of finding a compromise foreign policy.

Wilson hoped that the election of 1920 might decide the issue of the League of Nations for once and all, but it did not. The Republican National Convention, after some argument, adopted a platform endorsing some sort of international organization, but not Wilson's League. As death had removed Theodore Roosevelt from the scene in 1919, the race for the nomination was wide open. It was won by Warren G. Harding, an Ohio newspaperman, with Calvin Coolidge of Massachusetts as his companion on the ticket.

Harding, an impressively handsome man of extremely limited talents, took an ambiguous stand on the League issue. Since thirty-one prominent Republicans, including Hoover, issued a statement favouring a league of nations, while Lodge and the Republican 'irreconcilables' spoke strongly against it, no one could be quite sure what a vote for Harding meant in terms of international politics. The Democrats nominated James Cox of Ohio for President, Franklin Delano Roosevelt (Wilson's able young Assistant Secretary of the Navy) for vice-president, and pledged an absolute continuance of the Wilsonian foreign and domestic programmes. The public itself, weary of debate and oratory, wanted nothing so much as what Harding called 'a return to normalcy'. Harding won by a seven million majority, and carried a Republican Congress into office with him.

A genial, kindly man who liked to play poker with his friends, Harding was a perfect tool for the party politicians. Cursed with a curious inability to judge men and issues, he was shortly at the mercy of the most cynically corrupt set of rascals to appear in politics since Reconstruction days. Within two years one cabinet member went to prison, two more barely escaped it, and various minor government officials were either convicted of graft or forced to resign. Harding himself seems to have been untouched by the scandals, but he saw enough of what was going on to shake him severely. His health broke under the strain and he died during a trip to Alaska in August 1923. Calvin Coolidge, an impeccably honest man and a good administrator, cleaned up the mess and restored respectability to the Republican Party.

The Republicans meanwhile busied themselves with reversing the direction of Wilsonian policy. Congress swiftly withdrew the wartime powers it had granted the Chief Executive, dissolved the more powerful boards and commissions, and returned to the time-honoured McKinley principle of 'less government in business and more business in government'. Congress cut Federal expenditures, reduced corporation taxes, withdrew Federal controls from business, raised tariffs, subsidized new industries, and drew the teeth of the F.C.C., the I.C.C., and the Federal Reserve Act.

Coolidge phrased it succinctly – 'The business of America is business.' Big corporations grew bigger, bigger even than in McKinley's day, ending in a complex enormity that corporation executives themselves sometimes could not fathom.

In 1930 fifty per cent of the nation's corporate wealth was controlled by two hundred companies; the tobacco, utilities, aluminium, chemicals, dye, communications, and steel trusts eclipsed in size and power anything on the scene in 1900. Agriculture did not fare so well, for after a sharp recession in 1921 farm prices dropped while farm production increased. The farmers organized again – the Farmers' Union, the American Farm Business Federation, the Non-Partisan League, the revitalized Grange – and sent a strong 'farm bloc' to Congress without much encouragement from the Republican majority. Labour was restive. War left the unions powerful, and since the shift to a peace-time economy brought reduced wages and longer hours, hundreds of strikes plagued industry. Courts dusted off the injunction, reaffirmed the implications of the fourteenth Amendment, and followed a uniformly conservative course.

The nationalism generated by war carried over into the peace in the form of a campaign against 'Reds', incidentally aimed at labour and liberalism. The Russian Revolution provoked a Red-hunt in which the radical, the nonconformist, and the unorthodox were relentlessly tracked down by Federal and state authorities. Attorney General Palmer headed a drive to seize 'communists' (a term he tended to interpret very broadly) and gaoled some 6,000 persons, most of whom were released for lack of evidence. At the height of the scare robbers killed a paymaster during a Massachusetts factory hold-up. Nicola Sacco and Bartolomeo Vanzetti, both suspected anarchists, were arrested for the crime and tried in an atmosphere of anti-foreign, anti-radical rage. Though the majority of liberal opinion ranged itself on the side of the suspects, who behaved throughout with extraordinary dignity, the two were finally electrocuted in 1927. The wartime influx of Negroes to Northern cities touched off race riots; with the assistance of Henry Ford's Dearborn newspaper, anti-Semitism appeared on the scene. The Ku Klux Klan, dormant since 1900, was quickly revived. Nourished by anti-Negro, anti-Catholic, anti-Jewish, and anti-foreign patriots, the Klan claimed four million members by 1924 and held the balance of political power in several Northern states. By 1926 the wave of hysteria and intolerance had run its course, though a persistent small stream remained to swell into another flood after World War II.

The overwhelming fact about the twenties, though, was that they rolled in money. Presidential messages to Congress, someone remarked, sounded like the chairman of the board's report to stockholders. Except for agriculture, mining, and textiles, the national economy reached the highest level of profit yet recorded in American history – and the best thing was that it would never end, for American business leaders were convinced that 'prosperity is permanent'. The war impoverished Europe and destroyed much of its productive capacity; mass production and efficiency increased American production; instalment buying widened the purchasing market; new industries, such as the automobile, radio, and movies, made new jobs and new markets; the favourable attitude of the Federal government spurred business confidence and encouraged new ventures. Stock market speculation attracted thousands of new investors, leading John J. Raskob of General Motors to predict that any man who could invest $15 a week could within twenty years have $80,000 in cash and $400 a month income. America bulged with money and trusted those who had it. The public 'worshipped at the knees of business', remarked George Norris, the Nebraska insurgent, and made an oracle of Ford. The captain of industry enjoyed public confidence as never before. It was up to him, one commentator believed, 'to finish the work that religion, government, and war have failed to do . . .'

Calvin Coolidge, a New Englander with a reputation for silence, was shrewd enough to keep quiet and take the credit. The Republicans nominated him again for President in 1924 and promised four more years of 'Coolidge prosperity'. The Democrats, after a rowdy convention, could not decide between William McAdoo, a Californian from Wilson's cabinet, and Alfred Smith, the popular governor of

New York. Finally they compromised on John W. Davis, an able West Virginia corporation lawyer. Certain labour groups, socialists, discontented farm organizations, and Bull Moosers formed the Progressive party and ran Robert M. La Follette for President. But the time for old-fashioned political revolt was over; the American public was too confident of the future to listen to the old Wisconsin fighter. Coolidge slaughtered his opponents at the polls, beating Davis by seven million votes and La Follette by ten million. 'An air of optimism pervades the nation,' wrote a leading magazine after the election, and the country settled down with 'Silent Cal' and permanent prosperity.

The temper of the twenties was ambivalent. On the one hand it was officially confident and optimistic. The nation must move forward, said John Dewey, with 'faith in the active tendencies of the day' and 'the courage of intelligence to follow whither social and economic changes direct us'. Hoover thought that the country had 'finally eradicated the causes of poverty'; Bruce Barton showed that Christianity was the best basis for a 'business civilization'; people liked Émile Coué's popular formula of 'Every day in every way I am getting better and better.'

Yet it was also a time of doubt and cynicism, the result of war, confusion, and the increased tension and complexity of the post-war world. The war to end war ended in disillusion, 'normalcy' turned into corruption, the 'noble experiment' of prohibition produced drunkenness and gangs. For the first time since the founding of the Republic responsible thinkers questioned the efficacy of the American democratic process. H. L. Mencken jeered at the 'homo boobiens' who comprised the American electorate, Sinclair Lewis pilloried business and the small town in *Babbit* and *Main Street*, and Walter Lippmann's studies in public opinion indicated that the popular mind was irrational, gullible, easily misled. The *Army Training Manual* of 1928 listed the effects of democracy as 'mobocracy . . . demagogism, license, agitation, discontent, anarchy'. Church attendance fell off until by 1929 more people attended movies than churches. The United States, some intellectuals agreed, lacked a cultural tradition and suffered from commercialism; its moral inhibitions, provincialism, and herd-psychology stifled the creative intelligence.

One reaction was the desire to be 'emancipated'. War shattered the traditional codes of Puritan and Victorian morality by which Americans had lived, and there was nothing at the moment to replace them. Freud and Watson supplanted Darwin as a topic of conversation, reinforcing the popular preoccupation with extraversion and individualism. Old moral axioms disappeared in talk about glandular secretions, inhibitions and repressions, and stimulus-response patterns; ideas and desires once rarely mentioned became normal and healthy; moral doctrines once unanimously accepted were outmoded in terms of the new psychology. Bobbed hair, short skirts, and frank talk about sex marked the emancipated sophisticate, and there was a rise in the divorce rate as well as much discussion of 'companionate marriage'. Sports and spectacles became a national mania during the Golden Age of Jack Dempsey, Red Grange, Helen Wills Moody, and the 'million dollar gate'; of jazz, the 'shimmy', and the 'song hit'; of 'flappers' and sheiks', of Rudy Vallee, Rudolph Valentino, and the movie-star 'idol of millions'.

In sport the trend toward professionalism became stronger during the twenties, and the crowds attracted by football, baseball and basketball, made sporting events into highly lucrative ventures. The gate receipts of college football, particularly, converted the game into a business. College stadia, holding from 30,000 to 90,000 spectators, appeared in profusion and highly-paid coaches joined university staffs. Professional baseball organized an intricate interlocking system of major and minor league clubs which yearly grossed millions of dollars. The sports themselves, especially football and baseball, developed into mechanized games of extreme complexity. The modern American approach to sport is technological. Sports of personal prowess, with the exception of boxing, have become less popular than those emphasizing organized cooperation and a distribution of responsibility among specialists – in American terms, 'team play'. The particular player has in most games a special function to perform, at which he is often incredibly expert, while the manager or coach fits this function into the overall pattern of the game itself. American sport exhibits a chess-like rationale, requiring a tremendous knowledge of moves, countermoves, and of what players call 'the percentages' of success in any one. For this reason the coach or manager is of paramount importance in American sports; it is he who controls the play of each individual, plots strategy, and plans his 'attack' or 'defense' in semi-military fashion. Organized sport in America, as several commentators have pointed out, probably serves as a war-substitute of some importance. Possibly no other aspect of American life illustrates the American's respect for skill, efficiency, and technological organization. The American tradition in sport is a professional, not an amateur tradition. The approach is one of studied efficiency; popular heroes are in most cases professional or quasi-professional, not amateur athletes.

The temper of the twenties showed most clearly in its literature. Willa Cather's and Ellen Glasgow's sensitive novels of regional realism carried on the older tradition, and Edith Wharton continued in the path of expatriated Henry James. Robert Frost, the spiritual descendant of Whittier, Lowell and Emerson, wrote poetry in the New England tradition. Edwin Arlington Robinson's verse reflected the influence of Tennyson and Browning ('*Qui pourrais-je imiter pour être original?*' – the quotation from Coppée stands on the title-page of his first published volume); Vachel Lindsay, less a rebel than he thought, followed the course staked out by Whitman. But a whole set of 'new poets' appeared after Harriett Monroe founded *Poetry* magazine in 1912 – Amy Lowell, Sara Teasdale, Robinson Jeffers, Marianne Moore, T. S. Eliot, Edgar Lee Masters, Wallace Stevens, e. e. cummings, Carl Sandburg, Ezra Pound – all, in their own different ways, rebels against conventionalism and romanticism. A 'lost generation' of 'sad young men' wrote cynical, hedonistic, rebellious novels and plays – Ernest Hemingway, John Dos Passos, Eugene O'Neill, Maxwell Anderson, Sherwood Anderson, Elmer Rice, William Faulkner – while F. Scott Fitzgerald's novels of the 'jazz age' caught the flavour of contemporary life perfectly. Brilliant but brittle magazines such as *Esquire* and above all the *New Yorker* grew in popularity, literate, efficient and often informed with a conscience as lively as the eye and the typewriter of the author.

Artists exiled themselves to Paris's 'left bank' or New York's Greenwich Village, where they believed they could create in a friendlier, more emancipated, atmosphere. Eliot, like Henry James before him, became a British subject – and more British than the British. Critics engaged in sharp arguments over American tradition, Van Wyck Brooks and the 'radicals' contending that American cultural life was sterile, bloodless, hag-ridden by provincialism and Puritanism. In opposition, Babbitt at Harvard and More at Princeton condemned the literature of the day and called for a 'new humanism', a return to older standards of artistic harmony and restraint. While critics argued, the artists themselves experimented endlessly with style and technique, as Joyce, Gertrude Stein, Proust, and Eliot were experimenting in Europe. Before it ended, the twenties emerged as one of the most vital and stimulating periods in American literary history.

Calvin Coolidge could easily have had the Republican nomination for President in 1924, but when he announced that he 'did not choose to run' the mantle of succession fell on Herbert Hoover, his capable Secretary of Commerce. The party's platform simply re-stated the domestic and foreign policies of the preceding administrations, promising continued prosperity with not only 'a full dinner pail' but 'a full garage'. The Democrats nominated Alfred Smith of New York (know nationally as 'Al'), a New York City product, a Roman Catholic, and a 'wet' opponent of prohibition. Smith's record as governor of New York stamped him as a liberal and his Bowery accent and winning personality made him the favourite of millions, but the triple handicap of being a 'wet', a Catholic, and a New Yorker was too much. Hoover won by a huge majority in both electoral and popular vote, cracked the solid South, and carried a Republican Congress in with him.

Hoover entered the Presidency with a spotless reputation and solid public support. His wartime and post-war services as Chairman of the Belgian Relief Commission and Food Administrator had carried his name all over the world, leading the London *Nation* to call him 'the biggest man who has emerged on the Allied side'. His background, however, was chiefly in mining, business, and administration. He was unaccustomed to the give-and-take of politics, and his economic and political philosophy dated from the days of Carnegie and Sumner. He believed in strict individualism, open opportunity, and an unhampered profit system. An intelligent conservative, he conceived himself to be the defender of older ideals of economic enterprise, modified to meet the contemporary needs of financial and industrial life. He was also inflexible, doggedly holding to preconceived ideas, with a trace of the authoritarian in him. Yet he was an honest, able man, with internationalist views, capable of being a distinguished President. People had faith in 'The Great Engineer'.

Hoover's first move was to redeem two campaign promises. First, he established the Federal Farm Board and the Agricultural Marketing Act, both designed to stabilize farm markets and prices. At his suggestion Congress next plunged into a revision of the tariff bill, in which Hoover wanted 'limited changes'. Congressional protectionists, however, emerged with the Smoot-Hawley tariff which raised rates nearly 7 per cent over the already high tariffs of 1922. Hoover criticized the bill, but signed it over loud protests from abroad and from more than a thousand American economists. Hoover, in his inaugural address in March 1929 remarked, 'In a large view we have reached a higher degree of comfort and security than ever before existed in the world . . . I have no fears for the future.' Events soon proved him monumentally wrong, for the Big Prosperity Bubble burst in the autumn of 1929.

Even before it broke some economists were sceptical of the boom of the twenties. Over-production, the slow rise of real wages, and falling prices were straws in the wind as early as 1926. Stock prices built up in dizzying spirals (old-timers nostalgically remember R.C.A. shares at 549) but the few analysts who preached caution were shouted down. Wall Street went into a slow decline in early October 1929, and on 24 October the panic hit. Sixteen million shares changed hands, fifty leading stocks fell forty points a day, thousands of big and little investors were wiped out, messenger boys bought well-known stocks at a dollar a share.

Nobody really believed it. Hoover thought the break would end in sixty days or so. Secretary of the Treasury Mellon looked for 1930 to be 'a normal year', but nevertheless the recession spread. Both agriculture and industry had over-expanded; international trade was out of balance; artificial price levels were maintained by monopolistic control; credit, especially in instalment buying, had been badly overdone. The United States hit the bottom of the trough in early 1932, when the National Bureau of Economic Research drew an appalling picture of the national economy. Stock prices were down 83 per cent, productive output down 40 per cent, wages down 60 per cent, dividends down 57 per cent. Fifteen to seventeen million unemployed roamed the streets, credit froze at the source, money depreciated to half its value. The carnival of the twenties was over.

The Hoover administration did a good job in fighting the depression, but what it did was far from enough. Minimizing the seriousness of the situation in his public statements, Hoover urged 'business as usual' and waited for the depression to wear itself out. He raised the tariff and reduced taxes to encourage business, made Federal Reserve credit easier, and asked industry to expand production and retain wage levels. In early 1932 he established the Reconstruction

Finance Corporation to loan money to industry, banks, and farmers; near the end of his administration he expanded its powers and functions in an effort to get business going again. The difficulty was that Hoover, thinking in terms of 'rugged individualism', at no time threw the full weight of the Federal government into the battle against the depression. His programme was, in effect, a palliative designed to remedy temporary conditions until permanent prosperity reasserted itself – as he believed it must.

The depression hung like a cloud over the political conventions of 1932. Republicans faced the presidential election with something less than enthusiasm; they met, adopted a colourless programme, and nominated Hoover for another term. The Democrats met with the highest hopes in years. Their logical candidate, on the basis of his 1928 campaign record, was 'Al' Smith, but after some pre-convention horse-trading the nomination went to Franklin D. Roosevelt, Governor of New York. The platform the convention gave him was not much, but it mattered less than the man who ran on it.

Roosevelt's acceptance speech, the famous 'New Deal' speech, was a ringing promise to get something done. This was, he said, an industrial civilization, creating 'new problems for those who would remain free'. The great problem of the times was the 'new despotism' of 'industrial dictatorship', the rule of 'economic royalists'. Opportunity was stifled by monopoly; private enterprise was too private; it was privileged, not free and open. There were too many poor, too few well-to-do. 'Throughout the nation,' he continued, 'men and women, forgotten in the political philosophy of the government of the last years, look to us here for a more equitable opportunity to share in the distribution of national wealth.' 'I pledge you, I pledge myself,' he concluded, 'to a new deal for the American people.'

Roosevelt proved to be the best campaigner the Democratic party ever had. The New Deal, born in his Chicago acceptance speech, emerged as a sweeping, long-range political, economic, and social reorganization that, if instituted, would mark a major shift in the direction of American domestic policy. To Hoover the contest was between two widely different philosophies of government; the New Deal was 'a challenge to liberty' and its supporters 'exponents of a social philosophy different from the traditional American one'. The nation must choose, he said, between individualism and regimentation, between liberty and Federal bureaucracy. As the campaign wore on it was evident that Hoover planned a return to the happy, prosperous days of early 1929. Roosevelt planned a new, different kind of American society.

Roosevelt's lead in the balloting was never in doubt, and by midnight of election day it was certain that he had been elected by the largest vote then recorded in American history. Hoover carried only six states; both Houses of Congress went overwhelmingly Democratic. The landslide that carried Roosevelt into office, like the landslides that swept Jackson and Jefferson into the White House, was an expression of discontent. His vote was a victory for the depression, as well as a desperate nation's vote of confidence in a man who seemed to know where he was going.

Roosevelt's Inaugural Address on 4 March 1933 promised 'action, and action now' in this 'dark hour of national life'. 'The only thing we have to fear,' he said, 'is fear itself.'

We do not distrust the future of essential democracy. The people of the United States have not failed. In their need they have registered a mandate that they want direct, vigorous action. They have asked me for discipline and direction under leadership. They have made me the present instrument of their wishes. In the spirit of the gift I take it.

Thus began the New Deal.

CHAPTER 28

NEW DEAL, FAIR DEAL AND GLOBAL CONFLICT

FRANKLIN DELANO ROOSEVELT, a distant cousin of Theodore, was a wealthy, landed New Yorker descended from early Dutch settlers. His background included travel abroad, exclusive Groton School, Harvard, and Columbia Law School. In 1905 he married Eleanor Roosevelt, a sixth cousin, and in 1910, at thirty, he was elected to the New York State Senate, the first Democrat in a generation to hold a legislative seat from this rock-ribbed Republican district.

In 1912 Roosevelt strongly supported Wilson at the national convention. As a reward he was made Assistant Secretary of the Navy, where he did outstanding work in building up the service before and during World War I. A thorough believer in the 'New Freedom', young Roosevelt absorbed much of it during his Washington years, and in 1920, when he was paired with Cox on the Democratic presidential ticket, he gave Wilson a personal pledge to carry on his programme if elected. After the dismal Democratic defeat, he retired from politics to resume the practice of law.

Little more than a year later, at thirty-nine, Roosevelt was struck by poliomyelitis and paralysed from the waist down. Through a long six-year fight against illness he spent his time in correspondence, establishing a wide acquaintance with Democratic party leaders. He appeared in public but once, to nominate Al Smith at the 1924 National convention, but he was nevertheless a potent behind-the-scenes force in the party organization. In 1928 he ran successfully for the governorship of New York, and again in 1930. As governor, Roosevelt did a competent though not spectacular job. At the time of his nomination for President in 1932 he was known as a good party man with a fine radio presence (an

attribute that was beginning to be of major political significance), a 'safe' candidate, and a mild liberal.

When Roosevelt assumed the Presidency he possessed a
thorough knowledge of practical politics and limited administrative experience. His political philosophy was disorganized and unformed; not until the later stages of the
1932 campaign did he seem to arrange his ideas into a
coherent pattern, expressed most clearly in his book, *Looking
Forward*, in 1933. He possessed monumental self-confidence,
great mental and physical energy, a marked capacity for
growth, and (as one of his advisers said) 'a frightening
receptivity to ideas'.

Roosevelt was an intuitive politician, willing to experiment, working from day to day with a 'let's see if it will
work' technique. He was never a master planner, nor can
one find in his New Deal any unity of programme. His
greatest asset was his ability to discover, express, and translate into action the trends of popular opinion. Since Lincoln
no man in public life had a more sensitive finger on the
public pulse or a greater skill in seizing and exploiting the
opportune moment. And 1932, of course, presented a magnificent opportunity, with the nation confused, bewildered,
deep in the trough of depression.

The task of the moment in 1932 was to beat the depression, which Roosevelt promised to do with 'bold, persistent
experimentation'. From March to July, during the famous
'Hundred Days' of 1933, anti-depression measures passed
Congress with incredible speed. The Emergency Banking
Act loosened credit and increased the amount of money
issued by the Federal Reserve. The nation went off the gold
standard, placed an embargo on gold and silver exports,
and reduced the gold content of the dollar. The Banking
Act of 1933 guaranteed the safety of bank deposits through
the Federal Deposit Insurance Corporation; other agencies
were established to make credit easier; and a year later the
Securities Exchange Act appeared to control stock market
practices.

For farm relief, Congress passed the Agricultural Adjustment Act, governing farm production, prices, and surpluses. The State Department and Congress hastened to frame trade agreements with Canada and Europe, particularly in agricultural produce. Though invalidated in 1936 by the Supreme Court, the A.A.A. reappeared in more acceptable and expanded form in 1938. For direct relief of unemployed young men Congress authorized the Civilian Conservation Corps, later adding the National Youth Administration to assist deserving students by providing part-time jobs. The Federal Emergency Relief Act of May 1933 (later superseded by the Works Progress Administration) created relief jobs directly and indirectly by making grants available to state and local governments. The Reconstruction Finance Corporation, a Hoover hold-over, continued to extend loans to private business, while the Farm Credit Act, a corollary of the Triple-A, re-financed farm mortgages and eased farm credit.

For business and industry, Congress passed the National Industrial Recovery or 'Blue Eagle' Act in June 1933, intended to stabilize production, keep up wages, regulate hours and labour standards, and ban unfair trade and labour practices. By the time it was ruled unconstitutional in 1935, twenty million labourers worked under 500 different industrial codes. The N.I.R.A. also carried with it a gigantic relief programme, involving the Civil Works Administration, the Public Works Administration, and the Works Progress Administration, all of them designed to create jobs for nearly four million people. The Tennessee Valley Authority, born in May, 1933, was admittedly an experiment in Federally-owned public utilities, establishing a vast power empire cutting across seven states. After it in the next two decades came similar developments at Hoover Dam, Grand Coulee, Bonneville, Fort Peck, and elsewhere, as well as a Rural Electrification Act to carry electricity to isolated areas.

The ratification of the twenty-first Amendment in 1933, cancelling the eighteenth (Prohibition) Amendment, had no relation to the anti-depression or reform portions of the New Deal Programme, but was rather the result of disillusionment with a 'noble experiment'.

1934 and 1935 saw fewer relief measures and more 'bold experimentation'. The Social Security Act, the most far-reaching piece of social legislation in American history, ended thirty years of agitation for old-age pensions, unemployment insurance, indigent relief, maternity and child welfare, and public health benefits, but not health insurance. The Resettlement Administration of 1935 attempted to help the farmer by withdrawing marginal land from use, lending funds for homes, and re-financing mortgages. The Wheeler-Rayburn Act of 1935 gave the Federal government increased power over interstate utilities, and a new tax bill, known as the 'soak-the-rich' tax, increased corporation and undivided profits taxes. As Roosevelt's first term drew to an end, the list of measures passed by Congress and of executive orders issued from the White House made a total of twenty-one major bills and hundreds of minor ones.

Public confidence in unions, shaken in the twenties, grew in the thirties as the quality of labour leadership improved. The Supreme Court changed its personnel and its attitude toward labour legislation, and labour took advantage of the favourable policies of the New Deal to consolidate its gains. Many of the 'pump priming' measures of 1933 and 1934 were intended to give direct assistance to the workingman. Most helpful to unions was section 7A of the N.I.R.A. code, which granted labour the right to organize and bargain collectively 'without interference, coercion, or restraint by employers'. After a brief wave of strikes in 1932, Roosevelt in 1933 created the National Labor Board to mediate disputes arising from the N.I.R.A., superseding it with the National Labor Relations Board in 1934. After the Supreme Court invalidated the N.I.R.A., Congress passed the Wagner Act to safeguard 'the practice and procedure of collective bargaining' and authorized the N.L.R.B. to administer it. By 1937 the agency had handled 5,000 disputes, arbitrated 2,000 strikes, and conducted 1,400 union elections.

The A.F.L. added a million and a half members to its

rolls between 1932 and 1935. The A.F.L., however, organized on a craft-union basis, left untouched the masses of unskilled labour in the basic heavy industries. In 1936 a number of unions, led by John L. Lewis's United Mine Workers, organized the Committee for Industrial Organization to unionize mass-production industries such as automobiles, steel, textiles, rubber, and aluminium. After repeated internal squabbles the A.F.L. formally ejected the C.I.O. unions, who changed their name to the Congress of Industrial Organizations and proceeded in their campaign against big industries. The C.I.O., using more aggressive methods, soon outstripped the A.F.L. in membership and by the late thirties had succeeded in realizing most of its immediate objectives, though both Ford and 'Little Steel' held out against it for several more years. Stormy old John L. Lewis, who was succeeded by Philip Murray in 1940, finally pulled his U.M.W. out of the C.I.O. in 1942.

By 1936 opposition to Roosevelt had coalesced within the Democratic party, some of whose leaders accused him of fostering a 'New Deal' party within its framework, of overspending, of extending bureaucracy, of dangerously increasing Federal authority. Al Smith and other prominent Democrats bolted the party to join a group of wealthy businessmen in the American Liberty League, an organization charged with fighting 'the Red New Deal with a Soviet seal', as the Chicago *Tribune* called it. The Republican convention chose Governor Alfred Landon of Kansas as its presidential candidate, and the Democrats lost no time in re-nominating Roosevelt, with John Nance Garner of Texas as his running mate. The campaign was an uninteresting one, for there was little doubt of the outcome. Roosevelt won by 523 electoral votes to eight, with a popular majority of nine million, while Congress went overwhelmingly Democratic. The vote seemed a clear endorsement of the New Deal, and Roosevelt promised four more years of the same.

He started on his second term with renewed energy. The Supreme Court had killed much of the early New Deal legislation, and lawyers seemed to be casting glances at both the Social Security and the Wagner Acts. The 'Nine Old Men' of the Court, said Roosevelt, were 'miners and sappers' of the Constitution and foes of progress. In 1937 he suggested a plan for reforming the Federal judiciary, touching off a heated argument that took up most of the year. The Court itself settled the matter by shifting its direction ('a switch in time that saved nine', someone remarked) and when several aged Justices retired Roosevelt replaced them with his own appointees.

After Congress stymied several Roosevelt-sponsored bills, the President attempted in the congressional elections of 1938 to 'purge' the Democratic Party of its conservative, anti-New Deal elements, but failed. At the same time a sharp business recession in 1937 and early 1938 showed that the New Deal was not invulnerable. In late 1939 war broke out in Europe, and Roosevelt's domestic programme abruptly stopped. After September 1939 nearly all legislation introduced and debated in Congress, and all partisan political issues, were directly or indirectly influenced by World War II. The New Deal was finished.

The New Deal was not at all new. It was eclectic, borrowing from everything that had preceded it, representing the culmination of a half-century of political development. Roosevelt, taking office during a national crisis and working almost without opposition for three years, simply had an unparalleled opportunity for policy-making granted to none of his predecessors. Some of what he did was done hastily, some was frankly experimental, and much was primarily designed to rescue the American economy from the worst depression in its history. Older liberals complained that the New Deal 'Brain Trusters' paid little attention to the forms and techniques of true democracy. Conservatives claimed Roosevelt's policies were leftist; liberals criticized them as over-timid. Actually Roosevelt, in comparison to the administration that preceded him, followed a middle way. He was no doctrinaire, but ready always to try one plan, then another, or several simultaneously, sometimes veering to right or left but ending in the centre of the road.

The New Deal was by no means an attempt to change the capitalistic system of free enterprise. It was, Roosevelt said, 'a reform in order to preserve it', and to make it serve public ends more thoroughly. 'We seek,' he explained, 'to guarantee the survival of private enterprise by guaranteeing conditions under which it can work.' It must therefore be regulated in the public interest, to obtain stability, equilibrium, and 'balance in our economic system'. Neither Bryan, nor Theodore Roosevelt, nor Wilson, nor La Follette would have disagreed.

The New Deal failed, nevertheless, to arrest the trend toward consolidation in American economic life. The depression accelerated the growth of monopoly by driving weaker firms to the wall, to be absorbed by more durable corporations. At the same time monopoly was to some extent being replaced by oligopoly, that state of economic affairs in which so few sellers existed in particular fields that they dominated the market, despite theoretical competition with each other. In 1937, after five years of the New Deal, three firms produced 80 per cent of the nation's automobiles, three companies made 60 per cent of the steel, and one aluminium company controlled nearly 100 per cent of the output. About all that Roosevelt could do was to eliminate some of the more obvious violations of anti-trust legislation. Since the New Deal, the trend towards monopoly and oligopoly in American business life has continued.

The distinguishing trait of the New Deal was its broad extension of Federal authority over American life, and the assumption by the Federal government of large new areas of social and economic responsibility. In effect, it created a national state, powerful enough to define and enforce a national interest. The New Deal thus had its roots deep in the 1890s and early 1900s, in the agrarian revolt, in the Populist protest, in early Progressivism. In employing Hamiltonian means to achieve Jeffersonian ends, the New Deal looked more like Theodore Roosevelt's New Nationalism than Wilson's New Freedom. Roosevelt hoped, he said, ' . . . to remake national life after a fashion, which, whether the old prosperity returned or not, would yield a larger sense of social justice and meet the demands of a new democracy'. The Republican Party, on the other hand – the party which had won the War for the Union – was now forced into the role of resisting over-centralized government.

Only by a greater assumption of Federal authority did Roosevelt feel that he could achieve his ends. Of all the New Deal's principles, this had the most lasting influence on American politics. As the New York *Times* remarked in 1938, 'The unmistakable fact is that an increasing number of Americans, irrespective of party lines, have come to regard, as both necessary and desirable, a larger share of responsibility on the Government's part . . . '. The issue itself, refusing to die, has since provided a basis for continuing political debates over the merits of Truman's 'Fair Deal', Kennedy's 'New Frontier' and Johnson's 'Great Society', and their programmes. Did the New Deal extend and preserve the values of individualistic capitalism, as it claimed to do, or was it the entering wedge of an American collectivism, the first blueprint of a 'welfare state'?

The depression gave a distinct shock to American intellectual life. 'The climate,' wrote the President of the Carnegie Foundation, 'changed from one of optimism to one of acute pessimism.' If the standards and values of the twenties no longer seemed valid in a time of social disintegration, a re-examination of the ideological foundations of modern America was in order.

First to be questioned was the cult of the practical and pragmatic, in religion, philosophy, education, and business life. Quite possibly, some thinkers concluded, a pragmatic test of ideas to live by, if it produced war and depression, was insufficient. F. S. C. Northrop, Thurman Arnold, and others attacked the 'pragmatic realism' of contemporary philosophy and found it lacking in direction. President Robert Hutchins of the University of Chicago inveighed against pragmatism and ethical relativism in education, calling for a return to the speculative spirit of the medieval university and condemning the 'service station' concept of

American education. Catholic neo-scholastics, following the lead of Maritain and Gilson in France, regarded the rift between the intellectual and spiritual in contemporary society as productive of ethical insensitivity in social, political, and economic life. In Protestant theological circles a reaction set in against 'practical' religion. 'The middle-class paradise which we built,' wrote Karl Barth, 'is in decay', and like the Catholic Thomists he and others censured 'socialized' religion as a confusion of secular and divine. Reinhold Niebuhr, the most influential of the Protestant theologians, reaffirmed in new terms the old Calvinist doctrine of original sin, preaching a twentieth-century return to orthodoxy.

In the churches themselves, nevertheless, the trend toward socialized religion continued. Despite the warnings of Barth, Niebuhr, and the Neo-Thomists, many clerics believed that depression demanded even greater participation by the Church in everyday life. The Federal Council of Churches' creed of 1932 went far beyond its original statement of 1908, asking for 'social planning and control of the credit and monetary systems and economic processes for the common good'. The Central Conference of Rabbis adopted a Programme of Social Justice, and Pope Pius XI urged stronger Catholic participation in reconstructing the social order. Attendance in all but the highly ritualistic churches, however, continued to decline, while a bewildering variety of new sects appeared. Jehovah's Witnesses and other fringe denominations grew in membership; the fantastic 'I AM' movement of the mid-thirties claimed a million members; Father Divine's New York 'peace heavens' filled with disciples who chanted 'Father Divine is God, is God, is God'. The Buchmanite or Oxford Group, founded in England by an American Lutheran, attracted a respectably large following among intellectuals, and Catholicism made numerous converts.

During the depression the doctrines of Karl Marx held a particular attraction for rootless intellectuals, who searched not only for a solution to contemporary problems but for a centre of anti-fascist resistance. Marxist economic, social, historical, and aesthetic concepts were thoroughly explored by critics, writers, the 'little magazines', and *avant garde* political thinkers. The Bolshevik trials, the Hitler-Stalin pact, and the Russian invasion of Finland–alienated numerous Marxists and Marxist sympathizers, convincing disenchanted artists and intellectuals of communism's unadaptability to the American scene. Though the influence of Marxism in the United States was much less pervasive in the thirties than later investigators have assumed, interest in it contributed to a more careful reconsideration of contemporary problems in class relationships, economy, politics, and critical thought.

The rise of fascism was a matter of much deeper concern to the thinkers of the thirties. Some Americans returning from Europe voiced approval of the totalitarian methods of Hitler and Mussolini, although many were repelled by the anti-Semitic and anti-intellectual aspects of fascism. Native semi-fascist groups – the Bund, the Khaki Shirts, the Silver Shirts, the Crusaders – found encouragement in racist circles and even a few sincere thinkers expressed the belief that totalitarianism was perhaps a 'wave of the future' to which the United States must eventually adjust. Formal fascist organizations, however, attracted comparatively few members. The appeals of Huey Long of Louisiana for his 'Every Man a King' movement, and the Social Justice Crusade of Father Coughlin, a Detroit priest, aroused more enthusiasm. The slow recovery from hard times elicited a great deal of talk about the need for masculinity, discipline, and orderliness in American civilization, and evoked some popular admiration for the efficiency of totalitarian methods. Since neither Mussolini nor Hitler in the early and mid thirties seemed to pose a direct threat to American interests or security, the public in general remained largely indifferent to the spread of fascism in Europe.

To the creative artist, wrote Louis Adamic, the depression era was 'a time of transition and profound frustration . . .'. The spectacle of economic collapse at home, plus com-

munism and fascism abroad, aroused poets, novelists, drama-
tists, and critics to a re-examination of the native 'usable
past'. The negativism and hedonism of the 'lost generation'
disappeared in the depression. The novel in particular
turned into a favourite vehicle of social criticism and protest
in the early thirties. John Dos Passos's trilogy, *U.S.A.*, was a
savage indictment of the whole drift of American society
since the turn of the century. James T. Farrell drew a grimy
picture of adolescent vice and frustration in Chicago; John
Steinbeck, in a series of novels ending with *The Grapes of
Wrath* (1939) took up the cause of migrant workers and displaced 'okies' in the Far West; Erskine Caldwell's *Tobacco
Road* (1932) was a satiric handling of the Southern poor
white. Proletarian novels and poems, in which aggressiveness
of message often took precedence over art, appeared in
profusion.

By the end of the decade, however, with the threat of
fascism looming from abroad, many American artists turned
their eyes homeward. Nationalism, frowned on by the
writers of the twenties, became fashionable as World War II
approached and Left Bank refugees fled from Europe.
Expatriates, Marxists and aesthetes, surveying the native
tradition, discovered in it a set of values worth salvaging in
an unstable world. MacLeish, Sandburg, and Benét wrote
unashamedly American poems; Dos Passos found strength
and purpose in the democracy of eighteenth- and nineteenth-century America; Ernest Hemingway overcame his
youthful distrust of positive ideas; Thomas Wolfe, in the
manner of Whitman, found his inner life inextricably
entangled with the soul of America.

For the first time for more than a century, the South
produced literary leadership. The group originally founded
around *The Fugitive*, a little magazine published at Vanderbilt University, included writers of great distinction such as
John Crowe Ransom, Allen Tate, Laura Riding, Robert
Penn Warren and Marianne Moore. As Allen Tate wrote
for the 'agrarians' (as they called themselves), 'Only a return
to the provinces, to the small self-contained centres of life,

will put the all-destroying abstraction "America" safely to rest.' William Faulkner, although not one of the 'Fugitives', did launch on a long, complex study of his native South and despite his undoubted powers, he is at times so localized as to be almost incomprehensible to anyone who does not know Mississippi.

Negro writers, too, began to achieve literary eminence and broke away from the 'Uncle Tom' style that white America expected. Some, like William Braithwaite and Jessie Fausset, were, in their writings, indistinguishable from their white peers; others, above all James Weldon Johnson, Sterling Brown, Langston Hughes and Countee Cullen, attempted in the twenties and thirties to 'express the racial spirit by symbols from within rather than by symbols from without'. In the forties the temper of Negro writing changed. Richard Wright's *Native Son* (1940), a bitter, brutal novel based in part on the author's youth in Chicago, introduced an aggressive, militant note into Negro fiction. Wright's autobiography, *Black Boy* (1945) became an important document in this new Negro protest movement, followed by Chester Himes's novel *If He Hollers Let Him Go* (1945), Ralph Ellison's superbly written, introspective *Invisible Man* (1952), and James Baldwin's story of his Harlem boyhood, *Go Tell It On The Mountain* (1953). Baldwin's *Notes of a Native Son* (1955) and *Nobody Knows My Name* (1955) continued Wright's note of personal protest, and the tradition of Negro militancy in literature shows no signs of slackening.

Among the critics, Van Wyck Brooks, mellowing with the years, began a glowing, multi-volumed reappraisal of the native literary tradition, while Vernon Louis Parrington traced the development of American ideas in aggressively Jeffersonian–Jacksonian terms. The socially conscious novels of the early thirties faded before a new aestheticism which appeared in a resurgence of 'little magazines' and schools of 'new critics' who approached art in terms of its technical competence and the moral integrity of its ideas.

Painting, music, and architecture of the later thirties and early forties were concerned chiefly with attempts to find a means of grafting European modernism on native roots. In painting Grant Wood, Thomas Hart Benton, and John Steuart Curry (all Midwesterners) led a regionalist movement away from European inspiration; New York artists, such as Ben Shahn and Stuart Davis, tended to follow international rather than regional trends. Classicism still dominated American public architecture, though the influence of the Finn Eliel Saarinen and the Frenchman Le Corbusier reinforced Frank Lloyd Wright in his lifelong battle for American modernism. In designing homes, American architects discovered (as the painters had) numerous regional styles – the Western ranch-house, the Southern plantation house, the Pennsylvania Dutch house, the Cape Cod house of New England – and tried to evolve from them architectural designs adaptable to modern tastes and needs.

Musically the United States reached maturity in the thirties. The great popularity of the radio made the public at large music-conscious, and symphony concerts, complete operas, and recitals by the best artists came into millions of homes at the turn of a dial. Music appeared more often in public school curricula, and civic orchestras provided free concerts in smaller communities. American singers and performers, capable of holding their own with European artists, began to appear on opera and concert stages. American composers like Aaron Copland, Roy Harris, Walter Piston and Leonard Bernstein gained respect in their own right. Jazz, which lost its racial connotations in the twenties, flourished – on records, radio, and in theatres. A few composers, notably Gershwin and Blitzstein, hoped to graft it with traditional music, but both classical and jazz purists protested against their efforts.

Roosevelt's terms as President coincided with a period of ruthless aggression in Europe and Asia, beginning with Japan's invasion of Manchuria in 1931 and ending with Japan's defeat in 1945. Before Roosevelt's second term was well started it was apparent that foreign affairs must take precedence over domestic. Yet the American political system, both its parties and its institutions, were traditionally so geared as to subordinate foreign to domestic policy.

The American reaction to European and Asian events of 1935–9 was an overwhelming desire for peace and neutrality. The public regarded neither Hitler nor Mussolini as threats to American security, and until the invasion of Poland and the shooting war, nothing in Europe seemed to impinge directly on American affairs. Most Americans until 1941, the State Department later reported, 'did not accept the thesis that a European war could vitally affect the security of the United States, or that an attack on the United States by any of the Axis powers was possible'. Few Americans sympathized with German or Italian fascism, but at the same time the majority regarded the problem of fascism as something for Germans and Italians to settle. Disillusioned with memories of an earlier world war, fearful of entanglement in another, protected by two oceans, Americans simply believed it best for the United States to stay away and keep out. Congress, therefore, representing the drift of public opinion, consistently favoured an isolationist, neutral policy.

Roosevelt, Secretary of State Cordell Hull, and their advisers were far ahead of the public in their thinking – perhaps too much so. Roosevelt, after his 1935 warning that Americans could not 'hide their heads in the sand', frequently reminded the nation of its stake in world security. But his 'quarantine the aggressors' speech in Chicago in 1937 evoked such heated cries of 'warmonger' and 'hysterical internationalist' that he tempered his subsequent warnings considerably. Since he had to campaign in 1936 and again in 1940, and the Democratic Congress faced re-election in 1938, neither Roosevelt nor his party dared proceed too fast or too far. Both Roosevelt and Hull were internationally minded. Congress, particularly the Senate, was not. Foreign policy thus became a tug-of-war between the President and Congress after 1933, with Congress attempting to tie the Chief Executive's hands and Roosevelt trying equally hard to free them.

Roosevelt and Hull hoped to discourage the fascist nations

by improving machinery for collective security. As a step in this direction Roosevelt asked Congress in 1934 to pass the Reciprocal Trade Agreements Act to stimulate international trade with free countries by providing an expanding–contracting tariff. At almost the same time, as if in reply, Congress passed the Johnson Bill, forbidding loans to governments in default on previous debts, a direct slap at foreign financial entanglements. A year later Roosevelt and Hull urged greater collaboration with the League of Nations, asking for American entry into the World Court. This the Senate refused. In 1933 the President requested legislation permitting embargoes on trade with aggressor nations. Congress instead moved in 1935 to establish embargoes on trade with, and prevent loans to, *any* belligerent nation. Roosevelt signed the Neutrality Act of 1935 with reluctance, pointing out that since it did not discriminate between aggressors and victims, it assured European dictators of American non-interference. Nor did the Act itself work well, since it applied only to actual implements of war and failed to prevent shipment of useful materials to Italy after the Ethiopian invasion. Congress neverthe ess reaffirmed the Act in 1936 and 1937, and although both Roosevelt and Hull begged its reconsideration in early 1939, the Senate blocked its repeal.

The American reaction to the outbreak of war in 1939 was swift. Opinion was overwhelmingly sympathetic to the Allies, though most Americans hoped to avoid direct participation by serving as 'the arsenal of democracy'. With German militarism rampant in Europe, Congress revised the Neutrality Act to allow Britain and France to place huge military orders in the United States. But Under-Secretary of State Welles, after a trip abroad in January 1940, had a gloomy report to make; according to him, in both France and Britain morale was low, armaments short, preparations for war lagging. Later in the spring Germany overran Norway, Denmark, Holland, Belgium, and Luxembourg, cut across France to the Channel, nearly trapped the British and French at Dunkirk, and then turned toward Paris.

Paris fell on 14 June, four days later Italy joined Germany, and the great air war on Britain began.

The fall of France was a tremendous shock to the United States. Americans suddenly realized that Germany, Italy and Japan held control of Europe, Africa, and Asia (except for Russia) and that if Britain collapsed nothing remained between the United States and a totalitarian world. The nation faced the prospect of existing between the jaws of a nutcracker, never secure, always endangered, committed to a defensive, armed future. Answering cries for action, Roosevelt pledged swift rearmament, a bipartisan foreign policy, and immediate aid to Britain. Congress quickly appropriated funds to expand the army, navy, and air force and in September 1940 passed the first peace-time conscription bill in American history. Roosevelt by executive order transferred fifty over-age destroyers to the hard-pressed British fleet in return for a string of Atlantic bases; he sent rifles and surplus arms, tankers and cutters.

The presidential elections of 1940 came in the midst of pessimism and uncertainty, with Japan making threatening gestures in the Pacific, Europe nearly prostrate under the fascist heel, the Luftwaffe hammering at Britain. The single issue of the party conventions and the campaign was war. Republicans, sharply divided between isolationists and interventionists, chose Wendell Willkie, a dark horse corporation lawyer, after an extremely bitter convention-floor battle. Willkie's nomination represented a defeat for the isolationists, for he was in agreement with Roosevelt's foreign policy and repeatedly said so. The Democrats re-nominated Roosevelt for a precedent-shattering third term, with Henry Wallace of Iowa second on the ticket. Since both party candidates saw eye-to-eye on foreign policy, it was hard to find clear-cut issues in the campaign. Roosevelt won handily, carrying thirty-eight states, but Willkie polled more votes than any other Republican candidate up to that time.

After the 1940 election the split between isolationist and internationalist emerged more sharply than ever. Willkie after the election, openly threw his weight with Roosevelt and Hull, who believed that American involvement in the war on the side of the Allies was inevitable, and in case of further Axis victories, desirable; Frank Knox and Henry Stimson, both Republican appointees in Roosevelt's cabinet, agreed. A number of prominent men in political and private life, determined to keep the United States out of any war, believed that the Rooseveltian policy of 'aid to the Allies short of war' would assuredly drag the nation into it. Britain, they were convinced, was bound to lose, and the United States must not waste materials and money on a lost cause. America could live in peace with victorious fascist nations, whose aggressive intent had been, they thought, grossly exaggerated; living in a fascist-controlled world, in Herbert Hoover's opinion, 'would not be pleasant but it could be done'. In Congress Senator Robert Taft of Ohio and Senator Burton Wheeler of Montana led the opposition to Roosevelt's and Hull's foreign policy, while outside Congress Colonel Charles A. Lindbergh and Colonel Robert McCormick (publisher of the Chicago *Tribune*) gained wide support for the isolationists.

Roosevelt, however, consistently pushed his 'aid to the Allies' plan. In 1941 he suggested that a 'Lend-lease' programme, instead of the old 'cash and carry' system, be instituted in the purchase and shipment of arms abroad. This set off the most violent debate of the year. Opposed by potent isolationist forces in and out of Congress, and particularly by the powerful America First Committee, the Lend-lease plan consumed weeks of discussion before it finally passed Congress. 'Approval of this legislation,' said Senator Wheeler, 'means war, open and complete war. I therefore ask the American people before they supinely accept it, Was the last World War worthwhile?' Lend-lease also elicited Roosevelt's famous 'Four Freedoms' speech, outlining, as Wilson had with his Fourteen Points, America's aim in aiding the Allies – to insure in the post-war world freedom of speech, freedom of religion, freedom from want, and freedom from fear.

Lend-lease helped the Allies, but not enough to forestall a German invasion of Middle Europe and the Balkans or an Axis conquest of Greece and North Africa. In June 1941 the United States froze Axis assets, closed Axis consulates in the United States, and Germany launched its attack on Russia. Extension of the Lend-lease programme to Russia again precipitated protest, but since it was clear to the isolationists that a Russian defeat, however desirable, would serve only to increase the Axis threat to America, Congress voted to include the Soviet Union.

From June to December 1941 the record of American foreign policy was filled with un-neutral acts. In August Roosevelt and Churchill met on shipboard to prepare and sign the Atlantic Charter, a programme for world security after 'the final destruction of Nazi tyranny', thus placing the United States in the unique position of a neutral co-signer with a belligerent to a statement whose avowed purpose was the defeat of another belligerent. American destroyers patrolling the North Atlantic were frequently fired on by German submarines, and frequently fired back. After two destroyers and several merchant ships were lost, the Senate and the House agreed to revise the Neutrality Acts to arm merchant ships and to allow them to enter combat zones. Undoubtedly, by the autumn of 1941 the United States was engaged in an undeclared war with Germany. Though there was still hopeful talk of 'aid short of war', it was merely a question of time. Japan cut the time short.

Neither the United States nor the League of Nations had effectively opposed Japanese aggression in the Pacific since 1931. The Japanese Army seized Manchuria in the early thirties, and swept through China toward the East Indies while the United States and Europe were occupied with their own problems. Though Hoover denounced Japanese conquests, he also pointed out that so long as the Japanese committed acts which 'do not imperil the freedom of the American people', the United States would refrain from decisive action. Nor was Congress willing to apply pressure on Japan. Even after Japan's announcement of the 'New

Order' in Asia (which the United States officially refused to recognize) American opinion was still overwhelmingly neutral.

German and Italian successes impressed Japan's military leaders, and in September 1940 the three powers signed a military pact obviously aimed at the United States. Both Roosevelt and Hull, well aware of American unpreparedness, for the next eighteen months followed a careful course designed to gain time. By spring of 1941 Japan's Foreign Minister Matsuoka, convinced of imminent Axis victory in Europe, set his nation in motion for war. Prince Konoye, the leader of the peace party, was replaced by the bellicose Tojo, and on 25 November a Japanese naval task force, well briefed and well prepared, sailed for Pearl Harbor, Hawaii, the base of the United States Pacific Fleet. On 6 December Roosevelt sent a personal appeal for peace to Emperor Hirohito, a message intercepted and suppressed by the Japanese Army. On 7 December the Japanese surprise attack hit Pearl Harbor, almost completely shattering the base. Simultaneously an attack on the Philippines neutralized General MacArthur's air force, and three days later the British lost two battleships off Malaya. Japan, the master of the Pacific, could land its armies practically at will wherever it chose. The United States declared war on Japan on 8 December. Although their treaties with Japan did not oblige them so to do, Germany and Italy declared war on the United States on 11 December.

Pearl Harbor resolved in an hour the dilemma the American people had faced since 1939. The nation suddenly realized that it could not have peace and an Axis defeat at the same time. Since 1939 the United States had been a limited belligerent, true, but the Rooseveltian policy of partial participation did not of itself lead to final involvement in the war. The United States, as in 1917, was neither forced nor manoeuvred into war; it entered the war because it could not stay out. If America, from 1939 to 1941, had appeased the dictators, refused to lend its moral weight and its industrial might to the Allies, abandoned the European democracies and the Philippines, Pearl Harbor need not have happened. But the alternative – existence as an armed island, between the Rising Sun and the Swastika – was one the nation could not choose.

The strategy agreed upon by the Allies was based on two decisions: first, to defeat Germany while containing Japan; and second, to coordinate and unify all Allied economic, political, military, and diplomatic policies. In the opening phases of the war the United States, a late entry, was committed to a defensive strategy, its power in the Pacific damaged, its huge industrial potential only partially mobilized. Before it could shift to the offensive the nation had to organize and equip itself as swiftly as possible for a war in which its opponents already possessed the initiative.

The pattern of mobilization followed fairly closely that of World War I. The Office of War Mobilization, headed by James F. Byrnes, held the responsibility of working with the Army and Navy Departments to insure coordinated effort. The War Production Board, established in 1942 as the successor to the National Defense Advisory Commission, supervised the task of converting industry to a war-time basis, while the Defense Plant Corporation, a subsidiary of the R.F.C., planned and built government-owned war plants. By 1943 sixty per cent of American industry had been completely converted to war production, with a capacity at least equal to the combined total of the Axis powers. The Office of Civilian Defense trained air-raid wardens, auxiliary firemen and police, plane spotters, and emergency medical personnel. The Office of War Information handled news at home and propaganda abroad.

The wartime agencies that had most far-reaching effects on the daily life of the average American, however, were those directed by the Office of Economic Stabilization. The War Manpower Commission, which controlled both Selective Service and industrial employment, touched the destinies of nearly every American family. The Office of Price Administration established rent ceilings, rationed food, fixed prices, and battled with black markets, sometimes against strenuous opposition. The Office of Defense Transportation supervised nearly all public transportation; railroads, unlike the practice of World War I, remained in private hands subject to O.D.T. control. The War Labor Board, created to arbitrate in strikes and grievances, kept labour-management friction at a minimum; the most serious strikes were those of the United Mine Workers in 1943 and 1945. To finance the cost of the war, which was about four times that of World War I, Congress increased excise and income taxes sufficiently to cover 46 per cent of expenditures. The balance was raised by the sale of interest-bearing bonds to private investors, also a useful anti-inflation device for absorbing excess spending power.

In 1941 the United States, as General Arnold expressed it, held two advantages – the distance of oceans and precious time contributed by British resistance. Japan held virtually complete control of the Pacific, with China cut off from aid, India menaced, the Philippines, Singapore, and the strategic Pacific islands in Japanese hands. The problem of prosecuting even a defensive Pacific war was primarily one of supply, with 2,000 miles of sea between American industry and the fighting front. Under-manned British, Australian, New Zealand, Dutch and American forces fought savagely to hold their lines, and in the Solomons campaigns of 1942 they checked the Japanese advance for the first time. (The threatened invasion of India was also frustrated.)

The Battle of the Coral Sea and the Battle of Midway broke Japan's naval superiority in the Pacific. In late 1942 and early 1943 United States Marine and naval forces began an offensive on Guadalcanal, turned back a Japanese counter-attack in New Guinea, and after six months of hard fighting consolidated strong positions in the islands. Australian, New Zealand, and American forces then began an island-hopping movement, sealing off or by-passing Japanese-held bases while their planes hammered at Japanese supply lines. By the end of 1943 the Allies, holding both sea and air supremacy, had evolved a long-range strategy – land forces under MacArthur were to advance along the New Guinea coast and eventually into the Philippines, while naval forces under Admiral Nimitz moved along the island chains twards Japan, establishing bomber bases for attacks on Japanese-held territory and on Japan itself.

Following these plans, landing forces began penetration of the Marshalls and the Mariannas, taking Saipan, Guam, and neutralizing the huge base at Truk while MacArthur's forces pushed into New Guinea. By the autumn of 1944 Allied planes were over the Philippines. In October assault boats landed at Leyte, and the United States Fleet, by defeating the Imperial Navy at the Battle of Leyte Gulf, virtually drove the Japanese from Philippine waters. American troops landed on the Philippine island of Luzon in late 1944 and in February 1945 took Manila. The fall of Iwo Jima the same month provided a new base for air strikes at Japan, and by spring the Allies had control of the air over Formosa and the China coast. Other landings at Okinawa placed Allied planes within 300 miles of the Japanese homeland. Throughout 1944 Chinese, British, Indian, Australian and American troops fought in Burma, hoping to open a supply line into China. British and Indian troops took Rangoon and Mandalay in 1945, and the Burma Road, hacked out of the jungle, opened a China route, though the war ended before the Chinese could be sufficiently trained and equipped to play an offensive part in the conflict.

Experimental atomic fission was achieved by European scientists before the war. British and American physicists began serious work in nuclear fission in 1939, while the fascist governments of Germany and Italy drove out several key scientists (among them Albert Einstein, Lise Meitner, and Enrico Fermi) who carried into exile valuable information and priceless research skills. Roosevelt in 1939 appointed an advisory committee on uranium, and in 1940 placed the committee under the jurisdiction of the National Defense Research Council. In the autumn of 1941 it was suggested that the United States, Britain and Canada pool resources. This was done, and when the project reached the production stage it was placed under the control of the United States Army and charged with the manufacture of an atomic weapon. After the expenditure of some 2,000 million dollars, the first atomic bomb was exploded at Alamogordo, New Mexico, on 16 July 1945.

A division of opinion existed from the first over the use of atomic weapons in warfare. The German surrender of May 1945 left Japan the sole enemy, and proponents of the bomb pointed out that a successful invasion of the Japanese homeland might cost between one and two million lives. On the other hand, many condemned a mass slaughter of civilians as the sort of barbarism the United Nations fought against, claiming that Japan, already under heavy air attack, was virtually at the point of surrender. A possible quick ending of the war, however, weighed heavily in the considerations of President Truman and his advisers, and the decision to use the bomb, concurred in by Churchill, was unanimous.

On 6 August 1945 a single Air Force B-29 dropped an atomic bomb on Hiroshima, leaving 128,000 dead, missing, and injured. Three days later another dropped on Nagasaki, one day after Russia, completing its Yalta pledge, declared war on Japan. On 10 August Japan asked for peace, and the next day the American Secretary of State, acting on behalf of the Allies, submitted surrender terms. Japan surrendered on 14 August, signing the final peace on 2 September.

Adolf Hitler, in December 1941, believed that the entrance of the United States into the war came too late to save Britain and France from defeat. The United States, however, was better organized for war than in 1917, its productive capacity expanded by Lend-lease, its Navy at wartime strength, one and a half million men in training under the conscription laws of 1940 and 1941. By June 1942 there were sufficient ground troops in Europe to justify formation of an American command under General Eisenhower, while American planes in increasing numbers operated with the Royal Air Force from England. In 1942 and early 1943 the British and Americans were able to clear North Africa, and in June an Anglo-American force invaded Sicily. The great invasion of Italy, beginning in September 1943, led to the capture of Rome in early 1944, after which an Allied army of various elements began the slow, bloody advance up the Italian boot.

After the German attacks of 1941 and 1942 dashed themselves to pieces on stubborn Russian resistance, Roosevelt, Churchill, and Stalin met at Cairo and Teheran to plan a general offensive. In July of 1943 the Russians began a two-month advance, while air strikes from Britian seriously damaged German war production. As part of the combined offensive strategy, Allied forces invaded France on 6 June 1944, landing in Normandy and securing the port of Cherbourg. German lines of defence and communication in France crumbled swiftly, and by August the German army was fighting desperately along the Seine. That same month the American Seventh Army landed in Southern France and began a swift slash up the Rhône Valley. With the fall of Paris a few days later, all invading Allied forces joined facing the German frontier, ready to begin a series of co-ordinate drives.

By early 1945 Hitler's armies were hopelessly caught between the Russians, advancing towards Berlin from the northeast, and the British, French, and Americans, from the southwest. By March the Russians were within thirty miles of Berlin, the Allies crossing the Rhine. German troops in Italy and Austria surrendered, and on 2 May Berlin fell. Five days later the German army made its unconditional surrender.

The impact of World War II on American foreign relations was much greater than that of World War I. In the Second World War the United States from the first committed itself more completely to international collaboration than ever before in its history. During the war and after it, the nation faced point-blank (as it had in 1920) the problem of world-wide collective security, and there is no evidence to show that either the government or the public shirked a decision. Throughout the war the American government worked closely with the Allies and with the heads of anti-Axis states, compiling an unprecedented record of international cooperation at Casablanca, Quebec, Moscow, Cairo, Teheran, Bretton Woods, Dumbarton Oaks, Yalta, and Potsdam. The Senate, traditionally an isolationist stronghold, in 1943 pledged the United States to join 'an international authority with power to prevent aggression and to preserve the peace of the world'. In April 1945, a few days after Roosevelt's death, the United Nations met in San Francisco to complete its organization with full American support, and in July the Senate ratified the U.N. Charter by a vote of 89 to 2, marking the end of a long isolationist road. 'Let us not hesitate,' said Truman in words both Wilson and Roosevelt would have approved, 'to join hands with the peace-loving nations of the earth . . .'

However, almost as soon as the Peace of Potsdam was signed some of the first flush of internationalist enthusiasm died away. The chief difficulty was Russia, a nation the United States had steadily avoided since 1919. The war-time alliance of America and the Soviet Union was uneasy, and Roosevelt bent every effort during the war to win the confidence of Russian leaders. At Yalta in 1945 he agreed to a great-power veto in the U.N. Security Council, Russian annexation of East Poland, Polish annexation of German territory, and Russian dominance in Yugoslavia and Manchuria. In addition, Yalta established the controversial partition of Germany into four military zones, and the four-power control of Berlin. Roosevelt contended that he could not have prevented these concessions, and it is true that he did receive in return a Russian pledge to enter the war against Japan and promises of post-war cooperation.

Russia's post-war policies were hardly designed to inspire confidence in her one-time allies. Friendly relations between the U.S. and the U.S.S.R. swiftly deteriorated, beginning with Russian violations of the Yalta agreements concerning Poland and Romania. The rush of Russian communism into the power vacuum left by the collapse of Germany and

Japan, and the rise of communist influence in France and Italy, excited apprehension in American diplomatic circles. At the Potsdam peace talks of 1946 Truman and Secretary of State Byrnes concluded that it was hopeless to expect further Russian concessions and that Russia intended to prolong post-war chaos as long as possible. With British and French support, the United States announced a 'get tough' attitude toward Russia. The Truman Doctrine of 1947 committed the United States to a policy of containment of Russian expansion, and to a policy of alliance with the remaining democratic and anti-communist nations, including some strange bedfellows such as Franco's Spain, Tito's Yugoslavia, and Perón's Argentina.

Under the terms of the Truman Doctrine the United States poured money into Greece and Turkey, while the 'Marshall Plan', or European Recovery Programme, budgeted 5,000 million dollars a year to anti-communist nations. In addition, in 1949 the United States signed the North Atlantic Pact, an eleven-nation alliance aimed directly at Russia; 'armed attack against one or more' of the member countries was to be 'considered an attack against them all'. The Russian counter-move to the Truman Doctrine was the establishment of the new Cominform in Warsaw in 1947, and of an Economic Mutual Assistance pact involving Russia and her satellite neighbours. Meanwhile, arguments over the interpretations of the Potsdam agreements caused increasing friction between Russia and the Allies in Germany. In protest against announced plans to set up a West German state, the Soviet ordered a blockade of Berlin in June 1948, and released it only after Britain, Canada, France and the United States supplied the city by air for nearly a year. Nevertheless, the West German state came into existence in 1949, with Russia immediately countering by creating the German Democratic Republic in its own zone of control.

The United States and Russia met again head-on in the Far East. At Yalta Stalin agreed to enter the war against Japan within three months of a German surrender, a promise kept to the day. Japan, however, was on the brink of defeat, and the United States refused to allow either Russia or China, whose contributions to the Pacific war were negligible, or, indeed, her other allies whose contributions had been great, to share in more than an advisory capacity in the post-war control of Japan. General Douglas MacArthur was designated as Supreme Allied Commander of the Far East, supported by a four-power council of representatives from the United States, Russia, Great Britain, and China. The United States, however, clearly dominated the council.

Until the end of 1946 MacArthur pursued a policy of liberal reform in Japan, whose new government was modelled closely on Britain's. By 1947, however, growing tension between the United States and Russia emphasized Japan's usefulness to the United States as an economic and military outpost against Soviet expansion. The Japanese government swung perceptibly to the right, the reform policies disappeared, and Japan began rearming under the terms of the peace treaty drawn up in 1951.

When the Japanese surrendered in August 1945, the Chinese Nationalist forces of Chiang Kai-shek and the Chinese Communist armies began a race for possession of the coastal areas and Manchuria. The United States gave some help to Chiang, while the Communists received some aid from Russia. After intensified fighting between Nationalist and Communist armies, President Truman in 1945 sent General George Marshall to China to attempt mediation. Marshall succeeded in arranging a brief truce, but in thirteen months of negotiation got nowhere in adjusting differences between the warring groups. On his return he advocated withdrawal of support to Chiang, a recommendation Congress refused to follow. Though the United States subsequently sent between two and four thousand million dollars' worth of aid to China, the Nationalist government steadily lost support and territory.

In 1949 and 1950 the Communists, sweeping through the coastal cities, drove Chiang's armies to Hainan and finally to Formosa, where they most certainly would have been trapped had it not been for American intervention. The Washington government, following the Truman Doctrine, declared Formosa vital to American Far Eastern defence and ordered the United States Navy to protect it from Communist invasion. The outbreak of war in Korea and the subsequent entry of Chinese Communists into it transferred the Chinese problem elsewhere.

World War II's experiences served to increase American interest in Central and South America. After 1941 the 'good neighbour' policy became something more than an expression of goodwill; hemispheric solidarity, American diplomats recognized, was a matter of political and military necessity. Widespread pro-Nazism in Brazil and Argentina, both with large German populations, led the State Department to make a sincere though belated courtship of South America, including the announcement that the United States was ready to lend seventy million a month to needy Latin American nations. The Act of Chapultepec, signed shortly before the San Francisco U.N. Conference, reaffirmed but modified the Monroe Doctrine. Instead of viewing hemispheric protection as the unilateral responsibility of the United States, it defined an attack on any American nation as an attack on all, and pledged all to joint responsibility for the common defence.

The Chapultepec agreement, however, did not settle all hemispheric differences. American tariff barriers against South American grain and meat were long-standing causes of friction, especially with Argentina, whose dictator-president, Colonel Juan Perón, was a consistent, clear, and open antagonist of 'Yankee imperialism'. Post-war economic adjustments with Argentina lessened tension appreciably. Though recognizing distinctly the totalitarian nature of Perón's regime, the State Department carefully worked out compromises that modified, at least, some of its anti-American bias.

Meanwhile, Soviet-American conflict in the United Nations continued. The U.S.S.R., with a minority of U.N.

support, used its veto freely to block action, even on minor matters; the United States, with majority support, sometimes forced decisions on questions the Russians were sure to veto. The Soviet representatives, however, were far more guilty of disrupting U.N. efforts to keep peace and encourage unity, often creating ill-feeling and disharmony in areas where none need exist. The titanic struggle for dominance in its councils has hampered U.N. efforts severely since 1946, and will continue to do so so long as the United States and the Soviet Union collide in foreign policy.

The effect of World War II on internal affairs in the United States has been extremely far-reaching. Even more than in World War I mobilization extended the power of the Federal government over every segment of American society, with the result that the historic issue of states' rights versus federalism became the most hotly-discussed political question of the post-war years. Public opinion, as expressed in every election since 1944, has been divided on the issue. If their voting records provide any indication, the American people want freedom of choice and open economic competition without undue federal interference; at the same time they want federal protection against inflation, price drops, unemployment, depression, social and economic dislocation. In effect, post-war America was moving toward a modified capitalism, with insurance against capitalism's risks as well as opportunity to enjoy its benefits. The current political problem is to find a reasonable balance between extremes of federalism and decentralization.

Socially the war marked a great forward step for racial and nationality minority groups, with the Negro making the greatest stride of all. A major population shift, beginning in 1919, placed 20 per cent of the American Negro population in the cities of the North and West by 1940. Serious racial tensions developed, and minor race riots occurred during the war years, culminating in a particularly violent outbreak in Detroit in 1943. Yet despite white-Negro friction, the Negro made distinct social and economic progress under wartime conditions. Industry, faced with an unprecedented demand for labour, opened doors previously shut to black men and women; the C.I.O. and the A.F.L., which had long adopted bi-racial policies, brought Negro workers by thousands into the labour unions. From 1932 the Negro voter had shifted his allegiance to the Democratic party and under the New Deal programme gained a great deal of political power. In a number of cities his vote is a decisive factor, and Negroes hold many elective offices as well as other positions of civic responsibility in North and South.

In 1941 Roosevelt forbade racial or religious discrimination in employment and appointed a Fair Employment Practices Commission to enforce his order, a practice copied in several Northern states. The Supreme Court during the forties upheld the right of Negroes to sit on juries, vote in primary elections, and to receive equal educational facilities. Truman's civil rights programme, recommended to Congress in 1948, failed against strong Southern opposition, but Southern states themselves recognized their responsibility to the Negro and began to modify old 'jim crow' laws and customs. 'White supremacy' in America is by no means dead, but on the racial issue the South is no longer so solid as it was before World War II.

Generally the American record toward minority groups in the Second World War was an improvement over that of World War I, except for the treatment of Japanese nationals and Japanese-Americans. Feeling against the Japanese after Pearl Harbor was intense and unselective, and Nisei, or American-born Japanese, of whom the West Coast had many, bore the brunt of war-time intolerance. As a measure of military security 100,000 men, women, and children of Japanese descent were evacuated from the Pacific Coast states to relocation camps in the interior, sometimes under conditions of extreme hardship. Long-smouldering racial hatred, stemming from economic rivalry between Japanese and white agricultural and business interests in the West, led to talk of permanently expelling Japanese from the area. After the war, however, most Japanese returned to their homes and businesses without appreciable difficulty.

The most striking consequence of the war on public opinion was a tremendous surge of anti-communist, anti-Russian feeling, intensified by the breakdown of Soviet-American relations in 1946 and by the outbreak of the Korean war. The existence of a tightly-controlled, Soviet-directed Communist Party in the United States, at a time when the United States and Russia were engaged in conflict over world leadership, posed a national dilemma. The United States was firmly committed to anti-totalitarianism, and revered its tradition of free thought and free expression. How far should restrictions on Communist or quasi-Communist activity go? How far might the accepted principle of 'free trade in ideas' be safely followed? The problem of establishing internal security while protecting civil liberty had troubled the nation before – in the days of the Alien and Sedition Acts, in the abolitionist controversy, in the Civil War, in World War I – but the 'red scares' of 1919 and 1920 seemed destined to be repeated in virulent form, aided by a favourable press.

The Smith Act of 1940 made it a crime to advocate the forcible overthrow of any United States government, to disseminate such doctrines in printed form, or to belong to any organization that advocated such action. The Federal Bureau of Investigation, an agency of the Justice Department, was granted broader powers to deal with espionage and subversion in 1945. Politicians found anti-Communism at attractive vote-getting device, and members of Congress and of state legislature, beginning in 1947, asked for 'loyalty oaths' among civil service employees, teachers, and government officials. Congressional and legislative committees probed labour unions, government agencies, schools, universities, the movies, and publishing houses for evidences of Communist infiltration, sometimes harrying suspects without proper regard for process of law or traditional civil rights.

The facts behind the 'red scare' were foreboding enough – Russian successes in eastern Europe and China, the Berlin blockade, Russian obstructionism in the U.N., discovery of

Communist espionage in atomic research in Canada and England, the conviction of Alger Hiss, a respected State Department official, for perjury. Yet the facts were never sufficient to account for the hysteria that struck the public during the period 1947 to 1952, nor for the toleration by the public and the press of frequent abuses of civil rights in the search for subversives. The culmination of anti-Red political activities came after 1950 with the work of Senator Joseph McCarthy, who made widespread charges (usually under senatorial immunity from suit) against private citizens and government officials. In the midst of the furore Justice Jackson of the Supreme Court ruled in 1950 that the Communist Party was a conspiracy rather than a political party, and a mounting number of legal decisions agreed. Local and state laws outlawing the Communist Party appeared in many states, some upheld, some disallowed by the higher courts. In 1950 Congress passed the controversial Internal Security (McCarran) Act over Truman's veto, making it unlawful to conspire to establish a totalitarian dictatorship such as a communist state.

The presidential elections of 1944 came as the tide of war turned in the Allies' favour. Roosevelt, ill and worn, was reluctant to run for a fourth term, but since there seemed to be no one to replace him he quickly accepted the Democratic nomination. Henry Wallace of Iowa, vice-president since 1940, impressed the party leaders as too unstable for another term, and at the convention the choice for second place fell to Senator Harry Truman of Missouri. The Republican National Committee eliminated Taft and Willkie (he was not even invited to speak at the convention) in favour of Thomas Dewey, whose record as a 'gang-busting' district attorney and as Governor of New York made his name known the nation over.

The campaign was lively. Roosevelt made only a few public appearances, but Dewey launched an aggressive attack against the New Deal as a quarrelsome, inefficient bureaucracy of 'tired old men', promising instead a youthful, energetic administration. The momentum of war and New Deal reform carried Roosevelt through. His electoral majority, though large, did not accurately reflect his smaller popular majority of three and a half million. Much of his strength lay in the urban vote and in the support given to him by the unions through the C.I.O. Political Action Committee, founded in 1944.

Three months after his inauguration, Franklin Roosevelt died. He had understood the intricacies of American politics better than most of his predecessors and had found his way through them with courage and with cunning that sometimes approached unscrupulousness. He knew the American people so that, in moments of crisis, he could edge even his opponents into alliance. He was much loved by many of his countrymen, resented by almost as many and hated by a significant minority. If his grasp of international consequences was less secure than that of the other two great protagonists, Stalin and Churchill, it was, for an American President, rarely professional and based upon long experience. He shared with Churchill the paradox of a mind keen to the political rhythms of the twentieth century and a personality which seemed to belong to an earlier age.

With his death, the preservation of the Alliance, the task of winning the War and the future success of the New Deal fell to a man of quite different character. Harry S. Truman, a product of Missouri machine politics, was a politician from the ground up, stubbornly loyal to his party, his friends and his benefactors. Sent to the Senate by powerful Kansas City bosses, he had a comparatively undistinguished record before he was placed on the national ticket as the only eligible Midwestern Democrat. A humble, sincere man, apprehensive at the responsibilities thrust upon him, he pledged an unflagging devotion to Roosevelt's principles and to the continuance of the New Deal.

Truman's path was hard. He inherited a dragging war, a sudden peace and a recalcitrant Congress. Politically he stood somewhat to the right of Roosevelt, and after a series of wrangles New Deal appointees left his administration in droves: Wallace, Burnes, Ickes and others. The end of the war brought popular demands to make peace quickly, drop price and wage controls, 'bring the boys home', and return life to normal as swiftly as possible. The spread of post-war inflation surged upward, and a plague of strikes and work stoppages struck industry. Truman's uncertain approach to post-war problems seemed to stamp him as an ineffective successor to the self-confident Roosevelt.

The Republicans in Congress took advantage of Truman's inexperience, mangling most of his proposals beyond recognition and blocking others. Congressional leadership on domestic issues fell to Senator Robert Taft of Ohio, Republican foreign policy to Senator Arthur Vandenberg of Michigan. Taft, a President's son already known as 'Mr Republican', was a deeply isolationist conservative opposed to almost anything smacking of the New Deal. Vandenberg, an isolationist turned internationalist, was a broader and more flexible man whose foreign policy resembled Roosevelt's and Truman's. The resurgence of the Republican party began in the congressional elections of 1946, which returned a Republican majority to Washington for the first time since 1928.

As if to show its partisan temper at the outset, Congress passed the Twenty-Second Amendment to the Constitution, which forbade election to the Presidency for more than two full terms, or for more than one term if the candidate had served over two years of an unfinished term. Ratified by the thirty-sixth state in 1951, the amendment, a posthumous rebuke to Franklin Roosevelt, was also a reflection of a widening uneasy belief that the powers of the Chief Executive in the twentieth century were now so great that the nation should not risk usurpation of them by a single powerful man. (The Republicans, however, had reason to regret their victory in 1960 when Dwight Eisenhower, an almost certain winner for a third term, was prevented from candidacy by the amendment.)

The struggle between Truman and Congress after 1946 occupied the remainder of Truman's term. Following

Vandenberg's advice, Congress accepted the Truman Doctrine and the Marshall Plan, but Old Guard Republicans, skilfully led by Taft, won most of the rounds on domestic issues. A wave of strikes in 1946 and 1947, with John L. Lewis's United Mine Workers leading the way, convinced a good many Congressmen that uncontrolled labour was as dangerous to economic stability as uncontrolled management. The Taft-Hartley Act of 1947 therefore established curbs on union powers, banned the closed shop, authorized injunctions in jurisdictional strikes, required union financial statements, demanded non-Communist affidavits of union officials and outlawed certain types of strikes. Unions attacked it vehemently (although admitting the validity of some of its provisions), Truman vetoed it, and Congress passed it over his veto. Both the C.I.O.-P.A.C. and the A.F.L.-P.A.C. entered the 1948 elections with the Act as their major target.

Taft was the organization's choice for nomination at the Republican convention of 1948, but Dewey, despite his loss in 1944, remained the popular idol. Dewey won the nomination and started a slashing, confident campaign. New Dealers in the Democratic party would have preferred to jettison Truman (there was talk of drafting General Dwight Eisenhower, then President of Columbia University) but no one could agree on a substitute. An unenthusiastic convention nominated Truman, while the Northern wing of the party rammed home a sweepingly liberal platform, including a strong civil rights plank that immediately alienated the race-conscious South. Dissident Southern Democrats formed a States' Rights (Dixiecrat) party and nominated Governor J. Strom Thurmond of South Carolina. The Progressive Party, a Communist-liberal coalition, ran Henry Wallace on a platform reaffirming the New Deal and advocating cooperation with Russia.

Republicans, viewing the split in the Democratic party and basking in the favour of an almost uniformly anti-Truman press, approached election day with supreme self-confidence. All public opinion polls gave Dewey a decided edge, and even Democrats privately admitted that Truman had no chance. But Truman refused to give up. His battles with Congress had forced him to liberalize his political thinking, sharpen up his political techniques, and evolve a positive programme of his own. He called Congress into special session, offered his programme, and when the Republican majority defeated it he took to the road on a 'whistle-stop' tour of the nation. Flaying the 'do-nothing' Congress in hamlets and cities, evoking admiring cries of 'Give 'em hell, Harry!' Truman turned into a forceful, rough-and-tumble political leader of real appeal. The election, a shattering upset, surprised everyone but Truman. Thurmond took four states, Wallace none, Dewey sixteen, and Truman the rest, though his margin of victory was less than two million votes out of forty-nine million cast.

Truman's Fair Deal programme, the centre of controversy during his second term, was born in his speech to Congress in January 1949. By a 'fair deal', he said, he meant the realization of 'the promise of equal rights and equal opportunities which the founders of our Republic proclaimed'. His programme had a familiar ring, since it comprised most of the unfinished business of his first term plus national health legislation – a civil rights bill, repeal of the Taft-Hartley Act, public housing, farm subsidies, price and wage controls, more T.V.A.-type power projects. The Fair Deal involved a greater extension of Federal authority and responsibility than even Roosevelt had asked, leading to Republican cries of 'socialist', 'welfare state', or as Hoover called it, 'a disguise for the totalitarian state'. After 1949 this accusation became one of the most effective Republican political weapons.

The Democrats, lacking a genuine mandate from the voters, fell on the defensive. The Republicans, denied a term of office to which they felt entitled, took up the role of an irreconcilable opposition. Nor did Truman control Congress. Anti-Truman Democrats, chiefly from the South, frequently joined Republicans to block Fair Deal legislation, and after the 1950 elections reduced the Democratic majority to vanishing point. Truman was virtually helpless. Most of the Fair Deal went down the drain, although he did succeed in passing through Congress a boost in the minimum wage law, some public housing, and extended coverage under the Social Security Act. In his foreign policy, until 1950, Truman fared somewhat better. Congress expanded the European Recovery Programme, ratified the North Atlantic Treaty, and gave the President power to revise tariffs under the Reciprocal Trade Agreements Act.

Determined to avoid Wilson's error, Roosevelt in 1940 had proclaimed a bipartisan foreign policy, consulted with Republican leaders on major decisions, and placed prominent Republicans in his cabinet. So long as Vandenberg remained in charge of Republican foreign policy this worked well, but when the Michigan Senator's illness removed him from an active role in Senate affairs (he died in 1951) bipartisanship broke down. After 1950 Congressional Republicans made increasingly bitter denunciations of Truman and his Secretary of State, Dean Acheson, and showed a marked reluctance to continue in the Vandenberg tradition. By 1951 the attack on Truman and Acheson involved five major criticisms: alleged softness toward Russia, blundering in China and in the U.N., failure to force European unity against Russia, waste in foreign aid, and Communist (or semi-Communist) infiltration of government agencies. After the beginning of the Korean conflict the Truman-Acheson foreign policy became the most important single political issue.

Well before the close of World War II, the Soviet Union, China, Great Britain, and the United States agreed to Korean independence after Japan's defeat. By an agreement made in August 1945, the thirty-eighth Korean parallel became the dividing line of responsibility, Russia to control the north, the United States and other nations the south. In South Korea, after internal flare-ups between Korean conservatives and radicals, the United States created the

Republic of Korea and held elections in 1946, with the result that Syngman Rhee and the rightist elements gained control of the government. Both the United States and Russia discussed a merger of the two zones, but since each wanted the merger under a government friendly to itself, no decision could be reached. An open election, the United States believed, would create a pro-American government; Russia evidently agreed, and hoping that the removal of foreign forces might assist a successful Communist coup, suggested withdrawal of all troops from both zones. Both sides began training and arming Koreans in preparation for the eventual withdrawal, the U.S.S.R. arming North Koreans better and faster. Russia recalled its forces in early 1948, the United States following six months after.

On 24 June 1950 North Korean army units crossed the thirty-eighth parallel in a drive toward the Korean capital of Seoul, announcing that they came to liberate South Korea from the rule of Rhee and unify all Korea. While the South Korean army rapidly dissolved, the United States at Secretary Acheson's behest introduced into the United Nations Security Council a resolution calling on the North Koreans to withdraw. Meanwhile President Truman ordered General MacArthur, the Supreme Allied Commander in Tokyo, to send air and sea forces into Korea, with ground troops to follow, an action, said Truman, 'taken as a matter of basic moral principle'. With Russia and its veto absent, the Security Council approved a resolution that all U.N. members furnish military aid to the South Korean Republic, asking unity of command under American auspices and designating MacArthur as Commander-in-Chief of the U.N. forces. Congress, supporting the Council, extended the draft, increased taxes, and speeded up armament production.

The R.O.K. army, however, lost ground rapidly to the well-trained North Koreans, until the combined South Korean and U.N. troops held only a small area about Pusan. MacArthur mounted an offensive in the summer of 1950 that drove the North Koreans back across the thirty-eighth parallel and by November had them pinned against the

Manchurian border. In that month Chinese Communist troops from Manchuria appeared in North Korean lines. On 24 November MacArthur ordered American units to attack Chinese positions. The counter-attack that followed drove the outnumbered U.N. armies back to the thirty-eighth parallel, where their lines held.

The entrance of Communist China into the Korean conflict on a 'volunteer' basis created a difference of opinion between MacArthur and Truman over the conduct of the war. Truman, convinced that Russia and not China was the real antagonist, favoured treating Korea as a holding action, committing only a portion of American strength to checking the Chinese while building up anti-Russia strength in European and other Far Eastern danger spots. Under no circumstances, he and his advisers believed, should the Korean action be allowed to develop into a full-scale war against China, leaving Russia free to continue its advance across Europe and the Middle East.

MacArthur, seeing sweeping victories denied him, voiced his disapproval of the plan determined by his superiors. He made an unauthorized truce offer to China, with the implied threat of extending the war to the Chinese mainland, and disregarded Department of Defense orders forbidding public statements of policy by army officers. In April 1951 he wrote a letter to Representative Joseph Martin, House Republican leader and a bitter foe of the Truman administration. Martin immediately published the letter, which expressed strong criticism of the Korean strategy, and on 11 April 1951, President Truman, with the unanimous consent of his military and civilian advisers, removed MacArthur as U.N. Commander and replaced him with General Matthew Ridgway.

MacArthur's dismissal created a bewildering uproar. The frustrations of cold war and Korean stalemate led many to see merit in MacArthur's simple, forceful approach, and numerous groups opposed to Truman and Acheson sprang to the General's defence. MacArthur staged a triumphal return to Washington, where Congressional committees conducted a curious, inconclusive investigation of State and Defense Department policies. MacArthur himself, after a dramatic exit speech to Congress, retired to private business and interest in him rapidly waned. Not long after his removal Russia's U.N. representative, Jacob Malik, proposed peace talks in Korea. Both North and South Koreans agreed, but after months of conferences nothing was accomplished.

As a result of the Korean war and *l'affaire MacArthur* the United States adopted a long-range militarization programme and a much more aggressive attitude toward Russian expansion. Congress speeded up economic aid to Europe, and the State Department worked energetically to consolidate European alliances and to unify American and European resources. The decisive action taken by the United States in Korea committed it irrevocably to intervention in global politics, for better or for worse. Seeing world politics as a race for authority between communism and democracy, America accepted full responsibility for free-world leadership.

At the close of World War II, as they had after World War I, the American people wished nothing more than to live at peace in an isolated hemisphere, untouched by European or Asiatic disturbance. America had everything any American could wish – wealth, personal and political liberty, high living standards, unexploited resources, a free and stable government – and nothing held more appeal to the average American than simply the preservation of the *status quo*. But it was clear that the isolationism of the twenties and thirties was both unworkable and undesirable in the post-war world. The Second World War released tremendous forces in the war-ravaged countries of Europe and Asia, where the *status quo* meant unreasoning nationalism, poverty, distress, oppression, and revolution. Of all the nations to emerge from World War II, only the United States and Russia were in a position to exert immediate, forceful leadership, and Russia, by reason of its totalitarian structure and imperialistic commitments, was in the better position to act. That the United States accepted world leadership against the new totalitarian threat, a leadership forced on it by inexorable events, is proof of its attainment of national maturity. No administration, during this or any foreseeable future generation, is likely to relinquish it willingly.

Throughout Truman's second term his relations with Congress steadily deteriorated. Their losses in 1944 and 1948, Republicans reasoned, stemmed from 'me-tooism', that is, promises to do what Roosevelt and Truman had done, but to do it better. After 1948 the party leaders adopted a frankly conservative, anti-New Deal, anti-Fair Deal line, concentrating their attack on the 'creeping socialism' and 'blundering foreign policy' of both Roosevelt and Truman. Some liberal Republicans did not like the tactics; some conservative Democrats did. Strange coalitions therefore appeared in Congress, Southern Democrats occasionally joining Northern Republicans to thwart Truman, liberal Democrats and Republicans rushing to his assistance.

Harry Truman was a rugged and stubborn fighter, but he did not possess Roosevelt's flair for the dramatic, and what Roosevelt would have made a crusade became in Truman's hands a political squabble. After 1950 rebellious anti-Truman Democrats and Republicans in Congress treated the President with little more than contempt; for the first time in 160 years Congress tried to force the resignation of a cabinet member (Secretary of State Acheson) and very nearly succeeded. Enthusiastically aided by the press, Republicans and their minority Democratic allies launched an offensive against the President unmatched for rancour since the days of Andrew Johnson. By the presidential conventions of 1952 Truman, who had at all events announced in March that he would not seek re-election, had been thoroughly discredited.

The disappearance from centre-stage of Harry S. Truman marked the disappearance of the outstanding ordinary man of his time. Not once, but a dozen times he surprised the world by acting with vigour and courage when he might have been expected to follow an easier course. But, the magnificent moment over, he slipped back into the role of a somewhat humdrum party politician, eager for power and yet nervous of decision. His battles with Taft over labour relations, with McCarthy and McCarran over witch-hunts, with MacArthur over Korean policy, with the China Lobby and with the 'Do-Nothing' Republican majority in the Eightieth Congress were all fought with a vigour as unexpected as the 'Give 'em Hell, Harry' speeches of the 1948 election campaign, but there was little stamina in his policies. His limited political education was most obvious in his foreign policy. Europe was beyond his comprehension. His view of the British Commonwealth was founded upon the myth that having 'pounded down the absolute monarchy of George III' (the words are his) America must continue the process. He held fast to the belief that in international affairs 'compromise' is a synonym for 'appeasement'. Nevertheless, armed with America's indisputable strength and his own undeniable courage, Truman rose above prejudice, ineptness and his own modest powers.

Perhaps Truman's greatest contribution to the Presidency was his refusal to allow the powers and the initiative of the Executive to be pre-empted by Congress. Faced by a strong and recalcitrant Congress, he fought furiously against its attempts to erode presidential power; he vetoed more bills (250 of them) than any two-term President in history. Often he went directly to the voters for support in his battle against the legislative branch; he based and won his campaign of 1948 on the deficiencies of the Eightieth Congress. In effect, Truman reaffirmed what Jackson, Lincoln and the two Roosevelts had already demonstrated: that while the three branches of government were presumably equal, the Executive was the first among equals.

Early in 1952, Taft, twice frustrated, declared himself a candidate for the Republican nomination and began a vigorous pre-convention campaign. However, a great deal

of sentiment had developed in favour of General Dwight
Eisenhower, then commanding the N.A.T.O. forces in Europe,
who made no political statements and refused for some time
to reveal his party affiliations. (The portents should have
been clear for all to read. Washington, Jackson, Grant –
after almost every war in its history the United States had
presented the White House to a successful general.) Eisenhower supporters among Republicans entered his name in
several state primary elections, and after noting that he did
well, in June 1952 the General resigned from the Army,
declared himself a Republican, and returned to give his first
frankly political speech at Abilene, Kansas. Taft's long
service in the Senate and his years of experience made him
the favourite of the conservative party leaders, but Eisenhower's military reputation and his wide popularity gave
him greater public support. At the Chicago convention in
July a violent struggle between Taft and Eisenhower
delegates ended in an Eisenhower victory.

Truman had announced in March 1952 that he would
not seek re-election, thereby leaving the field open to
numerous hopefuls, among them Senator Estes Kefauver of
Tennessee, Senator Richard Russell of Georgia, Averell
Harriman of New York, and Vice-President Alben Barkley
of Kentucky. Kefauver, nationally known for his televised
investigations of crime and racketeering, went to the convention a solid favourite. However, a last-minute mobilization of liberals swung the convention to Adlai Stevenson, the
Democratic governor of Illinois, a virtually unknown intellectual who had given his state an enlightened and progressive administration. After some hesitation, Stevenson
accepted the nomination, pledging a continuance of New
Deal and Fair Deal policies.

The 1952 campaign was extremely bitter, centring about
five major issues: high taxes; the so-called Fair Deal
'welfare state'; waste and corruption in Federal agencies;
alleged infiltration of pro-Communists into government
posts; and especially the Truman–Acheson foreign policy
with regard to Korea, Russia and European aid. Signifi-

cantly, both candidates agreed on an internationalist foreign policy, though minor isolationist groups appeared in both parties.

Republican promises to end the Korean stalemate, reduce taxes, and pursue a strong anti-Russian course proved to be decisive factors in the election. Eisenhower won a sweeping victory, with 449 electoral votes to Stevenson's eighty-nine and a popular majority of seven million. Undoubtedly Eisenhower's personal popularity provided the Republicans with their biggest advantage, since he ran far ahead of the rest of the Republican ticket; the Republicans on 5 November held a majority of but one in the Senate and three in the House. For the first time in twenty years the Republican party controlled the executive and legislative branches of the American government, and for the first time since Hoover the Republican party had both responsibility and the power to direct national policy.

Dwight Eisenhower entered the White House with tremendous popular support and little political experience. Virtually insulated from partisan politics during forty years of Army service, he had been far removed from the bitter battles between New Deal, Fair Deal and Old Guard. The dimensions of his popularity reflected the national mood; he seemed to be above politics, an affable, honest, personable man whose great asset was his ability to adjust differences. 'I have not much patience with the desk-pounding type of leadership,' he once said. 'Leadership is a matter of influencing people. I try to convince people by the logic of my position.' His cabinet appointments indicated the alignment of power centres within his administration; many came directly from business, chiefly from large corporations, and as one member of his cabinet frankly stated, 'We're here in the saddle as an Administration representing business and industry.' As its spokesmen defined it, the aim of the Eisenhower government was to encourage business expansion, to maintain a balanced budget, to favour corporate over public activity, and to support a rising level of economic growth. Yet the appointment of Martin Durkin, a Democratic labour leader, to the post of Secretary of Labor came as a surprise and led the labour unions to hope for favourable concessions.

Eisenhower's chief interest in the early days of his office centred on foreign affairs – the stalemated Korean war, the organization of the European Defence Community, the final phases of the North Atlantic Treaty Organization, the continuation of foreign economic aid, and the development of a world trade policy. John Foster Dulles, the new Secretary of State, was an internationally-minded and experienced diplomat. The death of Stalin and an apparent shift in Russian and Chinese policy enabled Dulles and the U.N. to negotiate a truce in Korea, on approximately the same grounds as those recommended earlier by Truman and Acheson. Indecisive as it was, the Korean agreement still provided a temporary solution to the tangled Asian problem and redeemed a Republican campaign pledge. For the first time since 1950 the State Department believed it had an opportunity to seize the initiative in Russo–American relations, and while continuing to deal cautiously with the new Malenkov regime, Dulles expressed hope of a better settlement. Eisehnower's dream of stimulating 'profitable and fair world trade', however, ran into stiff opposition from high-tariff Republicans. The fate of E.D.C., N.A.T.O., and foreign aid remained shrouded in uncertainty, and it seemed clear that the Administration's foreign policy was due to encounter rough going from the isolationist, nationalist wing of the Republican party.

The Republicans moved slowly during their first year in office, feeling their way after twenty years as a minority party. As one of their first acts (in retroactive revenge against Roosevelt) the Republicans initiated, and the necessary number of state legislatures passed, the twenty-second Amendment to the Constitution, limiting to two terms the office of the Presidency. But despite Eisenhower's popular victory, the party he represented was hardly unified, and from the beginning many Republicans showed signs of restlessness on matters of foreign and domestic policy. Some

Republicans thought that the President was too slow in breaking away from the foreign policy of the Democrats, particularly in relations with the Allies; others thought him tardy in reversing the Democratic trend to the 'welfare state'. Party factions asserted themselves even before Eisenhower's inauguration. For a time Senator Taft held the factions in line, but his death in mid-1953 left the party without an experienced leader.

In domestic affairs the Republican record during its first year was indecisive. Labour, a substantial segment of which had supported Eisenhower in expectation of obtaining revisions in the Taft-Hartley law, split with his administration within a few months. Durkin resigned, claiming violations of specific promises to amend the act, and the C.I.O. and A.F.L. both expressed annoyance at lack of action from the White House. Midwestern farmers and Western cattlemen, confronted by a serious drought and declining prices, displayed familiar signs of agrarian restlessness. Meanwhile attacks on the civil service system, suspension of the public housing and community development programmes, proposals to dispose of Federally-owned industrial and power projects to private business, and the transfer of offshore oil reserves from Federal to state ownership created fears that twenty years of social and economic progress might swiftly be cancelled. Others, after two decades of protests against an expanding Federal authority, welcomed a reversal of the trend begun by Franklin Roosevelt and continued by Truman. Many major issues – farm policy, trade, Taft–Hartley amendments – were passed over in 1954.

During Eisenhower's first term of office, the great Communist scare reached its first crest and began to recede. The Korean war and its stalemated peace were frustrating experiences for the American people. Confronted constantly and globally with the Soviet threat of expansion, the United States seemed destined to face an interminable future of 'police actions' and 'brush-fire wars'. Searching for explanations of apparent Russian diplomatic successes, some Americans decided that United States foreign and military policy had been betrayed by internal subversion. The discovery of a Canadian spy ring, which had passed information to Russian intelligence, seemed to provide a handy clue. A series of investigations revealed some evidence of Communist influence in policy-making circles, culminating in the spectacular trial and conviction for perjury in 1949–50 of Alger Hiss, a former State Department official. At almost the same time, the exposure of an atomic spy ring brought the execution in 1953 of Julius and Ethel Rosenberg, both convicted of espionage.

The American public, after a decade of war and tension, was particularly vulnerable to a demagogue who could play on its fears and frustrations. Well aware of the advantages to be gained by capitalizing on the national mood, Senator Joseph McCarthy, a Republican, assumed the mantle of chief communist-hunter. In February 1950, in a famous speech at Wheeling, West Virginia, he labelled the State Department as 'thoroughly infested with Communists', beginning a swiftly-publicized campaign of scurrilous attacks and unsubstantiated charges against political, military, and intellectual leaders – including a particularly vicious attack on General George Marshall, one of the most respected men in public life. Within a few months McCarthy had a large following, well financed, and already too powerful to dislodge or even discipline. Though some Republican leaders, including Eisenhower, looked at the man and his methods with distaste, his value to the Republican party as a campaign weapon against the Democrats was too great to disregard. The Republican convention of 1952 placed on its platform the accusation that the Democratic party had, 'by a long succession of vicious acts, so undermined the foundation of our Republic as to threaten its existence', while the Attorney-General of the United States himself even encouraged suspicions of ex-President Truman and others of his administration.

The Republican victory of 1952, in which McCarthy played a useful role, also made him chairman of the Senate

Permanent Subcommittee on Investigation where he went almost unchallenged, wreaking havoc in public life and producing hosts of lesser imitators in the states. As one of his biographers, Richard Rovere, pointed out, McCarthy specialized in the 'multiple untruth', the lie so complicated and irrational that it was impossible to refute it by either evidence or logic. Abroad the word 'McCarthyism' came to represent the symbol of an incipient American fascism, and at home many feared that McCarthy-bred hysteria might permanently damage the cherished American tradition of civil rights and due process. However, by degrees public opinion began to right itself, and McCarthy began to lose some of his adroitness. In 1954 an attack on the Army led to his sudden downfall after a series of televised investigations exposed his methods to an audience of millions and effectively destroyed him. In December of that year, noting the shift of public opinion, the Senate voted to 'condemn' his conduct and his influence rapidly declined. McCarthy died in 1957, leaving a legacy of incalculable harm to American life. Ironically enough, that same year the Supreme Court by its decisions in *Jencks v. United States*, *Yates v. United States* and *Watkins v. United States* erased some of that legacy from the legal records.

President Eisenhower during his first year placed no definite legislative programme before Congress. His own domestic and foreign programme could be inferred, however, from press conferences and occasional speeches. First, he seemed interested in removing much of the influence of the Federal government from domestic affairs. His attitude towards this, the major issue of American political life in our time, represented a compromise policy of retaining the concept of long-range Federal planning while keeping Federal authority over social and economic life at a minimum. As an avowed internationalist, Eisenhower was concerned with pursuing a somewhat stronger foreign policy than that of his predecessor, while at the same time hoping to avoid entrapment by its critics. Here, as Roosevelt and Truman before him, he faced the powerful nationalist bloc within the Republican Party which by its constant attacks imprisoned the State Department in a ring of criticism, robbing it of flexibility, morale and reputation.

Eisenhower believed that the Presidency was, in effect, beyond political partisanship, an office resembling that of chairman of the board of a corporation. As a product of the military staff system he believed in institutionalizing Presidential duties, devolving large shares of responsibility to trusted staff while reserving for the President the right to act on major policies. As months passed, he tended to delegate more and more authority to his subordinates, so that members of his Cabinet took a stronger role in government than under any President since Calvin Coolidge. Feeling that both Roosevelt and Truman had over-emphasized the importance of the executive, Eisenhower hoped to re-establish the identity of Congress by making it the ally and not the antagonist of the President. In Eisenhower's view, the President proposed and Congress disposed; he had no desire to be a strong executive in the tradition of Jackson, Wilson, or the two Roosevelts. The role of the Federal government he conceived to be as a kind of passive partner of *laissez-faire* individualism; the function of government was 'to stabilize the economy and encourage the free play of our people's genius for individual initiative', as he phrased it, while avoiding the 'creeping socialism' of his predecessors' 'welfare state'.

By the 1956 elections, the Eisenhower administration had developed a much more identifiable style. The President described his political philosophy as 'dynamic conservatism', or 'progressive conservatism', indicating his middle-of-the-road position – for, as he said, the 'middle of the road is the truly creative area' within which constructive action seemed likely. The Democrats once more nominated Adlai Stevenson to oppose Eisenhower, and although Stevenson made much the same type of campaign as before,

Eisenhower's popularity and the trend of events would have been too much for any opponent. Eisenhower's vice-presidential running mate, Senator Richard Nixon of California, added youth and Western support to the Republican ticket, which swept to a decisive victory, winning even six traditionally Democratic states in the South. However, Eisenhower's vote was testimony to his personal popularity rather than to his party's, for the Democrats took Congress by a narrow margin, which they increased in the 1958 congressional elections. At no time, in either of his terms, did Eisenhower have real party control of Congress. It was clear that the voters 'liked Ike' better than his cohorts.

With his popularity and prestige, Eisenhower could no doubt have pushed through Congress almost any programme he wished. Instead, he chose to exert his personal power but rarely, preferring to maintain easy relations with both sides of the House and Senate. Throughout his second term he had difficulty in controlling some of his own party, especially its conservative wing. A sharp and puzzling economic recession stunned the nation in 1958; in the same year Eisenhower lost his most trusted assistant, Governor Sherman Adams of New Hampshire, in a scandal; in 1959 the death of John Foster Dulles left him without his most valued adviser in foreign affairs. Nevertheless Eisenhower actually accomplished more positive legislative results during his second term than he had contrived during his first. His administration passed the National Defense Education Act, which furnished support for science, language study, and student loans to universities; created a Civil Rights Commission to study problems of racial discrimination; made needed amendments to the Atomic Energy Act to allow greater cooperation in research; and in 1959 admitted both Hawaii and Alaska to statehood.

The problems of foreign policy in the post-war world raised some confusing issues for Americans. The fruits of victory, the successful unleashing of atomic energy, the establishment of the United Nations (Americans have always placed great faith in dramatically conceived institutions), and consequent prospects of peaceful prosperity lent a kind of euphoria to America's foreign relations. The power of the United Nations, the atomic superiority of the United States, and the enlightened cooperation of the victorious powers, it was assumed, would all combine to maintain world peace. However, the situation changed with disheartening swiftness – in Russia, China, Korea, a divided Europe, and a disturbed Middle East. It was difficult for the average American to make sense and order out of subsequent events. Russian allies suddenly became potential enemies; former German enemies suddenly became allies. China and the United States had joined wartime forces against Japan; by 1950 the United States was strengthening Japan as a check against Chinese power. Nor did it seem that the European and Asian nations were steering any less erratic courses, especially Russia. The conflict of interests between expanding American and Russian foreign policy soon became so intense that the great danger of the fifties to American foreign policy was that anti-communism would become the exclusive theme. Within a few years after a war against totalitarianism, the United States found itself, on grounds of their anti-communism, supporting some of the world's choicest reactionaries, among them Franco in Spain, Chiang in Formosa, Batista in Cuba, Bao Dai in Viet Nam, and even communist Tito in Yugoslavia. The ardent internationalism of Roosevelt's era, which replaced the isolationism of the thirties, was itself during the fifties in danger of being replaced by a mood of disillusion, by sharply reduced expectations, and the acceptance of any combination of foreign policy decisions which might best serve the national interest in an unsteady and inconsistent world of foreign affairs.

Foreign policy during both Eisenhower administrations was under the direction of Secretary of State John Foster Dulles. For most of his life Dulles, a successful corporation lawyer, had prepared himself to be Secretary of State as his uncle had been under Wilson and his grandfather

under Benjamin Harrison. A stubborn, shrewd, moralistic
and tough-minded man, he dominated American foreign
affairs for six important years. Since criticism of Democratic
foreign policy had been a hotly-debated campaign issue in
1952, Dulles felt constrained to enunciate a new policy.
Proclamation was easier than accomplishment. He promised
an attitude towards the Soviet Union more aggressive
than the 'containment' policy of his predecessor Acheson.
He was, he announced, willing to take risks. 'The ability
to get to the verge without getting into war is the necessary art,' he once wrote. 'If you are scared to go to the brink,
you are lost.' Acting from these principles, Dulles embarked
on a series of trips throughout the world that made him
one of the busiest, and certainly the most travelled, Secretaries of State in American history.

Dulles's assumption of his post preceded by less than three
months the death of Joseph Stalin, which at first appeared
to forecast a softening of Russian cold-war postures. He
managed to keep a precariously friendly relationship
between the United States and the successive Russian
governments of Malenkov and Bulganin. In 1955, after
careful preparation, he engineered a 'summit' meeting in
Paris of the chiefs of state of Great Britain, France, the
United States, and the U.S.S.R. which, though indecisive
in results, pointed the way toward more fruitful subsequent
meetings. At the same time Dulles and Eisenhower felt
the pressing necessity of unifying European military and
economic affairs. Some nations saw advantages in increasing
the total armed power through N.A.T.O., but at the same
time France, in particular, found it difficult to agree to an
augmented West German army. After signing a European
Defence Community pact in 1952 with West Germany,
Britain, and the Benelux countries, France then withdrew.
Two years later the French agreed to join West Germany,
Italy, and the Benelux group in a Western European Union
if the Germans forswore nuclear arms. However, in 1957
the United States granted West Germany tactical atomic
weapons, though retaining control of their use.

While the United States manoeuvred in Europe, the Russians continued unsuccessfully to exert pressure on American, British, and French forces in Berlin, hoping to force them out and to absorb the city into East Germany. After Premier Khruschev's visit to the United States in 1960, Soviet–American relations seemed to improve to the point that another 'summit' meeting was scheduled to meet in Paris for further discussions of the German and other problems. Unfortunately, the Russians brought down a United States U-2 reconnaissance plane over Soviet territory shortly before the meeting, and Khruschev, in protest over admitted American espionage, walked out of the chamber.

Other problems for Secretary Dulles lay scattered about the world. In the Far East, the United States faced the dilemma of either supporting Chiang Kai-shek's Nationalist Chinese government, which was neither secure nor democratic, or negotiating with the Chinese Communist government on the mainland. When Dulles chose Chiang, the United States and Nationalist China signed a 'mutual defense' treaty on 1 December 1954, under the terms of which the United States agreed to protect Taiwan, the base of Chiang's government, while Chiang agreed not to attack mainland China and precipitate a possible American–Red Chinese conflict. Meanwhile France was rapidly losing Indo-China, where the American government was providing 70 per cent of French war costs. When the showdown came in 1954, with the French forces trapped at Dien Bien Phu, the United States decided not to intervene, agreeing at the Geneva conference to a partition of the former French colony into North and South Vietnam. Hoping to erect a barrier to further communist expansion in South East Asia, Dulles proposed an alliance which late in 1954 became the South East Asia Treaty Organization (Thailand, Pakistan, the Philippines, Australia, Great Britain, France, and the United States, later Laos, Cambodia, and South Viet Nam) pledged to defend the signatory nations from attack. S.E.A.T.O. proved helpful, though not always effective (since it did not include India or Indonesia), but it was no doubt the best alliance that Dulles could achieve in the circumstances.

No sooner was S.E.A.T.O. formed than trouble broke out in the Middle East, where the United States was deeply and paradoxically involved because of its investments in Arab oil and its commitments to the new state of Israel. In 1954 the revolt against the corrupt reign of Egypt's King Farouk (led ultimately by Colonel Nasser) caught the Western powers by surprise. To counter possible Russian penetration into those Middle Eastern nations whose instability made communist infiltration likely, Dulles persuaded Pakistan, Iraq, Iran, Turkey, and Great Britain to agree in 1955 to the weak but potentially useful Baghdad Pact. Egypt, however, had a long-standing grievance against Britain over the Sudan and against Britain and France over the Suez Canal. Nasser, playing the United States and Russia against each other, received promises of assistance from both, but when he began trading cotton for Russian weapons, Dulles withdrew American aid. Nasser retaliated by seizing the Suez Canal, purportedly to obtain funds for replacement, which also gave him control of the line of shipment for three-quarters of Europe's oil supply. Israel, Britain, and France, claiming lack of American support, registered strong disapproval of Dulles's wait-and-see policy, and Israel, anticipating a build-up in Egyptian arms, on 29 October 1956, launched a 'preventive invasion' of Egypt. Immediately British and French troops landed in the Canal area as a protective measure, designed among other things to topple Nasser.

Russia and the United States reacted quickly to the invasion for different reasons. There was, Eisenhower believed, real danger of a confrontation between the Western powers and Russia that might lead to full-scale war. Russia threatened to send 'volunteers' to Egypt's aid, proposing also that the United States and Russia take joint action against the invading forces unless a cease-fire and withdrawal were accomplished within three days.

This was rejected by the United States; Eisenhower, who wished to act only under the U.N.'s mandate and through its machinery, passed the issue to the United Nations, refusing to accept 'the use of force as a proper instrument for the settlement of international disputes'. Though Britain and France vetoed a cease-fire resolution in the Security Council, the General Assembly passed it, and at Canada's suggestion, a compromise truce was worked out under an internationalized U.N. force.

Shortly after Suez Eisenhower asked Congress to authorize the President to grant economic and military aid to 'protect the territorial integrity of any nation . . . requesting such aid against overt aggression from any nation controlled by international communism.' The new 'Eisenhower doctrine' had little effect on either Nasser or the Russians, who continued to ship arms to Egypt and Yemen and signed a pact with Syria. In 1958 when pro-Nasser forces took over Iraq, its neighbours Lebanon and Jordan feared similar *coups* in their own countries. The United States responded to Lebanon's request for American aid against its rebels with a small expeditionary force, at the same time that British troops entered Jordan. Though Nasser, after 1959, steered a middle course between Russia and the West, the Middle East remained unstable and inflammable.

Of greater potential danger to the security of the United States, however, was the explosive situation in Latin America, a portion of the world long neglected by American foreign policy makers. The Organization of American States, set up by Truman in 1948 to provide machinery for settling intra-hemispheric disputes, was a useful step, but after 1950 all Latin America except Mexico was deep in crisis. Nearly all Latin American nations were economically depressed and under-developed; a number suffered under corrupt and cruel dictatorships; totalitarian influence everywhere was strong and growing. Guatemala, Bolivia, Argentina, Peru, Colombia, and Venezuela all underwent revolutions before 1958. Juan Perón's dictatorship lasted until 1956 in Argentina with tacit American approval;

meanwhile the United States supported Cuba's Fulgencio Batista and the Dominican Republic's Rafael Trujillo Molina, both flagrant dictators, on the grounds that they were, at least, non-communist and there was nobody better in view. Trujillo fell in 1961, replaced by a hopefully earnest government which seemed to have a fair chance of success. Cuba provided the real problem.

Fidel Castro, who launched his revolution against Batista in 1956, finally came to power on 1 January 1959. At first Castro enjoyed a good deal of American popularity, for his seemed to be a genuine people's revolution. But whatever his early promise, Castro put thousands into jail, executed hundreds more, expropriated industries, banks, and lands, and in general began to display most of the familiar marks of the traditional Latin American dictator. Castro himself was a convinced Marxist, though not necessarily a communist, and there was a strong pro-Russian and communist influence among his Fidelistas. American policy toward Castro, during his first year of power, was both indecisive and clumsy, as was Castro's toward the United States. Neither country seemed to be able to make up its mind about future relations. When, to save his tottering economic system, Castro signed a number of trade agreements with Russia, the United States withdrew all economic aid to Cuba and cut off 95 per cent of its imports of sugar, thus throwing Castro firmly into the Russian orbit. As President Eisenhower prepared to leave office, the Cuban problem was undoubtedly the most prickly he bequeathed to his successor.

In 1960, the economist J. K. Galbraith coined a phrase, 'the affluent society', to describe the America of the years following the Second World War. As he illustrated, the United States was very probably the richest society in modern history, fairly exuding prosperity. During the twenty years from 1940 to 1960 the gross national product increased more than 100 per cent, though the population grew only 34 per cent. Marks of affluence were everywhere.

Automobile manufacturers made and sold eight million cars in 1965; 88 per cent of all homes had television sets; 120 million Americans held savings or investments; their earnings in wages and salaries rose almost 25 per cent from 1955. In 1904, 2.2 million Americans travelled in foreign countries, spending 350 million dollars in the process. For that matter, Americans that year spent more than 150 million dollars – more than the gross national income of some small countries – simply on going to the movies. The important fact about this was, however, that lower income groups shared proportionately as well as higher ones in this wave of well-being. Great masses of Americans moved up the income ladder, while the downward shift in income distribution furnished a base for mass purchasing power which itself helped to promote prosperity.

But, at the same time, it was clear that many Americans failed to share in this prosperity; in fact some were losing ground. The paradox of poverty within affluence stirred consciences and demanded explanations. Studies showed the existence of hidden islands of disadvantage – youths, the aged, the chronically ill, the uneducated, the Negro. Other studies showed whole regions by-passed by economic growth, areas where opportunities for advancement lagged or failed to exist; the Appalachian area, for example, had stagnated for the past fifty years. President Kennedy, shocked by conditions he met in West Virginia and Eastern Kentucky during his 1960 campaign, introduced legislation by which the Federal government, in co-operation with the states, could take steps to approach the problem. Under President Johnson, by the Economic Opportunity Act of 1964, Congress established a number of agencies designed to deal directly with it; a year later Congress passed the Appalachian Development Act, the first of a long-term 'poverty program' aimed at the rehabilitation of under-developed areas. There is nothing – even poverty – the American believes cannot be solved by the application of organization, education and money.

During the forties and fifties in America as elsewhere

there emerged another major social and economic problem: 'automation', a word coined to describe the use in production of self-regulating, unattended, automatic machinery, associated later especially with the use of the computer. The introduction of automation into industry on a large scale began shortly after the Second World War, and since that time automated processes have displaced human labour at an ever swifter pace. It is estimated that because of automation more than one and a half million American workmen were dropped from manufacturing payrolls in the five years between 1955 and 1961.

What happened in the coal-mining industry provided a spectacular example: from 1940 to 1958 the number of miners decreased by sixty per cent, while the output per miner more than doubled. As the rate of elimination from the labour market continued to increase, labour unions and government combined to work out arrangements whereby displaced workers might be retrained for other industries or for new especially created jobs. But the sharp decline in the need for human labour, far more drastic than anything before in American labour history, will require measures of social and economic adjustment greater than have thus far been conceived.

The impact of automation and technological improvement in industrial production had another important effect. Need for the unskilled labourer, or 'blue-collar' worker, lessened; demand for the skilled operator and technician, or 'white-collar' worker, proportionately increased. Employers needed specially-trained people with more education and technical training than ever before as new methods, new machines, and in some cases entirely new industries continued to change the requirements of the labour market. While, for example, the need for unskilled coal miners dropped, the new electronics industry was hiring three quarters of a million highly-skilled workmen; the two were, of course, not at all interchangeable.

Thus the composition of the labour force in the United States changed swiftly. In 1960, for the first time, 'white-

738

collar' workers and those in the service trades made up the majority of the nation's labour force. Also, for the first time, more women joined the working force than men; women now constitute the largest source of new workers. The changing nature and needs of the American labour market together present one of the most difficult and challenging problems for the future.

Allied to this, of course, was the fact that the United States, like the rest of the world, faced a population explosion already long under way. The rate of increase during the nineteen-fifties was three times that of the thirties, and was still rising in the sixties. In 1968, the American population stood close to 200 million, and projections show that it might well reach 300 million by the close of the century. The 1964 census showed, in addition, that the great westward shift of population still continued; the Southwest and West showed the greatest gains of any region, while in 1963 California passed New York to become the most populous state. Hawaii and Alaska, the two new states added to the Union in 1959, had increased their populations by fifty per cent in 1964.

Increases in population and drastic changes in the needs of postwar society placed great strains on the nation's educational system. Americans since the seventeenth century have held to the belief that education – more of it extended to ever more people – furnished the key to social progress and individual betterment. Until the twentieth century, education for the American youngster often ended at fourteen; during the twenties it was extended to the completion of high school, at about seventeen or eighteen; by the fifties it was becoming necessary for success, in any but menial roles, to continue post-high school education to perhaps twenty or twenty-one.

In 1958, Congress enacted the National Defense Education Act, which placed the Federal government squarely in the field of education; since then the Department of Health, Education and Welfare has expended millions on the local and state level for the improvement of schools. By 1968, over forty per cent of all people between the ages of seventeen and twenty-one were enrolled in post-high school educational institutions, an indication not only of the need for a highly-trained population but also the sign of an affluent society which held higher aspirations for its children. In addition, the tremendous increase in the size and quality of the Russian educational effort, dramatized by the flight of 'Sputnik' in 1957, spurred the United States to greater concern for its own schools.

The pressure on educational institutions at all levels has been enormous; the census of 1960 showed thirty-seven million young people in elementary and secondary schools, and (an increase of fifty per cent over 1940) more than three and a half million in institutions of higher education. Most spectacular has been the growth of a new kind of institution, the 'junior' or 'community' college, designed to provide either two years of additional education beyond the high school or a two-year preface to further study at a college or university. In 1970, there will be probably a thousand such institutions, enrolling more than a million students; the city of Detroit alone, for example, plans to have thirty such junior colleges in operation. Never before has the extension of educational opportunity seemed more essential to the average American, and never has its necessity as one of the components of a better society seemed more urgent.

Since Eisenhower could not be a candidate for a third term, the Republican party approached the elections of 1960 almost agreed on Vice-President Richard Nixon, who was known as a shrewd and flexible campaigner, and who (with the President's blessing) easily gained the nomination. Henry Cabot Lodge, the United States representative at the United Nations, was chosen as the vice-presidential nominee. The Democrats had no obvious choice. Stevenson, twice defeated, still retained a strong party following but not enough to guarantee nomination. Senators Kefauver of Tennessee, Lyndon Johnson of Texas, Hubert Humphrey of Minnesota, and John F. Kennedy of Massachusetts all seemed front-runners, but Kennedy's bold and astute pursuit of the nomination brought it to him on the convention's first ballot, with Lyndon Johnson as his running mate. Noticeably, for the first time in a Presidential contest, neither candidate had personal experience of politics before World War II.

The campaign was intense. Nixon spoke in all fifty states and Kennedy in forty-four. Since he enjoyed Eisenhower's personal endorsement and since the nation enjoyed peace and prosperity, Nixon was generally conceded to have the edge. Kennedy, on the other hand, faced several political disadvantages; he was personally rich, an intellectual (recipient of a Pulitzer Prize in history), a Roman Catholic, and the nominee of a party not only out of power but seriously split between Northern and Southern factions. Nevertheless Kennedy won in the closest election since Wilson's second term – by a mere 113,000 votes out of 68 million, although his electoral vote was a safe 303–219. In the Congressional elections, however, the Democratic majority was decisively heavy.

Kennedy's cabinet appointments indicated the shift of direction that might be expected of his administration. All were younger men, relatively fresh to national politics (with the exception of Luther Hodges, Secretary of Commerce, and Republican Douglas Dillon, Secretary of the Treasury) such as the President's younger brother, Robert, as Attorney-General; Robert McNamara, administrative expert from the Ford Motor Company, as Secretary of Defense; Arthur Goldberg, a brilliant labour lawyer, as Secretary of Labor; and Orville Freeman of Agriculture, Stuart Udall of Interior, and Abraham Ribicoff of Health, Education, and Welfare. Possibly because of the paper-thin margin of Kennedy's victory, his 'New Frontier' moved forward rather slowly in the early months of his term. It was also true that although the administration theoretically possessed a majority in both House and Senate, in actual practice a coalition of conservative Southern Democrats and Northern Republicans could block almost any legislation of which it disapproved.

It proceeded to do exactly this, defeating bills for Federal aid to education, a nationalized medical care programme, the creation of a cabinet post for urban affairs, and a number of other presumably 'new dealish' measures proposed by the Administration. Somewhat unexpectedly, the President himself often preferred to follow a course of watchful negotiation with his Congressional opposition rather than an open contest. His greatest tactical victory, perhaps, was the Trade Expansion Act of 1962, which marked the United States's first significant departure from its traditional high tariffs and expanded two-way trade with Europe.

Kennedy's 'grand design' for American policy in Europe involved three basic assumptions: that the United States and Europe should be as closely associated economically as on the military and political level; that the United States and Europe should act as a unit in sharing Western defences; and that the two should join more closely in aiding the progress of the under-developed and emergent countries of Asia, Africa, and Latin America, with Europe assuming a larger portion of responsibility than heretofore. The major problem of American and European foreign policy, in Kennedy's view, ought not to be their relationship to each other, but rather their joint relationship with the rest of the world. The major challenge to Kennedy's policy, as it was to Eisenhower's, was President de Gaulle's concept of a Western Europe dominated by France and increasingly independent of United States influence. While the common attachment of Europe to N.A.T.O. was never in real dispute, the French leader seemed committed to a plan for the political future of Europe that ran counter to Kennedy's belief in the need for increased unity between Europe and the United States.

Dean Rusk, Kennedy's Secretary of State, inherited a bundle of foreign policy problems from Christian Herter, Dulles's successor. Rusk gave priority to Latin America, and in 1961 announced the creation of an Alliance for Progress, signed by all Latin American nations except

Cuba, designed to improve conditions in those countries by making available some 20 billion dollars of aid, half from the United States and half from international financial sources. The recipient nations, for their part, were to respond with internal social, economic, and political reforms. Although such reforms were not always forthcoming, the Alliance helped to initiate changes in several nations and served notice, at least, that the United States was neither indifferent to Latin American welfare nor hostile to legitimately democratic nationalist aspirations.

The great Caribbean thorn, Cuba, remained. An attempt to invade the island by a badly-equipped Cuban refugee force, half-heartedly encouraged by the United States, simply strengthened Castro's alliance with Russia and thoroughly frightened the Cubans. In mid-1962 American intelligence reported a heavy influx of Russian soldiers, weapons and technicians into Cuba, including jet bombers and intermediate-range missiles easily capable of reaching Washington. President Kennedy reacted by announcing a blockade of the island in October, warning that Cuban-bound ships would be searched for offensive weapons, and demanding that such Russian weapons already in Cuba be removed. The Soviets, after a brief, tense wait, agreed. On the one hand, the exposure of the swift Russian build-up in Cuba shocked other Latin American countries which had underrated the dangers of Castro-ite and Soviet penetration into their half of the hemisphere. On the other, Kennedy's action convinced the world of his willingness to take decisive unilateral action if Russian movement toward Latin America seemed to threaten American interests. After the 1962 crisis, the American and Cuban governments evolved a kind of wary truce, in which neither provoked the other unnecessarily. In 1964, in fact, Castro began to allow refugees from his country free passage to the United States, with the result that thousands of Cubans have since emigrated and have been assimilated into American society.

The most urgent social and political internal problems

of the fifties and sixties derived from the racial issue in the United States. The years 1940 to 1960 witnessed both a great increase in the Negro population and its movement northward. During these decades the Negro population of the North grew from less than 3 per cent to more than 7 per cent, while that of the Southern states remained relatively stable. By 1963 there were more Negroes in the North than in the South. This sudden growth was almost exclusively an urban phenomenon. One quarter of the Negroes in the United States in 1963 lived in ten cities – New York, Chicago, Philadelphia, Detroit, Washington, Los Angeles, Baltimore, Cleveland, New Orleans, and Houston – while in 1961 Washington became the first major American city with a Negro majority. Not only did this exacerbate difficult urban problems of housing, education, employment, and welfare, but it meant that in the larger Northern cities the Negro often held the balance of political power. In Illinois, Michigan, California, and New York, for example, Negroes by 1964 made up more than 10 per cent of the state's voting power.

There were other reasons, too, for the Negro's sudden consciousness of his unrealized rights. World War II served as a trigger for the coming Negro revolt. As John Oliver Kellems, the Negro novelist, observed, 'The spectacle of Negroes fighting racism while members of a racist army . . . , of fighting for democracy while democratic freedoms were denied them at home – this was too much for Negroes to bear.' The period after the War saw also the emergence of a different kind of Negro leader – drawn from powerful groups of Negro businessmen, articulate Negro artists and intellectuals, and militant Negro ministers and churchmen.

In conjunction with Federal authority, this new and aggressive Negro leadership provided the Negro with greater advances towards the full possession of his civil rights than during any comparable period in American history. Truman's order of 1948, desegregating the Armed Forces, was the first and most important of a series of Presidential orders and court rulings affecting Negro rights. In 1957

Congress passed the first Civil Rights Act in three-quarters of a century, designed to protect Negro voting rights, and at the same time it created a Civil Rights Commission to explore the need for additional legislation. A second Civil Rights Act passed in 1960 intended to strengthen Federal authority in the field, but Southern opposition so weakened its provisions that, as Senator Sparkman of Alabama boasted, 'Its effects will be negligible.' Nevertheless, the two acts represented discernible progress, and under both Eisenhower and Kennedy the Attorney-General's legal staff pressed suits against Southern cities and counties which by subterfuge and intimidation had long discouraged Negroes from voting.

Meanwhile the National Association for the Advancement of Colored People began an assault in Federal courts on segregated schools in the South. The Supreme Court, in *Sweatt v. Painter* (1950) made the first breach in the wall of segregation in public education, followed by its historic decision in *Brown v. Board of Education of Topeka* (1954). This last decision overturned the *Plessy v. Ferguson* decision of 1896, which had validated the existence of so-called 'separate but equal' facilities for white and Negro citizens. In its 1954 decision, however, the Court ruled that 'in the field of public education . . . separate educational facilities are inherently unequal', which meant the end of segregated public schools and a tremendous shock to the South's carefully constructed social-educational system. A year later the Court augmented its decision with an order to the Southern states to proceed to implement the Brown ruling 'with all deliberate speed'.

Some portions of the South began in good faith, albeit reluctantly, the slow and difficult process of carrying out the Supreme Court's order. Most did not. Part of the reason lay in the fact that in 1956 one hundred Southern congressmen joined in a public statement to 'commend the motives of those states which have declared the intention to resist forced integration by any lawful means', thereby virtually abdicating leadership of the South to its extremist elements.

In response Southern legislatures were quick to promise 'massive resistance' to the Federal authority through interminable litigation or direct defiance of the courts. By 1957 fewer than 400 school districts out of the South's 6,000 were desegregated, chiefly those in the border states with smaller Negro populations.

There were a number of disturbances, but the first real challenge to Federal authority came in 1957 at Little Rock, Arkansas, where Governor Faubus called on state troops to prevent the entrance of Negro students into a previously all-white school. President Eisenhower, acting under the powers of his office, dispatched Army paratroopers to Little Rock and Faubus backed down. Appalled at the breakdown of law and order in Arkansas, Southern moderates promised at least token integration in heavily Negro areas and began to make belated plans for gradual – if extremely slow – compliance with the law. Their efforts were often hampered and nullified by rabid, racist, white-supremacist groups such as the White Citizen's Councils, and by their own inability to grasp the initiative from racist demagogues. Unfortunately, too few Southerners heeded the words of the great Southern writer, William Faulkner, who before his death asked his countrymen, 'in decency and fairness' to 'stand for the simple things which democracy means, and which we have got to show the world that we do mean if we are to survive'.

Whereas the assault on segregated education came through the courts, the Negro's attack on segregation in public services and facilities was much more direct. The Negro of the fifties and sixties displayed a far less tolerant attitude toward his position in American life than that of his father or grandfather. While the N.A.A.C.P. and the Urban League were willing to fight a long, slow battle for civil equality by legal means, younger Negro leaders were impatient with delays. Some violently anti-white extremist groups, particularly the Black Muslims, advocated complete separation of the Negro from American society as presently constructed, but others, though sympathetic to the Muslims' attempt to give Negroes a sense of racial identity and pride, favoured less revolutionary solutions. In 1955 the Negroes of Birmingham, Alabama – the most rigidly segregated city in the South – began a year-long boycott of segregated bus facilities that eventually ended in success. The boycott also projected into prominence a Baptist minister, Martin Luther King, Jr, who symbolized a new and aggressive kind of Negro crusade originating in the church, the most powerful and cohesive agency in Negro life. New leaders and organizations appeared in the churches, colleges and universities: the Southern Christian Leadership Conference, led by ministers and church laymen; the Student Non-Violent Co-ordinating Committee, organized by young Negroes in colleges North and South; the Congress of Racial Equality, led by Negroes prominent in public life. The non-violent demonstration (drawing heavily from both Gandhi and evangelical Christianity) and the boycott gave them potent weapons. Negroes in all parts of the South responded with 'sit-ins' at segregated restaurants, 'wade-ins' at segregated swimming-pools, 'walk-ins' at segregated theatres, and 'kneel-ins' at segregated churches, while 'freedom riders' tested desegregation on buses and trains in the South. Some Southern communities responded with restraint; others, especially in Alabama and Mississippi, retaliated with mass arrests, punitive legislation, and police brutality. Mass demonstrations in Alabama, Mississippi, Maryland, North Carolina and Virginia showed the rising temper of Negro feeling. At the same time, in protest against discrimination, in housing, employment and opportunity in the North, Negroes demonstrated in New York, Philadelphia, Washington and other cities. Token equality, it was clear, was no longer enough. What the Negro wanted, said Martin Luther King, could be put into three words – '*all, now, here*'. In response to what was clearly developing as an issue of real urgency, Kennedy sent to the Congress in 1963 a sweeping Civil Rights Bill, met by the usual delaying tactics of the Southern congressional bloc.

The success of the 'sit-in' and other forms of non-violent protest encouraged its use as a form of political pressure. Congressional debates over civil rights legislation in 1963 elicited the great 'March on Washington for Jobs and Freedom', where almost a quarter of a million people gathered to hear the spokesmen not only of Negro organizations but of labour unions and of Jewish, Catholic and Protestant churches, demand equality for the Negro. In 1965 there was another march, from Selma, Alabama, to the state capital, when some thirty thousand marchers walked fifty miles along the Jefferson Davis Memorial Highway to dramatize their protest against the brutality of Alabama police and the racism of Governor Wallace.

The Negro's battle for the vote is beginning to be won, but his battle for full equality, particularly for economic opportunity, is far from over. Whether it is advancing toward victory at a satisfactory rate depends on how one reads the reports. The Negro magazine *Tuesday* reported in 1966 that it found progress 'impressive': *per capita* income of Negroes actually rose faster than white income in 1963 and 1964; the median income of Negro families outside the South was eighty per cent of that of white families and even in the South the median income of Negro families rose almost $800 from 1961 to 1964. On the other hand, the same statistics can be used to tell a different story, for the median income of Negro families outside the South is still twenty per cent below that of whites after the longest period of prosperity in American history, and half the Negroes in the South live near or below the poverty line. To civil rights leaders the prospect is not all bright. The spectacle of more than ten million Negroes concentrated in ghettoes from New York to Chicago to St Louis to Los Angeles marks no progress. Segregated housing and schools in the cities begins a depressing cycle: inadequate education, inability to find jobs, economic weakness, political powerlessness to combat segregated housing and education. The Negro-led riots in Philadelphia, Los Angeles, Newark, Detroit, Washington and Baltimore during the years 1964 to 1968 were for the most part the lashing out of frustrated people at this vicious circle of discrimination. There needed to be, as President Johnson pointed out in his Howard University speech in 1966, a 'next and more profound stage' in the civil rights struggle, where equality means 'not just legal equity but human ability, not just equality as a right and a theory but equality as a fact and a result'.

The meaning and dimensions of the American struggle to achieve racial equality for all its citizens are hard for Europeans to appreciate. Certainly the travail and anguish which attend it are part of the price the United States must pay for proclaiming a society dedicated to the proposition that all men are created equal, and for trying to bring it into being. The immensely delicate and difficult problem of accepting and assimilating millions of Americans of Negro and Oriental origins into full citizenship and complete equality is a bold and visionary task, that is not yet solved, and most Americans realize more urgently than anyone else that the promise of American democracy must remain incomplete until it is. Yet to attempt to transcend, in one nation, the prejudices and injustices and irrationalities of a racism that has plagued human society from its beginnings carries with it tremendous potentialities for the future. If American society can succeed in its experiment in racial integration, quite possibly it can provide a pattern and an example for other societies of the world. As Gunnar Myrdal, the Swedish sociologist, wrote in his classic study of the American racial problem, if 'America can demonstrate that justice, equality, and cooperation are possible between white and colored people', then the dream of the patriots, 'that America should give to the entire world its own freedoms and its own faith', would come true.

The Supreme Court's 1954 ruling on the racial issue in education was one of two historic decisions which promise to have profound impact on American life. The other, *Baker v. Carr* (1962), concerned unequal legislative representation in the states. This decision (which overturned another of 1946) gave individuals the right to challenge the apportionment of state legislative districts which over-represented sparsely-settled rural areas and under-represented densely-populated urban centres. In a number of states rural-dominated legislatures had consistently neglected urban problems and overruled urban needs. In *Baker v. Carr* the Court decided that such inequality in legislative representation deprived citizens of these states of their constitutional guarantees of equal protection of the laws under the fourteenth Amendment. As a result, court challenges to district lines were filed in more than half the states, and the consequences of such suits have already shifted the balance of power in a number of them towards the urban centres, drastically changing the complexion of state political life.

One of the most striking developments in American life has been the emergence, since 1952, of the Supreme Court as a decisive factor in political, social and economic affairs. Not since the Roosevelt administrations has the Court exerted such a direct and powerful influence on American society. As the 1954 Brown case, and others, forced a recognition of the rights of ten per cent of the American population, so the Baker case brought to issue the clash of rural and small-town America with the great urban population that includes the overwhelming majority of citizens. The United States, throughout the twentieth century, has been changing into an urban nation, and the Court has been among the first to recognize it. Certainly one strong influence that made the Court aware of the relevant issues of contemporary America was the leadership of Chief Justice Earl Warren (retired in 1968), who took the branch of government traditionally most reluctant to change and, with the help of other recently-appointed Justices, turned it into an effective instrument of social change and progress. It may well be that in the view of future historians, the 'Warren Court' will be accounted the most influential element in shaping the course of American society during the latter half of the twentieth century.

Both Eisenhower's and Kennedy's administrations faced

urgent and pervasive military and moral problems created by the development of nuclear energy and the sudden breakthrough in the conquest of space. The explosion of the first atomic bomb over Hiroshima in 1945 opened the terrifying prospect of a future war of annihilation, as well as the breathtaking potentialities of peaceful uses of the atom. A year later the U.S.S.R. rejected in the United Nations an American plan for international control of atomic energy, even though it entailed the surrender by the United States of what was at the time its virtual monopoly of nuclear technology. In 1949 the Russians exploded their own bomb; in 1952 the United States detonated the first thermonuclear (hydrogen) bomb, followed by Russia's in 1953. That same year Eisenhower presented an 'Atoms for Peace' plan to the United Nations, proposing to channel scientific efforts of all nations toward peaceful uses of this great new source of energy. It too was rejected, and instead the nuclear arms contest between the United States and the U.S.S.R. continued unabated, with other nations such as France and China eager to join it. The same national interests which pushed the development of nuclear energy carried over into research in space. In 1957 the Russians achieved a major scientific success by orbiting the first earth satellite, next launching the first astronaut, and orbiting two at once in 1961. Early in 1962 the United States placed its first man in space, Lt-Colonel John Glenn, and the two nations settled down in a race for the first manned flight to the moon.

This magnificent achievement (which was to be followed in the next years by adventures in space that were even more fantastic and which was certain to make the inconceivable – a voyage to the moon – a fact before the end of 1969) was disrupted by one question-mark which set some Americans and many foreigners to wondering. At the time of Hitler's persecutions, the United States had shown great generosity to refugees of all kinds and had given a home and the possibility of continued work to some of the finest minds of Europe. In 1962 it seemed at least sardonic and even sinister that the scientific leadership of the American space-programme (as in some degree of its Russian equivalent) should be in the hands of other European expatriates, one of them the very man who had launched the war-time rocket-raids on London. Von Braun for Einstein seemed a not altogether satisfactory exchange. But in the second half of the sixties, as the space programme accelerated, Von Braun's influence declined.

The issues of nuclear weapons challenged the American sense of national purpose in a manner which the nation was unprepared to meet so swiftly and directly, as indeed no nation was. The United States has always been conscious of its power to affect the course of world events, and certain of its ability to use that power virtuously. Yet both its virtue and its responsibility were seriously put to the test by the dilemma of nuclear armament, initiated at Hiroshima, which might end in nuclear catastrophe. For the United States, the issue became particularly difficult, for Americans have always tended to assume (perhaps over-optimistically) that in international affairs reason could somehow be substituted for force and force controlled by reason, even through the ambiguities of two world wars. The nuclear situation challenged this directly, inextricably involving the United States in a web of global responsibilities which it had never before been called upon to assume.

The leaders of every nation had recognized by 1950 that two fearsome possibilities confronted the world: the danger of contamination of the earth itself by radioactive fallout from nuclear explosions; and the equal danger of massive total nuclear war. The new weapons developed so swiftly after World War II, unlike any other weapons in history, were as dangerous in peace as in war, and there were doubts among the informed that, unless they were controlled, the human race itself might not survive. The implications of unrestricted nuclear competition encouraged the heads of state of the United States, Great Britain, France, and the U.S.S.R. to meet at Geneva in 1955 to explore possibilities for some kind of controls. Eisenhower's 'open skies' proposal, which involved aerial and ground inspection of both American and Russian military bases, failed to find support. Subsequent Russian vetoes of nuclear controls continued to immobilize the United Nations, the single international agency capable of nuclear restrictions. As Kennedy pointed out in 1961, when he presented a new, comprehensive disarmament plan to the United Nations, the world 'lived under a nuclear sword of Damocles, hanging by the slenderest of threads'. His plan, however, was rejected; almost as if in reply, the U.S.S.R. broke a two-year truce on nuclear testing by detonating thirty bombs in a few months, substantially raising the atmospheric level of radioactivity and leading to the renewal of similar tests by the United States. Once more in 1963 Kennedy proposed that discussion begin toward international restraints on testing and disarmament. After meetings with Britain and Russia, the United States announced for the three an agreement to ban certain kinds of nuclear testing, open for signature to all other nations. By a decisive 80–19 vote, the Senate ratified the agreement in September, marking the first major agreement concluded by the East and West since the Austrian treaty of 1955 ended the occupation of that country.

The American Presidency is a paradoxical institution. The President is a party man who urges the policies of his party followers whilst serving as the impartial figurehead of a country where his opponents can outnumber his supporters. His office has by right of election comparatively little constitutional power but can be vested with near-autocratic influence by an incumbent who has the strength, the cunning, and the capacity for leadership to win over the will of the people, to manage, to outmanoeuvre or to evade the machinery of Congress and the Supreme Court and the cumbersome bureaucracy.

In the fifties and sixties the position of the American President in the affairs of the Western Alliance had begun to mirror this home-bred paradox. Might alone could not make his leadership irrefutable; he had no right. Character, guile and assiduity together could bring him the position of authority: the accepted leadership of what had come to be known as the free world.

As Kennedy's first term moved into its last year the President could look back with pride and forward with hope. He had survived the bumblings of the Cuba 'invasion' in his first weeks at the White House and had handled the second and far greater Cuban crisis with courage and refined judgement. He had brought closer to an end the tragedy of segregation which had from the beginning interrupted the noble intentions of American society. As the American President at a time of American supremacy he was inevitably a world figure of supreme importance but in a very short time Kennedy was close to achieving the remarkable feat of making his leadership acceptable to much of the free world.

But, as Kennedy opened the campaign which, it seemed, would take him back to the White House for his second term, there was much to be done before his Presidency could be numbered with the great.

The campaign began in Texas, home state of Vice-President Lyndon Johnson, once his principal rival for the Democratic nomination to the Presidency but now seemingly so much a supporter of Kennedy's policies that he and Mrs Johnson joined the President and Mrs Kennedy in this invasion of a state which had shown itself far from enthusiastic about the programmes of the New Frontier.

If all had gone forward as planned this would still have been a move of enormous significance, for in many respects the future of the Democratic Party (and perhaps therefore of America and the Alliance) depended upon the ability of Kennedy to make the Party whole, to ease the tensions between the two wings of an uncomfortable coalition, to bring together in spirit as well as electioneering convenience Democratic liberals and Democratic conservatives.

Progress had been made, the promise great. Then in a few seconds on Friday 22 November 1963 history stammered.

Kennedy was shot dead as his motorcade drove through Dallas, Texas, by a mentally disturbed young assassin who, himself fatally wounded later, carried the reasons for his act to the grave with him. The senseless death of a President who had only begun to try on the mantle of greatness shocked the world; not only the 'free world', but also – most heartening circumstance in a universally disheartening experience – the Soviet leaders mourned, and the ordinary citizen with them.

Lyndon Baines Johnson, brought to the Presidency by the tragedy at Dallas, was shrewd, proud and earthy. He showed from the start a great sensitivity to the ambiguities of his position. 'I shall do my best,' he said as he took office within minutes of Kennedy's death, 'that is all I can do.'

The first Southerner to occupy the White House since Wilson, his environment – the dry, hardscrabble ranch country of South Texas and the tough oil and cattle tycoonery of Houston, Dallas and Fort Worth was as different from Wilson's South as it was from the cosmopolitan background which had come to the White House with Kennedy. Not for Johnson the urbanity, the intellectualism, the grace which had been such notable features of the Kennedy administration.

Johnson had first entered Congress in 1937, an admirer of Franklin Roosevelt and a dedicated New Dealer who, before he worked his way to considerable wealth, had known at first hand the bite of poverty. In 1952 the Senate Democrats chose him as majority leader and in that role he proved himself a skilful and professional politician, expert at reconciling differences. 'Come, let us reason together' was his favourite Biblical quotation, and during the Eisenhower years it was most often Johnson who, placing national interest above partisan advantage, brought together on important issues the Republican administration and the Democrat-controlled Senate. He it was who in 1954 organized the Senate against McCarthy and it was Johnson, the Southerner, who, against the opposition of his fellow Southern Democrats, manoeuvred the 1957 Civil Rights

Bill through the Senate. He once said, not wholly humor-
ously, that he believed 'in marching forward, but never
getting both feet off the ground at the same time'.

Coming to office with behind him a workable party
majority, Johnson devoted what remained of Kennedy's
term to continuing his predecessor's unfinished programme.
The Eighty-eighth Congress responded to his lead. Having
first established public favour by a cut in taxation, Congress
then extended the National Defense Education Act with
millions of dollars of new appropriations. It passed the
National Wilderness Act protecting public lands. It established a National Commission on Technology and Automation to make a long-overdue study of an area of endeavour
which was already vital and fast becoming central to the
national function. Still more important in the legislation of
the Eighty-eighth Congress was the Equal Opportunity Act
which made the first steps towards upgrading those poverty-
stricken regions where economic and social opportunities
were restricted or virtually non-existent.

But most important of all – and the legislation which
undoubtedly gave most pleasure to the President – was the
passing of the Civil Rights Act of 1964. Eighty-seven days of
debate preceded the enactment of this, the strongest civil
rights legislation since Emancipation. The new Act not only
outlawed discrimination in public accommodation, employment and educational facilities but it also established
methods of enforcement.

Almost immediately the Act brought change throughout
the South. Although pockets of resistance exist to this day,
manned by vocal and occasionally ruthless segregationists,
steady pressure from Federal agencies has, for example,
moved Southern school-systems to compliance, so that by
1966 all but 170 of the South's 6,000 school districts had
begun to integrate classes. In 1965, at Johnson's request,
Congress passed another Civil Rights Act, this time providing for Federal supervision of voter-registration and elections.
This brought with it an immediate increase in the number
of Negroes eligible to vote and, in 1966, to the hitherto

inconceivable circumstance: a Negro nominee among the sheriffs in Alabama.

There was, of course, little doubt that Johnson would be the Democrats' choice for the 1964 Presidential Election and in due course he was chosen with, as his running-mate, the liberal-minded Hubert Humphrey of Minnesota.

The choice for the Republicans was less obvious. In the minds of many Republicans, Richard Nixon had not been disgraced in defeat and early in Kennedy's term Nixon had seemed once more the logical contender. However, a Republican of quite different character from Nixon soon began to attract attention. Senator Barry Goldwater, an affable and somewhat vague man, impressed many of his party by preaching a simple and frequently inconsistent conservatism that seemed to fit him for the mantle of Robert Taft and the Republican Party for a return of its happy days under Coolidge. Indeed, the nostalgia he demonstrated – for example, in his book *The Conscience of a Conservative* (1960) – seemed to promise America a return to the cheerful virtues of a nineteenth-century society, to the days before high taxation, trade unionism or racial strife. In this his *credo* and in some 600 speeches which he made between 1961 and 1963 Goldwater preached resistance to the extension of governmental authority, the return of government to the localities, and the elimination of high taxation. Behind him there fell into line all those frustrated conservatives who had long resented the moderation of such as Dewey, Willkie, Eisenhower and Nixon and the readiness and (as the conservatives saw it) complacency with which such Republican leaders had accepted bipartisan policies on many issues of national and international importance. To them Goldwater offered 'a choice, not an echo' and with them stood all those others who had cause to fear or hate change, tension and moderation: Southern racists, newly-rich entrepreneurs, dissatisfied labourers. At local level, Goldwater's support grew rapidly until by 1964, to the surprise of the Party hierarchy, Goldwater had the nomination safe in his pocket. At the Convention his forces swept aside all more liberal opposition.

The Democrats campaigned in a low key. Kennedy's achievements and Johnson's as his successor they emphasized and for the future they promised more in the same vein, more stability, greater and faster social progress. Goldwater, who had worked so successfully to secure the nomination, was now faced with an opponent who quickly stripped him of any appearance of competence that he may have had before the campaign. Caught by Johnson, by sentiment still high from Kennedy's death, by the sense of the electorate, even by resentments and rivalries within his own party, Goldwater blundered hither and thither and revealed himself with inconsistency and irrationality. Many a stalwart Republican could not bring himself to vote for Goldwater. The result was a rout – Goldwater carried only Arizona, his own state, and the five states of the Deep South, which voted not so much for Goldwater as against Johnson and his stand on Negro rights – breaking their traditional Democratic allegiance rather than support the Southerner who had in their view betrayed his origins. Johnson won sixty-one per cent of the popular vote, the largest margin of modern times. Lyndon Johnson was now President in his own right.

The elections gave the Democratic party such an overwhelming majority in Congress that the President's major proposals met little serious opposition. Johnson's long and close association with Congressional leaders of both parties and his fearsomely persuasive talents as a mediator also played a large part in securing approval of almost all of his programme. Few Presidents have proved to be so effective in their dealings with Congress, or so successful in enacting their proposals into law. Congress in 1965 passed twenty-one major pieces of legislation, some carrying far-reaching implications for the future. Passage of the Health Care Insurance Bill, popularly known as 'Medicare', climaxed the thirty-year struggle for Federal participation in a national health programme. The Housing and Development Act, again the product of a long campaign that stretched back to Franklin Roosevelt's time, placed the national government squarely in the battle to eliminate the slum and to renew a badly-decayed city environment. Another Civil Rights Act supplemented the epoch-making legislation of 1964; a Higher Education Act put the resources of the Federal government behind an over-pressed educational system. Another pioneering act created the National Foundation of Arts and Humanities, an unprecedented step in supplying Federal aid for the creative arts; while at the other end of the scale Congress authorized eight billion more dollars for the 'poverty program'. Almost all of this legislation harked back in principle to the New Deal, under whose auspices Johnson had first entered politics. In 1965 Lyndon Johnson finally brought the New Deal's political and social philosophy to fruition.

At midpoint in Johnson's political career, it seemed safe to say that almost all of the major goals of his domestic programme had been realized. The basic structure of his 'Great Society' as he named it – or of the 'welfare state' if one disapproved of it – were by 1966 firmly in place. His and the nations' most persistent and pressing problems were those of foreign policy.

Johnson's experience of foreign affairs, as he assumed the Presidency, was limited, though as Vice-President he had begun to gain a wider perspective. His inaugural address of 1965 showed his awareness of the pitfalls that beset foreign policy, as he referred to that 'world where change and growth seem to tower beyond the control and even the judgment of men'. Handicapped by the persistent image of Kennedy's dash and style, Johnson also inherited a complex bundle of foreign policy problems. America's continued commitment to Nationalist China and the intractable Chiang Kai-shek, to South Korea, and to S.E.A.T.O. seemed to draw the nation imperceptibly but inevitably deeper into the perplexing problems of South-east Asia and toward an unwanted confrontation with the emerging giant mainland China.

The United States became involved in the tangled affairs of Vietnam after the departure of the French, and after the

Geneva agreements of 1954. Intending at first to give non-military aid to Premier Ngo Dinh Diem, the United States soon found itself caught in the see-saw conflict between Diem and the rebellious communist Viet Cong, with American troops serving as 'advisers' to the South Vietnamese forces. In 1963 Diem was overthrown and assassinated, his oppressive government followed by a succession of ephemeral military coups, each hopefully supported in turn by American troops and aid. None of these governments proved able to win the confidence of the Vietnamese people, to meet the growing power of the Viet Cong, or to stem the infiltration of guerillas from the hostile North. When in 1964 General Khanh, the Premier of the moment, demanded a full-scale military effort against his enemies, Congress gave President Johnson blanket permission to proceed as he thought best. Johnson and his advisers (chief among them Secretary of Defense McNamara, an able holdover from Kennedy's Cabinet), though wary of deeper involvement, stepped up military assistance. Viet Cong successes, however, soon brought the shaky Vietnamese army to the edge of disaster. In 1965 the President decided that the United States must commit itself further, and as a direct participant; by late that year there were 200,000 American troops in Vietnam, compared with 23,000 a year earlier. These troops were no longer 'advisers' but engaged in combat with both Viet Cong and with the North Vietnamese army units which not long before had appeared in the South.

Through 1965 and 1966 American policy in Vietnam wavered. Committed by treaty, statement and action to the independence of South Vietnam, America could not withdraw without suffering an immense blow to her international prestige. But even if this could be faced it was more difficult to accept the very real possibility that the loss of South Vietnam might mean the deliverance of all of South-east Asia, even perhaps India, into communist hands. And it seemed that the United States could only stay in Vietnam by enlarging hostilities. By the middle of 1966 the American people found themselves involved in a war for which they had no real enthusiasm, which blurred their image even with their allies by laying them open to charges of imperialist intent, which seemed to have no clear purpose and from which there appeared to be no acceptable exit.

And behind Vietnam loomed the shadow of a powerful and relentlessly hostile China. The dread of Russian Communism had not vanished but Russia now seemed tractable. It is with China – not only in Asia but in the world affairs at large – that the United States must come to terms.

It was, of course, the American policy of containment of China in Southeast Asia which led to the United States' increasing commitment to South Vietnam, and which drew American military forces ever deeper into its conflict with North Vietnam. By late 1967 it was clear that the Vietnamese affair had developed into a massive stalemate, with both the United States and China unwilling or unable to withdraw support from their Southern and Northern Vietnamese commitments. Increasing American disenchantment with successive South Vietnamese governments; seemingly endless demands for soldiers, equipment, and money; year-in-year-out draft quotas, from 250,000 to 380,000 men each year; and general discouragement with what appeared to be a useless conflict created deeper and more bitter divisions of public opinion than any issue since the Civil War. By 1968 Vietnam had absorbed over half a million troops, to become the longest war in American history; by late 1969 American total casualties in Vietnam exceeded those of the First World War.

Vietnam became, somehow, the focal point for American unrest, uncertainty and violence; the war seemed to be not only the cause of the draft but also of poverty, dissent, Negro rights, and every other malaise of contemporary life. Throughout 1967 and 1968 'peace' marches, 'poverty crusades', demonstrations, 'confrontations', and violent protests made headlines, while militant young Negro leaders like Stokely Carmichael, H. Rap Brown, and James Farmer capitalized on the public mood to stir up divisiveness in the ranks of the Negro civil rights movement. The assassination of Martin Luther King, the most respected of black non-violent leaders, on 4 April 1968, by a Southern white man in Tennessee, brought the Negro protest movement dangerously close to serious violence. Swift apprehension, trial and conviction of the killer, however, and the establishment of control by moderate Negro leaders, averted a crisis.

A stubborn, proud, inflexible man, Lyndon Johnson, however much he sensed the drift of public unrest, bent his foreign policy very little. His offers to negotiate with Hanoi met either silence or vituperative refusal; while his admirable record of domestic accomplishments slowly lost ground in the public mind as his position of leadership was eroded. His popularity within his party declined rapidly, and when Senator Eugene McCarthy of Minnesota decided to seek the Democratic nomination for the 1968 elections, he uncovered an amount of anti-Johnson, anti-Vietnam sentiment that projected him into contention with surprising velocity. In early 1968 Senator Robert Kennedy, younger brother of the slain President, announced his candidacy, again on an anti-Johnson, anti-Vietnam platform. With signs of storm on the horizon, Johnson declared himself out of consideration as a candidate in March, 1968, indicating that his choice as successor was Senator Hubert Humphrey of Minnesota, whose solidly liberal record dated from the days of F.D.R. In an incredibly ironic twist of fate, however, Kennedy was shot by an assassin, a young Syrian who believed that the Senator's pro-Israeli stance threatened the future of the Arab nations in the Middle East. That Robert Kennedy's death removed a potentially powerful force from the political scene is undeniable; certainly it changed the whole campaign irrevocably, making Humphrey almost certainly the party's nominee.

Johnson's self-removal from political consideration freed him considerably for negotiations with North Vietnam and took his efforts out of a political context. While both parties jockeyed for pre-convention position, exploratory messages between Washington and Hanoi resulted in the establishment of at least preliminary talks in Paris involving the Viet Cong, South Vietnam, the United States, and the Hanoi government; talks which might presumably result in actual negotiations later. The Democratic party in August predictably nominated Humphrey, while the Republicans equally predictably chose Richard Nixon, who had fought his way back from defeat to a position of authority within the party. In a campaign marked by bitter internal arguments within the Democratic ranks and bland unity within the Republican, Nixon won handily, taking thirty-two states, although his margin in the popular vote was relatively small. To him fell the problems that plagued and dismayed mid twentieth-century America – unrest everywhere, violence among Negroes and students, urban blight, rural depression and the hideous paradox of creeping poverty within a blatantly affluent society.

Since contemporary American society is a mass society the question it has faced since the turn of the twentieth century is: Can individual integrity and individual values be preserved in a standardized civilization? The contemporary thrust toward orthodoxy in the United States is of course neither new nor distinctively American. It has characterized modern life since the completion of the industrial revolution, though the United States has perhaps found it more difficult to resist than older societies. The conformist trend has produced in American society a deep sense of insecurity, the effect of a widening dichotomy between a traditional belief in the validity of the individual and an equally strong traditional belief in the judgement of the crowd. There is as a result an inner conflict in American life, manifested in the major areas of social and intellectual endeavour, a struggle to maintain individuality in a mass-dominated, insecure world that the nineteen-sixties neither understands nor trusts.

The pressure to conform in a mass society is nowhere

better illustrated than in American newspaper and periodical publishing since 1930. The depression drove smaller independent newspapers, journals, and publishers either out of business or into more financially stable chains, with the result that the control of publishing, particularly of newspapers, gravitated into fewer and fewer hands. As advertising revenue and circulation profits became more important than ever to a newspaper's existence, publishers became more sensitive to outside pressures; the press that survived the depression was for the most part cautious and orthodox. There were and are, however, notable exceptions. Since 1932 coverage of foreign affairs has tended to be nationalistic and coverage of domestic affairs conservative, sometimes reflecting special interests rather than public attitudes. *Time* magazine, founded in 1923 by Henry Luce, began a new style of summarized news presented in distinctively styled prose, and elicited a host of imitators. Luce's *Life*, begun in 1936, made the picture magazine popular; combined with *Time* it gave Luce Publications a strong influence in journalism, inclined toward nationalism and conservatism. *The Reader's Digest*, founded in 1922 by DeWitt Wallace, presented 'digests' of the 'best' articles of the week. It too attracted dozens of imitators, including digests of summaries and summaries of digests, most of them as orthodox as their prototype.

The close of World War I saw the appearance of great new communication media – movies, radio, and later television – appealing to audiences in the millions. Entertainment became a transcontinental business, dominated by a few corporations and a relatively small number of executives, to whom box-office receipts and advertising fees were more important than originality, initiative, or art. The movies established the pattern for the entertainment industry in the twenties, followed with minor variations by radio and television, and it was assumed by all that their function was to provide the nation with vicarious pleasure, escape, or reassurance. Hollywood developed into a fantastic never-never land, a stylized version of the romantic dreams of the frustrated and repressed, its films following well-tried formulas and usually avoiding controversial issues. While sociologists have expressed fears that the unreal world thus presented daily to millions might make it difficult for the average American to adjust to reality, little has been offered to prove that their fears are justified.

After the close of World War II, television swiftly replaced radio as the most popular means of communication and entertainment. With the fifties, as mass-produced television sets came down in price, the American public purchased at the rate of seven million a year so that by 1968 there were sets in more than eighty million homes. (Surprisingly, the number of American homes that have television sets is greater than the number that can boast telephones, refrigerators or indoor toilets.) There are in the United States nearly 700 commercial stations and more than 100 reserved exclusively for educational institutions.

A major factor in persuasion from the moment when its availability became general, both because of its coverage of news and because of its utility for political campaigning and advertising, the use of the medium by a politician must now be regarded as an important weapon in his armoury. Just as Franklin Roosevelt had harnessed to his own ends the then comparatively new radio and by his supreme ability in the techniques of radio performance had made his Fireside Chats into a significant contribution to the presidential role, so did Kennedy use television. His famous television debate with his rival for office, Richard Nixon, gave advance notice of the skill he was later to demonstrate in his televised press conferences.

Not only politically but also culturally and educationally the mass of American viewers learned to accept from television much that was new to them and of value. Through television millions of Americans learned about painting, ballet and the theatre. Even those who never travelled looked in on foreign lands.

Nevertheless, with all that it has achieved, the record of

the American television industry must be regarded as a disappointment. The insistence and triteness of its advertising, the banality of much of its entertainment and its consistent appeal to the 'twelve-year-old mind' (its own assessment of the common denominator of public taste) weakened television's effectiveness and made it fall far short of its tremendous potential.

And, happily, there was one thing television did not achieve: it did not kill the reading habit. Despite the prophecies of Jeremiahs who saw in this new medium the murderer of the printed word (their predecessors had made the same forecast for the cinema and for sound radio) the use of books for enlightenment grew phenomenally. The public library service enlarged and grew ever more effective but even more encouraging was the willingness of large sectors of the American public to buy books. Already in the thirties and forties book-ownership had received impetus from the book-clubs but it was the arrival on the scene of the paperback which changed the reading habits of America.

The first American paperback firm was founded in 1937 (only two years after the birth of the modern paperback in England) but even at the beginning of the fifties, although there were good titles available and many that were indifferently bad, the general impression of a paperback rack in drugstore or bookshop would have led an observer to believe that the American people would only read if their books were presented to them as pornography. Even the classics were decorated with undressed girls! By 1965, although the parade of nubility continued, the paperback industry had grown up. There were 25,000 titles in print and the sales approached one million copies a day. Sex and sadism were almost lost in the general quality. History, literature, philosophy, current affairs and the world's literary masterpieces were on sale not only in bookshops but also at pharmacies, gas stations, grocery stores, airports and bus terminals. It is not merely hard salesmanship but also a sign of intellectual growth when a traveller passing through, for example, Detroit's Metropolitan Airport can buy there not only mystery stories and popular novels but also Plato, Proust, Shakespeare, Ibsen and *Principia Mathematica*. With the development of the paperback (and with the general growth of education) went improvement in hardcover sales. In 1965 the American book publishing industry – the industry that had been condemned to death three times in one generation – grossed almost 2,000 million dollars.

According to some social analysts, there has occurred within the past generation a more drastic shift of values in American life than at any other period in its history. The most marked value shift is what social psychologists such as Clyde Kluckhohn and William Whyte have called 'the decline of the Protestant ethic'. In contrast to their grandfathers, Americans tend now to have a 'present-time' orientation, that is, they no longer place so much stress on planning for the future, but prefer to attend to the present. In addition, critics feel, they have shifted from an emphasis on the traditionally Puritan work-values toward those of leisure, recreation, and expression. Then too, others believe, American society has begun to display an orientation toward group rather than individual values, toward what David Riesmann has called 'other direction' and Erich Fromm 'the market-place personality'. The aim of many educational authorities, for example, has become the teaching of 'adjustment to life', the necessity of social approval, and the ready acceptance of majority values by the individual. Those who seem to provide reassurance of the individual's integrity in this modern predicament, and who furnish society with apparently explicit values – such as Monsignor Fulton Sheen or popular minister-philosopher Norman Vincent Peale – have built large followings.

Under the stresses of World War II and the confusion of the postwar world, American religion underwent a remarkable resurgence. Less than half of the American population belonged to a church in the mid-twenties; thirty years later church membership had risen to more than sixty per cent. The increase was greatest in the older, orthodox evangelical churches, particularly the Baptist and Methodist, but there were also great gains among newer fundamentalist sects such as the Church of the Nazarene, the Assembly of God, Jehovah's Witnesses and others. The Reverend Billy Graham, preaching fundamentalist conversion in the time-honoured American tradition that reaches back to Edwards and Wesley, draws millions to his sermons and has carried his 'Crusade for Christ' to England and Europe with equal success. At various levels, the power of religion in American life since the forties has been undeniably on the rise.

Despite the current concern over conformity, observers of the contemporary scene have noted strong counter-tendencies to indicate the persistence of individualism in the American scale of values. Studies of American university students, for example, show that they have greater tolerance for diversity in others, and prize diversity as a value more than Asian, European, or African students at the same age and level. Change and diversity, of course, have been principles of American life since its beginnings; the stability required for the existence of a homogenous society is simply impossible to maintain in an American milieu. At the same time, the present-day American has had much greater actual personal contact with the rest of the world than any of his predecessors, and a much wider experience with cultural diversity. A vast number of Americans have seen other cultures – almost twenty million of them in the armed services alone, not counting millions of tourists, exchange students, businessmen – so that the number of Americans who have some experience of Europe and Asia is far greater than the number of Europeans or Asians with experience of American life. The cumulative result of such experiences is that the United States is not a provincial nation, and that heterogeneity is becoming a much stronger principle in its social and cultural life.

Whatever the twentieth-century pressures toward conformity that appear in American life, there still exist in today's United States powerful counterbalances to standardization. Since the forties there has been a continual reassessment of the traditional positions of 'liberal' and 'conservative'.

None of the philosophical or political conservatives, satisfied the frustrated followers of McCarthy, left leaderless since 1957. The most influential follower of the Wisconsin Senator, however, was Robert Welch, a retired candy manufacturer who in 1960 established the John Birch Society (named after a young American killed in Communist China) dedicated to the exposure and destruction of 'anti-American tendencies' everywhere in contemporary society. Welch's announcement of his 'firm belief that Dwight Eisenhower is a dedicated, conscious agent of the Communist conspiracy' (an accusation which he levelled also at Dulles and Truman) out-McCarthyed the late Senator by some distance. Yet despite the absurdities of Welch's charges, the Society gathered significant support among right-wing extremists.

The liberalism of the sixties is of a more thoughtful, less ebullient variety than that of the brashly confident thirties. It is less doctrinaire and ideological than European liberalism; it is sceptical, pragmatic, flexible, aware of the feasibility and inevitability of change.

A major influence on mid-century American liberal thought has been the neo-Calvinist movement in theology, represented by Paul Tillich and especially Reinhold Niebuhr. Niebuhr's books, among them *Moral Man and Immoral Society* (1932), *Children of Light and Children of Darkness* (1945), and *The Irony of American History* (1952), exerted a powerful influence on the political thinking of the post-World War II generation. The younger liberal learned to temper his father's optimism about the improvability of human nature and the infallibility of reason, and to estimate more coolly the limits of the possible.

The dividing line between liberal and conservative in the sixties, unlike that of the thirties, is likely to cut across economic and political interests, governed less by their positions on economic and political than on ethical and international issues. There are still heated arguments over the role of government in society, over labour and capital, taxation and the distribution of wealth, the 'welfare state' and 'socialized medicine', but they are less strident and more academic in tone than before. The issues which divide liberal from conservative tend to derive from such things as foreign aid, the role of the United Nations, the relationship of American society to the emergent nations of Africa and Asia, civil rights for minorities at home and abroad, the nature of 'Americanism', and similar questions. Marxism, the class struggle, the rights of labour, and other topics popular in debate on college campuses thirty years ago have been displaced by discussions of the Peace Corps, 'freedom riders' in the South, or world federalism.

The United States is a big country, so populous that the acts and ideas of a minority may give a false impression that they constitute a sweeping movement, particularly to European eyes. Gangs in Chicago, divorces in Reno, or Klans in the South represent nothing more than fractional divergences from the main stream of American life. It is also a tremendously diverse country, a tangled skein of sections, localities, and groups to which the citizen holds powerful allegiances. There is no such thing as 'a typical American', for dissimilarities of background, geography, politics, race, environment, religion, and economic status prevent his existence. The customary European question, 'What do Americans think about this or that?' is unanswerable. Americans think in terms of multiple allegiances and not infrequently as individuals – much to the despair of politicians, advertisers, publishers, businessmen, and labour-leaders. They also possess a healthy scepticism and a stubborn independence. The television commercial may go unnoticed and the advertising slogan unread, the political exhortation may pass easily in at one ear and out of the other, the charlatan may disappear at the turn of a radio or television dial. No matter what evidence may be cited as proof of American crowd-mindedness, it is significant to note that the single most popular form of recreation in the United States is Walton's lonely sport of fishing.

The sum of America and Americans has been traditionally difficult for Europeans and Asians to grasp, even for those more perceptive observers who detect the words but not the tune of American life. The key to an understanding of the United States lies in the fact that it is an experiment in the making, never made. It is a society of change and movement, a highly diversified society operating fluidly within a framework of compromises. The core of the American experiment is that principle expressed in a long tradition of slogans (which Americans love) beginning with the Declaration of Independence itself and its phrase 'the pursuit of happiness', which is still the basis of its society. Conceived in the eighteenth century as an individual search, the pursuit has come to be understood in the twentieth century in larger social terms. The quest may sometimes have been diverted into blind alleys or perverted into meaningless activity, but again it has also been charted and channelled toward better ends.

The problem of recent American history has been to adapt its powerful sense of national purpose, derived from the Puritan concept of the New World as God's 'city set upon a hill' and from that optimistic view of the future glimpsed by Jefferson's Enlightenment and Jackson's commonwealth of equality, to twentieth-century changes and challenges. On the one hand, this conviction of purpose has sometimes hampered the United States in adjusting its relations to other nations which themselves have strong national drives. The American belief in the sanctity of its mission, as Reinhold Niebuhr has pointed out, has made it difficult for Americans 'to believe that anyone could think ill of us, since we are persuaded that our society is so essentially virtuous that only malice could prompt criticism of any of our actions'. This same belief has also proved bothersome in the establishment of relations with new, unsophisticated emergent nations, for though Americans have always believed deeply in the self-determination of peoples and the right of the governed to choose their own frame of government, they are equally convinced that the American way is the best way and cannot understand the failure of any nation so to choose.

Sensitivity to suspicion or criticism bedevilled even the most sensational technological achievement of the American or any other people in this or any other century. When, on 20 July 1969, man landed for the first time on the moon, the American people exploded into a natural euphoria of pride and excitement. Much of the rest of the world sat before its television screens or listened to bazaar radios, shared the excitement and was in no way behind the Americans in admiration for the courage of the men on the moon or the ingenuity that had placed them there. But some abroad (and not a few in the United States) had nagging doubts about the propriety of spending vast sums on a moon-shot when the world's more immediate problems of hunger, disease and war were still far from solution. Even the thrills of the night that belonged to Apollo 11 raised in some minds questions and fears. The prepared speeches of the first man-in-the-moon and of President Nixon were so carefully right: this was a triumph for mankind and not merely for America. But the shrill accompaniment of applause which came from America to the listening and watching world was, to some foreign observers, patently and hysterically chauvinistic and on the moon one other rehearsed gesture, the raising of the American flag, was sufficiently reminiscent of earlier imperialistic ventures to remind many observers that noble and courageous exploration has often been a prelude to bitter conflict and vicious hate.

Expressions of such doubts and fears puzzled most Americans and exasperated many who had already been brought to the brink of their collective patience by world-wide and vociferous criticism of America's behaviour in Vietnam. Convinced that their national mission is benevolent, they were hurt and even angered by the perversity that read malevolence even into their most fabulous achievement.

Others might write question marks against the validity of the American mission, but it remains true that this sense of mission exists and lends force, dignity, and conviction to the national purpose, for Americans still believe, in the twentieth century as in the eighteenth, that they bear the dual responsibility of creating a society which achieves the maximum of liberty and democracy for each man, and of assisting the rest of mankind to achieve it by the American example. As the poet Philip Freneau in 1775 conceived the future America to be 'a new Jerusalem, sent down from heaven..., a pattern to the world beside', so President Kennedy in 1963, shortly before his death, reaffirmed the vision:

Whether we like it or not, this is a time of change. As a people who set out to change the world, I think we should like it, however difficult the challenges. For no nation is at its best except under great challenges. The question for us now is whether in a changing world we will respond in a way befitting 'the land of the free and the home of the brave' – whether we will be at our best in these crucial years of our world leadership – whether we will measure up to the task awaiting us. The iron of the new world being forged today is now ready to be moulded. Our job is to shape it, so far as we can, into the world we want for ourselves and our children and for all men.

BIBLIOGRAPHY

It would be impossible to select from among the many general histories of the United States. Suffice it to say that Samuel Eliot Morison and Henry Steele Commager, *The Growth of the American Republic* (rev. ed. 1962, 2 vols.) and John Richard Alden, *Rise of the American Republic* (1963) are good general surveys. A British historian, Frank Thistlethwaite, has added a useful introduction, *The Great Experiment* (1955). Louis B. Wright *et al.*, *The Democratic Experience: A Short American History* (1963) is a concise yet scholarly book written by ten prominent historians, each writing about the particular period or aspect of American history in which he is a specialist. Another short study, Gilman M. Ostrander, *A Profile History of the United States* (1964) is especially good for social and intellectual developments. One of the most recent additions to the seemingly inexhaustible supply of general histories, John A. Garraty, *The American Nation: A History of the United States* (1966) is well written and well illustrated. *The Statistical History of the United States: from Colonial Times to the Present*, published by the Social Science Research Council in collaboration with the U.S. Census Bureau in 1963, is an indispensable reference work; so too is the Library of Congress bibliography, *A Guide to the Study of the United States of America*, first published in 1960.

Daniel J. Boorstin (ed.), *The Chicago History of American Civilization* (1956–64, 21 vols.) is ideally suited to the needs of the general reader, while the volumes of Henry Steele Commager and Richard B. Morris (eds.), *The New American Nation Series* (1954–65, 40 vols.) are generally longer and more detailed in nature. In addition, Arthur M. Schlesinger and Dixon Ryan Fox (eds.), *The History of American Life* (1927–44, 12 vols.) is still worth consulting.

For materials for the study of Negro life and literature, see the continuing series *The American Negro: His History and His Literature* (1968). On the early history of racial attitudes there is a recent book, Winthrop D. Jordan, *White Over Black: American Attitudes Toward the Negro 1550–1812* (1968).

Merle Curti, *The Growth of American Thought* (3rd edition 1964) has tended to eclipse Vernon L. Parrington's stimulating *Main*

Bibliography

Currents in American Thought (1927–30, 3 vols.) as the standard account of American intellectual development, though Stow Persons, *American Minds* (1958) and Ralph H. Gabriel, *The Course of American Democratic Thought* (2nd edition 1956) are good general studies, while Arthur M. Schlesinger, Jr. and Morton White (eds.), *Paths of American Thought* (1963) is a recent series of stimulating essays on American thought.

Samuel Flagg Bemis, *A Diplomatic History of the United States* (5th edition 1965) and Thomas A. Bailey, *A Diplomatic History of the American People* (7th edition 1964) are two standard works. For a concise recent analysis, see Robert H. Ferrell, *American Diplomacy: A History* (1959).

Wilfred E. Binkley, *American Political Parties: Their Natural History* (rev. ed. 1958) is a lively and well-written account of politics for the general reader, while William B. Hesseltine, *Third-Party Movements in the United States* (1962) is an excellent historical survey of American political protest movements. Richard Hofstadter, *The American Political Tradition and the Men Who Made It* (1956) contains incisive essays on men and events in American politics from Washington to Franklin Roosevelt. Denis W. Brogan, *Politics in America* (1960) is a perceptive analysis of American political development written by a British observer, while Alfred H. Kelly and Winifred A. Harbison, *The American Constitution: Its Origin and Development* (rev. ed. 1963) and Carl B. Swisher, *The Growth of Constitutional Power in the United States* (1963) combine to form an intelligent introduction to American constitutional history.

The standard history of American education is Ellwood P. Cubberley, *Education in the United States* (rev. ed. 1962). A good recent analysis is William M. French, *America's Educational Tradition: An Interpretive History* (1964). Rush Welter, *Popular Education and Democratic Thought in America* (1962) is a systematic and thought-provoking study of the interactions between the American commitment to education and American political theory.

Anson P. Stokes, *Church and State in the United States* (rev. ed. 1964) is a solid study, while Clifton E. Olmstead, *History of Religion in the United States* (1960) is a good recent addition. William W. Sweet, *The Story of Religion in America* (2nd rev. ed. 1950) is especially written for the layman, and Willard L. Sperry, *Religion in America* (1946) is especially written for the British layman. Dixon Wecter, *The Saga of American Society: A Record of Social Aspiration* (1957) is an entertaining book on manners, fashions, and social behaviour. Harvey Wish, *Society and Thought in Early America* (2nd edition

Bibliography

1962) and *Society and Thought in Modern America* (2nd edition 1962) are penetrating and comprehensive treatments of intellectual history as a phase of social development.

Herbert W. Schneider, *A History of American Philosophy* (2nd edition 1963) is unique for the way in which philosophical ideas are fitted into the general framework of American historical development. Anton Chroust, *The Rise of the Legal Profession in America* (1965, 2 vols.), and James W. Hurst, *Law and Social Process in United States History* (1960) are two of the better treatments of the history of American law. Perry Miller's *The Legal Mind in America* (1962) is an excellently edited collection of documents illustrating the development of American law and legal philosophy from the Revolution to 1860.

Harold U. Faulkner, *Economic History of the United States* (8th edition 1960) is probably the best one-volume treatment. Joseph Dorfman, *The Economic Mind in American Civilization* (1946–59, 5 vols.) is more sophisticated but still fascinating, while Seymour E. Harris, *American Economic History* (1961) and John Chamberlain, *The Enterprising Americans: A Business History of the United States* (1963) are valuable and readable. Thomas C. Cochran, *The Age of Enterprise: A Social History of Industrial America* (1961), Robert W. Fogel, *Railroads and American Economic Growth* (1964), Roger Burlingame, *March of the Iron Men* (1960) and *Scientists Behind the Inventors* (1964), and Foster Rhea Dulles, *Labor in America* (2nd rev. ed. 1960) are studies of particular aspects of economic history. The two books by Burlingame are particularly well suited to the average reader.

Robert E. Spiller, *et al.* (eds.), *The Literary History of the United States* (3rd rev. ed. 1963, 2 vols.) is an exhaustive study by a group of scholars, particularly valuable for its excellent biographies. Much shorter but equally important is Spiller's *The Cycle of American Literature: An Essay in Historical Criticism* (1955) and Marcus Cunliffe, *The Literature of the United States* (3rd ed. 1967). Supplementary to these are Carl Van Doren, *The American Novel 1789–1939* (1940) and Arthur H. Quinn, *A History of American Drama* (2nd edition 1951). Edmund Wilson (ed.), *The Shock of Recognition: The Development of Literature in the United States Recorded by the Men who Made It* (1955) is unique in that it gives the opinions of American writers of their literary colleagues, while James D. Hart, *The Popular Book: A History of America's Literary Tastes* (1950) treats literature from a different angle. Reference should also be made to Frank L. Mott, *American Journalism: A History of News-*

777

papers in the United States Through Two Hundred and Sixty Years, 1690–1950 (3rd edition 1962) and *A History of the American Magazine* (1938–57, 4 vols.). Vernon Loggins, *The Negro Author: His Development in America to 1900* (1964) is a most useful book. A very useful bibliography, T. G. Rosenthal (ed.), *American Fiction*, is published by the National Book League (London).

No entirely adequate history of American music has been written, though Wilfred H. Mellers, *Music in a New Found Land: Themes and Developments in the History of American Music* (1964) is a recent account worth consulting. Oliver W. Larkin, *Art and Life in America* (2nd edition 1960) is a brilliantly illustrated history of painting, sculpture, and architecture; John Walker writes a provocative introduction and some excellent notes to the panorama of two hundred years of American painting in *Paintings from America* (1951). Also see Edgar P. Richardson, *Painting in America: From 1502 to the Present* (1965). For the lighter side of American life, Foster Rhea Dulles, *America Learns to Play: A History of Popular Recreation* (2nd edition 1966) is an entertaining study

Frederick Jackson Turner, *The Frontier in American History* (1920), is important both to the state of American history and to the state of American historiography. It has had many fruits, among them, Ray A. Billington and James B. Hedges, *Westward Expansion: A History of the American Frontier* (2nd edition 1960). For views hostile to Turner's frontier hypothesis see, for example, Dixon Ryan Fox (ed.), *Sources of Culture in the Middle West* (1934).

Each of the minority groups has had its histories. While recent literature on the Negro in American history is voluminous, John Hope Franklin, *From Slavery to Freedom: A History of American Negroes* (3rd edition 1967) and Roi Vincent Ottley, *Black Odyssey* (1949) remain the most outstanding general studies. Leslie H. Fishel and Benjamin Quarles, *The Negro American: A Documentary History* (1967) is a convenient and well-chosen collection of source materials. S. P. Fullinwinder, *The Mind and Mood of Black America: Twentieth Century Thought* (1968) is a study of recent trends both in militant and conservative thought among the Negroes. For materials on the study of Negro life and history the most complete source is the New York Times, Arno Press Series, *The American Negro: His History and His Literature* (1968). Reference can also be made to the recent book which won a National Book Award, Winthrop D. Jordan, *White Over Black: American Attitudes Toward the Negro 1550 to 1812* (1968). Jack D. Forbes, *The Indian in America's Past* (1964), William T. Hagan, *The Indian in American*

Bibliography

History (1963), and Irvin M. Peithmann, *Broken Peace Pipes* (1964) are among the more readable recent accounts of the American Indian. Alvin M. Josephy, *The Indian Heritage of America* (1968) is an excellent socio-anthropological study. Alvin M. Josephy, *The Patriot Chiefs* (1959) is a fascinating study of two centuries of Indian leadership; Alden T. Vaughan, *New England Frontier* (1964) analyzes the colonists' attitudes toward and relations with Indians; and Ralph Andrist, *The Long Death* (1963) is a chronicle of the decline of Indian power in the West. Oscar Handlin, *Race and Nationality in American Life* (1957) is more comprehensive and general in scope. Carl Wittke, *We Who Built America: The Saga of the Immigrant* (rev. ed. 1964) and Oscar Handlin, *The Uprooted* (1957) and *Immigration as a Factor in American History* (1959) are the best studies available on immigration and immigrants.

For printed documents see Henry Steele Commager (ed.), *Documents of American History* (7th edition 1963) and for maps, James Truslow Adams and R. V. Coleman, *Atlas of American History* (1943) remains the best available.

There are several excellent reading lists designed primarily for the general reader; Herbert Herskowitz and Bernard Marlin, *A Guide to Reading in American History* (1966) and John E. Wiltz, *Books in American History* (1964) are two of the best.

An excellent account of the period immediately following the War of 1812 is George Dangerfield, *The Era of Good Feelings* (1963). Dangerfield's *The Awakening of American Nationalism, 1815–1828* (1965) is briefer and generally as informative as his larger study. Herbert J. Clancy, *The Democratic Party: Jefferson to Jackson* (1962) is a good detailed political history, and Charles M. Wiltse, *The New Nation, 1800–1845* (1961), Edward D. Branch, *The Sentimental Years, 1836–1860* (1965), and Carl Russell Fish, *The Rise of the Common Man, 1830–1850* (1937) are also useful.

Although controversial, Arthur M. Schlesinger, Jr, *The Age of Jackson* (abridged ed. 1964) is a superb account of the Jacksonian era. More detailed and well-written is Glyndon G. Van Deusen, *The Jacksonian Era, 1828–1848* (1963). The meaning and implications of Jacksonian Democracy are discussed in a number of books, among them Gilman M. Ostrander, *The Rights of Man in America, 1606–1861* (1960), Edwin C. Rozwenc, *Ideology and Power in the Age of Jackson* (1964), and Marvin Meyers, *The Jacksonian Persuasion* (1960).

Biographical studies of Jackson and his contemporaries are numerous. Marquis James, *Andrew Jackson: Border Captain* (1959)

Bibliography

and *Andrew Jackson: Portrait of a President* (1959), and John William Ward, *Andrew Jackson: Symbol for an Age* (1964) provide the reader with accounts of Old Hickory, while Samuel Flagg Bemis, *John Quincy Adams and the Foundations of American Policy* (1949) and *John Quincy Adams and the Union* (1956), Glyndon G. Van Deusen, *The Life of Henry Clay* (1963), and Russel B. Nye, *George Bancroft: Brahmin Rebel* (1944) are good for the life and times of some of Jackson's most illustrious contemporaries.

Perry Miller, *The Life of the Mind in America, from the Revolution to the Civil War* (1965) is a useful introduction to the social and intellectual history of the period. Daniel Boorstin's study of emerging cultural nationalism, *The Americans: The National Experience* (1965); and William R. Taylor, *Cavalier and Yankee: The Old South and The National Character* (1961) are outstanding studies. For the numerous reform movements which permeated American intellectual affairs between the Revolution and the Civil War, the reader should consult Alice Felt Tyler, *Freedom's Ferment: Phases of American Social History from the Revolution to the Outbreak of the Civil War* (1962), Henry Steele Commager, *Era of Reform, 1830–1860* (1960), and Ray A. Billington, *The Protestant Crusade, 1800–1860* (1964). Arthur Ekirch, *The Idea of Progress in America, 1815–1860* (1951) and the relevant chapters of Edward McNall Burns, *The American Idea of Mission: Concepts of National Purpose and Destiny* (1957) provide additional insight into the social and intellectual temper of the era. For the development of American literature see Benjamin T. Spencer, *The Quest for Nationality: An American Literary Campaign* (1957), Francis O. Matthiessen, *American Renaissance* (1941), and Van Wyck Brooks, *The World of Washington Irving* (1944) and *The Flowering of New England* (1936). Good biographies of literary figures include Ralph L. Rusk, *The Life of Ralph Waldo Emerson* (1949), Lewis Mumford, *Herman Melville: A Study of His Life and Vision* (1963), William R. Bittner, *Poe: A Biography* (1962) and Edward C. Wagenknecht, *Nathaniel Hawthorne: Man and Writer* (1961).

On the war with Mexico see Bernard A. DeVoto, *The Year of Decision, 1846* (1961), Robert S. Henry, *The Story of the Mexican War* (1961), and Otis A. Singletary, *The Mexican War* (1960), the latter volume especially suited to the general reader.

A number of good general studies cover the period from the Compromise of 1850 to the Compromise of 1877. James G. Randall and David Donald, *The Civil War and Reconstruction* (2nd edition 1961) is a more than adequate condensation of a vast amount of material, while other studies include Dumas Malone and Basil Rauch, *Crisis of the Union, 1841–1877* (1964), Roy Franklin Nichols, *The Stakes of Power, 1845–1877* (1961) and William A. Barker, *The Civil War in America* (1961). Robert W. Johannsen (ed.), *The Union in Crisis, 1850–1877* (1965) is a recent source-book for the tumultuous era, well worth reading.

Among studies of the decade preceding the Civil War, Avery Craven, *The Coming of the Civil War* (rev. ed. 1959) and Roy F. Nichols, *The Disruption of Democracy* (1962) are outstanding. The political and philosophical battles of the prewar era and the general theme of war causation are treated in Avery Craven, *An Historian and the Civil War* (1964), William and Bruce Catton, *Two Roads to Sumter* (1963), Henry H. Simms, *A Decade of Sectional Controversy, 1851–1861* (1941) and in a number of 'problems' books: Norman A. Graebner (ed.), *Politics and the Crisis of 1860* (1961), Norton Garfinkle (ed.), *Lincoln and the Coming of the Civil War* (1959) and Edwin C. Rozwenc (ed.), *The Causes of the American Civil War* (1961) and *Slavery and the Breakdown of the American Consensus* (1964). The reader should also see Paul I. Wellman, *The House Divides* (1966), and Allan Nevins, *Ordeal of the Union* (1947, 2 vols.), followed by Nevins' *The Emergence of Lincoln* (1950–51, 2 vols.), a detailed and colourful account of the immediate pre-war years.

No real understanding of the causes of the American Civil War is possible without a corresponding understanding of Southern civilization and temperament in the half-century preceding that conflict. Useful general introductions include Charles S. Sydnor, *The Development of Southern Sectionalism, 1819–1848* (1957) and Avery O. Craven, *The Growth of Southern Nationalism, 1848–1861* (1953). No serious reader will want to miss Wilbur J. Cash's classic, *The Mind of the South* (1960) for an intelligent, at times sophisticated, analysis of Southern civilization. Additional studies worth reading include Clement Eaton, *The Growth of Southern Civilization* (1961), John Hope Franklin, *The Militant South, 1800–1861* (1956), Rollin G. Osterweis, *Romanticism and Nationalism in the Old South* (1949), and Margaret L. Coit, *John C. Calhoun* (1961). Charles M. Wiltse's three-volume work, *John C. Calhoun* (1949–54), may well prove to be the definitive treatment.

The issue of slavery and the corresponding issue of the anti-slavery movement have had an impressive amount of historical attention devoted to them. Ulrich B. Phillips, *Life and Labor in the Old South* (1929) is especially well-written and is still worth

Bibliography

reading, though some of its conclusions have been disputed. Kenneth M. Stampp, *The Peculiar Institution: Slavery in the Ante-Bellum South* (1956), is an excellent sample of current thinking on the subject, while Stanley M. Elkins, *Slavery: A Problem in American Institutional and Intellectual Life* (1963) adopts a comparative approach and presents several interesting hypotheses. These specialized accounts should be balanced by William S. Jenkins, *Pro-Slavery Thought in the Old South* (1935), a sympathetic general exposition of the Southern position on slavery. On the sometimes controversial anti-slavery movement see Louis Filler, *The Crusade Against Slavery, 1830–1860* (1960), Russel B. Nye, *Fettered Freedom* (1949) and *William Lloyd Garrison and the Humanitarian Reformers* (1955), and Dwight L. Dumond, *Antislavery* (1961).

The bibliography of the Civil War itself is enormous and there has been a spate of additions occasioned by the Centennial. An adequate one-volume military history of the War is Fletcher Pratt, *Ordeal by Fire: A Short History of the Civil War* (1956). At greater length, Bruce Catton has produced one trilogy on the Army of the Potomac, *Mr. Lincoln's Army, Glory Road*, and *A Stillness at Appojamtox* (1962) and another designated as the Centennial History of the Civil War, *The Coming Fury, Terrible Swift Sword*, and *Never Call Retreat* (1961–65). For men and events of wartime politics, see Ellis M. Coulter, *The Confederate States of America, 1861–1865* (1950), B. Irvin Wiley, *Embattled Confederates* (1964), and Burton J. Hendrick, *Lincoln's War Cabinet* (1961). Biographical studies of military leaders include the massive accounts of *Robert E. Lee* (1934–35, 4 vols.) and of *Lee's Lieutenants* (1942–44, 3 vols.) by Douglas Southall Freeman, as well as Lloyd Lewis' *Sherman: Fighting Prophet* (1958). Lewis' *Captain Sam Grant* (1950) was to be the first of a three-volume study, continued by Bruce Catton, *Grant Moves South* (1960), and as yet unfinished. An interesting comparative study of northern and southern military leadership is John F. C. Fuller, *Grant and Lee: A Study in Personality and Generalship* (1957). Biographies of Lincoln and Jefferson Davis are numerous. A good introduction to Lincoln, however, is Paul M. Angle (ed.), *The Lincoln Reader* (1947), while Benjamin P. Thomas, *Abraham Lincoln* (1952) is a superb one-volume biography. Carl Sandburg, *Abraham Lincoln: The Prairie Years* (1926, 2 vols.) and *Abraham Lincoln: The War Years* (1939, 4 vols.) have been condensed by the author into a one-volume edition published in 1954. Roy P. Basler (ed.), *The Collected Works of Abraham Lincoln* appeared in eight volumes in 1953. The best biographical study

Bibliography

of the President of the Confederacy is Hudson Strode's recently completed *Jefferson Davis* (1955–64, 3 vols.).

Competent recent studies of the Reconstruction era are John Hope Franklin, *Reconstruction After the Civil War* (1961) and Kenneth M. Stampp, *The Era of Reconstruction, 1865–1877* (1965). A British historian, W. R. Brock, has added a useful if somewhat specialized study, *An American Crisis: Congress and Reconstruction, 1865–1867* (1963). Excellent recent books on specialized topics during this period include George R. Woolfolk, *The Cotton Regency: The Northern Merchants and Reconstruction, 1865–1880* (1958), Joel Williamston, *After Slavery: The Negro in South Carolina during Reconstruction, 1861–1877* (1965), and Joe M. Richardson, *The Negro in the Reconstruction of Florida, 1865–1877* (1965).

The immediate post-Civil War era witnessed an increased westward transmigration unparalleled in modern history. There have been scores of interesting books written on the various phases of this westward movement; some of the best include Walter P. Webb, *The Great Plains* (1959), Robert E. Riegel and R. G. Athearn, *America Moves West* (4th edition 1964), Ray A. Billington, *The Far Western Frontier* (1962) and Norman A. Graebner, *Empire on the Pacific* (1961). More specialized accounts include Oscar O. Winther, *Transportation Frontier: Trans-Mississippi West, 1865–1890* (1964), J. Frank Dobie, *The Longhorns* (1957), Mari Sandoz, *The Cattlemen* (1961), and the several books written by George R. Stewart, which include, among others, *Ordeal by Hunger* (1962), *California Trail* (1962), and *Donner Pass* (1960). In addition, the general reader will find Dick Everett, *Vanguards of the Frontier* (1965), Ernest S. Osgood, *The Day of the Cattlemen* (1960), and Rodman W. Paul, *California Gold: The Beginning of Mining in the Far West* (1965) interesting and at times exciting reading.

The social and intellectual history of the second half of the nineteenth century does not have an intensive bibliography, though there are several outstanding studies worth consulting. Perry Miller (ed.), *American Thought: Civil War to World War I* (1964) is a useful introduction to intellectual matters, while Lewis Mumford, *The Brown Decades: A Study of the Arts of America, 1865–1895* (1955) is good social and cultural history. Henry Steele Commager's *The American Mind* (1959) contains penetrating essays on intellectual trends at the turn of the century, while Oscar Cargill, *Intellectual America* (1941) is particularly useful for its treatment of American–European cultural relations during the

783

Bibliography

period. More specialized are Richard Hofstadter, *Social Darwinism in American Thought* (1960), A. Hunter Dupree, *Science, and the Emergence of Modern America, 1865–1916* (1963), and Thomas Beer, *The Mauve Decade* (1961). Biographies of the literary figures of the period include Gay W. Allen, *Walt Whitman as Man, Poet, and Legend* (1961), Oscar W. Firkins, *William Dean Howells, A Study* (1963), Edward C. Wagenknecht, *Mark Twain: The Man and His Work* (rev. ed. 1961), and Edgar Pelham, *Henry James: Man and Author* (1964).

Samuel P. Hays, *The Response to Industrialism, 1885–1914* (1963) and Harold U. Faulkner, *Politics, Reform and Expansion, 1890–1900* (1963) are good introductions to the history of the last two decades of the nineteenth century, while John D. Hicks, *The Populist Revolt* (1964) and Russel B. Nye, *Midwestern Progressive Politics* (rev. ed. 1959) are excellent sources of information concerning the political upheavals of the eighties and nineties. The rise of 'big business' is treated in Thomas C. Cochran and William Miller, *The Age of Enterprise: A Social History of Industrial America* (1961) and Harold U. Faulkner, *The Decline of Laissez-Faire, 1897–1917* (1951) and *The Quest for Social Justice* (1931). L. D. White, *The Republican Era, 1869–1901: A Study in Administrative History* (1958) traces the federal administration during this period. Burton J. Hendrick, *Andrew Carnegie* (1932) and Allan Nevins, *Rockefeller: A Study in Power* (rev. ed. 1953) are good biographies, though Carnegie's own writings, still easily available, give an even better view of the industrialist psychology.

For the Spanish–American War and the corresponding emergence of America as a world power see Foster Rhea Dulles, *America's Rise to World Power, 1898–1954* (1963), Harold K. Beale, *Theodore Roosevelt and the Rise of America to World Power* (1963) and Frank Freidel, *The Splendid Little War* (1958), a splendid little book for the general reader. Richard W. Leopold, *The Growth of American Foreign Relations* (1964) carries the narrative from 1889 to the present.

General accounts of United States history during the twentieth century include David Shannon, *Twentieth Century America* (1963), Harvey Wish, *Contemporary America* (3rd edition 1961), and Henry B. Parkes and Vincent Carosso, *Recent America* (1963, 2 vols.). Oscar Handlin, *American People in the Twentieth Century* (1963) is a good general study which emphasizes the role of immigration as a factor in American history. More specialized accounts of twentieth-century American development include Herbert Schneider,

Bibliography

Religion in Twentieth Century America (1963), Thomas C. Cochran, *The American Business System: A Historical Perspective, 1900–1955* (1962), Wayne H. Morgan, *American Socialism, 1900–1960* (1964), Frederick Lewis Allen, *The Big Change* (1961) and Selig Adler, *The Isolationist Impulse: Its Twentieth Century Reaction* (1961).

On the Progressives and the Progressive Era there are a number of excellent recent studies. Louis Filler, *Crusaders for American Liberalism* (rev. ed. 1961) is a sound account of the muck-rakers and other reformers, while the sweep of reform from 1865 through to the mid-twentieth century is brilliantly done by Eric Goldman, *Rendezvous with Destiny* (1956). For additional insight, the later chapters of Nye, cited above, survey the conflict between conservatism and liberalism in the early years of the twentieth century. George Mowry, *The Era of Theodore Roosevelt and the Birth of Modern America* (1962) is a good study of the early phases of Progressivism, while La Follette's *Autobiography* (1913) and Wilson's *The New Freedom* (1913) are essential to an understanding of the politics of the pre-World War I years. Elting E. Morison and John M. Blum have edited *The Letters of Theodore Roosevelt* (1951–54, 8 vols.), and Blum's *The Republican Roosevelt* (1964) is an astute study of T. R. as a politician. For the administrations of Wilson, Josephus Daniels, *The Wilson Era* (1946, 2 vols.) and Arthur S. Link, *Woodrow Wilson and the Progressive Era, 1910–1917* (1963) are valuable sources of information. Link's book is a condensation of his longer and more comprehensive *Wilson* (1964, 4 vols.). Biographical studies of other major Progressives include Paul W. Glad, *The Trumpet Soundeth: William Jennings Bryan and His Democracy, 1896–1912* (1960), Lawrence W. Levine, *Defender of the Faith, William Jennings Bryan: The Last Decade, 1915–1925* (1965), Ray Ginger, *Eugene V. Debs: A Biography* (1962), and Belle and Fola La Follette, *La Follette* (1953, 2 vols.).

Although preceding the period of American involvement, Barbara Tuchman's *The Guns of August* (1963) is especially well-written and illustrative of the European origins of the First World War, while a good short military history is Hanson W. Baldwin's competent *World War I* (1962). Laurence Stallings, *The Doughboys: The Story of the American Expeditionary Force, 1917–1918* (1964) provides some interesting sidelights; American participation in the war is further discussed in Herbert J. Bass (ed.), *America's Entry into World War I* (1964) and, at greater length, Benedict Crowell and Robert Wilson, *How America Went to War* (1917–21, 6 vols.). The peace conference and the debate over the League of Nations

Bibliography

are superbly described in Thomas A. Bailey, *Woodrow Wilson and the Great Betrayal* (1963) and *Woodrow Wilson and the Lost Peace* (1963). The most important intellectual history of America during the war years is Henry F. May, *The End of American Innocence: A Study of the First Years of Our Own Time, 1912–1917* (1964).

Frederick Lewis Allen's *Only Yesterday* (1964) and *Since Yesterday* (1961) are charmingly written social histories of life between the first and second World Wars, while Frederick J. Hoffman, *The Twenties: American Writing in the Postwar Decade* (rev. ed. 1962) does a fine job of integrating the literary and social trends of the period. Perhaps the best general treatment of the twenties is William Leuchtenburg's *The Perils of Prosperity, 1914–1932* (1963). For political and economic events leading up to the Great Crash of 1929 and the Great Depression which followed, see Harold U. Faulkner, *From Versailles to the New Deal* (1950), Arthur M. Schlesinger, Jr, *The Crisis of the Old Order* (1958), John Kenneth Galbraith, *The Great Crash, 1929* (1961) and H. G. Warren, *Herbert Hoover and the Great Depression* (1959).

Denis W. Brogan, *The Era of Franklin D. Roosevelt* (1950) is the best British study of the New Deal era, while the two volumes by Arthur M. Schlesinger, Jr, *The Coming of the New Deal* (1959) and *The Politics of Upheaval* (1960) are the best American studies, although they take the story only to 1936. William E. Leuchtenburg, *Franklin Roosevelt and the New Deal* (1963) is generally considered the best one-volume treatment of the entire era, whereas James M. Burns, *Roosevelt: The Lion and the Fox* (1956) is the best one-volume biography of Roosevelt. Additional studies worth consulting include Broadus Mitchell, *Depression Decade* (1947) for economic affairs, Dixon Wecter, *The Age of the Great Depression* (rev. ed. 1959) for social affairs ,and Dexter Perkins, *The New Age of Franklin Delano Roosevelt, 1932–1945* (1957) for an interpretative approach to the entire period. The definitive multi-volume biography of F.D.R., Frank Freidel's *Franklin D. Roosevelt* (1952–56, 3 vols.) remains unfinished and carries Roosevelt's life only to 1932. For the years after 1932, Robert E. Sherwood, *Roosevelt and Hopkins* (rev. ed. 1960) remains a useful source. Samuel Rosenman has edited *The Public Papers and Addresses of Franklin D. Roosevelt* (1948–50, 3 vols.), but B. D. Zevin (ed.), *Nothing to Fear* (1946) is an easily available one-volume collection of Roosevelt's major speeches. Jane D. Ickes (ed.), *The Secret Diaries of Harold Ickes* (1955, 3 vols.) provides a fascinating though highly personalized picture of New Deal inner politics, and William S. White, *The*

Bibliography

Taft Story (1954) is a competent study of one of the New Deal's bitter opponents.

On interwar diplomacy in general and Rooseveltian foreign policy in particular, see Allan Nevins, *The New Deal and World Affairs* (1950), Basil Rauch, *Roosevelt from Munich to Pearl Harbor* (1950), Herbert Feis, *The Road to Pearl Harbor* (1962), and William L. Langer and S. Everett Gleason, *The Challenge to Isolation: The World Crisis of 1937–1940 and American Foreign Policy* (1964, 2 vols.). Edwin O. Reischauer, *The United States and Japan* (1964) and A. Whitney Griswold, *The Far Eastern Policy of the United States* (1964) are especially good for American–Japanese relations between the World Wars. Among the primary sources for the period, Cordell Hull's *Memoirs* (1948), Walter Millis (ed.), *The Forrestal Diaries* (1951), Sumner Wells, *The Time for Decision* (1944), and the United States State Department, *Peace and War: United States Foreign Policy, 1931–1941* (1942) are important.

The historical literature on World War II is voluminous. For the general reader, Louis L. Snyder, *The War: A Concise History, 1939–1945* (1964), John L. Snell, *Illusion and Necessity: The Diplomacy of Global War, 1939–1945* (1963), and Vincent J. Esposito (ed.), *A Concise History of World War II* (1964) are good introductory studies. Kenneth S. Davis, *The Experience of War: The United States in World War II* (1964) is superb. No interested reader should neglect reading at least a volume or two of Sir Winston S. Churchill's *The Second World War* (1962, 6 vols.). A. Russel Buchanan, *The United States and World War II* (1964, 2 vols.) and Don Lawson, *The United States in World War II* (1964) are excellent on American participation in the war, while Dwight D. Eisenhower, *Crusade in Europe* (1961), James J. Fahey, *Pacific War Diary, 1942–1945* (1963), and Omar N. Bradley, *A Soldier's Story* (1964) are accounts by important American participants. Leo Giovannetti and Fred Freed, *The Decision to Drop the Bomb* (1963) is the best account of that decision yet to appear, while Herbert Feis, *The Atomic Bomb and the End of World War II* (1966) is more comprehensive. Longer and more specialized studies of the war include the United States Army's official but not yet completed *History of World War II* and Samuel Eliot Morison's semi-official *History of Naval Operations in World War II* (1947–62, 15 vols.).

For postwar foreign policy and the development of the Cold and Korean Wars see John W. Spanier, *American Foreign Policy since World War II* (1962), Eric F. Goldman, *The Crucial Decade – And After* (1961), Herbert Agar, *The Price of Power* (1957), Davis Rees,

Bibliography

Korea: The Limited War (1964), John A. Lukacs, *A History of the Cold War* (1962), Denna F. Fleming, *The Cold War and Its Origins* (1961) and W. W. Rostow, *The United States in the World Arena* (1960). Two good books, Herbert Feis, *The China Tangle* (1953) and A. D. Barnett, *Communist China and Asia: Challenge to American Policy* (1960), deal exclusively with American relations with the Far East since 1945, while Reischauer's study on American–Japanese relations, cited above, carries the story into the postwar years. America's role in the reconstruction of postwar Europe is excellently described in Joseph M. Jones, *The Fifteen Weeks* (1964), H. B. Price, *The Marshall Plan and Its Meaning* (1955), and R. E. Osgood, *NATO: The Entangling Alliance* (1962). On the Korean War see David Rees, *Korea: The Limited War* (1964) and John Spanier, *The Truman–MacArthur Controversy and the Korean War* (1965). Moreover, Truman's *Memoirs* (1956) and Eisenhower's *Mandate for Change* (1963) give the average reader a great deal of insight into the inner workings of the American Presidency during the Cold War. For more recent events in the conduct of American foreign policy see Roscoe Drummond and Gaston Coblenz, *Duel at the Brink* (1960), a study of John Foster Dulles, and Richard Tregaskis, *Viet Nam Diary* (1964). Bernard Newman, *Background to Viet Nam* (1965) considers the history of American involvement; by far the best recent analysis is that by the Franco-American journalist, Bernard Fall, *Viet Nam Witness: 1953–1966* (1966). Tad Szulc, *The Winds of Revolution* (1965) is a good consideration of Latin American and Mexican involvement there.

Among the better biographies of postwar political leaders are Alfred Steinberg, *The Man from Missouri* (1962) and Cabell Phillips, *The Truman Presidency* (1966), on Truman; Dean Albertson (ed.), *Eisenhower as President* (1963), Emmett John Hughes, *The Ordeal of Power* (1963), Robert J. Donovan, *Eisenhower: The Inside Story* (1956), Merlo J. Pusey, *Eisenhower: The President* (1956), on Ike; John M. Burns, *John Kennedy: A Political Profile* (1960) and Theodore Sorenson, *Kennedy* (1965), on J.F.K; and Jack Bell, *The Johnson Treatment* (1965), William S. White's adulatory *The Professional: Lyndon B. Johnson* (1964) and Philip Geyelin, *Lyndon B. Johnson and the World* (1966), on L.B.J. In addition, see White's biography of Taft, cited above, William Costello, *The Facts about Nixon* (1960), Richard H. Rovere, *Senator Joe McCarthy* (1959), and Noel F. Busch, *Adlai Stevenson of Illinois* (1952). Truman's own book, *Mr. Citizen* (1953), and Adlai Stevenson's *What I Think* (1956) are revealing self-portraits.

Bibliography

McCarthyism and the Alger Hiss affair, as well as the entire post-war 'loyalty' question, are discussed in Alan Barth, *The Loyalty of Free Men* (1951), Alistair Cooke, *A Generation on Trial* (1950), William F. Buckley, *McCarthy had His Enemies* (1954), Whittaker Chambers, *Witness* (1952) and J. W. Caughey, *In Clear and Present Danger* (1958). The conservative–liberal debate which reached a high point in the late fifties and early sixties is best viewed through Russell Kirk, *The Conservative Mind* (1953), Clinton Rossiter, *Conservatism in America* (1962), Louis Hartz, *The Liberal Tradition in America* (1955), and Arthur M. Schlesinger, Jr, *The Vital Center* (1949). Jeffrey Hart, *The American Dissent* (1966) is a summary of the most recent conservative position.

Social and intellectual trends in modern America have been the subject of innumerable historical, economic, and sociological studies, For discussion of the development of mass-entertainment media in recent times, for example, see Gilbert Seldes, *The Great Audience* (1950) and *The Public Arts* (1957), Lewis Jacobs, *The Rise of the American Film* (1939), Llewellyn White, *The American Radio* (1947) and Gary A. Steiner, *The People Look at Television* (1963). John K. Galbraith, *The Affluent Society* (1958) and *American Capitalism* (1962), Leo Fishman (ed.), *Poverty and Affluence* (1966), Thomas C. Cochran, *The American Business System* (1957) and Adolf A. Berle, *Power Without Property* (1959) are especially relevant to the study of contemporary economic trends, while David Riesman *et al.*, *The Lonely Crowd* (1950), C. Wright Mills, *White Collar* (1951) and Louis Kronenberger, *Company Manners* (1954) are good on the nature of the American character. For modern American literature, consult Alfred Kazin, *On Native Grounds: An Interpretation of Modern American Prose Literature* (1956) and Heinrich Straumann, *American Literature in the Twentieth Century* (3rd rev. ed. 1965). For studies of individual novelists, poets, critics and others, consult the Library of American Biography series (40 vols.) and *American Men of Letters* series (22 vols.), as well as the introductions to the *Portable* series of anthologies, especially Malcolm Cowley's *Portable Faulkner* (1946) and *Portable Hemingway* (1944).

Studies of the recent South and the Negro rights problem include Robert Highsaw, *The Deep South in Transformation* (1964); Louis Lomax, *The Negro Revolt* (1962), Louis Harris, *The Negro Revolution in America* (1964), Martin Luther King, *Why We Can't Wait* (1964), Anthony Lewis (ed.), *Portrait of a Decade* (1964), C. Eric Lincoln, *The Black Muslims* (1962), and Benjamin M. Ziegler (ed.),

Bibliography

Desegregation and the Supreme Court (1958). Elizabeth Miller, *The Negro in America* (1966) provides an analytical bibliography of four thousand books, articles, and pamphlets on the civil rights movement since 1954, while Francis Broderick and August Meier have compiled an excellent collection of documents, *Negro Protest Thought in The Twentieth Century* (1966).

INDEX

Index

Index

Committees of Correspondence, 177, 187, 201, 378

Committees of Safety, 177, 198, 225

Committee of Secret Correspondence, 225, 226

Common Sense (Paine), 216, 217, 219

Communications, effects of new means of, 644–5

Communism, increased influence of, 706; anti-communism, 710–12, 731, 769; world politics and, 720; American fear of, 726–7; and Latin America, 736; and problem of Vietnamese war, 760

Compromise of 1850, 443, 446, 447, 448, 450

Corncord, 116, 197

Condorcet, Marie Jean Antoine Nicolas Caritat, Marquis de, 211

Confederacy, or sovereign union, 456; Southerners and, 457; blockade of, 480, 494, 511–12; and Britain, 531–7; Radical Republicans attitude to, 563–4

Confederate Congress, 483, 523

Confederate States of America, constitution of, 471; difficulties of imposing unity on, 478; its army, 479; shortage of arms and rolling stock, 479–80; fight a defensive war, 480

Congregationalism, 'New Lights' and 'Old Lights', 346; Congresionalist-Unitarian controversy, 347; 'Plan of Union', 348; and revivalism, 349, 411; circuit-riding ministers, 366; and perfectionism, 412; and temperance, 416; becomes more liberal, 646

Congress of United States, at York, 222; and Dr Price, 237; problems facing, 242; and Treaty of Paris, 252; seeks greater powers, 252; and Philadelphia Convention, 259, 260; and Constitution, 260, 263; Hamilton attempts to weaken power of, 264; passes Aliens & Sedition Act, 268; debates site of Federal centre, 269–70; Embargo Acts, 300, 301, 305; votes for war with Britain, 305; representation in, 373; Whigs seize control of, 395; declares war on Mexico, 436; balance of power, 442–3, 444; Kansas-Nebraska bill, 450; rancorous debates over Kansas, 451; Lecompton constitution presented to, 460; Homestead Law, 504, 551, 559; sends wheat for Britain, 537; and Indian affairs, 560–61; Wade-Davis bill, 564; Southerners in, 564; Joint Committee on Reconstruction, 566; Tenure of Office Act, 567; corrupt during Grant Administration, 570–72; Amnesty Act, 572, 573; and Klu Klux Klan, 574; and 1876 election, 576;

Sherman Anti-Trust Act, 579, 587, 627, 643, 651; Gold Standard Act, 627; and Spanish War, 629, 630; and Philippines, 633; under Wilson administration, 643; and World War I, 657, 658, 661, 663; and League of Nations, 664; Acts to remedy depression, 682–4; isolationist policy, 694–5; agrees to rearm, 696; reluctantly votes Lend-Lease programme, 697, 698; and Truman administration, 714–15, 716–17, 721, 752; Economic Opportunity Act, 737, 756; blocks Kennedy legislation, 742; under Johnson administration, 756

Connecticut, 89; Colony of, 45; settlement, 53; charter for, 54; and Massachusetts, 55; attitude to Crown, 80–81; and the West, 116; constitution of, 249; opposed to 1812 War, 307

Constitution, American, 213; Franklin and, 151; Hamilton and Adams on, 212; Madison and basis of, 255; Philadelphia Convention and, 256–60; comes into effect, 262–3; ultimate defence of, 263–4; clumsy and inefficient, 264; and Aliens and Sedition Act, 268; Marshall on, 289, Hertford Convention and, 317; Amendments, 416, 417, 455, 565, 566–7, 584, 646, 662, 714, 725; and slavery, 422, 423–4, 426; interpretation of, 456; and electoral votes, 575

Constitutional Union party, 467, 468

Constitutions, state, 249–51, 255

Continental Congress, First, 187, 260; Second, 198, 203, 206, 207, 219, 220, 221, 225

Cook, James, 125, 126

Coolidge, Calvin, 676; on Allies' debt to U.S., 667; supports International Court of Justice, 667; on American self-sufficiency, 669; Hardings' running-mate, 669; and death of Harding, 670; on business, 670; re-elected, 672–3

Cooper, James Fennimore, 344, 405–6

Cooper, Thomas, 426

Copland, Aaron, 693

Copland, Reverend Patrick, 31, 32

Copley, John Singleton, 283

Coral Sea, battle of (1942), 701

Corinth, battle of (1862), 509

Corn Laws, repeal of, 588

Cornwallis, Charles Cornwallis, 1st Marquis, 232, 236, 239, 240

Corruption, 567–8, 570–72, 573, 670

Cortés, Hernando, 3–4

Corton, Samuel, 53

Cotton (*see also* Textiles), 457, export rights of N. Carolina, 68; under

Index

Index

xiii

Index

England—cont.

67–9; New Netherland falls to, 100;
Hudson's Bay Company, 117; imports
raw cotton, 372; working class sympathy
for Union, 531; governing class
sympathy for Confederacy, 532, 533
European Defence Community, 725
Evangelism, 349–50
Evarts, William G., 611
Everett, Edward, 414, 468, 488, 519
Ewell, Richard Stoddert, 500, 516–17

Farmers, force redrafting of state constitutions, 371; the Grange, 573, 615; grievances of, 614–15; and Populist party, 617, 619
Farmers' Alliance, 616–17
Farming, 587–8; decreases in Northeast, 385; in Northwest, 386; in South, 386; effect of Civil War on, 504, 506; cattle, 558; buffalo and plains farmers, 561; prices fall, 614, 616, 619; and Depression, 619; under Eisenhower administration, 726
Farragut, Admiral David Glasgow, 499
Farell, James T., 691
Fascism, American attitude to, 690, 694
Faulkner, William, 676, 691, 692, 746
Faussett, Jessie, 692
Federal Government, chief cause of power of, 264; constitutional authority of, 289; and new Western states, 363; creates Second Bank of United States, 368; and problem of slavery, 372; Jackson, Marshall and, 383; and states' rights, 455–7; South fears power of, 458
Federalism and Federalists, Madison's attitude to, 253, 255, 258; anti-Federalists, 260, 261; Washington and, 261; leadership respected, 261; The Federalist, 262; attitude to Britain and France, 267; identified with British cause, 305; and United States Bank, 307; 'Bluelight Federalist', 338; Republican party attracts, 351; and Monroe administration, 355; in constitutional law, 356; Federalist party by 1824, 374; Jacksonian attitude to, 383, 384; Jeffersonian attitude to, 384; state sovereignty and, 476; post-war problems of, 709; Eisenhower's policy on, 728–9
Fénelon, François de Salignac de la Mothe, 150
Fermi, Enrico, 702
Field, James, 617
Fillmore, Millard, 442, 444, 454
Finney, Charles Grandison, 411–13, 415
Fish, Hamilton, 611–12, 613

Fithian, Philip, 145–6
Fitzgerald, F. Scott. 676
Fitzhugh, George, 428, 457, 462, 477
Fitzhugh, William, 70
Flint, Timothy, 347
Florida (see also South), 1528 expedition lands in, 5; Spaniards in, 8, 17, 118; Raleigh's reconnaissance, 17; Oglethorpe renders impotent, 121; ceded to Britain, 128; Napoleon demands, 292; Monroe negotiates for, 293; becomes American property, 354; slave state, 439; secedes, 470
Ford, Henry, 644, 671, 685
Foreign policy, American (see also Imperialism), dictated by War of Independence, 225 et seq.; during first half of 19th century, 340; under Monroe administration, 354–5; Panama Canal, 440–41; from Appomattox to Spanish War, 611–14; turning point in, 630–31; prefers arbitration to war, 654; in 1941, 698–9; under Truman, 717; under Roosevelt, 717; in 1952 election, 724; in post-war world, 730–31; under Eisenhower and Dulles, 731–6; under Kennedy and Rusk, 742–3; under Johnson, 759–61
Formosa, 708
Forrest, Nathan Bedford, 490, 492, 525, 574
Foster, Stephen, 649
Fourier, Charles, 413, 414
Fox, Charles James, 238, 241
Fox, George, 83, 84
Frame, Richard, 89
France, her ships in N. Atlantic, 8–9; and Spain, 9, 117; trade, 11, 299, 302; colonial expansion, 95, 114, 117–18; imperial power shattered, 115; and exploration of Mississippi, 116–18; and Holland, 117, 228; and guerilla warfare in N. America, 119–20; military strength sapped, 120–21; and War of Austrian succession, 121; and Britain, 120–27, 235, 267, 290, 293; in War of American Revolution, 193; recognizes American independence, 224; ally of Americans, 225, 226, 340; treaties with United States, 226–7; aid to United States, 228, 231, 239; American view of French, 236; Jackson administration and, 394; and Mexico, 614; and United States and World War I, 653, 656, 660; post-war national debt, 666–7; Pacific pact, 667; and World War II, 695, 696, 704; West European Union, 732; loses Indo-China, 733; and Suez Canal, 734–5; discusses nuclear controls, 752

xiv

Index

Index

Index

Index

Index

Index

XXV

Index

Index

Index

Index

Index